WILD WOMEN

Mariella Frostrup is one of the UK's leading journalists, broadcasters and critics. She was born in Norway, raised in Ireland and has lived her adult life in the UK. Her lifelong love of travelling and scuba diving has taken her from Papua New Guinea to the Magellan Straits, Liberia to northern Iceland, Madagascar to Mozambique. She writes a monthly Travel column for the *Telegraph* and has described her many journeys in a host of other newspapers and magazines. She co-founded the GREAT initiative, an advocacy organisation for gender equality. Also a champion of literature and the arts, she presents *Open Book* on Radio 4 and *The Big Painting Challenge* on BBC1. Mariella lives in Somerset and London with her husband and two children.

and their Amazing Adventures over Land, Sea and Air

EDITED BY

MARIELLA FROSTRUP

An Anima Book

This is an Anima book, published in the UK
in 2020 by Head of Zeus Ltd

All excerpts have been reproduced according to the styles found in the original works.
As a result, some spellings and accents used can vary throughout this anthology.

9 7 5 3 1 2 4 6 8

A catalogue record for this book is available from the British Library.

ISBN (XTPB) 9781788540025
ISBN (E) 9781788540001

Research by Nadia Whiston
Typeset by Adrian McLaughlin

Printed and bound in Great Britain by
CPI Group (UK) Ltd, Croydon CRO 4YY

Head of Zeus Ltd
First Floor East
5–8 Hardwick Street
London EC1R 4RG

WWW.HEADOFZEUS.COM

For my daughter Molly Mae
and the adventures that lie ahead

CONTENTS

INTRODUCTION

Mariella Frostrup

Travel is a great liberator, freeing us from the responsibilities of home, widening our horizons and testing our strengths and capabilities outside the confines and comforts of our daily lives. No wonder that over the centuries women have proved themselves such eager adventurers, embarking on epic journeys of discovery that have tested their endurance and helped us in mapping the globe. The explorer Felicity Aston spoke for so many of her sex when she wrote 'the fact that I had crossed Antarctica, despite the tears and the fear and the alone-ness, deepened my belief that we are each far more capable than we give ourselves credit for. Our bodies are stronger and our minds more resilient than we could ever imagine.'

Yet despite the great journeys women have embarked on, it's the exploits of male explorers that have been well trammelled and jubilantly celebrated throughout history – from Odysseus's mythological voyage to Ferdinand Magellan; from Marco Polo to Vasco da Gama. We're taught in our formative years about Richard Burton and John Speke discovering the source of the Nile, Edmund Hillary conquering Everest, Jacques Cousteau exploring our oceans and so the list goes on. Even failures are celebrated; Christopher Columbus believing he'd reached the 'West Indies' and Ernest Shackleton getting himself marooned on the Antarctic ice are but two examples.

When it comes to famous female travellers tripping with similar ease off our tongues, we are less well endowed. You could be forgiven for thinking only the likes of Mary Wollstonecraft or Gertrude Bell ever left hearth and home under their own steam with a hunger for exploration. It seems the names of the men who mapped our planet have loomed so large for centuries that they've (no doubt unwittingly) blocked the light from the equally intrepid members of the opposite sex who set out on similar expeditions, breaking with convention, defying their families and societal expectations by setting off unfettered to the four corners of the Earth.

Despite the rightfully indignant, equality-demanding #MeToo-society we presently inhabit, you could be deluded into thinking that aside from a few eccentric pioneers like Cleopatra and Boadicea, until the 19th century women didn't leave their kitchens unless it was to accompany their husbands, teach the word of God or pay for a crime by being shipped away to penal colonies across the seas. It's one of the many yawning chasms increasingly being exposed in past history; whether in science or arts, politics, invention or exploration, where the contributions women have made have been overshadowed by male triumphs and are only now being burrowed out, dusted down and re-evaluated.

It was an impulse to fill one of those empty spaces, where women explorers belonged, that prompted me to collect together and celebrate some gripping travelogues from those who dared to roam while so many of their sex were constrained to hearth and home.

Take Aloha Wanderwell, the aptly named adventuress dubbed 'the world's most travelled girl' who, in the 1920s when still a teenager, hopped into a Model T-Ford and whizzed her way across 75 countries. Stranded in Brazil, she lived with the Bororo people; when stuck for fuel she ingeniously combined bananas and animal fat to power her car. Later her husband died in mysterious circumstances so she chopped off her hair and joined the French Foreign Legion. In Indonesia she shot her way out of a herd of angry elephants; she flew a seaplane and despite it all died in obscurity. How is it possible that this real life Indiana Jones isn't better celebrated today? Where's the Hollywood movie or Canadian Airport to bear her name?

My passion for travel writing was spawned when I discovered the now sadly defunct Travel Bookshop in my west London neighbourhood in the early 1980s, long before it was immortalised (but sadly not saved) by the Richard Curtis hit movie *Notting Hill.* Most Saturdays I'd be in its narrow aisles perusing wide-roaming shelves, helpfully divided by continents (to which this book pays homage), deciding where I would journey to next from the comfort of my sofa.

Thanks to that much-missed, tiny portal to the big wide world, I chanced upon, and read greedily through, a host of contemporary travellers and masters of the genre. From Patrick Leigh Fermor to Eric Newby, Wilfred Thesiger to Redmond O'Hanlon, Charlie Nicholl and Edward Behr, whose brilliantly titled but sadly out of print *Anyone Here Been Raped and Speaks English?* remains a comic favourite. Back then the writers I enjoyed had two things in common: their thirst for adventure and their sex. With barely a stamp on my pristine passport I expanded my knowledge of the world and fed my desire to explore it with their encounters. It didn't occur to me to stop and wonder whether women too had ventured forth and lived to tell similar tales.

In the intervening decades I have journeyed far and wide but never against the odds and with the total disregard for personal safety, comfort, convention, or family ties displayed by the pioneers here. Indeed I'm ashamed to admit that an encounter with a suggestive, baton-stroking prison guard in Zanzibar was all it took to banish my plans for driving a Land Rover the length of Africa!

The need to override such fears and find ways to protect yourself are far more imperative for the woman traveller and represent one of the extra layers of adversity they have to confront. The continuing prevalence of sexual violence, the threat of which in the 21st century remains as real as it was 500 years ago, continues to make solo travelling for the female of the species a particularly daunting prospect.

Viewing the world as an inherently threatening place is a protective instinct that's nurtured from birth and restricts so many of us from pursuing our intrepid dreams. The underlying intangible fear that is every woman's lifelong companion is as hard to articulate as it is to live with. For that reason the courage of so many of these women is as impressive as their actual travels, and represents a rallying call to put our apprehension of venturing forth into a more realistic perspective. Despite visiting the remotest – and in some cases most inhospitable – of places on Earth, the explorers in this book found only the adventures they were seeking, rather than experiences they were not, despite moments where it seemed otherwise!

Lois Pryce is a good example. Forget Che Guevara's revered motorcycle diaries, Pryce has travelled across the Americas, Africa and Iran by motorbike and in this collection describes being forced to journey alone on an overnight train from Brazzaville full of drunken soldiers. It's a passage that takes some beating for nail-biting, adrenaline-fuelled suspense and the articulating of the deep-rooted terror that is a constant companion to the lone female traveller. As with so many of the adventures contained in this anthology Pryce's hell-raising experience is documented with an absence of bravado that is a particularly rare element in the annals of male exploration. Junko Tabei, the Japanese mountaineer and first woman to climb Everest, offers further proof of such feminine restraint. Reaching the summit of the world's highest peak after months of preparation and a final six arduous hours climbing, she declares with simple relief 'here is the summit. I don't have to climb any more'!

The idea for the collection came when a sepia-tinted photograph of Adela Breton caught my eye in a local Somerset newspaper. Dashingly dressed in equine velvets, she sat proudly on her mule while her trusty travelling companion (of 20 years standing), a Mexican guide named Pablo Solorio, held the reins. The article drew attention to an exhibition in Bath featuring watercolours by this lifelong singleton, in which she diligently recorded and recreated the frescoes of the Aztecs and their ancestors in remote parts of Mexico. Breton's obscurity despite her pioneering journeys through Mexico, and her undisclosed but obviously unusual life story, got me wondering about how many other women with similar wanderlust might be gathering dust in out of print publications and museum archives. To my delight, a little bit of searching uncovered a wealth of amazing travelogues written by extraordinary, inspiring women that, collected together in this anthology, will, I hope, elevate these dashing dames to a more prominent position in the popular imagination.

Wild Women is really just an appetiser, because although these explorers themselves have too often been overshadowed, the wealth of writing and experiences there was to choose from was actually overwhelming. I'd urge readers excited by what they find in these pages to seek out the books from which so many of these wonderful accounts are extracted and experience an extended and still too rare view of the wider world through a female lens. These women battled not just to survive in remote, solitary and forbidding landscapes but also back home, where far from being celebrated, their ambitions often set them at odds with society and exposed lifestyles that were disparaged. Beryl Markham was the first woman to fly east to west across the Atlantic and thankfully her crash landing in Newfoundland failed to put her off further journeying. Ernest Hemingway called her book *West With the Night* a 'bloody wonderful story', yet her adventures as a pioneering bush aviator and the first female racehorse trainer in Africa are even less well remembered than her romantic scrapes, including with one Prince Henry, the Duke of Gloucester!

By turning their backs on the conventional, restricted existence on offer and embracing exploration and travel as a means to learn about the world beyond and also about themselves, these women were more often censured than applauded. What did American society make of a girl like Juanita Harrison I wonder? She's certainly not celebrated as she should be for her remarkable journeying. This 36-year-old African American, in the early days of the 20th century, only 35 years after slavery was abolished, began a solo trip around the world, which she documented in her only publication, the exuberantly titled: *My Great, Wide, Beautiful World.* Harrison may be particularly noteworthy for her unique experience and her disarmingly frank and humour-filled prose, but there are so many other travellers' tales here that have inspired me and continue to haunt my imagination.

In these pages you can find out what it was like to travel through Iran in the 1970s disguised as a man, as Sarah Hobson describes in *Through Persia in Disguise*. Best mates Mildred Cable and Francesca French were surely early champions of girl power, spending the first part of the 19th century traversing remotest China in a horse and cart, crossing the Gobi Desert five times in the course of their travels. I was totally seduced by aviator Jean Batten's description of her magical solo flight to Rio de Janeiro, where, flying low over the jungle, she's assaulted in the cockpit by 'a strong exotic perfume' which turns out to be from the orchids below her in the steaming rainforest, wafting upwards after a tropical deluge. Among her countless flights traversing the globe, this enterprising pilot conducted the first solo flight from England to New Zealand in 1936 in the most basic of aircraft.

To feel empowered to shape something more ambitious out of your life it helps to have role models to look to for inspiration. For women today, considerably closer to establishing their rightful place in the world than many of their predecessors in these pages, putting past heroines back on the historical map is increasingly imperative. In this collection I found myself spoilt for choice. Take Isabelle Eberhardt, who was born in 1877 and died aged 27 in a flash flood, yet managed to cram a startling amount in before her demise. A bite-sized biography reveals her as the illegitimate daughter of Russian anarchists who moved to Algeria. She became deeply involved in Algerian politics, converted to Islam and lived her short life dressed as a man, travelling North Africa extensively and writing stories, giving away her inheritance in such quantities that she died destitute. Or Robyn Davidson, who trekked 1,700 miles across the deserts of Western Australia with only a dog and four camels for company in the 1970s.

These are just a few examples of the many extraordinary women whose adventurous spirits and determination to live life on their own terms are highlighted here. It seems crucial that as we shape this brave new equal world, we elevate those who have forged paths to our own place in it and draw attention to the abundant stories of women's achievements that have been overlooked over the centuries. It's my great hope that this collection of writing will offer the same thrilling, edge-of-the-seat reading experience for you as it did for me as I compiled it. These inspiring female accounts took me on a whistle-stop tour of the globe in the finest company, opening my eyes not only to what they saw, but to places and cultures that are lost to us today. Particularly poignant in the light of the current political landscape is the freedom and hospitality once experienced by the likes of Gertrude Bell and Freya Stark in countries like Saudi Arabia, Iraq, Syria and Afghanistan, where today civil war and fundamentalist religious intolerance have, in some places, driven women's position back centuries.

It's my pleasure to introduce here a cast of great, intrepid, fearless women who are neither unique nor rare but part of a clamorous crowd who've been shamefully underexposed. They risked society's disapproval but were determined to expand their horizons on their own terms. I'm delighted to have been able to gather 50 of these incredible female pioneers together in one volume, celebrating their indispensible contribution to mapping the world as we know it today. From our earliest beginnings brave, unique, adventure-hungry women have traversed wild frontiers and journeyed to the furthest reaches of the Earth, their exploits arguably requiring greater bravery and pioneering spirit than the men we celebrate so much more loudly. Escaping the confines imposed on them by restrictive societies across the centuries, these women found the possibility for freedom and self-expression in the remotest wilderness and documented those experiences in lively and engaging accounts that for too long have sat gathering dust.

I hope intrepid and armchair travellers alike will enjoy crossing continents simply by dipping into these pages or find inspiration to embark on adventures of their own. Celebrating the achievements of this gaggle of gallivanting gals while propelling them to their rightful place in exploring history feels like a service long overdue!

Mariella Frostrup
Somerset
12th October 2018

PART ONE
AFRICA

JUNGLE PORTRAITS

Delia Akeley

Delia Akeley (1869–1970), known as 'Mickie', was born in Wisconsin, USA. She married three times; her first and third husbands were a barber and businessman respectively, but it was Husband No.2, a taxidermist, who set her on the path of exploration. She joined him on expeditions to collect exhibits for the American Museum of Natural History's African Hall, killing a bull elephant herself. But let's not hold it against her – it was 1906, and conservation hadn't been invented. Between husbands 2 and 3, she explored the desert between Kenya and Ethiopia, negotiated Kenya's Tana River in a dugout canoe, wrote *Jungle Portraits* and spent a few months hanging out with pygmies. Perhaps she should have stayed single?

The Flamingos of Lake Hannington

Finally, after loitering along and thoroughly enjoying ourselves, we came to a strip of dense thorn bush that reached to the water's edge and cut off our view of the lake beyond. Lying flat on the ground we wormed our way beneath the vine-entangled obstructions. This mode of travel is grilling work, especially in a tropical forest where it is hot and the thorns are vicious. Therefore, just before reaching the other side I stood up in an open place to stretch my aching muscles. Suddenly, while my hands were raised above my head, I heard a peculiar hissing noise. Although I was familiar with the sound, having heard it many times on our first expedition while collecting water birds around Lake Elementita and Lake Naivasha, I turned inquiringly to my boys for confirmation, and almost in chorus they whispered, "*endege menge*" (many birds).

With all possible speed we crept forward to the edge of the bush and the sight which greeted us caused me to hold my breath in sheer ecstasy. There before us, with the dazzling sunshine playing over their bodies, enhancing and dulling the colors, were acres of beautiful pink birds. There must have been at least a million feathered creatures in that vast assembly, for the entire colony had, during the night, moved over to the western shore and were now noisily feeding on the tiny Crustacea which thrive in the mud on the floor of this volcanic lake.

With business-like persistence they dredged for food; balancing their uptilted bodies with long, gently waving legs, they thrust their heads beneath the water and scooped up the mud with inverted bills. Quickly righting themselves, they brought their find to the surface. Still holding their bills in an inverted position, they washed the dirt from their food with a hissing, swishing sound before raising their heads high in the air and gulping it down.

It was quite evident that some of the birds were doing sentinel duty while the others fed. This precaution is characteristic of all the African birds or animals that live in large flocks or herds. As these guards stood alert and watchful in a sea of reversing pink bodies, their big purple and scarlet bills, topping their long slender necks, looked like the buds of some strange tropical plant ready to burst into bloom.

Two species of flamingo were represented in the feathered multitude. The small and more brilliantly colored *Phoenicopterus minor* was in the majority, although the larger species, *Phoenicopterus roseus*, was well represented by both immature and adult birds.

Lying with elbows resting on the ground, I watched the amazing scene through focused glasses. My pleasure was tempered, however, by thoughts of Mr. Akeley's disappointment and his fatiguing journey along the bush-covered wall of the eastern shore.

How long I remained in my uncomfortable position on the ground I do not know. But suddenly one of the porters, who had fallen asleep, startled us all by giving a loud sneeze that went echoing around the lake.

Instantly the watching sentinels sounded the alarm by uttering a loud "kronk, kronk." Like a vast number of athletes performing in unison, the feeding birds righted their bodies. Craning their necks and cocking their heads at a ridiculous angle, the brilliant assemblage listened intently for a few seconds. Then as if the sea of pink had been rocked by a gentle wave, the birds began to move and flip their wings. With absurd dignity those on the outskirts began to strut leisurely back and forth. Stepping high, they perked their heads, drooped their wings, and slowly swayed their glistening bodies from side to side like mannequins displaying the latest modes at a fashion parade.

They seemed to have no sense of the direction of the danger, however, and after milling and strutting about in an effort to locate the cause of the excitement their agitation ceased.

Before settling down and resuming their feeding each bird took a cautious last look around. Then apparently satisfied, they gave forth a subdued guttural "kronk" before thrusting their heads beneath the surface of the water. It was not until they had all settled down that I realized, with a pang, that I had forgotten all about taking a picture.

Eager though I was to secure records of the wonderful sight, I waited until they were quiet again. Then rising from the ground and brushing the ants off my clothing, I made a few shots from the shelter of the bush. The click of the shutter did not seem to disturb them, so I walked deliberately out on the beach in full view of the birds and made another picture.

The sentinels saw me at once, and immediately sounded the alarm. This time it was not a "kronk, kronk" of suspicion, but a deep, sharp, unmistakable "kronk, kronk, kronk" of command. Instantly answering "kronks" came from a million pink throats, and two million pink and black wings flashed in the air and crashed against wings as the seething mass of startled birds crowded one another in an effort to rise from the water.

As they milled about, kronking and hissing and beating their wings against one another, the noise was deafening. And as their feet churned the foul mud on the floor of the lake a sickening, almost overpowering stench rose from the water. The nauseating odor drenched the stifling hot atmosphere. It clung to our nostrils and got into our mouths; the porters spat on the ground in an effort to find relief.

Only the birds on the outskirts had room enough to get the running start necessary to raise their weight in the air, but one followed the other in rapid succession. As they rose in their stupendous numbers the thunder of their wings, mingled with their incredible hissing and kronking, was like the roar of a tropical hurricane, and the sound was heard by some of our boys over a mile away.

By the time the last bird had risen from the water the first ones had recovered from their fright and were settling in midlake. Presently I noticed that the main body of birds was drifting slowly in our direction. With camera in readiness, I sat down in the shadow of an acacia tree at the edge of the bush to watch and wait, hoping and praying that the birds would return to their feeding ground.

The heat was terrific and the delicate leaves on the acacia tree under which I sat were little protection against the smiting rays of the sun. While my temples throbbed and the perspiration oozed from every pore and drenched my garments, the porters slept peacefully.

There was hardly a sound to break the silence, save when the grunting bellow of a hippo rolled across the water, or when one of the feathered marshals flanking the oncoming multitude of birds kronked a command. Rarely indeed had the peace of these birds been disturbed by the intrusion of human beings, and as I sat and watched their approach I shuddered to think of their fate when the record-breaking game hunters from America, with the first-person complex, found them out.

In about an hour most of the birds had returned and were busily kronking and gossiping with one another in bird fashion. As they bobbed their heads and shifted their positions the sunlight played over their shimmering feathers and changed the colors. Some of them showed great curiosity and came close to the shore. Caution ruled their movements, however, for as they came slowly toward me they stopped frequently to stretch their necks and cock their heads to look and listen.

Twenty-four times my graflex clicked that afternoon and still the friendly creatures were not frightened. When I had finally exposed all my plates, and it was time to make our way back to camp, we walked right down to the water's edge, expecting that the birds would repeat the glorious spectacle of the morning. To my surprise and delight they only jostled one another, craned their necks, hissed, and bobbed their heads as if in friendly greeting.

I know of no other bird on the African continent that will delight the eye of the traveler or lend itself to the camera or brush of an artist more effectively than the flamingo. Their plumage is exquisitely beautiful. The long neck and body feathers of an adult bird shade from a pale pink to a rosy hue. The curiously shaped beak is scarlet and purple, and the long slender legs, which seem so inadequate for the weight of the excessively fat body, are deep pink with a blending of purple and scarlet. This remarkable coloring penetrates even the bones and the marrow of the legs. The feathers under their black-pinioned wings are crimson, and the same lovely color tips the wing coverts on the upper side of the wings.

There is a great contrast between the adult and the young birds. The latter are a grayish white, which changes to pink as the bird matures.

Like ducks and geese, the flamingo are extremely clannish, and congregate in immense flocks. They often form into units and follow a leader on a tour of the neighboring lakes.

At Lake Elementita, and also at Lake Naivasha, where we spent several months in 1905–1906, one of my chief interests was watching the arrival and departure of the feathered tourists.

I soon learned that large flocks of young flamingos were being piloted on these tours by a number of older birds, and, judging from the way they remained together at these stopover stations, their leaders were as conscientious and careful of their charge as councilors of a Boy or Girl Scout organization could possibly be. Although the young birds seemed very restless and were constantly rising from the water, as if trying their wings, they never left the main flock.

Their food consists of minute particles of animal matter found in the mud on the bottom of the lakes. When feeding they thrust their large, curved beak, upside down, into the mud and scoop up both dirt and food like an excavating shovel. Still holding the bill upside down they bring it to the surface, and, with a loud hissing sound, swish it through the water to separate the mud from their food, through a sieve-like arrangement on the side of the bill.

There is nothing in the bird world more ludicrous than a flock of frightened flamingos. They kronk and hiss and crowd one another like a panicky mob of human beings. When preparing for flight their ungainly movements remind one of an overloaded aeroplane trying to take off on a rough field. Stretching their long necks in front of them they beat the water with their wings as they gallop clumsily for a short distance over the mud. When they have gained sufficient momentum to raise their weight in the air, the neck and legs are quickly thrust out in a straight line with the body. It is then, when their black pinions are spread, that the crimson wing feathers are exposed and flash in the sunlight with each graceful sweep of their wings.

It was long after dark when the porters and I returned to camp on that memorable day at Lake Hannington. As we stumbled over the hot rocks toward the tents, I could see in the light of the kitchen fire Abdulla, the cook, bending over the steaming pots. The tent boys, dressed in clean white kanzus and red-tasseled caps, were gathered about him, waiting for my arrival to serve dinner. By the light of a lantern hanging in the veranda of my tent I could see the table with its white cloth and three camp chairs waiting for their owners.

In the background under the acacia trees the tiny tents of the porters could be seen by the light of many fires. The hot, sultry air was filled with the odor of wood fires and cooking food. The sound of melodious voices raised in conversation, snatches of song, and now and then bursts of happy laughter, told us that the comedian of our safari was entertaining his companions.

I found Mr. Akeley and Mr. Stephenson sitting silently, as hungry men will, before their tents. They had had a grilling day. Traveling over miles of lava rock in the stifling heat and blistering sun, they had dodged rhino and buffalo. They had seen greater kudu, kongoni, and impalla from a distance, but not a flamingo. Mr. Akeley's disappointment over his failure to find the birds or add a kudu to our scientific collection was so keen that I hadn't the heart to enthuse just then over my own good fortune. But later, over our coffee, I told them in detail of my experiences and Mr. Akeley consented to let me pilot him to the same spot in the morning. Before retiring we loaded our cameras and prepared for an early start.

Blessed indeed is he who can make plans and follow them to the letter in the jungle. The following morning an attack of malaria kept Mr. Akeley in camp. Mr. Stephenson wanted to add a kudu to his bag of rare trophies, so he started at dawn to hunt for the animals among the boulders along the escarpment.

As our time was limited at Lake Hannington, I left Mr. Akeley reclining on his cot under an acacia tree by the stream and went back to make motion pictures of the birds.

With the exception of a few flocks which were scattered over the lake, the majority of the birds were in the same place noisily feeding. When I walked out on the beach to set up my tripod they arose with a rush and a roar of wings that deafened the senses, and I was obliged to shout into my gun bearer's ear the instructions about placing my tripod.

After circling gracefully over the lake a few times, however, they returned and settled down without fear. As they came slowly, floating in a compact mass, toward us, they looked exceedingly foolish, hissing and bobbing their heads like talkative human beings. We talked aloud, and our voices echoing over the water did not deter their advance. Even our laughter over their ludicrous appearance did not frighten them.

The most inquisitive ones came so close to the shore that the boys ran out and waved their arms to keep them back within range of the lens.

The following day we were obliged to leave Hannington to meet the train for Nairobi, so we left the beautiful birds and the stifling valley to their solitude.

When we developed our plates and film a few days later we were so delighted with the results that we decided to make another journey to Hannington in May, when we hoped to find the flamingos nesting.

Although we made this journey, and went direct to the north end of the lake, following the old caravan trail, we were just about six weeks too late.

The old nests, which the birds reconstruct year after year by piling up mud with their bills a foot or more high, covered a vast, desolate mud plain which was dazzlingly white under a salt-encrusted surface. The torrid atmosphere reeked with the frightful odor of rotting egg-shells, putrid fish, and an age-old deposit of guano. No human being knows, nor has the boldest of our theorizing travelers even dared to guess, how many generations of flamingos have seen the light of the African day from this remarkable, though unsavory, community nursery.

Our disappointment over our failure to secure records of what must surely be one of the most amazing bird nurseries in the world was very keen. But Africa is no place in which to waste time over vain regrets. Therefore we heaved a sigh for the pictures we might have taken had we arrived a few weeks earlier, took a last look at the deserted nests, and started off to find the feathered colonists.

It was horribly hot and the stifling atmosphere reeked with the sickening odors from the nursery. While there are not so many hot-water springs and geysers along the margin of the water at the north end of the lake the stones over which we walked were just as hot as in the southern region. In fact they were so very hot there was no need to urge the porters to step lively with their burdens.

We found the birds in almost exactly the same spot as when I photographed them on our previous visit. We watched them for some time before Mr. Akeley went out on the beach to photograph them. Then with a rush and a mighty roar of flapping wings, the sea of pink rose in the air and after circling the lake settled on the water a few hundred yards in front of us.

Hastily building a crude blind with a few branches Mr. Akeley hid behind them to wait until the birds came closer while I, accompanied by the porters, sought the shelter of the trees.

In less than a half hour there was a general movement of the birds in our direction and it wasn't long before Mr. Akeley was recording the spectacular scene on his film. He soon learned that he had no need for caution with these friendly, inquisitive creatures. So he left the blind and placed his camera at the very edge of the water. Before he had time to turn the crank the birds crowded up, stepping on each other's toes and kronking queerly as they craned their necks to look at the shining lens. They came so close that we had to throw sticks and stones into the water to shoo them back into the field of the lens.

A THOUSAND MILES UP THE NILE

Amelia Edwards

Amelia Edwards (1831–1892) launched a career in journalism to support her ageing parents, enjoyed success as a novelist and ended up dedicating the last years of her own life to protecting Egypt's ancient sites. She'd already written several novels before she made the epic journey that would inspire her famous travelogue, *A Thousand Miles Up the Nile* (1877) and sparked her lifelong passion for Egypt. As well as being dedicated to conserving its ancient sites, she co-founded the Egypt Exploration Fund and gave birth to what we now know as Egyptology – in the process she building an extensive library and collection of antiquities. Quite a legacy.

Cairo to Bedreshayn

A rapid raid into some of the nearest shops, for things remembered at the last moment – a breathless gathering up of innumerable parcels – a few hurried farewells on the steps of the hotel – and away we rattle as fast as a pair of rawboned greys can carry us. For this morning every moment is of value. We are already late; we expect visitors to luncheon on board at midday; and we are to weigh anchor at two P.M. Hence our anxiety to reach Boulak before the bridge is opened, that we may drive across to the western bank against which our dahabeeyah lies moored. Hence also our mortification when we arrive just in time to see the bridge swing apart, and the first tall mast glide through.

Presently, however, when those on the look-out have observed our signals of distress, a smart-looking sandal, or jolly-boat, decked with gay rugs and cushions, manned by five smiling Arabs, and flying a bright little new Union Jack, comes swiftly threading her way in and out among the lumbering barges now crowding through the bridge. In a few more minutes, we are afloat. For this is our sandal, and these are five of our crew; and of the three dahabeeyahs moored over yonder in the shade of the palms, the biggest by far, and the trimmest, is our own dear, memorable 'Philae.'

Close behind the Philae lies the 'Bagstones,' – a neat little dahabeeyah in the occupation of two English ladies who chanced to cross with us in the 'Simla' from Brindisi, and of whom we have seen so much ever since that we regard them by this time as quite old friends in a strange land. I will call them the M. B.'s. The other boat, lying off a few yards ahead, carries the tricolor, and is chartered by a party of French gentlemen. All three are to sail to-day.

And now we are on board, and have shaken hands with the captain, and are as busy as bees; for there are cabins to put in order, flowers to arrange, and a hundred little things to be seen to before the guests arrive. It is wonderful, however, what a few books and roses, an open piano, and a sketch or two, will do. In a few minutes the comfortless hired look has vanished, and long enough before the first comers are announced, the Philae wears an aspect as cosy and home-like as if she had been occupied for a month.

As for the luncheon, it certainly surprised the givers of the entertainment quite as much as it must have surprised their guests. Being, no doubt, a pre-arranged display of professional pride on the part of dragoman and cook, it was more like an excessive Christmas dinner than a modest midday meal. We sat through it unflinchingly, however, for about an hour and three quarters, when a startling discharge of firearms sent us all running upon deck, and created a wholesome diversion in our favour. It was the French boat signalling her departure, shaking out her big sail, and going off triumphantly.

I fear that we of the Bagstones and Philae – being mere mortals and Englishwomen – could not help feeling just a little spiteful when we found the tricolor had started first; but then it was a consolation to know that the Frenchmen were going only to Assuan. Such is the *esprit du Nil.* The people in dahabeeyahs despise Cook's tourists; those who are bound for the Second Cataract look down with lofty compassion upon those whose ambition extends only to the First; and travellers who engage their boat by the month hold their heads a trifle higher than those who contract for the trip. We, who were going as far as we liked and for as long as we liked, could afford to be magnanimous. So we forgave the Frenchmen, went down again to the saloon, and had coffee and music.

It was nearly three o'clock when our Cairo visitors wished us 'bon voyage' and good-bye. Then the M.B.'s, who, with their nephew, had been of the party, went back to their own boat; and both captains prepared to sail at a given signal. For the M.B.'s had entered into a solemn convention to start with us, moor with us, and keep with us, if practicable, all the way up the river. It is pleasant now to remember that this sociable compact, instead of falling through as such compacts are wont to do, was quite literally carried out as far as Aboo Simbel; that is to say, during a period of seven weeks' hard going, and for a distance of upwards of eight hundred miles.

At last all is ready. The awning that has all day roofed in the upper deck is taken down; the captain stands at the head of the steps; the steersman is at the helm; the dragoman has loaded his musket. Is the Bagstones ready? We wave a handkerchief of inquiry – the signal is answered – the mooring ropes are loosened – the sailors pole the boat off from the bank – bang go the guns, six from the Philae, and six from the Bagstones, and away we go, our huge sail filling as it takes the wind!

Happy are the Nile travellers who start thus with a fair breeze on a brilliant afternoon. The good boat cleaves her way swiftly and steadily. Water-side palaces and gardens glide by, and are left behind. The domes and minarets of Cairo drop quickly out of sight. The mosque of the citadel, and the ruined fort that looks down upon it from the mountain ridge above, diminish in the distance. The Pyramids stand up sharp and clear.

We sit on the high upper deck, which is furnished with lounge-chairs, tables and foreign rugs, like a drawing-room in the open air, and enjoy the prospect at our ease. The valley is wide here and the banks are flat, showing a steep verge of crumbling alluvial mud next the river. Long belts of palm groves, tracts of young corn only an inch or two above the surface, and clusters of mud huts relieved now and then by a little whitewashed cupola or a stumpy minaret, succeed each other on both sides of the river, while the horizon is bounded to right and left by long ranges of yellow limestone mountains, in the folds of which sleep inexpressibly tender shadows of pale violet and blue.

Thus the miles glide away, and by and by we approach Turra – a large, new looking mud village, and the first of any extent that we have yet seen. Some of the houses are whitewashed; a few have glass windows, and many seem to be unfinished. A space of white, stony, glaring plain separates the village from the quarried mountains beyond, the flanks of which show all gashed and hewn away. One great cliff seems to have been cut sheer off for a distance of perhaps half a mile. Where the cuttings are fresh, the limestone comes out dazzling white, and the long slopes of debris heaped against the foot of the cliffs glisten like snow-drifts in the sun. Yet the outer surface of the mountains is orange-tawny, like the Pyramids. As for the piles of roughhewn blocks that lie ranged along the bank ready for transport, they look like salt rather than stone. Here lies moored a whole fleet of cargo boats, laden and lading; and along the tramway that extends from the river-side to the quarries, we see long trains of mule-carts coming and going.

For all the new buildings in Cairo, the Khedive's palaces, the public offices, the smart modern villas, the glaring new streets, the theatres, and foot-pavements, and cafés, all come from these mountains – just as the Pyramids did, more than six thousand years ago. There are hieroglyphed tablets and sculptured grottoes to be seen in the most ancient part of the quarries, if one were inclined to stop for them at this early stage of the journey; and Champollion tells of two magnificent outlines done in red ink upon the living rock by some master-hand of Pharaonic times, the cutting of which was never even begun. A substantial new barrack and an esplanade planted with sycamore figs bring the straggling village to an end.

And now, as the afternoon wanes, we draw near to a dense, wide spreading forest of stately date-palms on the western bank, knowing that beyond them, though unseen, lie the mounds of Memphis and all the wonders of Sakkarah. Then the sun goes down behind the

Libyan hills; and the palms stand out black and bronzed against a golden sky; and the Pyramids, left far behind, look grey and ghostly in the distance.

Presently, when it is quite dusk and the stars are out, we moor for the night at Bedreshayn, which is the nearest point for visiting Sakkarah. There is a railway station here, and also a considerable village, both lying back about half a mile from the river; and the distance from Cairo, which is reckoned at fifteen miles by the line, is probably about eighteen by water.

Such was our first day on the Nile. And perhaps, before going farther on our way, I ought to describe the Philae and introduce Reis Hassan and his crew.

A dahabeeyah, at the first glance, is more like a civic or an Oxford University barge, than anything in the shape of a boat with which we in England are familiar. It is shallow and flat-bottomed, and is adapted for either sailing or rowing. It carries two masts; a big one near the prow, and a smaller one at the stern. The cabins are on deck, and occupy the after part of the vessel; and the roof of the cabins forms the raised deck, or open-air drawing-room already mentioned. This upper deck is reached from the lower deck by two little flights of steps, and is the exclusive territory of the passengers. The lower deck is the territory of the crew. A dahabeeyah is, in fact, not very unlike the Noah's Ark of our childhood, with this difference – the habitable part, instead of occupying the middle of the vessel, is all at one end, top-heavy and many-windowed; while the foredeck is not more than six feet above the level of the water. The hold, however, is under the lower deck, and so counterbalances the weight at the other end. Not to multiply comparisons unnecessarily, I may say that a large dahabeeyah reminds one of old pictures of the Bucentaur; especially when the men are at their oars.

The kitchen – which is a mere shed like a Dutch oven in shape, and contains only a charcoal stove and a row of stew-pans – stands between the big mast and the prow, removed as far as possible from the passengers' cabins. In this position the cook is protected from a favourable wind by his shed; but in the case of a contrary wind he is screened by an awning. How, under even the most favourable circumstances, these men can serve up the elaborate dinners which are the pride of a Nile cook's heart, is sufficiently wonderful; but how they achieve the same results when wind-storms and sand-storms are blowing, and every breath is laden with the fine grit of the desert, is little short of miraculous.

Thus far, all dahabeeyahs are alike. The cabin arrangements differ, however, according to the size of the boat; and it must be remembered that in describing the Philae, I describe a dahabeeyah of the largest build – her total length from stem to stern being just one hundred feet, and the width of her upper deck at the broadest part little short of twenty.

Our floor being on a somewhat lower level than the men's deck, we went down three steps to the entrance door, on each side of which was an external cupboard, one serving as a storeroom and the other as a pantry. This door led into a passage out of which opened four sleeping-cabins, two on each side. These cabins measured about eight feet in length by four and a half in width, and contained a bed, a chair, a fixed washing-stand, a looking-glass against the wall, a shelf, a row of hooks, and under each bed two large drawers for clothes. At the end of this little passage another door opened into the dining saloon – a spacious, cheerful room, some twenty-three or twenty-four feet long, situate in the widest part of the boat, and lighted by four windows on each side and a skylight. The panelled walls and ceiling were painted in white picked out with gold; a cushioned divan covered with smart woollen reps ran along each side; and a gay Brussels carpet adorned the floor. The dining-table stood in the centre of the room; and there was ample space for a piano, two little bookcases, and several chairs. The window-curtains and portieres were of the same reps as the divan, the prevailing colours being scarlet and orange. Add a couple of mirrors in gilt frames; a vase of flowers on the table (for we were rarely without flowers of some sort, even in Nubia, where our daily bouquet had to be made with a few bean blossoms and castor-oil berries); plenty of books; the gentlemen's guns and sticks in one corner; and the hats of all the party hanging in the spaces between the windows; and it will be easy to realise the homely, habitable look of our general sitting-room.

Another door and passage opening from the upper end of the

saloon led to three more sleeping-rooms, two of which were single and one double; a bath-room; a tiny back staircase leading to the upper deck; and the stern cabin saloon. This last, following the form of the stern, was semicircular, lighted by eight windows, and surrounded by a divan. Under this, as under the saloon divans, there ran a row of deep drawers, which, being fairly divided, held our clothes, wine, and books. The entire length of the dahabeeyah being exactly one hundred feet, I take the cabin part to have occupied about fifty-six or fifty-seven feet (that is to say, about six or seven feet over the exact half), and the lower deck to have measured the remaining forty-three feet. But these dimensions, being given from memory, are approximate.

For the crew there was no sleeping accommodation whatever, unless they chose to creep into the hold among the luggage and packing-cases. But this they never did. They just rolled themselves up at night, heads and all, in rough brown blankets, and lay about the lower deck like dogs.

The Reis, or captain, the steersman, and twelve sailors, the dragoman, head cook, assistant cook, two waiters, and the boy who cooked for the crew, completed our equipment. Reis Hassan – short, stern-looking, authoritative – was a Cairo Arab. The dragoman, Elias Talhamy, was a Syrian of Beyrout. The two waiters, Michael and Habib, and the head cook (a wizened old *cordon bleu* named Hassan Bedawee) were also Syrians. The steersman and five of the sailors were from Thebes; four belonged to a place near Philae; one came from a village opposite Kom Ombo; one from Cairo, and two were Nubians from Assume. They were of all shades, from yellowish bronze to a hue not far removed from black; and though, at the first mention of it, nothing more incongruous can well be imagined than a sailor in petticoats and a turban, yet these men in their loose blue gowns, bare feet, and white muslin turbans, looked not only picturesque, but dressed exactly as they should be. They were for the most part fine young men, slender but powerful, square in the shoulders, like the ancient Egyptian statues, with the same slight legs and long flat feet. More docile, active, good-tempered, friendly fellows never pulled an oar. Simple and trustful as children, frugal as anchorites, they worked cheerfully from sunrise to sunset, sometimes towing the dahabeeyah on a rope all day long, like barge-horses sometimes punting for hours, which is the hardest work of all yet always singing at their task, always smiling when spoken to, and made as happy as princes with a handful of coarse Egyptian tobacco, or a bundle of fresh sugar-canes bought for a few pence by the river-side. We soon came to know them all by name – Mehemet Ali, Salame, Khalifeh, Riskali, Hassan, Musa, and so on; and as none of us ever went on shore without one or two of them to act as guards and attendants, and as the poor fellows were constantly getting bruised hands or feet, and coming to the upper deck to be doctored, a feeling of genuine friendliness was speedily established between us.

The ordinary pay of a Nile sailor is two pounds a month, with an additional allowance of about three and sixpence a month for flour. Bread is their staple food, and they make it themselves at certain places along the river where there are large public ovens for the purpose. This bread, which is cut up in slices and dried in the sun, is as brown as gingerbread and as hard as biscuit. They eat it soaked in hot water, flavoured with oil, pepper, and salt, and stirred in with boiled lentils till the whole becomes of the colour, flavour, and consistence of thick pea-soup. Except on grand occasions, such as Christmas Day or the anniversary of the Flight of the Prophet, when the passengers treat them to a sheep, this mess of bread and lentils, with a little coffee twice a day, and now and then a handful of dates, constitutes their only food throughout the journey.

The Nile season is the Nile sailors' harvest-time. When the warm weather sets in and the travellers migrate with the swallows, these poor fellows disperse in all directions; some to seek a living as porters in Cairo; others to their homes in Middle and Upper Egypt where, for about four pence a day, they take hire as labourers, or work at Shaduf irrigation till the Nile again overspreads the land. The Shaduf work is hard, and a man has to keep on for nine hours out of every twenty-four; but he prefers it, for the most part, to employment in the government sugar factories, where the wages average at about the same rate, but are paid in bread, which, being doled out by unscrupulous inferiors, is too often of light weight and bad quality. The sailors who succeed in getting a berth on board a cargo-boat for the summer are the most fortunate.

Our captain, pilot, and crew were all Mohammedans. The cook and his assistant were Syrian Mohammedans, the dragoman and waiters were Christians of the Syrian Latin church. Only one out of the fifteen natives could write or read; and that one was a sailor named Egendi, who acted as a sort of second mate. He used sometimes to write letters for the others, holding a scrap of tumbled paper across the palm of his left hand, and scrawling rude Arabic characters with a reed-pen of his own making. This Egendi, though perhaps the least interesting of the crew, was a man of many accomplishments – an excellent comic actor, a bit of a shoemaker, and a first-rate barber. More than once, when we happened to be stationed far from any village, he shaved his messmates all round, and turned them out with heads as smooth as billiard balls.

There are, of course, good and bad Mohammedans as there are good and bad churchmen of every denomination; and we had both sorts on board. Some of the men were very devout, never failing to perform their ablutions and say their prayers at sunrise and sunset. Others never dreamed of doing so. Some would not touch wine – had never tasted it in their lives, and would have suffered any extremity rather than break the law of their Prophet. Others had a nice taste in clarets, and a delicate appreciation of the respective merits of rum or whisky punch. It is, however, only fair to add that we never gave them these things except on special occasions, as on Christmas Day, or when they had been wading in the river, or in some other way undergoing extra fatigue in our service. Nor do I believe there was a man on board who would have spent a para of his scanty earnings on any drink stronger than coffee. Coffee and tobacco are, indeed, the only luxuries in which the Egyptian peasant indulges; and our poor fellows were never more grateful than when we distributed among them a few pounds of cheap native tobacco. This abominable mixture sells in the bazaars at sixpence the pound, the plant from which it is gathered being raised from inferior seed in a soil chemically unsuitable, because wholly devoid of potash.

Also it is systematically spoiled in the growing. Instead of being nipped off when green and dried in the shade, the leaves are allowed to wither on the stalk before they are gathered. The result is a kind of rank hay without strength or flavour, which is smoked by only the very poorest class, and carefully avoided by all who can afford to buy Turkish or Syrian tobacco.

Twice a day, after their midday and evening meals, our sailors were wont to sit in a circle and solemnly smoke a certain big pipe of the kind known as a hubble-bubble. This hubble-bubble (which was of most primitive make and consisted of a cocoa-nut and two sugar-canes) was common property; and, being filled by the captain, went round from hand to hand, from mouth to mouth, while it lasted.

They smoked cigarettes at other times, and seldom went on shore without a tobacco-pouch and a tiny book of cigarette-papers. Fancy a bare-legged Arab making cigarettes! No Frenchman, however, could twist them up more deftly, or smoke them with a better grace.

A Nile sailor's service expires with the season, so that he is generally a landsman for about half the year; but the captain's appointment is permanent. He is expected to live in Cairo, and is responsible for his dahabeeyah during the summer months, while it lies up at Boulak. Reis Hassan had a wife and a comfortable little home on the outskirts of Old Cairo, and was looked upon as a well-to-do personage among his fellows. He received four pounds a month all the year round from the owner of the Philae – a magnificent broad-shouldered Arab of about six foot nine, with a delightful smile, the manners of a gentleman, and the rapacity of a Shylock.

Our men treated us to a concert that first night, as we lay moored under the bank near Bedreshayn. Being told that it was customary to provide musical instruments, we had given them leave to buy a tar and darabukkeh before starting. The tar, or tambourine, was pretty enough, being made of rosewood inlaid with mother-of-pearl; but a more barbarous affair than the darabukkeh was surely never constructed. This primitive drum is about a foot and a half in length, funnel-shaped, moulded of sun-dried clay like the kullebs, and covered over at the top with strained parchment. It is held under the left arm and played like a tom-tom with the fingers of the right hand; and it weighs about four pounds. We would willingly have added a double pipe or a cocoa-nut fiddle* to the strength of the band, but none of our

* Arabic – *Kemengeh*.

men could play them. The tar and darabukkeh, however, answered the purpose well enough, and were perhaps better suited to their strange singing than more tuneful instruments.

We had just finished dinner when they began. First came a prolonged wail that swelled, and sank, and swelled again, and at last died away. This was the principal singer leading off with the keynote. The next followed suit on the third of the key; and finally all united in one long, shrill descending cry, like a yawn, or a howl, or a combination of both. This, twice repeated, preluded their performance and worked them up, apparently, to the necessary pitch of musical enthusiasm. The primo tenore then led off in a quavering roulade, at the end of which he slid into a melancholy chant to which the rest sang chorus. At the close of each verse they yawned and howled again; while the singer, carried away by his emotions, broke out every now and then into a repetition of the same amazing and utterly indescribable vocal wriggle with which he had begun. Whenever he did this, the rest held their breath in respectful admiration, and uttered an approving "Ah!" – which is here the customary expression of applause.

We thought their music horrible that first night, I remember; though we ended, as I believe most travellers do, by liking it. We, however, paid them the compliment of going upon deck and listening to their performance. As a night-scene, nothing could be more picturesque than this group of turbaned Arabs sitting in a circle, cross-legged, with a lantern in the midst. The singer quavered; the musicians thrummed; the rest softly clapped their hands to time, and waited their turn to chime in with the chorus. Meanwhile the lantern lit up their swarthy faces and their glittering teeth. The great mast towered up into the darkness. The river gleamed below. The stars shone overhead. We felt we were indeed strangers in a strange land.

WEST WITH THE NIGHT

Beryl Markham

Beryl Markham (1902–1986) was unmissable – six feet tall with blonde hair and blue eyes – she chalked up some major achievements and some glorious scandals. She grew up in Kenya where, aged only 18, she was the first woman to acquire a racehorse training licence in Africa. Diversifying briefly into aviation, in 1936 she was the first woman to fly solo over the Atlantic against the prevailing winds, writing up her account in *West with the Night* which turned Ernest Hemingway into a fan. As for those scandals – if you're going to take lovers, why not include an English prince and two famous authors?

He Was a Good Lion

One day, when we were riding to Elkington's, my father spoke about lions.

'Lions are more intelligent than some men,' he said, 'and more courageous than most. A lion will fight for what he has and for what he needs; he is contemptuous of cowards and wary of his equals. But he is not afraid. You can always trust a lion to be exactly what he is—and never anything else.'

'Except,' be added, looking more paternally concerned than usual, 'that damned lion of Elkington's!'

The Elkington lion was famous within a radius of twelve miles in all directions from the farm, because, if you happened to be anywhere inside that circle, you could hear him roar when he was hungry, when he was sad, or when he just felt like roaring. If, in the night, you lay sleepless on your bed and listened to an intermittent sound that began like the bellow of a banshee trapped in the bowels of Kilimanjaro and ended like the sound of that same banshee suddenly at large and arrived at the foot of your bed, you knew (because you had been told) that this was the song of Paddy.

Two or three of the settlers in East Africa at that time had caught lion cubs and raised them in cages. But Paddy, the Elkington lion, had never seen a cage.

He had grown to full size, tawny, black-maned and muscular, without a worry or a care. He lived on fresh meat, not of his own killing. He spent his waking hours (which coincided with everybody else's sleeping hours) wandering through Elkington's fields and pastures like an affable, if apostrophic, emperor, a-stroll in the gardens of his court.

He thrived in solitude. He had no mate, but pretended indifference and walked alone, not toying too much with imaginings of the unattainable. There were no physical barriers to his freedom, but the lions of the plains do not accept into their respected fraternity an individual bearing in his coat the smell of men. So Paddy ate, slept, and roared, and perhaps he sometimes dreamed, but he never left Elkington's. He was a tame lion, Paddy was. He was deaf to the call of the wild.

'I'm always careful of that lion,' I told my father, 'but he's really harmless. I have seen Mrs. Elkington stroke him.'

'Which proves nothing,' said my father. 'A domesticated lion is only an unnatural lion—and whatever is unnatural is untrustworthy.'

Whenever my father made an observation as deeply philosophical as that one, and as inclusive, I knew there was nothing more to be said.

I nudged my horse and we broke into a canter covering the remaining distance to Elkington's.

It wasn't a big farm as farms went in Africa before the First World War, but it had a very nice house with a large veranda on which my father, Jim Elkington, Mrs. Elkington, and one or two other settlers sat and talked with what to my mind was always unreasonable solemnity.

There were drinks, but beyond that there was a tea-table lavishly spread, as only the English can spread them. I have sometimes thought since of the Elkingtons' tea-table—round, capacious, and white, standing with sturdy legs against the green vines of the garden, a thousand miles of Africa receding from its edge.

It was a mark of sanity, I suppose, less than of luxury. It was evidence of the double debt England still owes to ancient China for her two gifts that made expansion possible—tea and gunpowder.

But cakes and muffins were no fit bribery for me. I had pleasures of my own then, or constant expectations. I made what niggardly salutations I could bring forth from a disinterested memory and left the house at a gait rather faster than a trot.

As I scampered past the square hay shed a hundred yards or so behind the Elkington house, I caught sight of Bishon Singh whom my father had sent ahead to tend our horses.

I think the Sikh must have been less than forty years old then, but his face was never any indication of his age. On some days he looked thirty and on others he looked fifty, depending on the weather, the time of day, his mood, or the tilt of his turban. If he had ever disengaged his beard from his hair and shaved the one and clipped the other, he might have astonished us all by looking like one of Kipling's elephant boys, but he never did either, and so, to me at least, he remained a man of mystery, without age or youth, but burdened with experience, like the wandering Jew.

He raised his arm and greeted me in Swahili as I ran through the Elkington farmyard and out toward the open country.

Why I ran at all or with what purpose in mind is beyond my answering, but when I had no specific destination I always ran as fast as I could in the hope of finding one—and I always found it.

I was within twenty yards of the Elkington lion before I saw him. He lay sprawled in the morning sun, huge, blackmaned, and gleaming with life. His tail moved slowly, stroking the rough grass like a knotted rope end. His body was sleek and easy, making a mould where he lay, a cool mould, that would be there when he had gone. He was not asleep; he was only idle. He was rusty-red, and soft, like a strokable cat.

I stopped and he lifted his head with magnificent ease and stared at me out of yellow eyes.

I stood there staring back, scuffling my bare toes in the dust, pursing my lips to make a noiseless whistle—a very small girl who knew about lions.

Paddy raised himself then, emitting a little sigh, and began to contemplate me with a kind of quiet premeditation, like that of a slow-witted man fondling an unaccustomed thought.

I cannot say that there was any menace in his eyes, because there wasn't, or that his 'frightful jowls' were drooling, because they were handsome jowls and very tidy. He did sniff the air, though, with what impressed me as being close to audible satisfaction. And he did not lie down again.

I remembered the rules that one remembers. I did not run. I walked very slowly, and I began to sing a defiant song.

'Kali coma Simba sisi,' I sang, 'Asikari yoti ni udari!—Fierce like the lion are we, Askari all are brave!'

I went in a straight line past Paddy when I sang it, seeing his eyes shine in the thick grass, watching his tail beat time to the metre of my ditty.

'Twendi, twendi—ku pigana—piga aduoi—piga sana!—Let us go, let us go—to fight—beat down the enemy! Beat hard, beat hard!'

What lion would be unimpressed with the marching song of the King's African Rifles?

Singing it still, I took up my trot toward the rim of the low hill which might, if I were lucky, have Cape gooseberry bushes on its slopes.

The country was grey-green and dry, and the sun lay on it closely, making the ground hot under my bare feet. There was no sound and no wind.

Even Paddy made no sound, coming swiftly behind me.

What I remember most clearly of the moment that followed are three things—a scream that was barely a whisper, a blow that struck me to the ground, and, as I buried my face in my arms and felt Paddy's teeth close on the flesh of my leg, a fantastically bobbing turban, that was Bishon Singh's turban, appear over the edge of the hill.

I remained conscious, but I closed my eyes and tried not to be. It was not so much the pain as it was the sound.

The sound of Paddy's roar in my ears will only be duplicated, I think, when the doors of hell slip their wobbly hinges, one day, and give voice and authenticity to the whole panorama of Dante's poetic nightmares. It was an immense roar that encompassed the world and dissolved me in it.

I shut my eyes very tight and lay still under the weight of Paddy's paws.

Bishon Singh said afterward that he did nothing. He said he had remained by the hay shed for a few minutes after I ran past him, and then, for no explainable reason, had begun to follow me. He admitted, though, that, a little while before, he had seen Paddy go in the direction I had taken.

The Sikh called for help, of course, when he saw the lion meant to attack, and a half-dozen of Elkington's syces had come running from the house. Along with them had come Jim Elkington with a rawhide whip.

Jim Elkington, even without a rawhide whip, was very impressive. He was one of those enormous men whose girths alone seem to preclude any possibility of normal movement, much less of speed. But Jim had speed—not to be loosely compared with lightning, but rather like the speed of something spherical and smooth and relatively irresistible, like the cannon balls of the Napoleonic Wars. Jim was, without question, a man of considerable courage, but in the case of my Rescue From the Lion, it was, I am told, his momentum rather than his bravery for which I must forever be grateful.

It happened like this—as Bishon Singh told it;

'I am resting against the walls of the place where hay is kept and first the large lion and then you, Beru, pass me going toward the open field, and a thought comes to me that a lion and a young girl are strange company, so I follow. I follow to the place where the hill that goes up becomes the hill that goes down, and where it goes down deepest I see that you are running without much thought in your head and the lion is running behind you with many thoughts in his head, and I scream for everybody to come very fast.

'Everybody comes very fast, but the large lion is faster than anybody, and he jumps on your back and I see you scream but I hear no scream. I only hear the lion, and I begin to run with everybody, and this includes Bwana Elkington, who is saying a great many words I do not know and is carrying a long kiboko which he holds in his hand and is meant for beating the large lion.

'Bwana Elkington goes past me the way a man with lighter legs and fewer inches around his stomach might go past me, and he is waving the long kiboko so that it whistles over all of our heads like a very sharp wind, but when we get close to the lion it comes to my mind that that lion is not of the mood to accept a kiboko.

'He is standing with the front of himself on your back, Beru, and you are bleeding in three or five places, and he is roaring. I do not believe Bwana Elkington could have thought that that lion at that moment would consent to being beaten, because the lion was not looking the way he had ever looked before when it was necessary for him to be beaten. He was looking as if he did not wish to be disturbed by a kiboko, or the Bwana, or the syces, or Bishon Singh, and he was saying so in a very large voice.

'I believe that Bwana Elkington understood this voice when he was still more than several feet from the lion, and I believe the Bwana considered in his mind that it would be the best thing not to beat the lion just then, but the Bwana when he runs very fast is like the trunk of a great baobob tree rolling down a slope, and it seems that because of this it was not possible for him to explain the thought of his mind to the soles of his feet in a sufficient quickness of time to prevent him from rushing much closer to the lion than in his heart he wished to be.

'And it was this circumstance, as I am telling it,' said Bishon Singh, 'which in my considered opinion made it possible for you to be alive, Beru.'

'Bwana Elkington rushed at the lion then, Bishon Singh?'

'The lion, as of the contrary, rushed at Bwana Elkington,' said Bishon Singh. 'The lion deserted you for the Bwana, Beru. The lion was of the opinion that his master was not in any honest way deserving of a portion of what he, the lion, had accomplished in the matter of fresh meat through no effort by anybody except himself.'

Bishon Singh offered this extremely reasonable interpretation with impressive gravity, as if he were expounding the Case For the Lion to a chosen jury of Paddy's peers.

'Fresh meat'... I repeated dreamily, and crossed my fingers.

'So then what happened...?'

The Sikh lifted his shoulders and let them drop again 'What could happen, Beru? The lion rushed for Bwana Elkington, who in his turn rushed from the lion, and in so rushing did not keep in his hand the long kiboko, but allowed it to fall upon the ground, and in accomplishing this the Bwana was free to ascend a very fortunate tree, which he did.'

'And you picked me up, Bishon Singh?'

He made a little dip with his massive turban. 'I was happy with the duty of carrying you back to this very bed, Beru, and of advising your father, who had gone to observe some of Bwana Elkington's horses, that you had been moderately eaten by the large lion. Your father returned very fast, and Bwana Elkington some time later returned very fast, but the large lion has not returned at all.'

The large lion had not returned at all. That night he killed a horse, and the next night he killed a yearling bullock, and after that a cow fresh for milking.

In the end he was caught and finally caged, but brought to no rendezvous with the firing squad at sunrise. He remained for years in his cage, which, had he managed to live in freedom with his inhibitions, he might never have seen at all.

It seems characteristic of the mind of man that the repression of what is natural to humans must be abhorred, but that what is natural to an infinitely more natural animal must be confined within the bounds of a reason peculiar only to men—more peculiar sometimes than seems reasonable at all.

Paddy lived, people stared at him and he stared back, and this went on until he was an old, old lion. Jim Elkington died, and Mrs. Elkington, who really loved Paddy, was forced, because of circumstances beyond her control or Paddy's, to have him shot by Boy Long, the manager of Lord Delamere's estates.

This choice of executioners was, in itself, a tribute to Paddy, for no one loved animals more or understood them better, or could shoot more cleanly than Boy Long.

But the result was the same to Paddy. He had lived and died in ways not of his choosing. He was a good lion. He had done what he could about being a tame lion. Who thinks it just to be judged by a single error?

I still have the scars of his teeth and claws, but they are very small now and almost forgotten, and I cannot begrudge him his moment.

SOUTH FROM THE LIMPOPO

Dervla Murphy

Dervla Murphy (1931–present) is an Irish touring cyclist. Her first major adventure, begun in 1963, took her through Europe and beyond to her eventual destination: India. She was armed with a pistol, waved warningly at potential attackers, and a journal, published as the first of many books. She was later accompanied on her travels by her young daughter. Murphy's life has been inspirational and the only woman who wouldn't want to be her is apparently Murphy herself, who wishes she were the Anglo-Italian explorer Freya Stark.

Surplus People

Maclear – Matatiele – Pietermaritzburg – Johannesburg – Home

> Some people plead that the right to own land should be granted to Bantu living in White areas... If these concessions are granted such a population will not be satisfied with social rights only, but will certainly insist on the franchise and make further demands... My department would view the alienation of White land as a nail in the coffin of the White nation and of the fundamental principle of apartheid. We shall therefore be only too glad to assist those Bantu who are interested in buying land in towns in their respective homelands.
>
> I.P. van Onselen, Secretary for Bantu Administration and Development (1972)

Maclear, 26 July 1993

When Jim switched on the TV news this morning we saw a bloodstained church floor strewn with blanket-covered bodies. It is assumed APLA killed those eleven people, and grievously maimed many more, in last evening's gun and grenade attack on Kenilworth church in Cape Town. The Hurters exclaimed that only blacks would slaughter people at prayer, within a church building, but I had to contradict them. Northern Ireland has endured an identical atrocity in a rural church in Armagh.

Over the forty-five mountainous miles from Elliot to Maclear a formidable gale blew either against or across me. Here all the telephone lines being down has closed both banks – most improbably there are two – and I must live on credit in this friendly no-star hotel where the last guest checked out sixteen days ago.

Maclear is a dispirited little place. One can't buy cheese, butter, yoghurt, amasi, even sardines – or a daily newspaper in any language. The Jo'burg *Sunday Times* arrives on Wednesdays, the bread is stale and black/white relations are extremely uneasy. In part, this has to do with the township's grazing land having been seized only a few years ago for yet another commercial forestry plantation. (Approaching Maclear, one sees a landscape devastated by this development.) However, some local blacks supported the seizure; South African Paper and Pulp Industries (SAPPI) gave much desperately needed employment while the land was being cleared and planted. But now fewer jobs are available and the grazing is gone for ever – or until such time as there is a revolution more radical than anything envisaged by the ANC.

Tonight the hotel business is booming; I have three fellow-guests – two Xhosas and an Afrikaner – all employees of a cane-spirit company. (One of the favourite township drinks: cheap and nasty.) Here is affirmative action in practice, the white rep training blacks in a dorp ladies bar. An interesting tableau, the English-speaking regulars being carefully polite, the blacks ill-at-ease behind an over-jolly façade. One farmer has just returned from his first journey overseas, a visit to cousins in Wales. South Africans, he assured us, don't know what *real* apartheid is – they should see how things are between the

English and the Welsh! He saw it for himself when an Englishman entered a pub and everyone spoke Welsh to exclude him – how's that for racism? The blacks registered shock/horror and agreed no such thing could ever happen in South Africa.

The same, 27 July

Sheer 1,000-foot table-tops almost completely surround Maclear and on one is concealed the township. When I climbed up this morning, invited by Mrs Ntloko who runs the clinic, I found an extremity of destitution that makes Zola seem affluent. Mrs Ntloko introduced me to several men who, having found their first job on the forestry project and become accustomed to earning, are now again unwaged and seething with anger; recently they had to sell their cattle for lack of grazing. Equally angry are the hundreds of ex-miners, sacked during the past few years from worked-out Rand gold mines. This community, like countless others, was dependent for generations on miners' wages. But South Africa never ceases to surprise. Even the angriest of the men apologized to me, as a white, for the Kenilworth slaughter. 'We are very sorry, that was bad, we don't like it.'

At noon the bank opened but no cash was available until 3.30. The manager tried hard to put me off the Transkei. 'They'll steal your bike in Mount Fletcher! And that track is so rough you'll be days getting there. Why not let me give you a lift back to Elliot? You could go on to Jo'burg through the Free State.'

Tomorrow I mean to take the sort of precautions that always make me feel silly. Normally my journal travels in a pannier-bag, my camera around my waist and the binoculars over a shoulder. While in the Transkei I'll carry my journal over a shoulder (under my shirt) and the camera and binoculars in a pannier-bag. This apprehension is uncharacteristic but Maclear's blacks are – it has to be admitted – slightly unsettling.

In the bar this evening a young man put on the Mandela turn, a popular entertainment. From under the counter came one of those shockingly realistic rubber masks that cover the whole head, not just the face. These are repulsively clever caricatures, the unmistakable Mandela features modified to present a monkey-man. The wearers mockingly mimic Mr Mandela's voice, making Winnie-related speeches which provoke guffaws of ribald laughter, or putting PAC and APLA slogans into the mouth of their President-to-be. Among the white hoi polloi no distinction is drawn between the ANC and the PAC, a symptom of their uninterest in their own country's political evolution.

Mount Fletcher, 28 July

This is being written under the influence of drink. A lot of drink, consequent upon the locals' determination fittingly to celebrate the arrival of a *white tourist*! It's unlikely they'll shoot me hereabouts: alcohol poisoning is the main hazard. I can't imagine what the potation is (not any form of beer) – it comes out of a ginormous tin kettle and my liver will take weeks to recover. When I arrived, free-wheeling down the steep main street, the whole town came to a halt. Stopping at the bottle-store, I was at once surrounded by ten or twelve grim-faced young Comrades. (By now I can tell a Comrade at a glance; they have a persona all their own.) But quarter of an hour later everyone was smiling and I had been persuaded to spend two nights here.

The same, 29 July

The above entry was curtailed by the contents of that kettle.

Yesterday's thirty-seven miles were the most exhausting – and among the most beautiful – of this whole journey. First, a very steep two-mile climb from Maclear to a wide plateau where the sun rose over a distant range of strangely peaked mountains, the peaks all leaning sideways as though pushed out of shape. In that slanting light and clear air each colour was vibrant: the red-gold of grassy slopes, the dark yet glowing green of trees marking watercourses, the brown-gold of maize fields.

Over the next eight miles I met no one. Then from the plateau's edge appeared the Transkei beyond a deep valley: countless tiny dwellings on barren hillsides. The Halcyon Drift 'border' post was manned by two white soldiers, three black police officers and an Alsatian tethered to an armoured vehicle. The white cyclist enraged this creature; he literally foamed at the mouth and almost broke his chain in a frenzied effort to get at me. One soldier glanced at my passport, handed it back, then asked my nationality. His mate described as 'suicidal' my entering the Transkei unarmed.

Slowly I pushed Lear out of the valley on one of the worst roads I have ever endured. Here a truckload of Mount Fletcher folk, who had stopped to pee, gave me a heart-warming welcome, counteracting the recent build-up of 'Transkei tension'. Immediately I knew this was going to be a happy experience, a feeling reinforced when Joel joined me, full of curiosity and chat. Elsewhere in Africa such encounters occur daily, here they are very rare.

Joel, a 23-year-old road worker, wants to be a teacher but has had to take a menial job to feed the family: parents in poor health, an elder sister crippled by polio, plus a wife and two children. As we walked to the ridge-top he told me about his three cows whose calves were stillborn because of the drought. Drought-stricken white farmers receive government aid – more than R3 *billion* last year – but blacks must suffer their losses unaided.

As we passed a gigantic new earth-mover abandoned by the wayside, Joel mentioned a plan to tar this Maclear–Mount Fletcher road. When work began some months ago he was one of the team breaking rocks and scattering them on the surface as a foundation. But the money ran out; under Transkei's grotesquely corrupt puppet regime such crises are common. I had to walk the next twenty-five miles, dragging Lear over these large, loose, sharp fragments of mountain.

Although in white terminology Katkop is a 'village' it extends over several square miles (or rather, long miles) and here live uncounted thousands, far from water, without electricity, chronically short of firewood and grazing. About one-third of the dwellings are round thatched huts – the most skilful thatching I've seen since Cameroon – the rest are tiny oblong shacks, their tin roofs stone-anchored. Many are brightly painted – duck-egg green the favourite shade, but also lemon, pale pink, buff, sky blue. Some external walls are decorated with elaborate traditional designs in red, black, brown, white. Some minuscule windows wear incongruous suburban lace curtains tied back with pretty bows. Every few miles a tiny 'café' or huxter shop offers basic sustenance. The local litter consists almost entirely of plastic bags fluttering in the breeze on rusty wire fencing, itself a form of litter left over from the days when this land was white-owned.

Here the heights and depths are truly awesome. This is a red-rock landscape, deeply riven by irregular gorges below 2,000-foot precipices – a topographical chaos of visual splendour leaving little space for human habitation or cultivation. Yet in an emotionally muddled way I rejoiced to be in an area where some traces of 'normal' African life remain. Little herd-boys sat on high boulders guarding their pitifully small herds of cattle, others walked behind a flock of goats on a contour footpath, coloured blanket draped gracefully over a shoulder. Women were laundering blankets in scanty streams, then children carefully spread them to dry on tennis-court widths of smooth polished rock, blanket-wrapped men rode small sturdy Basuto ponies up and down precipitous slopes sitting straight-backed, their feet almost touching the ground. White South Africa's landscapes, however beautiful, remain memorials to apartheid – their unpeopled spaces cruel, black activity channelled towards the *baas*'s enrichment.

Beyond Katkop came a mysterious region of crumpled dark-grey rocks, uncannily resembling giant crocodiles or prehistoric monsters. Then we crossed a high pass, the gradient making my struggle to drag Lear over that surface like some medieval penance for the most heinous of sins. But my reward was a scene of the wildest splendour – the opposite mountain walls golden in the noon light, against an intensely blue sky. I half-regretted getting to the top, from where could be seen the next 'village', Lalangubo, very far below.

Four (mostly downhill) hours later Mount Fletcher appeared in a wide valley, bounded to east and west by long low ridges.

As the Comrades escorted me from the bottle-store to the Castle Rocks Hotel we were followed by excited children and adolescents, some exclaiming at my achievement (as well they might!) and shouting friendly questions. Unsurprisingly, no washing water was available until morning. Then Mr Nxesi – a one-eyed raggedly dressed elder who speaks near-perfect English – swept me off to his kraal of thatched huts on a distant hillside. There that potent kettle was produced and an impromptu party laid on for the 'brave lady from Ireland'. (Xhosa songs and dances – shades of Mafefe!)

Before the contents of the kettle took effect (a brief period: my tummy was very empty) we discussed regional politics. Said Mr Nxesi, 'Comrade Mandela isn't tough enough, he'll never control our robbers in Umtata [Transkei's capital]. Money is power. And our Mafia is numerous, thousands will fight to keep jobs and perks. Poverty isn't the worst thing the Bantustans did to us. The worst is corruption – *so* much money from Pretoria! Our leaders and their hangers-on are destroyed. Destroyed in their souls.'

I refrained from questioning Mr Nxesi about his fluent English, a question with the implied corollary, 'How come an educated man lives in such poverty?' But I had my suspicions confirmed today. He lost an eye, and his job, in a drunken brawl; not so long ago he was head of the English department in a black university. The kraal is his ancestral home; last year he had to sell a bungalow built in happier times. And his wife has left him. Sad…

The Castle Rocks Hotel – and Mount Fletcher in general – could be said to prove a white point. Once this was a typical small-town hotel, its two rows of bedrooms overlooking a wide lawn. Now everything is ramshackle. And the lavatory is inaccessible; one has to find the person with the key – and who is that? At any given moment, where is s/he to be found? When those questions prove unanswerable I use my mug as a jerry and tip it out the window, as did many London citizens in the seventeenth century to Pepys's distress. Here no distress is caused, only astonishment on the part of adjacent livestock: hens, geese, goats and a pathetically lean cow. I'm writing this with my room door open and a hen and ten fluffy chicks have just wandered in to hoover the floor – expecting, and finding, numerous crumbs left by the last occupant. In Mount Fletcher, with fowl busily pecking around my bedroom floor and that cow scratching her neck against my windowsill, I feel more at ease than I ever could in a dorp hotel.

Also, R30 covers the cost of supper, room and breakfast, for which one pays at least R130 in 'South Africa'.

In contrast to the dorps' crowded hotel bars, neither bar here is much used. Both are dingy, ill-lit, stale-smelling, their shelves almost bare, equipped only with three unsteady stools and two glasses (one each!). Most customers sit on the stoop's parapet, high above the main street where noisy geese, minute black piglets and another bony cow nibble and root in the short brown grass. The pavement slabs have long since been removed to serve some other purpose.

At present Mount Fletcher is sorely afflicted by political dissension, its ANC activists disunited. The Mafia of whom Mr Nxesi spoke may be encountered in government offices overmanned by incompetent officials. In the ANC office – which, rather confusingly, doubles as a doctor's private clinic – Dr P— pointedly ignored my arrival while continuing to operate his computer, the screen showing a list of expensive drugs. Then, having put Whitey in her place, he delegated Mrs Sokhupa, who describes herself as a 'social worker', to show me round the hospital founded in 1934 by a philanthropic Englishman. The original single-storey dark-brick building is pleasant enough, the jerry-built addition less so. The nursing staff impress more by their kindness to patients than by their knowledge. They complain, with good reason, about shortages: of medicines, bandages, oxygen, bed-pans, wheelchairs. The wards and corridors were cleanish but only *ish*. Nobody seemed sufficiently AIDS-aware to take seriously the need for unwavering vigilance. Yes, it's a bad disease. But Transkei people don't get it. The main worry is an increase in TB deaths.

The hospital's director is a Kampala doctor, amiable and courteous – much taller and darker skinned than the average Xhosa. He invited us to drink tea in his roomy, comfortably furnished bungalow on the edge of the compound, with a fine view of the town below and the hills beyond. On the way we passed through a colony of flimsy rusting caravans parked close together: the nurses' quarters, each small caravan accommodating two.

The doctor had felt no scruples about taking this job in 1985 when State repression was at its worst – the Last Stand. In Uganda he couldn't earn such a salary and he had to think of his family: four motherless children to be educated, a dependent father and aunt... Remembering how implacably much of the white world boycotted South Africa – cutting its citizens off from the BBC and isolating academics from the latest research – it is ironic that so many blacks were then hurrying south to support apartheid directly by availing of good job offers in the 'Bantustans'.

Today the secondary school is closed; either the teachers or the pupils are on strike – maybe both. 'The teachers are so ignorant it doesn't matter,' said Mrs Sokhupa. 'They can't even keep the kids sitting down. This year I'm sending my two sons to Elliot, to a good white school. The other kids treat them badly but I say it doesn't matter. There they can learn – if I pay big money!'

According to Mr Nxesi, the under-30 generation hereabouts is largely illiterate. Many children don't start school until they are 8 or 9; only then can they walk the necessary distances, up to sixteen miles daily. Even more detrimental, most boys drop out after circumcision at the age of 16. It would be too humiliating for *men* to have to accept the authority of their own age-group – any teacher under 40.

There was much rejoicing today when light rain fell for an hour; this morning the hotel dishes were rinsed in my washing water – *after* I had washed. Out of a similar water shortage came my (and my daughter's) Madagascan hepatitis-A.

This is a soothingly silent town; most people are too poor to afford ghetto blasters.

Matatiele, 30 July

I had just commented on Mount Fletcher's tranquillity when the party started. A newly arrived army platoon was celebrating its last night of freedom before barrack life closed in. End of tranquillity.

Yesterday morning a bucket of steaming water and a teapot of coffee (no tea available) were brought to my room by a buxom young maid with a smile like the sunrise. Later, I enjoyed a substantial breakfast of fried eggs and liver. But this morning – nothing. The dining room was shambolic, the entire staff AWOL. As I packed, several hungover teenaged soldiers, clad only in underpants, came wandering in and out of my room – fascinated by Lear's panniers – and deplored no water, no breakfast... The lack of water seemed to bother them most. Soon they had to report for duty and how could they be expected to don uniforms before washing?

On the road to Matatiele – new and velvet-smooth – the taxi traffic was heavy and the concomitant litter repulsive. For South Africa's prodigiously littered countryside all races are to blame. James Bryce, visiting 'white' Beaufort West in 1897, noted, 'Most of its houses are stuck down irregularly over a surface covered with broken bottles and empty sardine and preserved meat tins.' A century later, cyclists are seriously at risk when speeding motorists open windows to dispose of bottles.

This small market town is just over the 'border' in Natal. During my afternoon's dander I saw only two whites, apart from busy storekeepers. Xhosas throng the streets, many wrapped in colourful blankets, and the pavements are piled with hawkers' goods. The whole scene – noisy, bright, animated, scruffy – is the very antithesis of your average dorp.

Matatiele is reputed to be an APLA/PAC stronghold and by sunset a dozen young APLA warriors had occupied the ladies bar. Already they knew all about me (slightly disconcerting if not surprising) and were keen to publicize their Africanist ideology. The most articulate and forceful favoured anonymity, so let's call them Tom, Dick and Harry.

'We don't believe in killing foreigners,' explained Tom. 'Not in the Transkei or anywhere else. It's the boere does those murders, then blames us.'

'But we do believe in "One Settler, One Bullet",' said Dick. 'Why not? Settlers have a legal right to our land, they tell us, through "armed conquest", OK, to get it back we use violence – right?'

Harry boasted, 'We've more and more township kids joining our struggle.' (This is untrue.) 'They don't trust the ANC, they know the capitalists have bought them. A new South Africa – what's new? Without armed action there's nothing in it for the exploited. Who's negotiating for them? We're only violent because the whites won't back down, not really, unless we fight.'

*

Underberg, 31 July

Today I broke a rule, arriving here an hour after sunset. Reason: a strong relentless headwind over the eighty-five hilly miles from Matatiele.

For hours commercial forestry frustrated me, completely concealing one of Africa's most splendid mountain ranges. These pines and bluegums, covering the lower slopes of the Drakensberg like some disfiguring disease, retain the water that previously filled rivers and are an ecological and social disaster. Each tree's roots reach down some sixty feet to groundwater level and each absorbs more than 100 litres a day. Largely because of the activities of SAPPI and MONDI, South Africa's dwindling rivers have become an international problem, threatening the survival of countless peasant farmers in southern Mozambique.

In Underberg's hotel bar a party of transplanted Rhodies gave me a heroine's welcome.

'From Matatiele today on that bike? Hey, you're some woman!' Wenwes like action and physical stamina and what they imagine to be daring deeds – like cycling through a very small area of the Transkei.

Ixopo, 1 August

More plantations today, including miles of nurseries – proof that SAPPI and MONDI are planning ahead, confident of being unhampered in the new South Africa. To escape, I took a narrow dirt track along the edge of a small separate segment of the Transkei which the APLA warriors had warned me to avoid. (Hence my Underberg detour, instead of the direct route through Kokstad and Umzimkulu.) This track overlooks a series of deep, wide, winter-brown valleys – far below, densely populated, with bulky blue-hazy ranges beyond. Then suddenly, high among superb unplanted mountains, I found myself over the 'border'; there was no roadblock, perhaps because this area is so remote. Here shacks crowded the steep slopes and the atmosphere was distinctly unwelcoming, as predicted by APLA. Pushing Lear up one long hill I felt quite vulnerable as young men scowled speculatively at the panniers.

In this sort of terrain a cyclist does not have the advantage of speed; turning to freewheel away from any difficulty would simply take me back to the base of an equally steep hill. I was halfway up when three youths began to shout at me aggressively – a nasty moment. But then an elder with an air of authority emerged from his neat little bungalow and silently shook hands (he spoke no English) before escorting me to the edge of the settlement. From there the track dived into a boulder-strewn, uninhabited valley.

The Eastern Cape is hilly enough but Natal is outrageously hilly; here is no such thing as a short climb or a gentle slope. On the main roads wayside notices warn that the next hill is five or six miles long with a gradient requiring trucks to take Special Precautions.

What must the first British settlers have made of this terrain when they arrived by the boatload between 1849 and 1851? But soon they were flourishing and marvelling at Natal's fertility: lush grass growing five feet high, an abundance of free building timber in the kloofs, soil suitable for growing sugar-cane, cotton, tobacco, indigo and yielding two crops a year. All that plus a climate they incredulously described as 'perpetual summer' – and thousands of dispossessed 'Kaffirs' reduced to working for a pittance. (In 1848 five 'native locations' had been demarcated on land 'unsuitable for European occupation'.) By 1853, families who had been starving in Britain a few years earlier were living in relative comfort, many killing their own mutton – the ultimate criterion of prosperity.

On this Sunday afternoon Ixopo (to pronounce it correctly you must make a choking sound) was moribund. A pleasant little town, its suburbs are even leafier than the norm, its homes and gardens spacious and English-looking. The bigger hotel is closed. The other, also big, has recently been bought by a cheerful Indian with no hang-ups about selling alcohol at 4 p.m. on the Sabbath. Yet again I'm the only guest and in Ixopo even the bar-trade is feeble. But Mr Moosa (Billy to his friends) remains resolutely optimistic.

'This time next year things will be better. By then we'll all feel we're simply *South African*. A historic change is coming, a psychological change. Even Natal will be better, even kwaZulu.'

I wonder... This province is blood-soaked like no other. Last weekend saw sixteen murders: a 'normal' statistic. Men, women, children and babies are routinely butchered, by the dozen. Weapons abound and intimidation is general. Fear, hate, suspicion, bitterness, grief and wild demoralizing rumours have corroded the black communities and to some extent infected everyone.

Later, Billy and I were joined by Rudi, a middle-aged Coloured friend of the Moosa family. Ixopo, he informed me, is the Zulu word for the sound cattle make when withdrawing hooves from mud. Rudi has white skin, grey-green eyes and crinkly light-brown hair. 'Wearing a wig' – he grinned – 'I could've passed for white if I'd wanted to. But the way things were as I grew up, you'd be ashamed to be white.'

Billy then took charge of an elfin 3-year-old daughter while her mother Seetha, a primary-school teacher, made scrumptious samoosas in the kitchen from where she shouted comments at intervals.

As a building contractor, Rudi worries about the immediate future. 'Everything is at a standstill, I've no work for my men. Hey, it's tough! They can't live on sunshine, I have them on half-pay. But after the elections business will improve all round. The ANC won't be having any more scary revolutionary ideas. There's no risk here of a mess like up north.'

'We're solid behind the ANC,' called Seetha from the kitchen, 'us and all our families – though living here we don't say so. Only to foreigners!'

Billy nodded. 'Now no one else can run the show – politically, I mean. And we have our white tribe to run the economy.'

Seetha brought us a mountain of samoosas and a packet of paper napkins. 'As I see it,' she said, 'our only danger now is too many whites hating and distrusting Mr Mandela. We don't, we can respect him.'

'But let's talk straight,' said Rudi. 'Most Indians and Coloureds are anti-black. It's a gut thing. All the same, it's not like white racism. We're only anti-black in bulk – see what I mean? Doesn't stop most of us having some good black friends – real friends. How many whites can honestly say they've a black friend, a real friend? Maybe a few up in the university world, but damn few!'

*

Richmond, 2 August

Miles of swift freewheeling took me down to the Josephine Bridge (who was Josephine?) across the Umkomaas, altitude 1,800 feet. The river is low, yet this lush narrow valley yields an abundance of fruits and vegetables all the year round.

Between there and Richmond (4,500 feet) my sweat-loss was sensational and on the outskirts of the town, in Websters Garden Stall, I drank two litres of amasi while a garrulous Anglo-Irishman chose his flowers, fruits and herbs. Long ago he left a mouldering Big House in Co. Cork and he has done well for himself in Natal. He excoriated the media. They report local black-on-black violence as happening in Richmond. It's not happening in *Richmond*, it's happening in Richmond's townships. But the media can't spell those names so they say 'Richmond'. Consequently, property prices have halved and the two hotels have closed. Then there's the drought. When they can't cultivate, farmers find it's best to go on long holidays to cheap Mauritius instead of staying in expensive South Africa. Many have sold their livestock and are giving all their water to the orange orchards. But the '93 crop is dwarfed – unsellable. This victim of drought has just returned from a three-month holiday on Mauritius.

Beyond Websters I noticed a signpost to Byrne, a nearby village named after J.C. Byrne who in his lifetime was loathed by the hapless emigrants he cheated with such ease. Mr Byrne, operating from a smart London office, was among the many con-men who planned large-scale emigrations to Natal for their own profit.

During 1850 Natal – hitherto virtually unknown in Britain – suddenly became the fashionable colony. Some 'independent' emigrants, travelling cabin class, brought agricultural implements and a few farm animals. But most early settlers were destitute labourers who eagerly took advantage of such schemes as the Earl of Egremont's Petworth Emigration Society. When the Duke of Buccleuch dispatched a shipload of surplus tenants they settled around Richmond. Numerous noble lords were only too pleased to get rid of their 'distressed tenantry' by paying £10 per head for fares and outfits consisting of clothing for two years. Also, as Britain was then in a panic about overpopulation causing 'unrest', the Poor Law allowed parishes to assist emigrants from the rates. Quite often, assistance became compulsion. Imprisoned felons' families being dependent on the rates, many thieves and footpads were offered a choice: conviction or emigration.

Richmond's tree-lined main street (Shepstone Street – no Voortrekkers here please!) proves how quickly the settlers recreated England. Natal's first Anglican church was built here in 1856 and its rectory stands on the site of Natal's first girls' school (1869). Country crafts are now on sale where James Hacklands was making wagons by 1862. The court house began to dispense British justice in 1865. The Freemasons Lodge opened in 1884 (it seems the apostrophe had already fallen into disuse locally) and in 1897 came the railway station, at the end of a branch fine from Pietermaritzburg.

Along Chilley Street you can smell the chillis. The Indian colony took root in the late 1860s and has been quietly flourishing ever since; Billy and Seetha were both born here. Can there really – I wondered, looking at the shops – be so many Patels in South Africa? Or has 'Patel' been adopted in lieu of names too long and unwieldy for settler tongues? I was seeking a *Weekly Mail,* nowhere to be found since I left Cape Town. By now the national media's morbid navel-gazing has completely cut me off from the rest of the world; the only widely available global news concerns either sport – chiefly rugby and cricket, soccer is the blacks' game – or the British Royal Family. The latter fixation defeats me; why should South Africans – including Afrikaners – be so riveted by the minutiae of royal deeds and misdeeds?

Mr A.P. Patel sells the *Weekly Mail* and Mrs Patel, remarking that I looked tired – I felt humidity exhausted – invited me into a back room for cinnamon tea and home-made sweetmeats. She had heard all about me from Seetha; one doesn't travel quite anonymously through rural South Africa.

Richmond's motel is closed but was bought a few weeks ago by a young English-speaking couple who have just reopened the bar and offered me a free bed in a garden shed. At the bar sat four Afrikaner SAP officers, unwinding after a stressful foray into a township. They competed to stand me beers and for my entertainment swapped the latest jokes – for example, 'How many poles does it take to kill a Hani?'

Then they recalled various horrors in which they or their friends have been involved. Like the slaughter of eighteen Inkatha Freedom Party (IFP) supporters in nearby kwaShange. And the night an important Zulu chief was assassinated outside his Pietermaritzburg home – the very same night an equally important chief and two of his followers were shot dead in northern Natal. On one of the worst nights, twenty-three were killed in Richmond. Soon after, two women were hacked to death with pangas in a local IFP leader's house. This led to nineteen being arrested, including a member of the SADF. When an IFP member talked aloud about having proof of heavy white involvement in all this violence, he was shot dead next day – the very day Chief Ndlovu, known to be working hard for peace in the Richmond area, was assassinated near Ixopo. By now hundreds – no, thousands! – have joined both the ANC and the IFP in an effort to protect themselves.

The truth's elusiveness compounds the terror aroused by the present crisis. It is impossible to establish the facts about any crime or to distinguish information from disinformation. Even in those rare cases when impartial Peace Monitor witnesses are present, they can observe only a fragment of the action and have little hope of obtaining reliable evidence from either side about motives, provocations, methods, consequences. This opacity is unnerving for the mass of politically uninvolved township dwellers – helpless victims of divisive rumours, accusations, denials and reprisals.

My kind hostess brought me, unasked, a large plate of boerewors and chips. As I ate, a fifth SAP officer joined us, an English-speaker in his early twenties. Soon Charlie was explaining, 'My background is liberal – DP parents – and at school I used to stand up for blacks when that was risky. I'd notions about helping to reform the police. Now I hate blacks. After seeing how they treat each other, I hate them all. Last week only a few hundred came to an ANC demo in the town centre so the bully-boys toured the townships. Three hours later we'd 3,000 to control! Richmond's two townships, Magoda and Pateni, had 30,000 blacks. Now there's less than 15,000, most ANC have fled to the Rand or the Cape.'

George arrived next, in a Mercedes, the 24-year-old son of one of those hard-hit local farmers. Three years ago he was appointed manager of a large sawmill and he reported a recent 'sensible' SAPPI directive to all managers: 'Employ only whites in the important jobs to keep production up.' He reckons he's sorted out all that subversive trade-union nonsense. 'I told them, "If you put your trade-union subscription into the bank instead, you'll soon have something to show for it. Why should you pay for a fine car for some trade-union dictator? Soon the bank will give you more money than you'll ever get fighting with your employers." It's like always with blacks, you've got to think for them...'

Last year George heard the shots when his uncle was being murdered in his garage after 'they' had pillaged the house. 'He wasn't even trying to catch the bastards, he'd just driven in, they killed him for fun – or spite or something...'

It is hard to cope with South Africa's relentless daily death-toll. Yet an extraordinary feature of this transition period is the overall normality of everyday life from the traveller's point of view – while for the majority of citizens law and order is rapidly breaking down.

Pietermaritzburg, 3 August

Leaving Richmond at dawn, I wondered how the new South Africa will change the town. Surely it cannot continue to look as though neatly excised from Victorian England, carefully packaged and shipped to Natal.

Soon I had the Sugar Hill Racing Stable on my right and the Baynesfield Estate on my left. This estate was established in 1863 by Joseph Baynes, on 24,000 of the region's most fertile acres; Mr Baynes, we gather, travelled cabin class. Next came miles of canefields and dairy pastures and then, near Pietermaritzburg, I passed thousands of shacks crowded on a wide mountainside which may or may not be fertile – there is no space left for cultivation. Speeding down the final slope – Natal's capital lies in a hollow surrounded by high wooded hills – I noted a penumbra of pollution. Yet cities do have their compensations, like the Africana second-hand bookshop, my first halt. There I lost all self-control and a large parcel of rare vols is now on its way to Ireland.

I'm staying here with Glynis and Steve Bach, first met in Vosburg – staying only two nights because my return flight is booked for 17 August and I plan to return to Natal next April.

The same, 9 August

The fourth of August 1993 is a date I shall never forget. Early that morning I heard deeply distressing news from home and for the first time – being in a state of shock – neglected adequately to guard Lear. Two hours later he was stolen from my friends' back garden.

Two black workmen in an adjacent garden witnessed the theft. When they questioned the intruder he claimed Steve owed him money but had refused to pay so he was taking Lear instead. The workmen must have known this was nonsense but they said no more. Were they afraid lest the thief might pull a gun? Or did they feel some sympathy for his enterprise?

Everything possible has been done to retrieve Lear but I never had any hope. At Steve's insistence, a dim-witted Coloured police officer came that evening to take a statement. However, it would at present be unreasonable to expect the SAP to exert themselves in pursuit of a cycle thief. I offered a R500 reward – NO QUESTIONS ASKED – on the front page of the *Natal Witness*, this being the local price of a new mountain-bike. To publicize my loss the *Witness* also ran a half-page interview complete with a pathetic photograph; I didn't have to feign looking stricken. The SABC did a long radio interview, broadcast countrywide. The local Zulu-language radio station gave a detailed description of Lear (but how easy it is to change a bicycle's appearance!) with a passionate plea for his return and much emphasis on the reward. The local ANC offices displayed enlarged photographs of Lear accompanied by further passionate pleas. All, predictably, to no avail.

It is ironical that after months of dodging the sort of publicity likely to attend a female sexagenarian's bicycle tour of South Africa in 1993, that journey has had to end under the spotlight. In consequence, some of my readers have surfaced and a new friend has nobly offered to lend me her bicycle – a precious machine, so I am touched and flattered.

But now I lack heart (and time) for the last lap to Jo'burg. Tomorrow, Margaret and Jennifer are driving down to collect me; Margaret had already planned this trip to visit an aunt in Greys Hospital.

I am absurdly upset. On the practical level a bicycle is just a machine, an inanimate object easily replaced. But not so on the emotional level. To me Lear was a friend, my only companion on quite a long journey that started in Nairobi. I feel utterly desolate without him. (What would a shrink make of this admission?) One could argue – I have to try to make excuses – that a bicycle is not, after all, 'just a machine' as is a motor car. The cyclist and the bicycle form a team; they work together as the motorist and motor car do not. Perhaps other cyclists exist, somewhere out there, who can understand this. Or perhaps not. Maybe I'm uniquely dotty.

Now I must count my blessings. In fact only one is visible at the moment: that this journal was not stolen. It might have been, as it lives in a pannier-bag. But having rummaged through both panniers and found nothing of value to him, the thief ripped them off, no doubt fearing they might arouse suspicion (obvious 'tourist property') as he sped away. The only balm on my wound is the certainty that he needs Lear, in material terms, more than I do. A similar theft at home would have enraged me: you can't feel enraged in South Africa when a black steals from a white.

In the air over the Transvaal, 17 August

However little they may deserve it, the whites do at present arouse sympathy – emotional earthquake victims, their whole world collapsing, fear of bloody chaos a dark shadow, incomprehension of blacks distorting their view of the future. An incomprehension nonetheless heartbreaking for being inevitable, in South Africa – and of course vehemently denied. How often I've had to listen to both Afrikaners and English-speakers explaining why they understand blacks so very well – because as children they had no other playmates and went off to boarding school speaking better Sotho/Xhosa/Zulu than Afrikaans or English. The implied insult to African culture is breathtaking.

Imagine a Chinese child growing up to the age of 10 on some remote nineteenth-century European farm, playing only with the children of illiterate, impoverished labourers and on the basis of that experience claiming as an adult that he understood Europeans very well. People would laugh at his stupid arrogance.

Why am I already eagerly looking forward to my return on 1 April '94? I seem to be entangled in a love-hate relationship with South Africa, a baffling emotional involvement with its variegated tribes and their tragic problems. Now I care about what happens to them – all of them – to an extent I would not have believed possible six months ago.

RED TAPE AND WHITE KNUCKLES

Lois Pryce

Lois Pryce (1973–present) was born in Aberdeen, Scotland. In 2003, she went on a 20,000-mile solo motorcycle ride, journeying across the Americas from Alaska at the top to Tierra del Fuego at the southern tip of the continent. She enjoyed it so much that in 2006 she embarked on another epic solo ride from London to Cape Town, South Africa. A mere 10,000 miles this time, but she was following a particularly hazardous route, and the title of her account – *Red Tape and White Knuckles* – says it all. She has since 'done' Iran – twice. Where next Lois?

Fourteen

Loutété was just a little dot on the map, halfway between Dolisie and Brazzaville, but it was surprisingly busy, centred as it was on the railway. It was the typical collection of breezeblock buildings, tumbledown shacks, market stalls and general disorder. The streets were bustling with activity, but even among this scene of industrious hustle my arrival caused the now familiar furore, with people stopping in their tracks to point and shout and run after me, trying to sell me all manner of goods. I rode on through the town, making my standard gestures of what I hoped were non-committal friendliness, waving and smiling at the staring faces. The railway tracks cut through the middle of the town and as I approached the level crossing I was halted by the screech of a policeman's whistle. I had spotted their checkpoint hut but was taking my usual approach of not stopping unless ordered to do so. This method often worked in my favour with a lazy official waving me on, and I had even managed to pass by unnoticed on a few occasions, blending into the general hubbub. But not this time.

'Where are you going?' demanded the policeman, and as he stepped in front of the bike I noticed that half of his right arm was missing. The sleeve of his jacket was pinned up just above where his elbow had once been.

'Brazzaville.'

'You cannot continue.'

I was expecting the usual inspection of papers and possibly a request for '*un cadeau*', but not this. I wondered if it was a roundabout method of extortion, but I decided to hold tight until he asked outright.

An inquisitive crowd had already gathered around me and the noise of their animated chatter was at such a level that I could barely hear him speak.

'You cannot continue,' he repeated, motioning with his severed arm at the road ahead.

'Why not? Is there a problem with the road?' I asked.

He launched into a volley of high-speed French which I struggled to understand over the racket of the onlookers.

'I'm sorry, can you speak slower, I don't understand...'

'You cannot continue! It is dangerous! I must not allow you!' He spoke at a more measured pace, but his tone was tinged with irritation.

'But why?'

'Why? Why? Because of the Ninjas! The Ninjas!' he shouted, as if I was the most stupid person he'd ever had the misfortune to flag down. 'The Ninjas! They are rebels! The Ninjas! The road to Brazzaville, they control this area!' He waved his one-and-a-half arms around, suggesting the scale of the Ninjas' operation.

I knew of the Ninjas; they were the former prime minister's own personal militia, but I didn't know to what extent they were still at large, and I didn't know what to believe. In my suspicious frame of mind, I wondered if it was all a big scam. Why should I trust this angry, bullying policeman?

'What do they do, the Ninjas?' I asked him. 'Hold up vehicles? Rob people?'

He stepped closer and stared into my eyes.

'Madame, they will kill you.'

Sure enough the policeman had an alternative plan all worked out for me.

'You must take the train to Brazzaville, you will put your motorcycle on the train.'

It was difficult knowing who to trust and what to believe, but the last thing I wanted to do was get on a train. I was here to ride my bike and that's what I was going to do, and if that meant running the gauntlet with the Ninjas, then so be it.

'No thank you,' I insisted politely. 'I'll continue on the road.'

'YOU CANNOT CONTINUE! YOU MUST TAKE THE TRAIN!' roared the policeman, utterly frustrated at my lack of compliance.

Fortunately at this moment a statuesque man dressed in an ankle-length white robe pushed his way through the throng. He was holding the hand of his tiny daughter, who looked at me shyly before burying her face in the folds of his robe.

'My name is Spencer, I speak English,' he said to me. 'Please, what is the problem?'

I liked him immediately; he had an air of calm authority about him that reminded me of Abba, the village chief at the Niger border post, and I guessed he was high up in Loutété's pecking order by the way the policeman acquiesced to him. I introduced myself and explained my predicament.

'I'm on my way to Brazzaville, but he won't let me carry on.'

Spencer and the policeman entered into a lively discussion which involved much flailing of the policeman's stump.

'I am sorry, but he is right, you cannot continue on the road,' said Spencer. 'The Ninjas are very dangerous. After the civil war they refused to hand over their arms, and they control this area, here.' He pointed on my map. 'The road to Brazzaville is very dangerous now. Many people have been attacked and robbed. It is for his sake too,' he said, motioning to the policeman, who was looking thoroughly vexed. 'He cannot let you go – if something happens to you, it is his fault. You understand?'

It was unlikely that the expression 'covering your arse' had made it into the Congolese vernacular, but that's exactly what the policeman was doing.

The crowd had now swelled to the extent that they were taking up the entire width of the road and were looking on, laughing and shouting things I didn't understand, while the policeman tried to disperse them, yelling orders which went largely ignored. Frustrated at his ineffectiveness, he marched up to me and Spencer, exerting his authority.

'You, madame!' he said gripping my upper arm. 'You take the train. Come with me to buy ticket.'

The policeman was pointing to a building made of rusty corrugated iron, sited between the road and the train tracks.

I looked at Spencer but he just shrugged helplessly.

'You must go with him.'

I started pushing my bike over to the building but I barely had time to think before I was being shoved across the street, caught up in the swarm of bystanders. The crowd had burst into action and I was being mobbed by people who wanted to 'help'.

'I buy you ticket for train!'

'You pay me, I lift bike on train.'

'No! I put on bike on train – you pay me!'

'You need rope to tie bike to train – I have rope!'

'No, I have rope! You buy this rope!'

It was almost impossible to make any headway through the mob, and before long a couple of men had wrestled my bike from me and were lifting it over the railway sidings to the waiting train.

'Stop! Wait!' I shouted, but no one was listening. The policeman was striding ahead towards the building and I looked around for Spencer, but he was nowhere to be seen.

'Stop! Where are you going?' I shouted. 'Bring back my bike!' But nobody took any notice and through the crowd I could see a group of three men pushing it towards the train.

Several men in uniform appeared from out of the corrugated iron shack, shouting instructions at me.

'They've got my bike!' I shouted back at them, flustered by the way the situation was spiralling out of my control. I didn't know who to turn to for help; it certainly wasn't the policemen, and I couldn't see Spencer anywhere.

'There is no problem, madame, they will put your motorcycle on the train,' said the one-armed policeman, as if I was making a fuss about nothing. 'They are not stealing it,' he added witheringly.

But it's all I've got, I wanted to shout, it's not just a bike, it's my home too, everything I have is on that bike! Without it, I'm lost! I'm stuck! But I knew he wouldn't understand, or care.

'You! Madame! Come in here! You must buy ticket,' yelled a voice from inside the shack.

I stepped into the dingy, windowless room to find four uniformed men staring at me with grim expressions. One of them kicked the door shut behind me, leaving just the weak glow of a bare bulb illuminating their faces and glancing its dirty yellow light off their brass buttons.

'You go to Brazzaville, you must buy ticket,' said a man sitting behind a desk. He was obviously the one in charge here, as he sported the most stripes, badges and medals on his jacket. 'Forty thousand francs.'

'Look, I don't want to take the bloody train!' I protested one more time.

'The Ninjas! They will kill you!' bawled the one-armed policeman, utterly sick of me by now.

'And you must buy ticket for bike, thirty thousand francs,' continued the man behind the desk.

Seventy quid for me and the bike! I calculated, seething with frustration.

'And you must pay the men who lift your bike on to train,' added another.

'And you must pay the men who tie your bike to the train.'

I stood there in silence, trying to take everything in, not knowing what to say.

'But…'

'You pay the man now for the tickets,' said the one-armed policeman from the corner. It was an order. 'He is the chief of police,' he added.

'I don't have seventy thousand francs,' I told them, trying to keep my voice calm.

There was silence.

'How much do you have?'

My mind raced through my options, thinking about where I kept my cash and how I could avoid handing the whole lot over to these thugs. I reached into the inside pocket of my jacket, where I knew there were a couple of 10,000-franc notes. I kept them in case I ran into the likes of the Ninjas, but these guys weren't much different, they were just Ninjas in uniform. I fished out one of the notes and handed it to the man behind the desk. He looked at it, smoothed it out, placed it on the desk, and without saying anything, offered his hand again. His cronies watched in silence.

'You have more,' he said eventually. I wasn't sure if this was a question or a statement.

'No,' I lied.

'You give him more money,' said the one-armed policeman, with a meaningful look.

The four of them stared at me, succeeding in their attempt at intimidation. I fished out the other tenner.

'You must give him more,' he yelled, 'for the train ticket!'

'I don't have any more money,' I said very slowly in French, not making any attempt to keep the frustration out of my voice. '*Vous comprends?*'

'More! More money!' he shouted again.

Overcome with rage and frustration, I shouted back at him, even louder: 'I don't have any more!' My voice ricocheted around the metal walls.

They looked at each other, shrugged and muttered something unintelligible. The chief pocketed the two notes and nodded towards the door.

'Go,' he said.

I pushed open the door. I never thought to ask for the ticket and it never materialised.

As soon as I stepped outside someone was tugging at my sleeve, demanding more money to lift the bike on to the train; another was grabbing me, shouting about the rope he had bought. I was being propelled through the chaos, overwhelmed by all the yelling and pushing and shoving. The situation had slipped away from me – it was now completely out of my control and I felt overwhelmed with confusion. Then to my relief, I saw Spencer, standing among the chaos, his daughter still clinging on to his hand.

'Where's my bike?' I asked him desperately.

'It is over there, they are putting it on the train, but please, hurry, you must come quick, the train must leave soon. You have your ticket?'

'No, well, I mean yes, I mean I paid for it, but I don't have a ticket.'

'Never mind, you must come quick.'

'You must come now…' bawled someone in an army uniform, grabbing my arm, as I was swept along with the crowd of passengers that were pushing their way to the waiting train.

I was hauled over the sidings to find a couple of soldiers lifting my bike up on to a flatbed wagon at the rear of the train and lashing it to a metal post.

'You sit here,' said Spencer, pointing to a jerrycan that was wedged up against my bike, and I realised that I would not be travelling in a carriage, but out here on the wagon. That was OK, at least I'd be next to my bike and be able to keep an eye on my belongings, but as a rush of passengers climbed aboard I also realised that I would not be travelling alone out here. As well as me and my bike, the wagon was transporting a platoon of forty Congolese soldiers to Brazzaville, all of them wielding Kalashnikovs and sporting bandoliers of bullets slung around their upper bodies. I watched in mounting horror as they leapt on to the wagon, clutching bottles of whisky, shouting and laughing in drunken high spirits, and bellowing out army chants. I felt physically sick as the reality of my situation began to sink in.

'Hurry! Hurry! The train is leaving!' a policeman was screaming at me.

There was nothing else to do but clamber up on to the wagon and take my seat on the jerrycan. My embarkation prompted a rowdy cheer from the soldiers and I felt my stomach churn.

'It is OK, Lois,' said Spencer, seeing my face cloud over with despair. 'You must be strong.'

'But… but…' I bit my bottom lip, trying desperately to hold back tears of fear and anger and frustration. Spencer and his daughter stared up at me from the rubbish-strewn tracks.

'And Lois,' he said, beckoning me to crouch down so he could whisper, 'the military, the soldiers, they all smoke marijuana, OK?'

I nodded, thinking that this was the least of my problems, but he looked at me with a serious expression. 'It is OK. You understand what I am saying?'

I didn't really, but I guessed he was telling me to keep my mouth shut, not that I was in any mood for striking up a conversation with my fellow passengers.

Somewhere down the tracks a whistle blew and the big diesel engine shuddered into life.

'Be strong, Lois, you must be strong!' Spencer insisted, as the train began to chug slowly out of Loutété station; tears rolled down my cheeks as I surveyed my new surroundings and, worse, my new travelling companions, who had been foisted upon me so suddenly. I nodded helplessly and managed a choked 'Thank you.' He stood there with his daughter, the two of them watching me and the marauding soldiers disappear off down the tracks into the jungle. I was taking the train, whether I liked it or not.

The jerrycan was leaking from the filler cap, and every bump and sway of the wagon sloshed a bit of diesel out until I could feel it soaking through my trousers. I could have sat on the floor but I couldn't bring myself to move a muscle. My arrival had caused quite a commotion and some of the soldiers had tried to engage me in conversation, but I pretended I couldn't speak French and ignored their attempts at a parley. A few of them entertained their colleagues with comments about me that I genuinely didn't understand, but which prompted raucous laughter and backslapping among them, and paranoid terror in me. I felt sick with dread, and my gut-feeling was to stay perfectly still in the pathetic hope that the soldiers would forget I was there. This response was strangely at odds with my usual approach to sticky situations – I normally relied on smiling, flattery and being ultra-polite to get me out of trouble. But this was different; something innate in me warned against making any kind of connection with these men. I knew what drunken soldiers got up to in the Congo and the very thought made me shudder with raw fear. *I'm not equipped for this,* I thought, *this wasn't meant to happen, I'm not cut out for this.* I felt a terrible, hopeless dread and, like a hunted animal, my instinct was to remain motionless until the danger had passed. But that was going to be an awfully long time.

Spencer had said the train to Brazzaville took eight or nine hours, at least twice as long as it would have been by road, even battling through the mud of the Route Nationale 1. I yearned to unleash my bike and for us to jump off and flee into the jungle; even if it meant dodging the Ninjas, at least I would be in charge of my own destiny. As I fantasised about my great escape, I realised why, along with the obvious sheer terror of what could happen to me over the next nine hours, I also felt so upset and angry. I had been robbed of my independence, one of the great joys and main reasons for travelling by motorcycle. My autonomy was gone; now I was at the mercy of a semi-derelict public transport system and a platoon of drunk, armed Congolese soldiers. It had all happened so quickly – within a matter of minutes the freedom of the road had been snatched away from me and I felt as if my bike and I had been taken prisoner.

The train was old and rickety and moved at a painfully slow pace, winding its way through dark, thick rainforest where tenacious vines coiled around the vast tree trunks and the swampy jungle floor never saw the light of day. Occasionally we would stop at a little halt that seemed to service nothing but a couple of shacks in the middle of nowhere but was overrun with people. They looked as if they'd crawled out of the bush, and maybe they had. They stood by the tracks, half-naked, barefoot and muddy, hollering and waving at the train. The soldiers would shout back at them but I couldn't understand if this was an exchange of greetings or if they were protesting about something. The only other time the train stopped was for the passengers to answer the call of nature, grinding and creaking to a standstill while the soldiers jumped off, took a leak by the side of the tracks and hauled themselves back up before it set off again on its excruciating crawl. I was desperate to make use of these toilet breaks, but I couldn't bring myself to join in with the soldiers, so I just sat there, crossing my legs and praying for the nightmare to end.

As predicted by Spencer, the soldiers were soon passing round giant spliffs, and mixed with the whisky their bullish spirits reached bursting point. They sang in raucous discord, shouted mock insults and threats at each other, pretending to push one and another off the train in play fights. Most of them still wore their AK47s slung on their backs, but a few of them had removed their weapons, casually discarding them on the floor. Occasionally one of the soldiers would direct a comment at me and they would all burst out laughing, but I did my best to ignore them or at best, managed a weak smile. It was like being trapped on the world's worst stag night. I had never felt so small and acutely female. I had grown up with two brothers, I've always had male friends and plenty of fruity language has passed my lips, but this was too much machismo for my tender heart; I was drowning in a sea of testosterone.

It wasn't the yelling and shoving that bothered me, or the boozing and smoking, it was the call and response army chants that chilled me to the core. I don't go for men in uniform, quite the opposite in fact, and as a champion of individuality I have a deep-rooted mistrust of most organised group activities. A friend of mine almost persuaded me to join a yoga class once, but just the sight of everyone doing the same thing at the same time sent me running for the door; it was all a bit Hitler Youth for my tastes. Ergo, the armed forces and I were never going to hit it off, and the mindless, boorish chanting of my travelling companions epitomised everything I loathed and feared in our species.

I didn't know what else to do but sit there on the jerrycan and avoid all eye contact with the soldiers. I stared at my bike, tied up next to me, and concentrated on its smallest details, its scratches and scrapes, each one telling a story, reminding me of happier times. Although I've never been one for bestowing names or human characteristics on my vehicles, at this moment just having my bike next to me gave me comfort. It was more than merely a means of transport; it had become my home over the last few months but most of all it represented fun and freedom, two things that were sorely absent from my current situation.

The time dragged by with unbearable slowness and after a while I could hardly bring myself to look at my watch. But every minute that passed by without incident gave me hope and I knew that I was another minute nearer to Brazzaville and the end of this nightmare. However, my hope that I would blend into the background was way off the mark and a couple of young soldiers, tired of shouting and pushing each other around, looked to me for their entertainment. They were probably as bored as I was, but bored young men plus booze plus drugs does not make for a pretty combination, as any English town centre on a Saturday night will attest. I froze with unadulterated fear as one of them sat down on another, vacant jerrycan and put his arm around my shoulders. I had spotted him earlier when he had climbed on to the wagon; he was one of the youngest of the soldiers, probably in his late teens, and a brash, aggressive show-off. He was the loudest, the cockiest, and I despised him already for his attention-seeking behaviour. His entire upper body was slung with rows of brass bullets over his black, string vest and his machine gun swung around carelessly, hanging from his right shoulder.

'What is wrong with you?' he said in French. 'Don't you like us?'

I could smell the whisky on his breath. I didn't know what to do or say, I didn't know if he was being facetious or genuine.

'What is wrong with you?' he said again. 'Why don't you speak?'

'I'm fine,' I muttered. 'Just tired.' It was a lame answer, but the last thing I wanted to do was to engage in conversation with him.

His friend was examining my bike with great interest, looking at the luggage and opening and closing my panniers. I turned away from the younger soldier so I could keep an eye on the bike, but just this move was enough to provoke him.

'You think he will steal something?' he said, and gave a harsh, loud laugh. 'She thinks you are stealing from her!' he said to his mate, who shouted something back that I didn't understand and spat on the floor of the wagon.

The rest of the platoon were still carousing, shouting and chanting, but the young soldier's arm remained around my shoulders and I could feel the hard metal ridges of his bullets pressing through my clothes. My stomach was knotted tight and I was desperate to shake off his arm but instead I sat there, tensed for what might happen next. His tone and his eyes scared me; he was that dreadful combination of young, cruel and vainglorious, and I feared the lengths to which he would go to impress his fellow soldiers.

As I sat there perfectly still, breathing heavily and trying to stay calm, the train groaned and screeched as it slowed down and then jolted to a sudden stop. The soldiers lurched and steadied themselves and there was a loud clamour as they leapt off the train and busied themselves in the bushes. The young soldier stood up to follow them and grabbed my arm.

'Get off!' I shouted, and my sudden burst of anger caused him to jump in surprise. It was the loudest noise I had made in hours, and even though I had spoken in English, he had not failed to understand. He laughed in a patronising way, as if to say, 'Calm down love, no need to make a fuss,' but all the time he stared at me with cold, furious eyes and his friend, who had become bored with my bike, turned and grabbed hold of his arm.

'*On y va! On y va!*' said his friend, and without looking at me he hauled him away off the train, leaving me sitting there trembling.

Mercifully I was left alone once we started moving again, and after a couple of hours the weed finally had the effect I had hoped for and my companions started to mellow out. Reassured by the calmer mood among the soldiers, I made a tentative move towards my panniers, where a packet of chocolate biscuits awaited me. It was late afternoon, I hadn't eaten since breakfast and I was feeling distinctly weak with hunger. Although I was still nervous about attracting attention to myself, my hunger prevailed over my fear. It was bad enough that I wouldn't be able to go to the loo for nine hours, but I was damned if I was going to let these meathead buffoons come between me and my chocolate biscuits.

I moved slowly and quietly, turning round in my seated position until I could reach the buckles of my pannier bags. Unfastening them as gently as possible, I rummaged around inside until I felt the cylindrical foil packet in my hand. Oh joy! I secreted it swiftly inside my jacket, hoping that the noise of the train would drown out the telltale crackly sound of my opening the packet. But I had underestimated the eagle eyes of my travelling companions, and my covert operation had not passed unnoticed. What did I expect? These men were trained to kill, to stake out their enemies in the impenetrable jungle of the Congo Basin. Did I really think I would get away with such a clumsy manoeuvre?

As I nibbled away on the first biscuit I could feel my blood sugar levels returning to normal, but my relief was tempered by the fact that an enormous soldier sitting opposite me was watching my every mouthful. I avoided his gaze and crammed in a couple more biscuits, staring down at the floor while I chewed, but although I was pretending to ignore him, I could feel his eyes boring into me. Reassured by the fact that I had managed to at least get the biscuits out of the pannier without causing too much commotion among the troops, I thought I might as well try to make the most of this train journey and read a book while it was still light. I went back into my luggage and dug out my current read, which Pete had given to me in Lambaréné, a paperback about a murderous Colombian drugs baron who, in comparison to my current travelling companions, seemed like quite a mild-mannered fellow. A good book and a packet of choccie biccies, what more could a girl want? It was pure Bridget Jones, but I just couldn't relax with the brutal eyes of the soldier opposite trained on my biscuits.

The mammoth joints were still doing the rounds, and as the soldiers became more stoned they were predictably getting the munchies. Eventually it was too much to bear for my giant hulking soldier. He stood up, stepped towards me, and without speaking pointed to where my biscuits were stashed beneath my jacket. I resented his bullying approach and couldn't bring myself to indulge him so readily, so I pretended I didn't understand what he wanted. Towering over me, he pointed again at the location of my hidden biscuits and stared at me with a look so intimidating that my skin prickled in cold fear. I shrugged my shoulders in false incomprehension and he resorted to his ultimate tactic. With a shimmy of his powerful shoulders, he swung his Kalashnikov round from his back so that it was now dangling by his side and with a light movement he flipped it into his right hand so that it was swinging, not exactly pointing, but swinging in front of my face. 'You only had to ask,' I wanted to say, but I handed over the biscuits silently.

CALL TO ADVENTURE!

Aloha Wanderwell

Aloha Wanderwell (1906–1996) was nicknamed 'the world's most travelled girl' – this feisty Canadian hopped into a Model T-Ford and raced her way across 75 countries in the 1920s while still a teenager. Stranded in Brazil she lived with the Bororo people; stuck for fuel she ingeniously combined bananas and animal fat so she could continue her journey. In later life her husband died in mysterious circumstances after which she chopped off her hair and joined the French Foreign Legion. In Indonesia she shot her way out of a herd of angry elephants, she also regularly flew a seaplane. Yet, despite all these achievements, she died in obscurity. Perfectly named her life is a filmscript-in-waiting.

Adventure Calling

With pockets empty and a light heart, I went ashore at Port Said, and in all Port Said I could find no trace of Cap. I enquired at hotels, theaters and shipping offices. Someone was bound to remember if two cars as distinctive in style as those of our expedition had been embarked aboard ship for India. I feared that Cap might have had to go on without me, that I might have missed another message from him sent to Paris.

No one in Port Said shipping circles had seen the cars leave; the American Express office clerks thought the expedition was still in Cairo.

My feet burned in my high leather boots, and my body sweltered in my uniform jerkin under the North African sun. I was hungry; it seemed I always was hungry. I considered wiring Cap in care of the Cairo American Express and taking a chance that he might call in for mail. Meanwhile I needed food and lodging and I lacked even the price of a third-class fare by train to Cairo. I toyed with the idea of sending an S.O.S. to Mother at Nice, but it seemed a shame; I had convinced her six months before that she should consider me as the man of the family who was out to retrieve the family fortunes. I knew even the lessening of my school expenses must make the financial strain lighter, and Moms had enough to bear since my father had been killed in the World War. That tragedy, her poor health, and my sister Meg and I had all contributed to our being in Nice on the lucky day when the chance came for me to join this expedition. I thought of Mother now and her unselfishness, covering her natural anxiety, in letting me go. But the plan seemed such a solution of everything for me. Young as I was, I was sure I had the qualifications. I knew how to be a secretary, in a way; I knew I could wear a uniform, and I knew I would not want to get married within three years. I knew, too, that I could rough it in Europe, Asia and Africa or wherever else the specially built, snub-nosed torpedo-shaped flivvers might happen to go. I knew I could learn to work before and behind a movie camera, and I could speak several languages besides English, which was a big advantage.

But here I was wandering aimlessly round Port Said and wondering how best to reach Cairo, the expedition crew and Cap. Of course it was quite simple in the end. I went to the Consulate and showed my papers, told my story, and the young vice-consul with fatherly benevolence gave me the price of a first-class passage on the Cairo train.

I went to Cairo third-class, under protest from train officials. Only natives travel third-class. I knew that, but I had no mind to go hungry, and the difference in the money meant eating.

At last, Cairo. I was thrilled to be in the land of the Pharaohs, Cleopatra, Joseph and Moses, of veiled women and ancient civilization. The whole thing was a mighty jumble in my mind; I felt in the middle of romance when a mob of brown-skinned urchins followed me from the station along the Chara ab Din, pointed at my breeched legs and cried:

"Baksheesh—Baksheesh!"

I had nothing to give them, for I had already tried several hotels and Cap was registered at none of them. I despaired a little, but at the same time that familiar throb of exultancy was pulsing through my veins.

I was excited merely by walking amid this potpourri of humanity. There were tall, dark-skinned Egyptians in red fezzes, proud-looking men, defiant and somber; I recognized Copts pushing through the crowds on donkey-back, and I could pick out the copper-tinted Arabs with their classic features. There were Moslems in turbans, some green turbans among them, on those who had visited Mecca. Peasant women trailed black skirts in the dust, and their chains of barbaric jewelry swung and clinked with each step. I had a queer feeling of kinship, a feeling which comes back to me over and over when I set foot in the strange, out-of-the-way places of the world. I knew that I loved Cairo.

Darkness was falling and I was still wandering along the streets, when I heard the unmistakable note which is as ear-compelling as the call of a sea gull over the sea.

"Allah Akbar," rang from side to side of the city, and I knew it was the muezzin calling the faithful to prayer. I watched the people shake out little prayer mats, kneel and place their foreheads to the ground.

Now I sought the theaters of the city, for I believe Cap might be giving an exhibit of the films; he could not be far away, for the Express Company reported that he called occasionally for mail. The first three theaters drew a blank, but the fourth had contracted with Cap for picture-showing, but not for another week. The manager, who spoke bad French, did not know where Cap stayed.

I was really discouraged when I asked to be directed to a quiet hotel. Before going in to register I turned to take a last look at the procession of nations in the roadway. It was then that a familiar voice came to me, speaking in English:

"Hi there. Aloha!"

It was Cap, with his big, enfolding smile and his hand grasping mine.

"We're in camp at the foot of the pyramids—I did not expect you until tomorrow," Cap explained all in a breath, and then we were in one of the cars, arriving at the edge of the desert where the tents were pitched, and everything was quiet.

I could not bear to sleep. I sat on a sand dune and watched the full moon sail in a sky that was like an upturned goblet of dark, blue glass. There were trillions of stars, and not far away I could see the outline of the Sphinx, smiling and sightless.

Cap strolled by. "I'm taking my last turn round the camp," he said. "I've made a habit of it, because the men's tents are some distance from yours. Let's climb the shoulder of the Sphinx; we can see quite well with the moon as full as it is—I want to tell you that I'm glad you're back."

Cap told me of incidents of their travel since I had left the expedition, of the new members of the crew and how they would not be eligible to travel after Aden. He told of being drenched with rains in Rumania and hurrying through Greece and Turkey, Bulgaria and the other Balkan countries; they had touched Syria and then from Palestine had come into Egypt. I seethed with an agony of regret at what I had missed, and I rededicated myself to the success of the enterprise. I felt uplifted and old as the hills, and I was really horribly young.

"We must make enough money here to carry us on to Aden," explained Cap. "I have already begun to seek permission from the authorities to let us travel on a pilgrim ship to Jidda and join a caravan there so that we can get within sight of the walls of Mecca—I know we cannot go any further, but that will be something. Then from Arabia to India—I have an ambition there, Aloha, that you should be the first girl to drive a car herself from Bombay to Calcutta—I believe it could be done."

"Mecca, Cap," I said, not half hearing the plans about India, "has any but the true Moslem ever been into Mecca?"

But Cap was already thinking of something else and wanting to know how I had traveled to Egypt. He exclaimed with horror at the risk I had taken.

"Aloha what would your mother say?"

"Don't tell her, by letter anyway," I implored, and then as a sudden chill desert breeze blew up I clambered down to the sand.

"Good night, Cap," I called as I disappeared into the tent assigned me. It was as if I had never been away, for I felt so utterly at home and safe.

I found that the only member of the original European crew still with the expedition was Jarocki. He greeted me boisterously as I went over to the spot where, in the early morning coolness, I had seen two

Arab lads spreading a canvas and placing food of dates, oranges and eggs for our breakfast.

"Allo, Mademoiselle Aloha, Allo!"

Jarocki, short, thickset and typically Polish, was glad to see me. He beamed.

"No. 2's engine purrs like a kitten," he said, reporting on the car which was mine to drive, and which he had handled while I was away. Jarocki broke off his speech abruptly, for, coming from the small tent which stood next to the one I had occupied overnight, was a tall, fair-haired girl so like myself in appearance that I could not help being startled.

"This is Marisha," said Jarocki as the girl approached, and I held out my hand to her in greeting. Cap had told me of her the night before. In appearance she was a splendid substitute for me on the stage, but there the resemblance stopped, for her life story was pitiful. She was a product of the Red Russian revolution, in which she had seen her family slaughtered. She then was passed from hand to hand in the easy marriage and divorce of the early Soviet, until the fourth such experience had driven her to dare escape. Somehow she reached Turkey, and it was in Constantinople that someone had told Cap about her. She was half starved and almost in rags. Her appearance secured her the position, but she did not want to go around the world nor to have adventures.

"Peace and quiet are all I seek," explained Marisha to Cap and myself when she told us she was to remain behind in Cairo. She was going into the harem of a wealthy young Egyptian Moslem as his third wife, and she was taking his religion. The handsome young man had seen her first in my role in the stage work at a Cairo theater; he paid her court. It was all quite in order, and many times since then I have visited Marisha in her curious cloistered life. She is contentedly happy, with that peace and quiet which she so desired.

But the call of the open road was mine. Very quickly I fell into the expedition routine, and took over the adjutant work which had been part of my duties before.

"Cap," I asked one day near the end of our stay in Cairo, "will you show me the city?"

All these days I had been feeling the intense call of the strange place.

There were the Yashmaed women, the hawk-eyed Arabs in flowing burnous, the fantastic blending of colors in fez and turban, the clash of religions, creeds, races—touching but never mixing. I walked with Cap along Chara ab Din and I glanced fearfully down the dark arched alleys.

"We'd better turn back," said Cap suddenly, but my eyes had been everywhere and I had grasped the significance of the sign ahead of us as quickly as had Cap. "Out of bounds for British soldiers," the words were.

Of course—Cairo's red-light district.

"Cap—Cap, I want to see the best and worst of Cairo," I protested.

It was a shrouded, narrow and garish lane that we entered, and there all of raucous Cairo strutted; the meager width of the place was filled to overflowing. An Arab in a long white robe sauntered along and blew on a small reed pipe which made a sing-song buzz. From open doorways came shrill voices of singing girls; there was high laughter, the reek of perfumes reached our nostrils, of spices and a warm, cloying air.

Cap flatly refused to let me look inside any of the latticed windows.

"I'm a fool to humor you this much," he said, and added, "I only take you along because I know you'd try to come alone if I did not!" Cap certainly understood young people who have romantic imaginations—he let those of us traveling with him at varying times see all we wanted to see, within reason, and then there was no mystery, so everyone was satisfied.

Along the Cairo alley, framed in dark archways, were groups of scantily clad girls who talked and giggled. Many were really beautiful as the dim lights of lanterns caught their features. All were painted of face and some had their bodies tattooed; once in a while a girl, overcome by excess of spirits or a desire to stimulate lagging trade, dashed out into the roadway and danced flauntingly. Cap went ahead at one point to open passage-way where the crowd was dense, and I got some steps behind him because of the congestion of people. Suddenly I felt my progress checked for a slim, brown hand had reached out from a doorway and was clutching my arm in a wiry vise. I could feel curious, black eyes glinting at me.

"Je suis une femme!" I exclaimed in French, hoping that I had been stopped by mistake. But the woman continued to hold me, and then brought up her other hand to feel my body.

"Cap!" I shouted. "Oh, Cap!"

Fortunately Cap heard me above the din of other voices, and came pushing his way back to catch my other arm.

"Take off my helmet, Cap," I said; "that should convince them I'm a girl," for now I was wedged in with a group of half-clad women chattering like excited monkeys.

My curls tumbled down in all directions, just as I meant it to happen.

"Femme en pantaloon!" said the old woman who held me, speaking very good French. She had recognized me as a girl, and dropped my arm to put her fingers on my hair. I took the chance of freedom, and pushed roughly with Cap through the crowd. The chattering girls gave way in surprise at the sudden movement.

"Whew!" said Cap. "I shouldn't have liked to fight that pack of harridans for you."

"The old woman meant no harm," I said. "Just seeing a white woman in breeches puzzled her," but I spoke out of bravado, for I was really frightened; it would not have been the first time a white girl disappeared into those purlieus of humanity and did not return.

The sides of the street we were on converged now and we found our progress stopped by a crescent-shaped archway where there was a native drinking house. Here was music and a girl was dancing. I saw an instrument shaped like a lyre in the hands of one of the squatting musicians; another played a tambourine. Others held reed pipes to their lips, and I recognized the minor wailing of the tabla, which I had heard before, and there were the staccato shrill notes of a flute. The reiteration of these shrill notes disturbed me. I felt exhilarated so that I stepped out buoyantly, and neither Cap nor I spoke until the hush of empty streets brought realization to us that somewhere we had taken a wrong turn and were lost in a labyrinth of dark arched alleys and unknown lanes.

A dark figure slipped stealthily before us, and disappeared like a wraith when Cap shouted to attract attention, for he wanted to enquire which turn to take. Terror, mingled with delight, chased thrills up and down my spine, and then as quickly as we had realized we were lost, we came out on the wide Chara ab Din, found the car and were on the way to camp.

I slept soundly, knowing that on the morrow we would stow the last of our dunnage on the cars, strike camp on the desert, and make for Port Suez.

Ten days later the pilgrim ship Burulos was sailing for Jidda, and already we held the special passenger permits, already we had the instructions about joining the caravan which would bring us within sight of the walls of Mecca—but no further. That "no further" was so emphatic it bothered me.

IN MOROCCO

Edith Wharton

Edith Wharton (1862–1937) was born in New York's Gilded Age into a family which belonged to the city's aristocracy. She was the first woman ever to win the Pulitzer Prize for Literature (1921). She enjoyed an excellent education, married a suitable man, developed a fondness for interior design and travelled extensively in Europe, the latter informing her most famous novel *The Age of Innocence*. The expression 'keeping up with the Joneses' (her maiden name) is said to have been inspired by her wealthy father's family. During the First World War, she carried out relief work in Paris and afterwards she visited Morocco, adding to her impressive body of literary works an account of her travels – named, somewhat prosaically, *In Morocco*.

Marrakech: The Way There

There are countless Arab tales of evil djinns who take the form of sandstorms and hot winds to overwhelm exhausted travellers.

In spite of the new French road between Rabat and Marrakech the memory of such tales rises up insistently from every mile of the level red earth and the desolate stony stretches of the *bled*. As long as the road runs in sight of the Atlantic breakers they give the scene freshness and life; but when it bends inland and stretches away across the wilderness the sense of the immensity and immobility of Africa descends on one with an intolerable oppression.

The road traverses no villages, and not even a ring of nomad tents is visible in the distance on the wide stretches of arable land. At infrequent intervals our motor passed a train of laden mules, or a group of peasants about a well, and sometimes, far off, a fortified farm profiled its thick-set angle-towers against the sky, or a white *koubba* floated like a mirage above the brush; but these rare signs of life intensified the solitude of the long miles between.

At midday we were refreshed by the sight of the little oasis around the military-post of Settat. We lunched there with the commanding officer, in a cool Arab house about a flowery patio; but that brief interval over, the fiery plain began again. After Settat the road runs on for miles across the waste to the gorge of the Oued Ouem; and beyond the river it climbs to another plain so desperate in its calcined aridity that the prickly scrub of the wilderness we had left seemed like the vegetation of an oasis. For fifty kilometres the earth under our wheels was made up of a kind of glistening red slag covered with pebbles and stones. Not the scantest and toughest of rock-growths thrust a leaf through its brassy surface; not a well-head or a darker depression of the rock gave sign of a trickle of water. Everything around us glittered with the same unmerciful dryness.

A long way ahead loomed the line of the Djebilets, the djinn-haunted mountains guarding Marrakech on the north. When at last we reached them the wicked glister of their purple flanks seemed like a volcanic upheaval of the plain. For some time we had watched the clouds gathering over them, and as we got to the top of the defile rain was falling from a fringe of thunder to the south. Then the vapours lifted, and we saw below us another red plain with an island of palms in its centre. Mysteriously, from the heart of the palms, a tower shot up, as if alone in the wilderness; behind it stood the sun-streaked cliffs of the Atlas, with snow summits appearing and vanishing through the storm.

As we drove downward the rock gradually began to turn to red earth fissured by yellow streams, and stray knots of palms sprang up, lean and dishevelled, about well-heads where people were, watering camels and donkeys. To the east, dominating the oasis, the twin peaked hills of the Ghilis, fortified to the crest, mounted guard over invisible Marrakech; but still, above the palms, we saw only that lonely and triumphant tower.

Presently we crossed the Oued Tensif on an old bridge built by Moroccan engineers. Beyond the river were more palms, then olive-orchards, then the vague sketch of the new European settlement, with a few shops and cafés on avenues ending suddenly in clay pits, and at last Marrakech itself appeared to us, in the form of a red wall across a red wilderness.

We passed through a gate and were confronted by other ramparts. Then we entered an outskirt of dusty red lanes bordered by clay hovels with draped figures slinking by like ghosts. After that more walls, more gates, more endlessly winding lanes, more gates again, more turns, a dusty open space with donkeys and camels and negroes; a final wall with a great door under a lofty arch – and suddenly we were in the palace of the Bahia, among flowers and shadows and falling water.

The Bahia

Whoever would understand Marrakech must begin by mounting at sunset to the roof of the Bahia.

Outspread below lies the oasis-city of the south, flat and vast as the great nomad camp it really is, its low roofs extending on all sides to a belt of blue palms ringed with desert. Only two or three minarets and a few noblemen's houses among gardens break the general flatness; but they are hardly noticeable, so irresistibly is the eye drawn toward two dominant objects – the white wall of the Atlas and the red tower of the Koutoubya.

Foursquare, untapering, the great tower lifts its flanks of ruddy stone. Its large spaces of unornamented wall, its triple tier of clustered openings, lightening as they rise from the severe rectangular lights of the first stage to the graceful arcade below the parapet, have the stern harmony of the noblest architecture. The Koutoubya would be magnificent anywhere; in this flat desert it is grand enough to face the Atlas.

The Almohad conquerors who built the Koutoubya and embellished Marrakech dreamed a dream of beauty that extended from the Guadalquivir to the Sahara; and at its two extremes they placed their watch-towers. The Giralda watched over civilized enemies in a land of ancient Roman culture; the Koutoubya stood at the edge of the world, facing the hordes of the desert.

The Almoravid princes who founded Marrakech came from the

black desert of Senegal; themselves were leaders of wild hordes. In the history of North Africa the same cycle has perpetually repeated itself. Generation after generation of chiefs have flowed in from the desert or the mountains, overthrown their predecessors, massacred, plundered, grown rich, built sudden palaces, encouraged their great servants to do the same; then fallen on them, and taken their wealth and their palaces. Usually some religious fury, some ascetic wrath against the self-indulgence of the cities, has been the motive of these attacks; but invariably the same results followed, as they followed when the Germanic barbarians descended on Italy. The conquerors, infected with luxury and mad with power, built vaster palaces, planned grander cities; but Sultans and Viziers camped in their golden houses as if on the march, and the mud huts of the tribesmen within their walls were but one degree removed from the mud-walled tents of the *bled*.

This was more especially the case with Marrakech, a city of Berbers and blacks, and the last outpost against the fierce black world beyond the Atlas from which its founders came. When one looks at its site, and considers its history, one can only marvel at the height of civilization it attained.

The Bahia itself, now the palace of the Resident-General, though built less than a hundred years ago, is typical of the architectural megalomania of the great southern chiefs. It was built by Ba-Ahmed, the all-powerful black Vizier of the Sultan Moulay-el-Hassan.* Ba-Ahmed was evidently an artist and an archæologist. His ambition was to re-create a Palace of Beauty such as the Moors had built in the prime of Arab art, and he brought to Marrakech skilled artificers of Fez, the last surviving masters of the mystery of chiselled plaster and ceramic mosaics and honeycombing of gilded cedar. They came, they built the Bahia, and it remains the loveliest and most fantastic of Moroccan palaces.

Court within court, garden beyond garden, reception halls, private apartments, slaves' quarters, sunny prophets' chambers on the roofs and baths in vaulted crypts, the labyrinth of passages and rooms

* Moulay-el-Hassan reigned from 1873 to 1894.

stretches away over several acres of ground. A long court enclosed in pale-green trellis-work, where pigeons plume themselves about a great tank and the dripping tiles glitter with refracted sunlight, leads to the fresh gloom of a cypress garden, or under jasmine tunnels bordered with running water; and these again open on arcaded apartments faced with tiles and stucco-work, where, in a languid twilight, the hours drift by to the ceaseless music of the fountains.

The beauty of Moroccan palaces is made up of details of ornament and refinements of sensuous delight too numerous to record; but to get an idea of their general character it is worth while to cross the Court of Cypresses at the Bahia and follow a series of low-studded passages that turn on themselves till they reach the centre of the labyrinth. Here, passing by a low padlocked door leading to a crypt, and known as the 'Door of the Vizier's Treasure-House', one comes on a painted portal that opens into a still more secret sanctuary: the apartment of the Grand Vizier's Favourite.

This lovely prison, from which all sight and sound of the outer world are excluded, is built about an atrium paved with disks of turquoise and black and white. Water trickles from a central *vasca* of alabaster into an hexagonal mosaic channel in the pavement. The walls, which are at least twenty-five feet high, are roofed with painted beams resting on panels of traceried stucco in which is set a clerestory of jewelled glass. On each side of the atrium are long recessed rooms closed by vermilion doors painted with gold arabesques and vases of spring flowers; and into these shadowy inner rooms, spread with rugs and divans and soft pillows, no light comes except when their doors are opened into the atrium. In this fabulous place it was my good luck to be lodged while I was at Marrakech.

In a climate where, after the winter snow has melted from the Atlas, every breath of air for long months is a flame of fire, these enclosed rooms in the middle of the palaces are the only places of refuge from the heat. Even in October the temperature of the favourite's apartment was deliciously reviving after a morning in the bazaars or the dusty streets, and I never came back to its wet tiles and perpetual twilight without the sense of plunging into a deep sea-pool.

From far off, through circuitous corridors, came the scent of citron-blossom and jasmine, with sometimes a bird's song before dawn, sometimes a flute's wail at sunset, and always the call of the muezzin in the night; but no sunlight reached the apartment except in remote rays through the clerestory, and no air except through one or two broken panes.

Sometimes, lying on my divan, and looking out through the vermilion doors, I used to surprise a pair of swallows dropping down from their nest in the cedar-beams to preen themselves on the fountain's edge or in the channels of the pavement; for the roof was full of birds who came and went through the broken panes of the clerestory. Usually they were my only visitors; but one morning just at daylight I was waked by a soft tramp of bare feet, and saw, silhouetted against the cream-coloured walls a procession of eight tall negroes in linen tunics, who filed noiselessly across the atrium like a moving frieze of bronze. In that fantastic setting, and the hush of that twilight hour, the vision was so like the picture of a 'Seraglio Tragedy', some fragment of a Delacroix or Decamps floating up into the drowsy brain, that I almost fancied I had seen the ghosts of Ba-Ahmed's executioners revisiting with dagger and bowstring the scene of an unavenged crime.

A cock crew, and they vanished... and when I made the mistake of asking what they had been doing in my room at that hour I was told (as though it were the most natural thing in the world) that they were the municipal lamp-lighters of Marrakech, whose duty it is to refill every morning the two hundred acetylene lamps lighting the palace of the Resident-General. Such unforeseen aspects, in this mysterious city, do the most ordinary domestic functions wear.

The Bazaars

Passing out of the enchanted circle of the Bahia it is startling to plunge into the native life about its gates.

Marrakech is the great market of the south; and the south means not only the Atlas with its feudal chiefs and their wild clansmen, but all that lies beyond of heat and savagery: the Sahara of the veiled Touaregs, Dakka, Timbuctoo, Senegal and the Soudan. Here come the camel caravans from Demnat and Tameslout, from the Moulouya and the Souss, and those from the Atlantic ports and the confines of Algeria. The population of this old city of the southern march has always been even more mixed than that of the northerly Moroccan towns. It is made up of the descendants of all the peoples conquered by a long line of Sultans who brought their trains of captives across the sea from Moorish Spain and across the Sahara from Timbuctoo. Even in the highly cultivated region on the lower slopes of the Atlas there are groups of varied ethnic origin, the descendants of tribes transplanted by long-gone rulers and still preserving many of their original characteristics.

In the bazaars all these peoples meet and mingle: cattle-dealers, olive-growers, peasants from the Atlas, the Souss and the Draa, Blue Men of the Sahara, blacks from Senegal and the Soudan, coming in to trade with the wool-merchants, tanners, leather-merchants, silk-weavers, armourers, and makers of agricultural implements.

Dark, fierce and fanatical are these narrow *souks* of Marrakech. They are mere mud lanes roofed with rushes, as in South Tunisia and Timbuctoo, and the crowds swarming in them are so dense that it is hardly possible, at certain hours, to approach the tiny raised kennels where the merchants sit like idols among their wares. One feels at once that something more than the thought of bargaining – dear as this is to the African heart – animates these incessantly moving throngs. The *souks* of Marrakech seem, more than any others, the central organ of a native life that extends far beyond the city walls into secret clefts of the mountains and far-off oases where plots are hatched and holy wars fomented – farther still, to yellow deserts whence negroes are secretly brought across the Atlas to that inmost recess of the bazaar where the ancient traffic in flesh and blood still surreptitiously goes on.

All these many threads of the native life, woven of greed and lust, of fetishism and fear and blind hate of the stranger, form, in the *souks*, a thick network in which at times one's feet seem literally to stumble. Fanatics in sheepskins glowering from the guarded thresholds of the mosques, fierce tribesmen with inlaid arms in their belts and the fighters' tufts of wiry hair escaping from camel's-hair turbans, mad negroes standing stark naked in niches of the walls and pouring down

Soudanese incantations upon the fascinated crowd, consumptive Jews with pathos and cunning in their large eyes and smiling lips, lusty slave-girls with earthen oil-jars resting against swaying hips, almond-eyed boys leading fat merchants by the hand, and bare-legged Berber women, tattooed and insolently gay, trading their striped blankets, or bags of dried roses and irises, for sugar, tea, or Manchester cottons – from all these hundreds of unknown and unknowable people, bound together by secret affinities, or intriguing against each other with secret hate, there emanated an atmosphere of mystery and menace more stifling than the smell of camels and spices and black bodies and smoking fry which hangs like a fog under the close roofing of the *souks*.

And suddenly one leaves the crowd and the turbid air for one of those quiet corners that are like the back-waters of the bazaars: a small square where a vine stretches across a shop-front and hangs ripe clusters of grapes through the reeds. In the patterning of grape-shadows a very old donkey, tethered to a stone-post, dozes under a pack-saddle that is never taken off; and near by, in a matted niche, sits a very old man in white. This is the chief of the Guild of 'morocco' Workers of Marrakech, the most accomplished craftsman in Morocco in the preparing and using of the skins to which the city gives its name. Of these sleek moroccos, cream-white or dyed with cochineal or pomegranate skins, are made the rich bags of the Chleuh dancing-boys, the embroidered slippers for the harem, the belts and harnesses that figure so largely in Moroccan trade – and of the finest, in old days, were made the pomegranate-red morocco bindings of European bibliophiles.

From this peaceful corner one passes into the barbaric splendour of a *souk* hung with innumerable plumy bunches of floss silk-skeins of citron yellow, crimson, grasshopper green and pure purple. This is the silk-spinners' quarter, and next to it comes that of the dyers, with great seething vats into which the raw silk is plunged, and ropes over-head where the rainbow masses are hung out to dry.

Another turn leads into the street of the metalworkers and arm-ourers, where the sunlight through the thatch flames on round flanks of beaten copper or picks out the silver bosses of ornate powder-flasks and pistols; and near by is the *souk* of the ploughshares, crowded with peasants in rough Chleuh cloaks who are waiting to have their archaic ploughs repaired, and that of the smiths, in an outer lane of mud huts where negroes squat in the dust and sinewy naked figures in tattered loin cloths bend over blazing coals. And here ends the maze of the bazaars.

PART TWO
ANTARCTICA

ALONE IN ANTARCTICA

Felicity Aston

Felicity Aston (1977–present) was born in a southern English village, but her favourite region of the world is Antarctica. Spending time in that wilderness was once a requirement of her work as a meteorologist, but she now voluntarily takes part in races and expeditions in places where it's literally arctic. In 2012, she was the first woman to cross the Antarctic land-mass alone on skis (hence *Alone in Antarctica*), with only a jar of peanut butter on her luxury list. She completed the 1,744km journey in 59 days, setting a Guinness World Record and confirming her place as an adventurer to be reckoned with.

Getting Out of the Tent

@felicity_aston Another awesome day skiing past a parade of beautiful mountains beneath crazy clouds. This last couple of days have certainly been my reward.
@felicity_aston Just in case I was in danger of feeling sentimental, a violent wind has appeared from nowhere and is beating the tent like the bad old days.

As my route brought me closer to Wilson Nunatak I was seized with the desire to climb to its summit. The idea was imprudent in many ways; I was within striking distance of completing a two-month, 1,700-kilometre journey that had stretched me physically and mentally. The last thing I needed was any extra exertion or an eleventh-hour injury. And yet, as the peak revealed itself in ever greater detail, the more I was drawn to it. The nunatak was shaped like a blunted sphinx, its perfectly smooth contours rising into a low summit joined by a gentle saddle to a second, higher summit. My sight drifted up over its back and settled on the flattened hilltop at its crown. It looked like an uncomplicated hike and the summit promised an elevated 360 degree view, the exhilaration of being able to see forever, the inexplicable draw of being at the undisputed 'top' of something. As if in encouragement, the sun settled directly above the higher summit and surrounded itself with a spectacular halo like a presenting peacock. It was 22 January and the distance to the coast appeared in single figures on my GPS. For the first time on the expedition, I had time to spare.

At the base of the nunatak patches of snow and ice were stranded in the spaces between boulders, petering out by degrees higher up. I dragged my sledges onto one of the larger snow islands, securing them carefully with my skis so that there was no chance of them moving without me. The lower flanks of the nunatak were a jumble of fractured ledges and platforms of frost-shattered stone striped with distinct bands of coloured rock; some dark, some pale, some blotched with dabs of quartz. At first it felt strange to be on solid ground, to be stepping rather than sliding, but soon I was hopping from ledge to ledge, enjoying the sense of freedom. Without the weight of my sledges dragging behind me, I felt unnaturally buoyant. The gradient was easily manageable even in my square-toed ski boots and, contouring around the slope at a slight angle, I soon found myself on the lower of the two summits. Along the saddle, belts of light and dark rock formed concentric circles, one on top of the other. I stopped to look closer at the splinters of rock that littered the ground coloured in vibrant orange and ruddy brown that looked gaudy compared to the pastel shades I was used to. With another short climb I finally approached the higher summit of Wilson Nunatak. The wind greeted me, blowing hard from the open space ahead, and I stepped onto the lip of a dreamy skyscape of pearlescent cloud. Below, the glossy snow was streaked with ribbons of blue ice. Above it, surrounded by a delicate silver halo and gossamer cloud, blazed my friend the sun in triumphant approval. I nodded my grinning appreciation in its direction before turning my attention to the horizon on my left which was bristling with dark purple mountains, low and triangular, crowded together in a dense band. The extent of the Ellsworth Mountain range took me by surprise. My private panorama of mountains that had seemed so extensive as I crossed the narrow open neck of Horseshoe Valley had been, in reality, barely a glimpse of the range's toenail.

I sat on a boulder and breathed deeply in quiet satisfaction. The whole of Antarctica seemed to be mapped out below me. Shifting my position I turned my back to the wind and gazed southward at the horizon I had skied over. My mind led me back over the miles to where I had begun all those weeks before, and then continued back in time over the longer path that had brought me here. I thought about the anguish over the decision to walk away from conventional employment, of the endless search for ways to make expeditions happen and of creating a viable living around them. There had been no roadmap and yet looking backwards it all seemed so obvious, every step appearing to be part of an ordered sequence of events designed for the sole purpose of enabling me to be on this summit on this day.

It hadn't seemed so clear and ordered at the time. In hindsight, I had spent much of my twenties floundering in uncertainty and timidity, not being able to see a way forward and held back by the suspicion that I was making terrible mistakes. If only I could speak to myself back then and give reassurance that I was on the right track, that the decisions I was making would lead me to good places. But no one can tell you the way, you have to find it yourself – and the way is never clear until you step forward.

My thoughts turned to the less metaphorical 'way' that lay immediately ahead. I inspected the view to the north for any sign of the coast. It was difficult in the layers of shimmer to be sure what was cloud and what was snow but I thought I could see a deep cleft in the landscape close to the horizon, a richer shading that indicated an incline of some sort. Might this be Hercules Inlet? The thought gave me the momentum to move from my perch. I gave one last, longing look around at the view below me and turned to leave. It struck me then that I had climbed quickly to the top of the nunatak without pause and without feeling even the slightest bit out of breath. A climb like this, even when training for an expedition, would normally have left me gasping for air and my muscles burning. The constant low-intensity exertion of skiing and the extended time at higher altitudes must have left me in much better fitness than I appreciated. As I trotted down the same slopes back to my sledges I felt charged with energy and just a little bit pleased with myself. Reconnecting my harness to the sledges I felt unstoppable, all the fatigue of the past weeks forgotten and the coast within what felt to be no more than a short stride away. Little did I know that in the short distance that lay ahead to the very edge of Antarctica I would face some of the most demanding terrain of the entire journey.

The difficulty started almost immediately. The ground from the edge of the nunatak fell away into an immense windscoop with slicks of blue ice pooled at the bottom. There was no way to go around the windscoop completely as it tailed directly across my path but at least the slope down into it that lay directly ahead looked less severe than the gradients further to the left or right. There was nothing for it but to go straight down. I set off, holding my skis rigidly parallel to each other, feeling the glide of the slope beneath me. The crusted snow surface was studded with circular sastrugi that rose in platforms like inverted wedding cakes, the wind having eroded all the softer snow from around their bases, and they were as tough as plaster. As I picked up speed my ski tips were deflected from them like a pinball wizard. I was jolted off balance several times before finally pulling myself into a halt. My sledges, which had bounced violently along behind me, swung around on the rope attached to the harness at my waist and jack-knifed on the slope a few feet below, pulling me roughly forward. I paused for a moment, suspended precariously on the slope and rethought. I couldn't risk being pulled over and injured by my own sledges thundering down the slope behind me. Instead, I allowed my sledges to slide ahead like an eager dog taking its owner for a walk, and angled my skis against the slope so that I made steady but laborious zigzags down the glacis. It was awkward, so I was relieved when the slope began to flatten out. Eventually I felt confident enough to release the sledges, overtaking them as I glided downward under gravity. There was still enough of a gradient to pick up some speed. I squealed in delight as I clattered over the uneven sastrugi followed in hot pursuit by my sledges. Reaching the bottom panting but grinning I glanced upward at the slope we'd just descended. Disappointingly, from this angle it looked like the gentlest of inclines betraying nothing of what had caused the anxious restraint of the last few hours.

The ground ahead was flat but covered with the same mushroom-like sastrugi which made it feel like I was skiing over cobbles (even though I skied around the worst) and slowed my progress. Again and again I came down steep slopes, although none of them as dramatic as the incline beneath Wilson Nunatak. I stopped frequently to try and make sense of the scenery around me and match it to the view I'd had from the summit. It was clear that I was edging my way downwards, losing a lot of height and up ahead I could see a long line of dusky-blue shading protruding towards me from the east. It looked like a deep valley with a flat floor. I couldn't think of anything else this could be other than Hercules Inlet. Heading towards it, the sastrugi had been completely scoured away by the wind, revealing a solid surface of opaline ice which had been cratered into fist-sized dimples by the sun. Light glinted from every surface magnifying the glare so that as I approached the lip of the next slope it wasn't difficult to spot a ribbon of matt white snaking across my path. It was a snow-covered crevasse.

I cautiously approached the near side of the crack to get a better look. The snow that sagged slightly over the gap looked deceptively solid but I remained wary. It was a relatively narrow crevasse but still wider than the length of my skis and too wide for me to be confident of making a safe leap to the other side, even if I took off my skis. I allowed my eyes to follow its trail, a softly curving line that darted across the landscape for as far as I could see in either direction and looked unchanging right along its length. With little to recommend turning right or left, I dithered for an instant before turning right (which at least looked slightly downhill). I skied along the edge of the crevasse for a little over a mile, stopping to inspect, then reject, several potential crossing places along the way. Finally the crevasse narrowed just enough for me to be able to place a tentative ski across the gap. My ski tip sat comfortably on the far edge while the back of my ski still rested securely on the near edge. I jabbed the ice on the other side hard with my ski pole to check that it felt as solid as it looked. Feeling confident I brought my other ski across so that my feet were suspended in parallel across the gap. Pausing like that for a moment I couldn't resist but plunge my ski pole into the snow bridge next to me, just to see what was beneath. The round basket at the end of my ski pole broke easily through the powdery snow and a chunk of the surface fell away like dust. Through the hole I could see the peculiar luminescent blue of light filtered through ice, and a glimpse of a terrifying blackness of a deep void. The glimpse was enough to make me step hastily onto the solid safety of the other side and drag my sledges quickly after me.

Glancing again at the hole I'd made with my ski pole I considered how lucky I was to have come across this crack in fine weather and clear sunshine in which every surface feature was as defined as an engineer's draft. The thought of what might have happened had I skied over this crevasse unknowingly in bad weather and flat light made my heart thump faster. I shuddered as if to shake off the thought and turned to look at the way ahead with renewed concentration. If there was one crevasse it was likely there would be more. Sure enough I crossed not one but two crevasses of a similar size, each time skiing along their edge until I found a safe place to cross. I felt confident but my anxiety increased as the hard icy surfaces ahead became covered by snowpack and low sastrugi. The snow would conceal any further crevassing in the ice beneath.

The plane being sent to collect me wouldn't be able to land on a slope; I had to reach flatter ground so I continued down slope after slope but I felt taut with nerves, worried that each step might send me plunging into a dark void. I ached to pitch camp, to be able to stay put and be safe rather than bear the excruciating suspense of what each stride might bring – but I couldn't stop where I was.

'Almost,' I told myself, noticing that my teeth were clamped tightly together in angst, my jaw taking the brunt of the nervous stress I felt.

The gradient ended abruptly on a narrow but flat plain surrounded on three sides by steep escarpments. This, I realised in amazement, was

Hercules Inlet. The snow surface I stood on was ice floating on water (which is why it was so flat), a slim tongue extending from the main Ronne Ice Shelf to the east, whereas the surrounding escarpments were snow-covered shoreline. I could see a crease of colour in the snow at the base of the escarpments – as clear a sign of the coast as I was going to get in Antarctica – and by skiing across it I had completed my traverse.

I had arrived.

The numbers on my GPS confirmed that I was significantly north of the eightieth line of latitude which traced the coast and had therefore moved beyond the edge of the continent – but still I kept skiing. I headed onwards towards the centre of the inlet, feeling that I needed to reach something that was a definitive endpoint, but there was no clear finish line, no camp, no people, no silver globe to touch as a finishing post. I spied the low profile of an island in the middle of the inlet, pear-shaped with a large flat area on top, and, in the absence of anything better, I headed for that. As I approached the centre of the island I slowed my pace, dragging each ski steadily and deliberately to elongate every stride, until finally I stopped.

I squinted up at the sun.

'It's over,' I said aloud, partly to the sun and partly to myself.

The sun was abnormally quiet for once, presumably as overcome by the surprise of the moment as I was. After counting the hours and the miles for so long it now all seemed to have come to an end too quickly. I reached for my water bottle and sat on my sledge in silence, gulping and watching the mountains. Having skied 1,744 kilometres in the previous fifty-nine days, I was now the first and only woman in the world ever to have crossed Antarctica alone.

I had traversed a continent.

I had skied across Antarctica.

The thought sounded absurd. It seemed barely credible to have skied so far, to have traversed an entire landmass, even though I could remember every stride, every moment, every inch. I imagined a map of Antarctica and my ski tracks leaving two unbroken parallel lines right the way across it. It was like looking down from the top of a ladder and realising for the first time how high I had climbed. While climbing you have to focus on each rung, absorbed by each new footing and only when safely at the top can you appreciate the view. Similarly, I had needed to be absorbed by each footfall, by the individual incidences of each day and only now could I start to see how far those footfalls had carried me. It was hard to take in. Just as the scale of the journey had prevented me thinking of the whole, now it prevented me from being able to appreciate what had been completed. I didn't feel triumphant and I wasn't filled with a sense of achievement; there was just surprise and perhaps a small sense of anticlimax. After all, I was still alone, just me and Antarctica, exactly as it had been for the past two months.

I pulled out my satellite phone and sat with it in my lap for a moment before calling Union Glacier. Beneath the congratulations, I could hear relief in Steve's voice that I was done and sensed that I was now one less concern in a hugely complex logistical picture he was wrestling with as the season drew to a close. They were going to send a plane for me within hours.

'I promise you that by this evening you'll be in the warm with a glass of red wine,' Steve told me.

As I rang off the thought of the promised comfort and imminent company broke through my sense of bewilderment and, at last, the tears came.

I was going home.

The alone-ness that had pressed down on me for so long and held me in taut high-alert would soon be replaced with the warmth and security of company. Within hours I would be able to release myself from mental hibernation and relax into a more familiar version of myself. All I had to do was sit tight.

I woke to cheerful sunlight filtering through the bright yellow lining of my faithful Hilleberg and felt rigidly tense. Then I remembered. Today I didn't have to leap out of my sleeping bag to chase the horizon – I was already where I had to be. I relaxed into the warmth and let my mind settle. The previous evening I'd set up my tent to wait for the plane and called Union Glacier on the hour every hour to report on the weather for the pilots – but each time I did so I was told that the plane had been delayed a little longer. Eventually Steve came back on the phone. Mindful of his promise of red wine by the end of the night, he was apologetic.

'I'm so sorry, Felicity, but the weather has deteriorated this end so we won't be able to come and get you tonight.'

The weather had played one last trick on me but I wasn't sorry. I needed a last evening alone with Antarctica. It felt appropriate. I needed time to digest the fact that my journey was over and to prepare myself for company again.

That morning I took my time making breakfast coffee from my meagre remaining rations while still nested in the comfort of my sleeping bag. I was aware of a deep relief unfolding and a steadfast sense of satisfaction spreading into every corner of my being but, through my contentment, an insistent thought rose adamantly to the surface. It was very similar to a thought that had occurred to me three years before when standing alone at the South Pole for the first time. The thought was the knowledge that on that morning, as on every morning for the last two months, I could have got on my skis and headed across the snow. Tired as I was I knew that my muscles were capable of another day. My mind imagined packing up and skiing away, which led quickly to the inevitable next question; if I was sure I could continue, how far would I be able to ski?

I tried to gauge what capability I had left in me both physically and mentally. Would I realistically be able to ski all day? Did I feel strong enough to ski for another week? Would it be conceivable to turn around and ski another 2,000 kilometres back to where I had started?

I expressed a silent, inward groan. These are the questions, this is the curiosity, that has led me back to the polar regions again and again. Within hours of finishing the most ambitious expedition of my life I was already being drawn on to think of new challenges and my heart sank a little with the weight of it. I could see how easily the bid to find extremes of capability could transform from a mode of motivation into a source of torment. Filling the hole left by an expedition with the seeds of a new adventure was a temptation I was wary of, knowing as I did both its compelling addiction and the fact that it has no end. But I couldn't avoid the question circling my brain. If I had succeeded in crossing Antarctica alone, did it mean that I was capable of more? After all, it is only when we have tried our best and failed that we know we have reached our absolute potential. Was what I had been searching for all this time not success but, in fact, failure?

I shook the thoughts from my head. I had come to Antarctica to explore my limits but I realised now that I had arrived with a preconception of what that limit would look like. I had envisaged falling to my knees in the snow with the conviction that I couldn't go on. I imagined that I would be able to describe my limit in terms of a number of miles and a number of days. I had been wrong. The last two months had taught me that a personal limit is not as defined as a line in the snow. No matter how far we travel or how hard we push, our bodies will keep moving forward and our minds will find ways to process. But in exploring those extremes we pay a price. I may have covered every mile in Antarctica from coast to coast but there had been mornings on the ice when I had felt in real danger of losing my mind, times when I had felt more desperate and desolate than at any other time in my life and I never wanted to experience that kind of despair again. There is a price I'm not willing to pay in order to discover the absolute extent of my personal limits. I have pushed far enough. Through the prism of Antarctica I had found my answer, I had found my limit. My limit was being alone.

By mid-afternoon I began to worry that I would need to eke my rations out over another night when I received word from Union Glacier that the plane was on its way and would be with me within the hour. I packed away all my belongings, leaving just the shell of my tent as a precautionary shelter, and stepped outside to wait. A constant breeze streamed past me from the north but the sun glared in heatless intensity through a loose patchwork of high cloud. Expectation raced through me as both excitement and panic; excitement that I was going home but panic at the thought of my expedition being over. I had longed for the plane to return ever since it had left me – but I had also dreaded it. Since leaving the Pole I had feared its appearance because it would mean I had run out of time. Now, I dreaded it because the plane heralded the passing of something that I would never experience again. My big adventure was over and, as demanding as it had been, there was a sadness in the finality of going home.

I pulled out my camera and started to take pictures. I took pictures of the horizon, of the tent, of myself. It wasn't as if I didn't already have a million images of almost precisely identical scenery but I think I knew even then that I wasn't taking pictures to capture the view. It was an instinctive act to try and capture something of the moment – as if the pixels of my camera could trap not just light but a sense of the experience too.

I heard it before I could see it. A faint drone barely perceptible above the fizz of silence. Scanning the horizon to the west I spotted the plane while it was still no more than a microscopic dot low over the mountains. It grew and expanded until I could see the dark slash of its wings and the distinctive silhouette of a Twin Otter. It brought back memories of standing beneath a different range of mountains on the opposite side of the continent and once again I couldn't quite untangle how it was possible that I'd skied across an entire landmass. I didn't have any special abilities, I wasn't superhuman and yet here I was on the far coast of Antarctica. It was clear to me that the success of my expedition had not depended on physical strength or dramatic acts of bravery but on the fact that at least some progress – however small – had been made every single day. It had not been about glorious heroism but the humblest of qualities, a quality that perhaps we all too often fail to appreciate for its worth – that of perseverance. Critical to skiing across Antarctica had been the distinctly unimpressive and yet, for me, incredibly demanding challenge of finding the will to get out of the tent each and every morning. If I had failed in that most fundamental of tasks, then my expedition would have been over.

The plane landed in a flash of glinting metal and a roar of thrumming engines. I sheltered my eyes from the sun to watch as it dragged a nebulous cloud of ice vapour around itself, before turning and trundling back towards me. As I watched, I made an internal pact with myself to remember that it is as vital to celebrate daily successes – even those as marginal as getting out of the tent – as it is to analyse failures; that one small success every day will eventually add up to a greater achievement; that looking back to fully appreciate how far we have come is as essential as looking forward to where we want to be.

The shadow of the plane's wing fell on the snow around me and the rush of backdraft from the engine lifted spindrift into the air. I stepped forward to dismantle my home on the ice for the very last time. While I rolled tent material and plucked anchors from the snow in a series of movements made slick and rapid by repetition over the last sixty days I sensed the impression of something important crystallising in my subconscious. The fact that I had crossed Antarctica, despite the tears and the fear and the alone-ness, deepened my belief that we are each far more capable than we give ourselves credit for. Our bodies are stronger and our minds more resilient than we could ever imagine. To entrench it in my brain and carry it with me out of Antarctica, I summarised this important realisation in one simple phrase:

Keep getting out of the tent.

If I can do that, each and every day, no matter the challenge, who knows where the next day will take me.

ON THE ICE

Gretchen Legler

Gretchen Legler (1960–present) was born in Salt Lake City, USA, and is a Professor of Creative Writing at the University of Maine. To get in the zone for writing her series of linked essays *On the Ice: An Intimate Portrait of Life at McMurdo Station, Antarctica*, Legler spent five months in that numbingly cold place on a US National Science Foundation grant. It certainly seems to have been worth enduring the hardships – Legler won an award for best environmental creative writing, *and* found love there.

An Antarctic Quintet

I.

I'd been lying on my back, taking notes, looking up into the crystals and into that blue that still amazes me—blue so blue it was as if my eyes had broken; blue so blue it was like gas that faded away into more and more intense blue violet; beauty so expansive I couldn't contain it—I had to break to let it in. The first time I'd been in an Antarctic ice cave, months earlier, the person who took me there said that often people who go down into crevasses and into ice caves are so overcome by the blue that it makes them cry. I remembered that as I lay there on my back, taking notes, trying to draw the crystals that hung like blooms of flowers above me, trying to figure out where the blue began and where it ended.

I'd gone with nine others on this expedition to the ice caves that were part of the Erebus glacier tongue, a long spit of ancient ice spilling out onto the frozen Ross Sea from the base of Mount Erebus, Ross Island's active volcano. The caves were about an hour's drive over the ice from McMurdo Station. We'd signed up for the field trip on a sheet of paper outside the galley—it was a jaunt, free to anyone who wished to go—electricians or galley cooks who had the afternoon off, a scientist who wanted out of her lab for a few hours. As the orange truck plodded across the frozen sea, heaving over humps in the ice, we passengers packed snugly inside rolled and bumped into one another like children on a carnival ride, smiling at each other over the great roar of the truck's engine.

We went to two caves. One of them was easy to get into. You climbed a hill of snow, wriggled through a rather large opening, and slid down a slight slope into a cavern about as big as an average living room. The other cave you would miss if you didn't know it was there. You kick-stepped your way up a steep incline, then pressed your body through an opening just large enough to fit your shoulders through. Then you slid down a thin, icy tube until you landed on a shelf of thick blue ice. Next, with the aid of a rope, you climbed up and around and through a maze of tight ice walls until you reached two larger caverns, luminous with the deep turquoise and violet of glacier ice, and still as a tomb. Standing on the cold, flat floor of this second cave I felt and heard a seal's high-pitched call bounce through the ice.

It was in the first cave, though, that I lay upon my back, so intent on studying the blue around me that I was startled when I sensed that I was alone. Suddenly everyone else was gone. I reluctantly packed up my notebook and rose to leave. Once I was out of my grotto, I realized there was another person left in the blue room. It was my friend Gary Teetzel, an engineer from the Crary Lab. He and I had spent time together weeks earlier in the observation tube—an eighteen-foot-long tube set by scientists into the cold sea near McMurdo, a tube you could climb down into and sit in and watch creatures in the dark ocean around you.

"Oh, it's you," I said to Gary, jokingly, as if, should there be anyone left in the ice cavern it would have to be *him,* and *me.* He seemed a kindred spirit—a lover of quiet and contemplation. We stood at opposite ends of this ice cavern for another ten minutes, until we heard a voice calling us to come away and board the vehicle.

As I stood, I cupped my hands around my eyes so that all I saw was the blue, and as I stared, my heart began to beat faster and my breath started to come faster and tears came to my eyes. It was that blue that made me cry. That blue. That blue violet that seems to pull you in, that makes you feel as if you're falling into it, that compels you somehow to look into it, even though it blurs your vision and confuses you. It was that blue, so enigmatic that for a moment you lose your balance in it. You don't quite know if you're in the sky, or underwater, or whether for an instant you might be in both places at once. The blue is like a frosty, vague, and endlessly deep hole in your heart. It has no edges, just color and depth. It's a color that is like some kind of yearning, some unfulfilled desire, or some constant, extreme joy. It just burns there, burns violet, burns blue.

II.

The helicopter hovered over the rugged, ice-carved mountaintop, whipping up gravel and sand. A hunched figure came running from a tent nearby, clutching a hat to its head. Out of the open helicopter door a cookstove was handed to the figure, who grabbed it and secured it under his arm. There were waves of the hand and nearly inaudible shouts of thanks, and we lifted up again, the tiny camp below us diminishing to no more than bright dots of color in the sweeping landscape of ice and stone.

I was with McMurdo technician Tracy Dahl on a morning helicopter ride up the Taylor Valley in Antarctica's Dry Valleys, the world's coldest desert—a landscape so alien it had become a testing ground for equipment the United States hoped one day to send to Mars. Dahl was to deliver the stove and other supplies to two graduate students who'd pitched their peaked, yellow canvas Scott tents on the top of a windy, gravely high plateau. The next stop was a pickup and delivery at Lake Bonney, farther up the valley, and then, finally, Dahl and I were set down outside the three uninhabited canvas jamesways that made up the Lake Fryxell camp, which Dahl was to prepare for a soon-to-be-arriving field party.

After the chores were done, Dahl and I sat beside the fuel stove in one of the jamesways and warmed our feet on its metal sides, tipped back in our chairs, drinking tea, passing the time until Dahl's helicopter arrived to take him back to McMurdo. Then I'd be on my own. I was equipped for a small expedition: radio, backpack with tent, stove, sleeping bag, extra food, and clothes. I would make my way back on foot to Lake Hoare, the field camp where I'd been staying for the week. Mine was an officially sanctioned several-hour walk. If I didn't arrive at Lake Hoare by dinnertime, there would probably be a helicopter sent from McMurdo to find me. Nevertheless, it felt like an adventure—a walk in Antarctica, a walk in the wildest place I'd ever been, a walk in what might yet be the wildest place on Earth.

Every walk, said Henry David Thoreau, that nineteenth-century American saunterer of woods and mind, is a sort of crusade—a westward going, a wildward going—a journey toward self-awareness, transformation, and the future. We should be prepared, he said, on even the shortest walk to go "in the spirit of undying adventure, never to return—prepared to send back our embalmed hearts only as relics to our desolate kingdoms." The name itself, walker, saunterer, Thoreau wrote, may have derived from the expression used to describe a person in the Middle Ages who wandered about the land, *à la Sainte Terre*, a pilgrim, heading toward the Holy Land. Or it might be rooted in the words *sans terre,* without a home, but everywhere at home.

I felt both as I set off across Lake Fryxell, my ice axe swinging like a walking stick at my side, its metal point pinging against the hard turquoise surface beneath me. The teeth of my crampons bit in as I walked: metal against ice. The blue lake ice was cut by geometric patterns of crazy white lines and rising white orbs. I felt homeless and at home in the universe, as if I, too, was a pilgrim, walking not toward, but *in* a holy land.

The flatness of the valley I was in was broken on each side by distant hills swathed in shades of brown and white, the ones to my back more mountainous and sharp, the ones facing me, softer. My way led across Lake Fryxell, so beautifully disturbed by the designs in its frozen surface, toward the edge of the Canada glacier, which spilled out of the mountains between Fryxell and Lake Hoare and which I would have to go around. I paused frequently on the walk, gazing, enthralled with patterns in the snow made by wind, so delicately and improbably shaped—like letters, like words, like whole sentences written in dark brown dust on snow. Often I would stop to simply gaze about me, down the valley where it spread out wide and met the blue and white cloud-spattered sky, behind me to see the tiny jamesways of the Fryxell camp receding, and the towering glacial wall, emanating coldness. Many times, when I paused, the glacier would crack and thunder and I would jump for fear I'd be smashed by a falling chunk of ice as big as a house, me like a fly beneath it.

Such openness I had never walked in, never traveled by foot in such intimacy with. One step at a time would take me back to Lake Hoare by evening. I savored each step, giddily feeling my strong legs hinge at the hips, feeling each stride, my lungs expanding fully, my arms swinging, my back bearing up the weight of the pack. The land here was bare bones, stripped-down, elemental, and beautiful; beautiful in the way the bleak, landless, endless ocean is beautiful to fishers; the way deserts are beautiful to Saharan nomads; beautiful in its smallness—the many-colored pebbles in my path, the ragged ice along the shore, the turquoise glass I walked upon; and beautiful in its largeness—the infinite reach of sky, the gigantic arc of the land. The land brought me back, as it did Thoreau, to my senses; back to my body, back to my self.

As I walked I pondered how the world was reached through the self, how the universal comes of the particular, the immense from the intimate. Thoreau called it "recreating self," and for it he went to the most dismal of places; he entered the darkest of woods, the swampiest of swamps; they were his sacred places, *sanctum sanctorum*—for they were the places that were truly wild. What would he have made, I wondered, of Antarctica?

The woods and meadows of nineteenth-century New England were Thoreau's wilderness. He called it a mythic land: "You may name it America, but it is not America; neither Americus Vespucius, nor Columbus, nor the rest were discoverers of it. There is a truer account of it in Mythology than in any history of America." That he walked in a mythic landscape meant to him that his journey took him into all time. Thoreau walking in his woods, me walking alone from Lake Fryxell to Lake Hoare, around the booming edge of the towering Canada glacier, was humankind, womankind, mankind walking, walking in an unknown land. You may name it Antarctica, but it is not Antarctica. All moments converge here in this place and time—all efforts at renewal, all quests for knowledge, all attempts at transformation and adventure collide here in this *solid* earth, in this *actual* world.

As I rounded the final protruding hunk of ice of the Canada glacier and came within sight of the Lake Hoare camp, I could see the tiny purple, blue, and yellow dots of the domed tents, and the glint of the sun off the small metal buildings. I pulled my radio out of the bulging deep pocket of my bibbed wind pants and called in. "W-002 calling Lake Hoare," I said, giving my Antarctic code name, the W standing for writer. The radio crackled and popped and then came the familiar voice of Bob Wharton, the head scientist at the camp. "Roger, this is Lake Hoare camp. How would you like your steak done?" It would be good to be back among them, but it had also been good to be out alone, walking in Antarctica, feeling that magical, paradoxical diminishment of self and enlargement of spirit that such a landscape brings—that feeling that one is in the presence of something that has been in existence long before you and will continue long after you, into all time; some spirit that is larger and older than the human mind, and that, in its power, comforts rather than terrifies, soothes rather than agitates.

"I believe in the forest, and in the meadow, and in the night in which corn grows..." wrote Thoreau. This is what he crusaded for, what he walked for—the *common sense,* the link between spirit and body, earth and self. I believed in this too—that there was a sublime power in this land that could mysteriously help a person reconnect with that subtle magnetism in wildness that would show her the way. I believed in this vast glacier-scoured landscape, this thundering ice, and in the impossible simplicity of the thin line between frozen earth and sky.

III.

Antarctica is famous for wind, wind that roars down the mountains from the polar plateau, spilling into the ocean; *katabatic* wind, fast wind, wind that carves ice into feathers and ferns; wind that carves rock into wind facts, *ventifacts,* signifiers of wind, something solid made of the workmanship of wild air.

The wind howling in around the seams in the McMurdo galley door is a sound I'll remember from Antarctica. Wind screaming in on stormy days, at a higher pitch than I could sing, sounding so much like a piece of machinery gone haywire, or an animal caught short, surprised or afraid. I'll remember the wind at the windows, knocking in a thick, padded, muffled way, so that you might imagine there was someone out there, wanting you to *open up, open up,* let them in. And the wind whistling down the hollow shaft of a bamboo pole, one in a line planted out there in the middle of nowhere showing the way to safety, the way home, the way around a deadly crack in the ice. The wind whistled down the shaft, as if the pole were a bamboo flute and wind was playing on it a merry, eerie tune.

I'll remember, too, the sound of the small cotton flags tied to those poles—red and green for follow me this way, black for go this way and you'll die—the flags, *slap, slap, slapping* in the wind, snapping against themselves, cracking like whips in the 100-degrees-below-zero air.

I'll remember the wind *whoop, whoop, whoop, whooping* through the electrical and telephone wires. In one spot, behind McMurdo's two bars, the winds whipped and howled and *moaned* and *moaned* and *moaned* around the buildings, into nooks and out again, eddying and swirling, dancing and buzzing through the wires overhead, playing the wires as if they were the strings of a deep bass, pushing me along, pushing me, hurrying me along so forcefully that I had to lean back into the strength of the wind to stand upright.

I'll remember the almost nothing sound of wind across the ice, smooth and moving fast, blowing from nowhere to everywhere, taking with it my breath, the snow at my feet, the fur of my parka hood, and all of my heat.

IV.

Siple Dome camp was simple and spare: a small runway, a collection of tents and canvas jamesways surrounded by mounds of snow-buried gear and supplies. Beyond that there was nothing familiar, nothing kind to human flesh or desire, only miles-thick ice and snow, only *the fresh and natural surface of the planet Earth, as it was made forever and ever.*

Thoreau's words came to me then, again, as I marveled at how *wild* the space around me was, how nobly spacious, how elemental, and how being here grounded me undeniably in my own flesh. Siple Dome, a scientific field camp on the West Antarctic Ice Sheet, was a place by all accounts in the middle of absolutely nowhere, where one could turn 360 degrees and not see the horizon alter its unwaveringly straight face; where one was surrounded by a wilderness of snow and ice stretching as far as the mind could imagine; wildness so extreme it could extinguish you in a blink, as quickly as if you were being drowned, as quickly as if you'd been set free in outer space with no oxygen.

Before the cooks, electricians, carpenters, and scientists at Siple Dome could even begin the work of setting up the field station and going about their research, they had to shovel the camp out from beneath yards and yards of snow that had buried it over the Antarctic winter. Now this unlikely village lay atop the snow and ice, looking ever so much like a nomadic encampment in a wide, icy desert, at any moment prone to being blown away, to being buried again, to being neatly erased from the face of the earth.

Kendrick Taylor, from the Desert Research Institute in Reno, Nevada, a man who studies ice, drove out with me on a sunny Sunday to a spot ten kilometers from the camp, following a line of green flags on bamboo poles that marked a safe route along the snow. When we reached the end of the flag line, we stopped our snowmobiles and Kendrick said to me, pointing into nowhere, at nothing, "Go ahead another two kilometers and turn off your machine and sit. I'll wait here."

I drove out toward a horizon like I'd never seen. I imagined that, had I kept going, I could have driven right off the edge of the planet. The only thing separating the land from the sky in this place was a thin white line and the faintest change in hue from white to pale blue. The snowy wind moved like a fog over the ground, a slinky, elegant, snaky thing, throwing off my sense of balance, blurring the edges of my vision.

I drove for two kilometers, watching the odometer as I went. Then I stopped, turned off the machine, and sat in the quiet. I looked behind me for Kendrick and saw only a dark speck in the distance, surrounded by an immensity of blankness, sky and ground inextricably fused. I got off the snowmobile and lay down in the snow. I spread out my legs and my arms as if I were making a snow angel. I could feel the hard coolness of the ice all along my back and legs. *Contact!* Here it was beneath me. Here I was upon it—Thoreau's *solid* earth! *Here was no man's garden, but the unhandseled globe.* All I heard was the sharp hiss of the wind blowing crystals of snow over me, past my ears, and across my face. All I felt was my body against matter. How comical I must have looked and how tiny; an amalgam of flesh and bone, nylon and rubber in the midst of that Titanic ice. But who would have seen? I shut my eyes and must have been lulled by the wind, hypnotized by the cold, because I was roused only when a snowmobile engine broke my reverie. It was Kendrick coming to get me. I looked down at my legs, my arms, my boots—they were covered with snow, the black of my wind pants now white. The snow had begun to conceal me, as it had buried the pallets of cargo lined up around Siple Dome camp, as it had drifted over the jamesways themselves. How easily, how effortlessly, I could have disappeared; how easily any of us could, and how inexplicably this knowledge of our smallness, of my smallness, filled me with joy.

V.

At the South Pole, I wandered out from the silver geodesic dome into the searing white light of late afternoon. It was always bright day outside at the Pole, the sun overhead, circling around and around and around this spot at the bottom of the world, hardly dipping, never setting. I wore snow goggles, my furred parka hood was cinched tight, leaving just a peephole, fur-backed gauntlets covered my hands and lower arms, a fleece neck gaiter protected my cheeks and nose from freezing. I breathed with difficulty in the thin, 10,000-foot-high air, and the gaiter over my face thickened with frost. It was the beginning of summer at the South Pole, and it was minus 75.1 degrees Fahrenheit.

When I looked to the horizon I saw only white and blue, separated by a subtle line between the ice and sky that bowed around, encircling me in the curve of the globe. I walked out from the geodesic dome toward the two most famous landmarks at the South Pole—the mirrored ball atop the red-and-white-striped barber pole ringed by flags that is the ceremonial pole, and the small, nondescript surveyor's marker that is the exact location of the geographical South Pole, the southern axis of the planet Earth. At the ceremonial pole, the flags slapped in the wind and added stunning color to the all-white landscape. The flags are those of the original nations that signed the Antarctic Treaty—a treaty that preserves Antarctica as the only continent on the globe free from national ownership, resource extraction, development, plundering, and wreck; a treaty meant to preserve the continent in perpetuity "for peaceful purposes."

A short distance away from the barber pole was the survey marker, about three feet high, a metal pole atop which sits a thick, gold-colored disk imprinted with an image of the Antarctic continent itself. Also pressed into the top of the disk are the words "Planet Earth. Geographical South Pole. 90 Degrees South. January 1, 1997." The marker is dated because the ice here shifts westward about thirty feet a year, making it necessary to replot the exact location of the pole on the first new day of each year. When I looked up and squinted into the distance, I could see a long line of such markers trailing away into the snowy flatness.

A friend had entrusted me, before I left my home in Anchorage, Alaska, with some ashes in a small glass vial. They were remains from her mother and sister. In the past she'd given such vials to others who'd gone to places such as the summit of Denali or to other ends of the earth. I said I'd find a place for her mother and sister at the bottom of the world, so I had the vial in the pocket of my red parka. I dug a small impression in the snow with the heel of my boot and, with my hands still in my ungainly mittens, fumbled the vial open and sprinkled ashes into the hole. I covered the spot and stamped it down, thinking that in weeks, months, next year, the ice would move on, taking the ashes with it, westward; one day they'd make it out to the continent's edge, fall into the sea, melt, be taken up by the circumpolar currents and make their way around the globe. Then they would be everywhere. I bowed toward the marker, toward the center, and I said a prayer—for my friend who'd lost her mother and sister, one to a heart attack and one to suicide; for me, whose sister also took her own life; for all of us, for all of our grief, for all of our delicate, human suffering.

Afterward, in the dull, stinging cold, I stared for a time at the words on the survey marker. "Planet Earth. Geographical South Pole." The geographical South Pole. The other end of the world from the place I lived. Everywhere I looked from here, from this exact spot, was north. If I walked around this spot, I'd be walking around the world, through all the time zones, from one day to the next, into the future, through the past and out again.... I did it. I put my mittened hand on the head of the marker, feeling the impression of the continent through the leather and lining, and I walked around it. I walked around and around and around the world, my steps creaking in the dry hard snow. I'd never felt so riveted in place, so exactly located, so precisely in one spot, and everywhere at once.

ACCESS ALL AREAS

Sara Wheeler

Sara Wheeler (1961–present) grew up in Bristol and studied Classics and Modern Languages at Oxford University. In the mid-1990s the US National Science Foundation, impressed by her travel writing about the Greek island of Euboea and Chile, offered her a seven-month post as their first female writer-in-residence at the South Pole. It might appear to have been more of a punishment than a prize, but Wheeler luckily relishes extreme environments, and recorded her adventures with great humour in *Access All Areas*.

The Igloo Papers

It was one damned thing after another in the igloo. You struggle out of the bag to solve one problem, and a battalion of others queue up for recognition.

There was a perfectly good high-altitude tent in my kit. But I was in a remote field camp on the West Antarctic Ice Sheet, and I spent two days building the igloo, helped by the team of bearded seismic geologists with whom I was camping, the weather having temporarily buggered up their chances of setting off bombs. As part of a long-term project to map the mountain range immured within a mile of ice beneath our tents, seismologists make holes in the ice—sounds easy, doesn't it?—pack them with nitroglycerine, stand well back, and light the fuse. A series of REF TEK computers laid on the ice measure the waves that bounce back from the earth's crust hiding somewhere below. It is a long job, with whiteouts imposing extended periods of inactivity.

When camping in the Antarctic, you take so many items into the sleeping bag to prevent freezing that there is barely room to get in yourself. You always need your water bottle in with you, and in crowd the baby wipes (the polar substitute for washing), camera, batteries for the tape recorder, underwear defrosted for the next day, and any odd scientific equipment that happens to be lying around. It is like sleeping in a cutlery drawer, in a deep freeze. In the igloo, the rake of the wall resulted in a shower of fine ice crystals down the back of the pajamas whenever one raised one's head from the *semifreddo* pair of wind pants doubling up as a pillow. One's nostrils hardened in the night. The toothpaste froze.

Having said all that, when I crawled out each day and blinked up at the blue lid of sky and the ice-crystal sun dogs shimmering alongside the high sun, and when I walked up my ice steps to the fluttering Union Jack the Beards made for me and crunched onto the welcome mat carved in the snow, and when I looked out over the plateau and scanned the 360-degree horizon and I saw the curvature of the earth, as if I were in space, and the sun a white stain on the blue, at that moment each day, I thanked God out loud for bringing me to the most heartbreakingly beautiful place on earth, and I forgot about the igloo. No five-star hotel could have provided an experience that even came close.

The liquid waste facility at the seismic camp consisted of a pee flag. It was in full view: otherwise in a blizzard you would die weeing. (A poor end to your obituary.) Not all camps involve quite such communally oriented urination. Once, when I was camping on sea ice with a small group of benthic geologists, the scientists drilled a hole ten feet down to the ocean and placed a wooden drop lav over it, topped with a warm polystyrene seat. With a windbreak set up behind, this luxurious khazi offered a world-class view over a glacier. Perfection. Until one morning a member of the team came skidding across the ice with his wind pants around his ankles. "Mike!" I cried. "Whatever's the matter?" "I was sitting on the john," he gabbled, "and a seal came up through the hole." Imagine: all that hot fishy breath.

My best-ever camp was on the ice just off Ross Island. With the munificent assistance of the U.S. Antarctic Program and the companionship of Lucia deLeiris, an accomplished Rhode Island artist, I set up a camp that later appeared on that season's sea-ice maps as "The Ant Art Chicks." As it was still only September, the scientists hadn't yet arrived. Lucia and I were the only people out camping in an area larger than the United States. It was the continent's brief cusp between darkness and light, and we had twenty minutes more light each day until October 22, when the sun failed to set and we lost all our diurnal clues.

Home consisted of two huts on ski-runners that we towed out from McMurdo, the American base camp, using a tracked vehicle. We positioned the huts in the lee of Mount Erebus, an active volcano, and opposite the Transantarctic Mountains. We called the camp Sea View as, when the weather was bad, sea was all we had to look at. It might have been frozen, but it was sea. The ambient temperature hovered around minus 40, and with wind-chill it plunged to minus 175°F. The huts were heated by drip-oil diesel stoves, though by morning a drift had always crept in past the blanket we hung over the doorjamb. When we threw a mug of boiling water in the air outside, it froze before it landed. Temperature inversion created mirages that shimmered around the horizon. When a whiteout blew in, Lucia had to paint me.*

We had drilled bamboo poles into the ice outside Sea View and strung out an aerial for our high-frequency radio, and once a day, at an appointed time, we checked in with McMurdo to tell them we were still alive. In the minus 20s we found it appallingly difficult to fix the antenna wire after a blizzard blew it down. It was impossible with gloves; without gloves, one's fingers turned to frozen chipolatas in under a minute. But we had to keep our radio schedule. If we didn't, the search-and-rescue team would launch a chopper. The risk involved in deploying a helicopter in the Antarctic in September conditions—well, it was easier to countenance losing a few digits.

For recreation, we crawled around the configuration of ice caves beneath the Erebus Glacier Tongue. The ice had formed arabesques like carvings in the slender windows of a mosque, and through them light fell, diffused through glimmering blue caverns. Had it been rock, it would have been a landscape painted by Leonardo, the pinnacles yielding to dreamy vistas of ice. If our landscapes were canvases, they

* See www.luciadeleiris.com for pictures of Sea View camp.

were conceived by a mind raised above the troubles that afflict the human spirit.

In late September we saw our first seals, illuminated by a gibbous moon. Four Weddells lay on the ice between Erebus and its glacier tongue, resembling, from Sea View, mouse droppings on a dinner plate. Until then we had been living in the silence between movements of a symphony. Lying in the bag at night, I heard seals calling to one another under the ice.

When it was clear, during the day the skies were diaphanous, frosting the Transantarctics in pinks and blues, the faces of each peak as sharply defined as the cuts of a diamond. And then, suddenly, Antarctica would shut down. The winds roared across the frozen sea, battering the glacier tongue and tossing walls of snow into the air. We were trapped inside for days, the windows sheets. At night, a particularly violent blast might shake the hut and jolt us upright, our hearts beating, like a volley of artillery fire. Then it would abruptly drop into silence, as if it had been turned off. "At last!" we would murmur and settle back into the bags. But it was just building up to a fresh attack.

When the storm ended, the world seemed new, and the huts shed their cladding of ice like the ark dripping water. The snow had been blown from the foothills of Erebus, revealing polished blue ice stuck fast to the rock that protruded like an elbow below the treacherously seductive crevasse fields. A thin band of apricot and gasoline blue hung over the Transantarctics, and the pallid sun shed a watery light over thousands of miles of ice. We could have been in the silent corner of savanna where man first stood upright.

The storms seemed to have bleached our interior landscapes too. We sat outside in the evening calm. Often we saw nacreous clouds, drifting high up in the infinite reaches of the sky.* There might be twenty-five of them, in twenty-five variations of opalescent lemons and reds and reedy greens. As Gertrude Stein said, "Paradise—if you

* High-altitude, low-temperature formations. Nacreous clouds are the most dramatic manifestation of polar stratospheric clouds but are rare in the warmer Arctic. They are typically visible in September. Ozone reduction only occurs when polar stratospheric clouds are present, which partially explains why ozone depletion is significantly lower in the north.

can stand it." The dignity of the landscape infused our minds like a symphony: I heard another music in those days. [1995]

The South Pole

"Great God," Captain Scott wrote in his diary in 1912 when he reached the southern axis of the earth. "This is an awful place."

In the death throes of the twentieth century, the American government maintains a scientific base at 90 south, and in a typical summer season up to 130 people work in it. About 40 are scientists, the rest support staff: cooks, electricians, engineers, and so on. I lived with them for several weeks.

South Pole workers make the eight-hour trip in a military Hercules C-130 from Christchurch, New Zealand, to McMurdo on the fringe of the Antarctic continent. From there another C-130 conveys them 850 miles inland, up over the Transantarctic Mountains and across the polar plateau. Planes land on skis on blue ice, and to avoid frozen paralysis, the pilots keep the engines turning while the crew refuel.

The heart of the station is a sapphire-blue geodesic dome, a fifty-five-foot-tall harlequin aluminum structure shaped like the lid of a wok. On top, a Stars and Stripes flaps among a small forest of antennas, and underneath a tunnel leads to half a dozen simple heated buildings with freezer doors. I cannot say that the station is ugly. It is too small and insignificant in that landscape to seem anything but vulnerable.

The mean annual temperature is minus 120°F. Nothing works in that kind of cold. Metal snaps. I have seen scientists in tears when the humidity barometer flutters between zero and one and all their instruments die. Yet many people at the pole work outside, bulldozing ice to make water or maintaining equipment.

The U.S. Antarctic Program lent me state-of-the-art gear. You know you're in a man's world when the long johns have willy slits. During my stay at the pole, 29 out of the 120 residents were women. Not until 1969 did Americans send their first women south—though that was years ahead of the British Antarctic Survey, and even then it incited the newspaper headline POWDER PUFF EXPLORERS INVADE THE SOUTH POLE. Liaisons inevitably develop, especially as relationships at home crumple under the strain of separation. On-station anxiety was concealed behind a mask of humorous resignation and encapsulated in the apocryphal e-mail message from home the blokes had pinned on the wall of the computer room: "Yours is bigger, but his is here."

The Amundsen-Scott South Pole Station doctor presides over a field medical facility. When I arrived, like many I suffered mild altitude sickness: the pole is at ninety-three hundred feet, which means you're standing on a layer of ice almost one-third of the height of Mount Everest. The combination of altitude and an exceptionally shallow atmosphere means that the human body receives about half its normal oxygen supply. The doctor put me on oxygen for two hours. I remember being marooned in a consulting room hung with posters of Neil Armstrong wobbling about on the moon. I asked the doctor if she'd be able to repeat the feat of the Soviet Antarctic doctor who, in 1961, removed his own appendix. "I've trained the others to do mine," she said. You have to use your initiative. Forty years ago a Swedish doctor took out a man's eye. He had never even seen an eye operation, but he was coached over the wireless by an ophthalmic surgeon in Sweden.

To minimize the risk of another ghoulish drama, everyone who goes south must undergo rigorous medicals. Before I went to the Antarctic, I created British fiscal history by claiming a syphilis test against tax.

My stay coincided with Christmas. A long-established tradition at the pole involved "A Race Around the World," a mile lap around the spot marking 90 south. We all did it, and we all got out of breath. Afterward we ate turkey in the galley.

The winter population shrinks to twenty-five. During eight months of darkness, temperatures plunge to the minus 100s. Until four years ago, when budget cuts prevailed, the U.S. Antarctic Program carried out a midwinter resupply airdrop. A C-141 plane flew over from Christchurch, refueled twice in midair, and tossed out boxes the size of upright pianos to twenty-odd people waiting in darkness on the polar plateau. One year they pushed out twelve hundred individually bubble-wrapped eggs, and only two broke.

Isolation and continual darkness hammer the psyche. American shrinks identified a "winter-over syndrome" in the Antarctic in which 72 percent of the sample reported severe depression and 65 percent had problems with hostility and anger. During one Antarctic winter, a Russian at Vostok Station killed a colleague with an ice ax during a row about a game of chess. To ensure it didn't happen again, the authorities banned chess.

It can be awful. But when the sun reappears and spring unfurls over the gleaming plateau, Antarctica isn't an awful place at all. Out on the ice the silence is so dense that you can hear the blood pumping around your head, and you look around and realize that this is the only place on the planet that nobody owns. "The stark polar lands," wrote Shackleton, "grip the hearts of the men who have lived on them in a manner that can hardly be understood by the people who have never got outside the pale of civilisation." [1999]

Postscript

The dome was sinking fast and has been decommissioned since I wrote this piece. The sixty-five-thousand-square-foot modular station that replaced it sits on thirty-six special hydraulic jack columns that raise the structure in ten-inch increments as snow and ice accumulate. To build it, the National Science Foundation flew in forty thousand tons of construction materials. New facilities include the IceCube telescope, a revolutionary search tool for the hypothesized dark matter that might clarify the currently anomalous accounts of the origins of the universe. IceCube is on the lookout for neutrinos, the subatomic particles created by deep-space events such as exploding stars, gamma ray bursts, and cataclysmic phenomena involving black holes and neutron stars.

I wish I could go back.

Frozen Ten Years

February 10, 1996. Mackay Glacier, Antarctica. Whiteout conditions. Spent most of the day supine in the tent, and was really looking forward to dinner. Anxieties about fuel running out resulted in me undercooking the pasta, then I had to spend ten minutes breaking up frozen lumps of Parmesan with a geology hammer. The label on the Parmesan tub says, "Matured ten months," and someone has written underneath, in red Biro, "FROZEN TEN YEARS." All five of us had a carrot for dessert—one each. A week ago, when the resupply helicopter came, we got a small sack of fresh food from New Zealand. I kept five carrots back, for a treat.

Food assumes a role of abnormal importance in this abbreviated environment. A naval commander who wintered over in Antarctica in the 1970s reported a group obsession with food and said his men cared desperately if meals weren't up to scratch as food had become a substitute for sex.

The first explorers fixated on culinary ingenuity. One man assured himself of lifelong popularity by producing minty peas, revealing later that he had squirted toothpaste into the pot. During the hard times out sledging, when meals were doled out, men played the game Shut-Eye, or Whose Portion Is This? Someone named the recipient of each plate with his eyes closed so the cook couldn't be accused of favoritism. It wasn't a game, of course: it was a peacekeeping mechanism. When rations dwindled, everyone had food dreams, and the man who actually got to eat in his dream, rather than waking up just as a steaming plate of Irish stew was placed in front of him, was threatened with short rations by his colleagues. They were hungry all the time in those days, and in the long hours holed up in the tent, a man would speak bitterly about the second helping of treacle sponge he had turned down years before.

Eight thirty, and no meals until tomorrow. Maybe I'll have a dried fig. Find myself obsessing about the fig scene in *Sons and Lovers*. Food is a poor substitute for sex on a number of fronts, one of them being that all the food down here is frozen. Someone living on base brought a plastic bag of ice cream out to our camp two weeks ago. We had to warm it up on the Primus stove before we could eat it. You couldn't act out a Häagen-Dazs ad in Antarctica. By the time you'd achieved anything like smearable consistency, everyone would have frozen to death. As for that scene in *9½ Weeks* in which Kim Basinger and Mickey Rourke do rude things to each other with ice cubes—I find ice ceases to be sexy when you're sitting on fifteen thousand feet of it and there's a foot more lurking in your sleeping bag. [1996]

None of these pieces mention the Cro-Magnon Walkman I carried throughout my Antarctic career. I massaged its batteries as lovingly as a baby so I could take refuge in Beethoven's late strings when storm clouds gathered literally, metaphorically, or, as sometimes happened, both at once. I do think music teaches us the thing we most want to know: that we are not alone. On the other hand—I reserve the right to be inconsistent—surely the only truth is that we are, in the end, alone. An Inuit at an ice hole means all that humanity means, so long as he is solitary. Add more figures and the picture becomes less human, not more so. Belonging is an illusion. Chesterton said something similar. Though not involving Inuit.

But here come some Inuit now.

When I wrote about the Antarctic in *Terra Incognita*, my life was ahead of me. I was closer to thirty than to forty. When, many years later, I tackled the Arctic in *The Magnetic North*—and this is not intended to be negative—my life as I perceived it was behind me: I mean that the die was cast, that the big decisions had been irrevocably taken, for better or worse. I was never going to be anything but a writer; I was never going to have a strong backhand or translate Rabelais or ice a Christmas cake. I say this without regret (well, with a touch of regret; who could say that she does not miss her younger self?), but perhaps it explains the distant melody of a requiem in that book, and in these two pieces too, works in progress that appeared in *Vanity Fair* and *Condé Nast Traveller.*

PART THREE
ASIA

SYRIA

Gertrude Bell

Gertrude Bell (1868–1926), the daughter of a minor English peer, she rejected the way of life she was born into. Instead, she gained a first-class degree in Modern History from Oxford and became a writer, traveller, archaeologist, linguist, mountaineer and a powerful political force in the Middle East. She has been described as 'one of the few representatives of His Majesty's Government remembered by the Arabs with anything resembling affection' which is no faint praise. Her account of her travels through Greater Syria in 1906 is a classic and Arabia and its people were the love of her life.

Chapter 4

There is an Arabic proverb which says: 'Hayyeh rubda wala ḍaif mudha' – neither ash-grey snake nor mid-day guest. We were careful not to make a breach in our manners by outstaying our welcome, and our camp was up before the sun. To wake in that desert dawn was like waking in the heart of an opal. The mists lifting their heads out of the hollows, the dews floating in ghostly wreaths from the black tents, were shot through first with the faint glories of the eastern sky and then with the strong yellow rays of the risen sun. I sent a silver and purple kerchief to Fellaḥ ul 'Isa, 'for the little son' who had played solemnly about the hearth, took grateful leave of Namrūd, drank a parting cup of coffee, and, the old sheikh holding my stirrup, mounted and rode away with Ġablān. We climbed the Jebel el 'Alya and crossed the wide summit of the range; the landscape was akin to that of our own English border country but bigger, the sweeping curves more generous, the distances further away. The glorious cold air intoxicated every sense and set the blood throbbing – to my mind the saying about the Bay of Naples should run differently.

See the desert on a fine morning and die – if you can. Even the stolid mules felt the breath of it and raced across the spongy ground ('Mad! the accursed ones!') till their packs swung round and brought them down, and twice we stopped to head them off and reload. The Little Heart, the highest peak of the Jebel Druze, surveyed us cheerfully the while, glittering in its snow mantle far away to the north.

At the foot of the northern slopes of the 'Alya hills we entered a great rolling plain like that which we had left to the south. We passed many of those mysterious rujm which start the fancy speculating on the past history of the land, and presently we caught sight of the scattered encampments of the Ḥassaniyyeh, who are good friends to the Da'ja and belong to the same group of tribes. And here we spied two riders coming across the plain and Ġablān went out to greet them and remained some time in talk, and then returned with a grave face. The day before, the very day before, while we had been journeying peacefully from Ṭneib, four hundred horsemen of the Ṣukhūr and the Ḥoweiṭāṭ, leagued in evil, had swept these plains, surprised an outlying group of the Beni Ḥassan and carried off the tents, together with two thousand head of cattle. It was almost a pity, I thought, that we had come a day too late, but Ġablān looked graver still at the suggestion, and said that he would have been forced to join in the fray, yes, he would even have left me, though I had been committed to his charge, for the Da'ja were bound to help the Beni Ḥassan against the Ṣukhūr. And perhaps yesterday's work would be enough to break the new-born truce between that powerful tribe and the allies of the 'Anazeh and set the whole desert at war again. There was sorrow in the tents of the Children of Ḥassan. We saw a man weeping by the tent pole, with his head bowed in his hands, everything he possessed having been swept from him. As we rode we talked much of ghazu (raid) and the rules that govern it. The fortunes of the Arab are as varied as those of a gambler on the Stock Exchange. One day he is the richest man in the desert, and next morning he may not have a single camel foal to his name. He lives in a state of war, and even if the surest pledges have been exchanged with the neighbouring tribes there is no certainty that a band of raiders from hundreds of miles away will not descend on his camp in the night, as a tribe unknown to Syria, the Beni Awājeh, fell, two years ago, on the lands south-east of Aleppo, crossing three hundred miles of desert, Mardūf (two on a camel) from their seat above Baghdad, carrying off all the cattle and killing scores of people. How many thousand years this state of things has lasted, those who shall read the earliest records of the inner desert will tell us, for it goes back to the first of them, but in all the centuries the Arab has bought no wisdom from experience. He is never safe, and yet he behaves as though security were his daily bread. He pitches his feeble little camps, ten or fifteen tents together, over a wide stretch of undefended and indefensible country. He is too far from his fellows to call in their aid, too far as a rule to gather the horsemen together and follow after the raiders whose retreat must be sufficiently slow, burdened with the captured flocks, to guarantee success to a swift pursuit. Having lost all his worldly goods, he goes about the desert and makes his plaint, and one man gives him a strip or two of goats' hair cloth, and another a coffee-pot, a third presents him with a camel, and a fourth with a few sheep, till he has a roof to cover him and enough animals to keep his family from hunger. There are good customs among the Arabs, as Namrūd said. So he bides his time for months, perhaps for years, till at length opportunity ripens, and the horsemen of his tribe with their allies ride forth and recapture all the flocks that had been carried off and more besides, and the feud enters on another phase. The truth is that the ghazu is the only industry the desert knows and the only game. As an industry it seems to the commercial mind to be based on a false conception of the laws of supply and demand, but as a game there is much to be said for it. The spirit of adventure finds full scope in it – you can picture the excitement of the night ride across the plain, the rush of the mares in the attack, the glorious (and comparatively innocuous) popping of rifles and the exhilaration of knowing yourself a fine fellow as you turn homewards with the spoil. It is the best sort of fantasīa, as they say in the desert, with a spice of danger behind it. Not that the danger is alarmingly great: a considerable amount of amusement can be got without much bloodshed, and the raiding Arab is seldom bent on killing. He never lifts his hand against women and children, and if here and there a man falls it is almost by accident, since who can be sure of the ultimate destination of a rifle bullet once it is embarked on its lawless course? This is the Arab view of the ghazu; the Druzes look at it otherwise. For them it is red war. They do not play the game as it should be played, they go out to slay, and they spare no one. While they have a grain of powder in their flasks and strength to pull the trigger, they kill every man, woman and child that they encounter.

Knowing the independence of Arab women and the freedom with which marriages are contracted between different tribes of equal birth, I saw many romantic possibilities of mingled love and hatred between the Montagues and the Capulets. 'Lo, on a sudden I loved her,' says 'Antara, 'though I had slain her kin.' Ġablān replied that these difficult situations did indeed occur, and ended sometimes in a tragedy, but if the lovers would be content to wait, some compromise could be arrived at, or they might be able to marry during one of the brief but oft-recurring intervals of truce. The real danger begins when blood feud is started within the tribe itself and a man having murdered one of his own people is cast out a homeless, kinless exile to shelter with strangers or with foes. Such was Amr ul Ḳais, the lonely outlaw, crying to the night: 'Oh long night, wilt thou not bring the dawn? yet the day is no better than thou.'

A few miles further north the Ḥassaniyyeh encampments had not yet heard of yesterday's misfortune, and we had the pleasure of spreading the ill-news. Ġablān rode up to every group we passed and delivered his mind of its burden; the men in buckram multiplied as we went, and perhaps I had been wrong in accepting the four hundred of the original statement, for they had had plenty of time to breed during the twenty-four hours that had elapsed between their departure and our arrival. All the tents were occupied with preparations not for war but for feasting. On the morrow fell the great festival of the Mohammedan year, the Feast of Sacrifice, when the pilgrims in Mecca slaughter their offerings and True Believers at home follow their example. By every tent there was a huge pile of thorns wherewith to roast the camel or sheep next day, and the shirts of the tribe were spread out to dry in the sun after a washing which, I have reason to believe, takes place but once a year. Towards sunset we reached a big encampment of the Beni Ḥassan, where Ġablān decided to spend the night. There was water in a muddy pool near at hand and a good site for our tents above the hollow in which the Arabs lay. None of the great sheikhs were camped there and, mindful of Namrūd's warnings, I refused all invitations and spent the evening at home, watching the sunset and the kindling of the cooking fires and the blue smoke that floated away into the twilight. The sacrificial camel, in gorgeous trappings, grazed among my mules, and after dark the festival was heralded by a prolonged letting off of rifles. Ḳablān sat silent by the camp fire, his thoughts busy with the merrymakings that were on foot at home. It went sorely against the grain that he should be absent on such a day. 'How many horsemen,' said he, 'will alight to-morrow at my father's tent! and I shall not be there to welcome them or to wish a good feast day to my little son!'

We were off before the rejoicings had begun. I had no desire to assist at the last moments of the camel, and moreover we had a long day before us through country that was not particularly safe. As far as my caravan was concerned, the risk was small. I had a letter in my pocket from Fellaḥ ul 'Isa to Nasīb el Aṭrash, the Sheikh of Ṣalkhad in the Jebel Druze. 'To the renowned and honoured sheikh, Nasīb el Aṭrash,' it ran (I had heard my host dictate it to Namrūd and seen him seal it with his seal), 'the venerated, may God prolong his existence! We send you greetings, to you and to all the people of Ṣalkhad, and to your brother Jada'llah, and to the son of your uncle Muḥammad el Aṭrash in Umm er Rummān, and to our friends in Imtain. And further, there goes to you from us a lady of the most noble among the English. And we greet Muḥammada and our friends.... &c., (here followed another list of names), and this is all that is needful, and peace be with you.' And beyond this letter I had the guarantee of my nationality, for the Druzes have not yet forgotten our interference on their behalf in 1860; moreover I was acquainted with several of the sheikhs of the Ṭurshān, to which powerful family Nasīb belonged. But Ḳablān was in a different case, and he was fully conscious of the ambiguity of his position. In spite of his uncle's visit to the Mountain, he was not at all certain how the Druzes would receive him; he was leaving the last outposts of his allies, and entering a border land by tradition hostile (he himself had no acquaintance with it but that which he had gathered on raiding expeditions), and if he did not find enemies among the Druzes he might well fall in with a scouring party of the bitter foes of the Da'ja, the Ḥaseneh or their like, who camp east of the hills.

After an hour or two of travel, the character of the country changed completely: the soft soil of the desert came to an end, and the volcanic rocks of the Ḥaurān began. We rode for some time up a gulley of lava, left the last of the Ḥassaniyyeh tents in a little open space between some mounds, and found ourselves on the edge of a plain that stretched to the foot of the Jebel Druze in an unbroken expanse, completely deserted, almost devoid of vegetation and strewn with black volcanic stones. It has been said that the borders of the desert are like a rocky shore on which the sailor who navigates deep waters with success may yet be wrecked when he attempts to bring his ship to port. This was the landing which we had to effect. Somewhere between us and the hills were the ruins of Umm ej Jemāl, where I hoped to get into touch with the Druzes, but for the life of us we could not tell where they lay, the plain having just sufficient rise and fall to hide them. Now Umm ej Jemāl has an evil name – I believe mine was the second European camp that had ever been pitched in it, the first having been that of a party of American archæologists who left a fortnight before I arrived – and Ġablān's evident anxiety enhanced its sinister reputation. Twice he turned to me and asked whether it were necessary to camp there. I answered that he had undertaken to guide me to Umm ej Jemāl, and that there was no question but that I should go, and the second time I backed my obstinacy by pointing out that we must have water that night for the animals, and that there was little chance of finding it except in the cisterns of the ruined village. Thereupon I had out my map, and after trying to guess what point on the blank white paper we must have reached, I turned my caravan a little to the west towards a low rise from whence we should probably catch sight of our destination. Ġablān took the decision in good part and expressed regret that he could not be of better service in directing us. He had been once in his life to Umm ej Jemāl, but it was at dead of night when he was out raiding. He and his party had stopped for half an hour to water their horses and had passed on eastward, returning by another route. Yes, it had been a successful raid, praise be to God!

and one of the first in which he had engaged. Mikhāil listened with indifference to our deliberations, the muleteers were not consulted, but as we set off again Ḥabīb tucked his revolver more handily into his belt.

We rode on. I was engaged in looking for the rasīf, the paved Roman road that runs from Ḳala'at ez Zerka straight to Boṣrah, and also in wondering what I should do to protect if necessary the friend and guide whose pleasant companionship had enlivened our hours of travel and who should certainly come to no harm while he was with us. As we drew nearer to the rising ground we observed that it was crowned with sheepfolds, and presently we could see men gathering their flocks together and driving them behind the black walls, their hurried movements betraying their alarm. We noticed also some figures, whether mounted or on foot it was impossible to determine, advancing on us from a hollow to the left, and after a moment two puffs of smoke rose in front of them, and we heard the crack of rifles.

Ġablān turned to me with a quick gesture.

'Ḍarabūna!' he said. 'They have fired on us.'

I said aloud: 'They are afraid,' but to myself, 'We're in for it.'

Ġablān rose in his stirrups, dragged his fur-lined cloak from his shoulders, wound it round his left arm and waved it above his head, and very slowly he and I paced forward together. Another couple of shots were fired, and still we rode forward, Ġablān waving his flag of truce. The firing ceased; it was nothing after all but the accepted greeting to strangers, conducted with the customary levity of the barbarian. Our assailants turned out to be two Arabs, grinning from ear to ear, quite ready to fraternise with us as soon as they had decided that we were not bent on sheep stealing, and most willing to direct us to Umm ej Jemāl. As soon as we had rounded the tell we saw it in front of us, its black towers and walls standing so boldly out of the desert that it was impossible to believe it had been ruined and deserted for thirteen hundred years. It was not till we came close that the rents and gashes in the tufa masonry and the breaches in the city wall were visible. I pushed forward and would have ridden straight into the heart of the town, but Ġablān caught me up and laid his hand upon my bridle.

'I go first,' he said. 'Oh lady, you were committed to my charge.'

And since he was the only person who incurred any risk and was well aware of the fact, his resolution did him credit.

We clattered over the ruined wall, passed round the square monastery tower which is the chief feature of the Mother of Camels (such is the meaning of the Arabic name), and rode into an open place between empty streets, and there was no one to fear and no sign of life save that offered by two small black tents, the inhabitants of which greeted us with enthusiasm, and proceeded to sell us milk and eggs in the most amicable fashion. Arabs who live at the foot of Ḥaurān mountains are called the Jebeliyyeh, the Arabs of the Hills, and they are of no consideration, being but servants and shepherds to the Druzes. In the winter they herd the flocks that are sent down into the plain, and in the summer they are allowed to occupy the uncultivated slopes with their own cattle.

I spent the hour of daylight that remained in examining the wonderful Nabatæan necropolis outside the walls. Monsieur Dussaud began the work on it five years ago; Mr. Butler and Dr. Littmann, whose visit immediately preceded mine, will be found to have continued it when their next volumes are given to the world. Having seen what tombs they had uncovered and noted several mounds that must conceal others, I sent away my companions and wandered in the dusk through the ruined streets of the town, into great rooms and up broken stairs, till Ḍablān came and called me in, saying that if a man saw something in a fur coat exploring those uncanny places after dark, he might easily take the apparition for a ghoul and shoot at it. Moreover, he wished to ask me whether he might not return to Ṭneib. One of the Arabs would guide us next day to the first Druze village, and Ḍablān would as soon come no nearer to the Mountain. I agreed readily, indeed it was a relief not to have his safety on my conscience. He received three napoleons for his trouble and a warm letter of thanks to deliver to Fellaḥ ul 'Isa, and we parted with many assurances that if God willed we would travel together again.

The stony foot of the Jebel Ḥaurān is strewn with villages deserted since the Mohammedan invasion in the seventh century. I visited two that lay not far from my path, Shabḥa and Shabḥīyyeh, and found them to be both of the same character as Umm ej Jemāl. From afar they look like well built towns with square towers rising above streets of three-storied houses. Where the walls have fallen they lie as they fell, and no hand has troubled to clear away the ruins. Monsieur de Vogüé was the first to describe the architecture of the Ḥaurān; his splendid volumes are still the principal source of information. The dwelling-houses are built round a court in which there is usually an outer stair leading to the upper story. There is no wood used in their construction, even the doors are of solid stone, turning on stone hinges, and the windows of stone slabs pierced with open-work patterns. Sometimes there are traces of a colonnaded portico, or the walls are broken by a double window, the arches of which are supported by a small column and a rough plain capital; frequently the lintels of the doors are adorned with a cross or a Christian monogram, but otherwise there is little decoration. The chambers are roofed with stone slabs resting on the back of transverse arches.

So far as can be said with any certainty, Nabatæan inscriptions and tombs are the oldest monuments that have been discovered in the district; they are followed by many important remains of pagan Rome, but the really flourishing period seems to have been the Christian. After the Mohammedan invasion, which put an end to the prosperity of the Ḥaurān uplands, few of the villages were re-inhabited, and when the Druzes came about a hundred and fifty years ago, they found no settled population. They made the Mountain their own, rebuilt and thereby destroyed the ancient towns, and extended their lordship over the plains to the south, though they have not established themselves in the villages of that debatable land which remains a happy hunting ground for the archæologist. The American expedition will make good use of the immense amount of material that exists there, and knowing that the work had been done by better hands than mine, I rolled up the measuring tape and folded the foot-rule. But I could not so far overcome a natural instinct as to cease from copying inscriptions, and the one or two (they were extremely few) that had escaped Dr. Littmann's vigilant eye and come by chance to me were made over to him when we met in Damascus.

To our new guide, Fendi, fell the congenial task of posting me up in the gossip of the Mountain. Death had been busy among the great family of the Ṭurshān during the past five years. Fāiz el Aṭrash, Sheikh of Ḳreyeh, was gone, poisoned said some, and a week or two before my arrival the most renowned of all the leaders of the Druzes, Shibly Beg el Aṭrash, had died of a mysterious and lingering illness – poison again, it was whispered. There was this war and that on hand, a terrible raid of the Arabs of the Wādy Sirḥān to be avenged, and a score with the Ṣukhūr to be settled, but on the whole there was prosperity, and as much peace as a Druze would wish to enjoy. The conversation was interrupted by a little shooting at rabbits lying asleep in the sun, not a gentlemanly sport perhaps, but one that helped to fill and to diversify the pot. After a time I left the mules and Fendi to go their own way, and taking Mikhāil with me, made a long circuit to visit the ruined towns. We were just finishing lunch under a broken wall, well separated from the rest of the party, when we saw two horsemen approaching us across the plain. We swept up the remains of the lunch and mounted hastily, feeling that any greeting they might accord us was better met in the saddle. They stopped in front of us and gave us the salute, following it with an abrupt question as to where we were going. I answered: 'To Ṣalkhād, to Nasīb el Aṭrash,' and they let us pass without further remark. They were not Druzes, for they did not wear the Druze turban, but Christians from Ḳreyeh, where there is a large Christian community, riding down to Umm ej Jemāl to visit the winter quarters of their flocks, so said Fendi, whom they had passed a mile ahead. Several hours before we reached the present limits of cultivation, we saw the signs of ancient agriculture in the shape of long parallel lines of stones heaped aside from earth that had once been fruitful. They looked like the ridge and furrow of a gigantic meadow, and like the ridge and furrow they are almost indelible, the mark of labour that must have ceased with the Arab invasion. At the foot of the first spur of the hills, Tell esh Shīḥ (it is called after the grey-white Shīḥ plant which is the best pasturage for sheep), we left the unharvested desert and entered the region of ploughed fields – we left, too, the long clean levels of the open wilderness and were caught fetlock deep in the mud of a Syrian road. It led us up the hill to Umm er Rummān, the Mother of Pomegranates, on the edge of the lowest plateau of the Jebel Druze, as bleak a little muddy spot as you could hope to see. I stopped at the entrance of the village, and asked a group of Druzes where I should find a camping ground, and they directed me to an extremely dirty place below the cemetery, saying there was no other where I should not spoil the crops or the grass, though the crops, Heaven save the mark! were as yet below ground, and the grass consisted of a few brown spears half covered with melting snow. I could not entertain the idea of pitching tents so near the graveyard, and demanded to be directed to the house of Muḥammad el Aṭrash, Sheikh of Umm er Rummān. This prince of the Ṭurshān was seated upon his roof, engaged in directing certain agricultural operations that were being carried forward in the slough below. Long years had made him shapeless of figure and the effect was enhanced by the innumerable garments in which the winter cold had forced him to wrap his fat old body. I came as near as the mud would allow, and shouted:

'Peace be upon you, oh Sheikh!'

'And upon you peace!' he bawled in answer.

'Where in your village is there a dry spot for a camp?'

The sheikh conferred at the top of his voice with his henchmen in the mud, and finally replied that he did not know, by God! While I was wondering where to turn, a Druze stepped forward and announced that he could show me a place outside the town, and the sheikh, much relieved by the shifting of responsibility, gave me a loud injunction to go in peace, and resumed his occupations.

My guide was a young man with the clear cut features and the sharp intelligent expression of his race. He was endowed, too, like all his kin, with a lively curiosity, and as he hopped from side to side of the road to avoid the pools of mud and slush, he had from me all my story, whence I came and whither I was going, who were my friends in the Jebel Druze and what my father's name – very different this from the custom of the Arabs, with whom it is an essential point of good breeding never to demand more than the stranger sees fit to impart. In At Ṭabari's history there is a fine tale of a man who sought refuge with an Arab sheikh. He stayed on, and the sheikh died, and his son who ruled in his stead advanced in years, and at length the grandson of the original host came to his father and said: 'Who is the man who dwells with us?' And the father answered: 'My son, in my father's time he came, and my father grew old and died, and he stayed on under my protection, and I too have grown old; but in all these years we have never asked him why he sought us nor what is his name. Neither do thou ask.' Yet I rejoiced to find myself once more among the trenchant wits and the searching koḥl-blackened eyes of the Mountain, where every question calls for a quick retort or a brisk parry, and when my interlocutor grew too inquisitive I had only to answer:

'Listen, oh you! I am not "thou," but "Your Excellency,"' and he laughed and understood and took the rebuke to heart.

There are many inscriptions in Umm er Rummān, a few Nabatæan and the rest Cufic, proving that the town on the shelf of the hills was an early settlement and that it was one of those the Arabs re-occupied for a time after the invasion. A delighted crowd of little boys followed me from house to house, tumbling over one another in their eagerness to point out a written stone built into a wall or laid in the flooring about the hearth. In one house a woman caught me by the arm and implored me to heal her husband. The man was lying in a dark corner of the windowless room, with his face wrapped in filthy bandages, and when these had been removed a horrible wound was revealed, the track of a bullet that had passed through the cheek and shattered the jaw. I could do nothing but give him an antiseptic, and adjure the woman to wash the wound and keep the wrappings clean, and above all not to let him drink the medicine, though I felt it would make small odds which way he used it, Death had him so surely by the heel. This was the first of the long roll of sufferers that must pass before the eyes and catch despairingly at the sympathies of every traveller in wild places. Men and women afflicted with ulcers and terrible sores, with fevers and rheumatisms, children crippled from their birth, the blind and the old, there are none who do not hope that the unmeasured wisdom of the West may find them a remedy. You stand aghast at the depths of human misery and at your own helplessness.

The path of archæology led me at last to the sheikh's door, and I went in to pay him an official visit. He was most hospitably inclined now that the business of the day was over; we sat together in the maḳ'ad, the audience room, a dark and dirty sort of out-house, with an iron stove in the centre of it, and discussed the Japanese War and desert ghazus and other topics of the day, while Selmān, the sheikh's son, a charming boy of sixteen, made us coffee. Muḥammad is brother-in-law to Shibly and to Yahya Beg el Aṭrash, who had been my first host five years before when I had escaped to his village of 'Areh from the Turkish Mudīr at Boṣrah, and Selmān is the only son of his father's old age and the only descendant of the famous 'Areh house of the Ṭurshān, for Shibly died and Yahya lives childless. The boy walked back with me to my camp, stepping lightly through the mud, a gay and eager figure touched with the air of distinction that befits one who comes of a noble stock. He had had no schooling, though there was a big Druze maktab at Ḳreyeh, fifteen miles away, kept by a Christian of some learning.

'My father holds me so precious,' he explained, 'that he will not let me leave his side.'

'Oh Selmān,' I began –

'Oh God!' he returned, using the ejaculation customary to one addressed by name.

'The minds of the Druzes are like fine steel, but what is steel until it is beaten into a sword blade?'

Selmān answered: 'My uncle Shibly could neither read nor write.'

I said: 'The times are changed. The house of the Ṭurshān will need trained wits if it would lead the Mountain as it did before.'

But that headship is a thing of the past. Shibly is dead and Yahya childless, Muḥammad is old and Selmān undeveloped, Fāiz has left four sons but they are of no repute, Nasīb is cunning but very ignorant, there is Muṣṭafa at Imātain, who passes for a worthy man of little intelligence, and Ḥamūd at Sweida, who is distinguished mainly for his wealth. The ablest man among the Druzes is without doubt Abu Tellāl of Shaḥba, and the most enlightened Sheikh Muḥammad en Naṣṣār.

The night was bitterly cold. My thermometer had been broken, so that the exact temperature could not be registered, but every morning until we reached Damascus the water in the cup by my bedside was a solid piece of ice, and one night a little tumbling stream outside the camp was frozen hard and silent. The animals and the muleteers were usually housed in a khan while the frost lasted. Muḥammad the Druze, who had returned to his original name and faith, disappeared the moment camp was pitched, and spent the night enjoying the hospitality of his relations. 'For,' said Mikhāil sarcastically, 'every man who can give him a meal he reckons to be the son of his uncle.'

I was obliged to delay my start next morning in order to profit by the sheikh's invitation to breakfast at a very elastic nine o'clock – two hours after sunrise was what was said, and who knows exactly when it may suit that luminary to appear? It was a pleasant party. We discussed the war in Yemen in all its bearings – theoretically, for I was the only person who had any news, and mine was derived from a *Weekly Times* a month old – and then Muḥammad questioned me as to why Europeans looked for inscriptions.

'But I think I know,' he added. 'It is that they may restore the land to the lords of it.'

I assured him that the latest descendants of the former owners of the Ḥaurān had been dead a thousand years, and he listened politely and changed the subject with the baffled air of one who cannot get a true answer.

The young man who had shown us our camping ground rode with us to Ṣalkhad, saying he had business there and might as well have company by the way. His name was Ṣāleh; he was of a clerkly family, a reader and a scribe. I was so tactless as to ask him whether he were 'ākil, initiated – the Druzes are divided into the initiated and the uninitiated, but the line of demarcation does not follow that of social pre-eminence, since most of the Ṭurshān are uninitiated. He gave me a sharp look, and replied:

'What do you think?' and I saw my error and dropped the subject.

But Ṣāleh was not one to let slip any opportunity of gaining information. He questioned me acutely on our customs, down to the laws of marriage and divorce. He was vastly entertained at the English rule that the father should pay a man for marrying his daughter (so he interpreted the habit of giving her a marriage portion), and we laughed together over the absurdity of the arrangement. He was anxious to know Western views as to the creation of the world and the origin of matter, and I obliged him with certain heterodox opinions, on which he seized with far greater lucidity than that with which they were offered. We passed an agreeable morning, in spite of the mud and boulders of the road. At the edge of the snow wreaths a little purple crocus had made haste to bloom, and a starry white garlic – the Mountain is very rich in Spring flowers. The views to the south over the great plain we had crossed were enchanting; to the north the hills rose in unbroken slopes of snow, Ḳuleib, the Little Heart, looking quite Alpine with its frosty summit half veiled in mist. Two hours after noon we reached Ṣalkhad, the first goal of our journey.

AROUND THE WORLD IN SEVENTY-TWO DAYS

Nellie Bly

Nellie Bly (1864–1922), born Elizabeth Jane Cochran in Pennsylvania, USA, was the epitome of female feistiness. In 1885, she penned an affronted, but eloquent response to a pejorative newspaper article entitled 'What Girls Are Good For'. She was promptly offered a job as a journalist, adopted the pseudonym Nellie Bly (from a song) and set about proving that Girls Are Good For Quite A Lot. Her articles tackled gritty subjects like slum life and corruption among officials in Mexico. She even went undercover as a patient in an asylum to expose the dire conditions there. But the highlight of Bly's career is recorded in *Around the World in Seventy-Two Days* – her successful attempt to upstage the relatively slothful fictional hero Phileas Fogg, who famously took 80 days.

One Hundred and Twenty Hours in Japan

After seeing Hong Kong with its wharfs crowded with dirty boats manned by still dirtier people, and its streets packed with a filthy crowd, Yokohama has a cleaned-up Sunday appearance. Travelers are taken from the ships, which anchor some distance out in the bay, to the land in small steam launches. The first-class hotels in the different ports have their individual launches, but like American hotel omnibuses, while being run by the hotel to assist in procuring patrons, the traveler pays for them just the same.

An import as well as an export duty is charged in Japan, but we passed the custom inspectors unmolested. I found the Japanese jinricksha men a gratifying improvement upon those I seen from Ceylon to China. They presented no sight of filthy rags, nor naked bodies, nor smell of grease. Clad in neat navy-blue garments, their little pudgy legs encased in unwrinkled tights, the upper half of their bodies in short jackets with wide flowing sleeves; their clean, good-natured faces, peeping from beneath comical mushroom-shaped hats; their blue-black, wiry locks cropped just above the nape of the neck, they offered a striking contrast to the jinricksha men of other countries. Their crests were embroidered upon the back and sleeves of their top garment as are the crests of every man, woman and child in Japan.

Rain the night previous had left the streets muddy and the air cool and crisp, but the sun creeping through the mistiness of early morning, fell upon us with most gratifying warmth. Wrapping our knees with rugs the 'ricksha men started off in a lively trot to the Pacific Mail and O. and O. Companies' office, where I met discourteous people for the first time since I left the P. & O. "Victoria." And these were Americans, too. The most generous excuse that can be offered for them is that they have held their positions so long that they feel they are masters, instead of a steamship company's servants. A man going into the office to buy a ticket to America, was answered in the following manner by one of the head men:

"You'll have to come back later if you want a ticket. I'm going to lunch now."

I stayed at the Grand Hotel while in Japan. It is a large building, with long verandas, wide halls and airy rooms, commanding an exquisite view of the lake in front. Barring an enormous and monotonous collection of rats, the Grand would be considered a good hotel even in America. The food is splendid and the service excellent. The "Japs," noiseless, swift, anxious to please, stand at the head of all the servants I encountered from New York to New York; and then they look so neat in their blue tights and white linen jackets.

I always have an inclination to laugh when I look at the Japanese men in their native dress. Their legs are small and their trousers are skin tight. The upper garment, with its great wide sleeves, is as loose as the lower is tight. When they finish their "get up" by placing their dish-pan shaped hat upon their heads, the wonder grows how such small legs can carry it all! Stick two straws in one end of a potato, a mushroom in the other, set it up on the straws and you have a Japanese in outline. Talk about French heels! The Japanese sandal is a small board elevated on two pieces of thin wood fully five inches in height. They make the people look exactly as if they were on stilts. These queer shoes are fastened to the foot by a single strap running between toes number one and two, the wearer when walking necessarily maintaining a sliding instead of an up and down movement, in order to keep the shoe on.

On a cold day one would imagine the Japanese were a nation of armless people. They fold their arms up in their long, loose sleeves. A Japanese woman's sleeves are to her what a boy's pockets are to him. Her cards, money, combs, hair pins, ornaments and rice paper are carried in her sleeves. Her rice paper is her handkerchief, and she notes with horror and disgust that after using we return our handkerchiefs to our pockets. I think the Japanese women carry everything in their sleeves, even their hearts. Not that they are fickle—none are more true, more devoted, more loyal, more constant, than Japanese women—but they are so guileless and artless that almost any one, if opportunity offers, can pick at their trusting hearts.

If I loved and married, I would say to my mate: "Come, I know where Eden is," and like Edwin Arnold, desert the land of my birth for Japan, the land of love–beauty–poetry–cleanliness. I somehow always connected Japan and its people with China and its people, believing the one no improvement on the other. I could not have made a greater mistake. Japan is beautiful. Its women are charmingly sweet. I know little about the men except that they do not go far as we judge manly beauty, being undersized, dark, and far from prepossessing. They have the reputation of being extremely clever, so I do not speak of them as a whole, only of those I came in contact with. I saw one, a giant in frame, a god in features; but he was a public wrestler.

The Japanese are the direct opposite to the Chinese. The Japanese are the cleanliest people on earth, the Chinese are the filthiest; the Japanese are always happy and cheerful, the Chinese are always grumpy and morose; the Japanese are the most graceful of people, the Chinese the most awkward; the Japanese have few vices, the Chinese have all the vices in the world; in short, the Japanese are the most delightful of people, the Chinese the most disagreeable.

The majority of the Europeans live on the bluff in low white bungalows, with great rooms and breezy verandas, built in the hearts of Oriental gardens, where one can have an unsurpassed view of the Mississippi bay, or can play tennis or cricket, or loll in hammocks, guarded from public gaze by luxurious green hedges. The Japanese homes form a great contrast to the bungalows. They are daintily small, like play houses indeed, built of a thin shingle-like board, fine in texture. Chimneys and fireplaces are unknown. The first wall is set back, allowing the upper floor and side walls to extend over the lower flooring, making it a portico built in instead of on the house. Light window frames, with their minute openings covered with fine rice paper instead of glass, are the doors and windows in one. They do not swing open and shut as do our doors, nor do they move up and down like our windows, but slide like rolling doors. They form the partitions of the houses inside and can be removed at any time, throwing the floor into one room.

They have two very pretty customs in Japan. The one is decorating their houses in honor of the new year, and the other celebrating the blossoming of the cherry trees. Bamboo saplings covered with light airy foliage and pinioned so as to incline towards the middle of the street, where meeting they form an arch, make very effective decorations. Rice trimmings mixed with sea-weed, orange, lobster and ferns are hung over every door to insure a plentiful year, while as sentinels on either side are large tubs, in which are three thick bamboo stalks, with small evergreen trees for background.

In the cool of the evening we went to a house that had been specially engaged to see the dancing, or *geisha*, girls. At the door we saw all the wooden shoes of the household, and we were asked to take off our shoes before entering, a proceeding rather disliked by some of the party, who refused absolutely to do as requested. We effected a compromise, however, by putting cloth slippers over our shoes. The second floor had been converted into one room, with nothing in it except the matting covering the floor and a Japanese screen here and there. We sat upon the floor, for chairs there are none in Japan, but the exquisite matting is padded until it is as soft as velvet. It was laughable to see us trying to sit down, and yet more so to see us endeavor to find a posture of ease for our limbs. We were about as graceful as an elephant dancing. A smiling woman in a black kimono set several round and square charcoal boxes containing burning charcoal before us. These are the only Japanese stove. Afterwards she brought a tray containing a number of long-stemmed pipes—Japanese women smoke constantly—a pot of tea and several small cups.

Impatiently I awaited the *geisha* girls. In the tiny maidens glided at last, clad in exquisite trailing, angel-sleeved kimonos. The girls bow gracefully, bending down until their heads touch their knees, then kneeling before us murmur gently a greeting which sounds like "Koinbanwa!" drawing in their breath with a long, hissing suction, which is a token of great honor. The musicians sat down on the floor and began an alarming din upon *samisens*, drums and gongs, singing meanwhile through their pretty noses. If the noses were not so pretty I am sure the music would be unbearable to one who has ever heard a chest note. The *geisha* girls stand posed with open fan in hand above their heads, ready to begin the dance. They are very short with the slenderest of slender waists. Their soft and tender eyes are made blacker by painted lashes and brows; their midnight hair, stiffened with a gummy wash, is most wonderfully dressed in large coils and ornamented with gold and silver flowers and gilt paper pom-pons. The younger the girl the more gay is her hair. Their kimonos, of the most exquisite material, trail all around them, and are loosely held together at the waist with an obi-sash; their long flowing sleeves fall back, showing their dimpled arms and baby hands. Upon their tiny feet they wear cunning white linen socks cut with a place for the great toe. When they go out they wear wooden sandals. The Japanese are the only women I ever saw who could rouge and powder and be not repulsive, but the more charming because of it. They powder their faces and have a way of reddening their under lip just at the tip that gives them a most tempting look. The lips look like two luxurious cherries. The musicians begin a long chanting strain, and these bits of beauty begin the dance. With a grace, simply enchanting, they twirl their little fans, sway their dainty bodies in a hundred different poses, each one more intoxicating than the other, all the while looking so childish and shy, with an innocent smile lurking about their lips, dimpling their soft cheeks, and their black eyes twinkling with the pleasure of the dance. After the dance the *geisha* girls made friends with me, examining, with surprised delight, my dress, my bracelets, my rings, my boots—to them the most wonderful and extraordinary things,—my hair, my gloves, indeed they missed very little, and they approved of all. They said I was very sweet, and urged me to come again, and in honor of the custom of my land—the Japanese never kiss—they pressed their soft, pouting lips to mine in parting.

Japanese women know nothing whatever of bonnets, and may they never! On rainy days they tie white scarfs over their wonderful hairdressing, but at other times they waddle bareheaded, with fan and umbrella, along the streets on their wooden clogs. They have absolutely no furniture. Their bed is a piece of matting, their pillows, narrow blocks of wood, probably six inches in length, two wide and six high. They rest the back of the neck on the velvet covered top, so their wonderful hair remains dressed for weeks at a time. Their tea and pipe always stand beside them, so they can partake of their comforts the last thing before sleep and the first thing after.

A Japanese reporter from Tokyo came to interview me, his newspaper having translated and published the story of my visit to Jules Verne. Carefully he read the questions which he wished to ask me. They were written at intervals on long rolls of foolscap, the space to be filled in as I answered. I thought it ridiculous until I returned and became an interviewee. Then I concluded it would be humane for us to adopt the Japanese system of interviewing.

I went to Kamakura to see the great bronze god, the image of Buddha, familiarly called Diabutsu. It stands in a verdant valley at the foot of two mountains. It was built in 1250 by Ono Goroyemon, a famous bronze caster, and is fifty feet in height; it is sitting Japanese style, ninety-eight feet being its waist circumference; the face is eight feet long, the eye is four feet, the ear six feet six and one-half inches, the nose three feet eight and one-half inches, the mouth is three feet two and one-half inches, the diameter of the lap is thirty-six feet, and the circumference of the thumb is over three feet. I had my photograph taken sitting on its thumb with two friends, one of whom offered $50,000 for the god. Years ago at the feast of the god sacrifices were made to Diabutsu. Quite frequently the hollow interior would be heated to a white heat, and hundreds of victims were cast into the seething furnace in honor of the god. It is different now, sacrifices being not the custom, and the hollow interior is harmlessly fitted up with tiny altars and a ladder stairway by which visitors can climb up into Diabutsu's eye, and from that height view the surrounding lovely country. We also visited a very pretty temple near by, saw a famous fan tree and a lotus-pond, and spent some time at a most delightful tea-house, where two little "Jap" girls served us with tea and sweets. I also spent one day at Tokio, where I saw the Mikado's Japanese and European castles, which are enclosed by a fifty foot stone wall and three wide moats. The people in Tokio are trying to ape the style of the Europeans. I saw several men in native costume riding bicycles. Their roads are superb. There is a street car line in Tokio, a novelty in the East, and carriages of all descriptions. The European clothing sent to Japan is at least ready-made, if not second hand. One woman I saw was considered very stylish. The bodice of a European dress she wore had been cut to fit a slender, tapering waist. The Japanese never saw a corset and their waists are enormous. The woman was able to fasten one button at the neck, and from that point the bodice was permitted to spread. She was considered very swell. At dinner one night I saw a "Jap" woman in a low cut evening dress, with nothing but white socks on her feet.

It would fill a large book if I attempted to describe all I saw during my stay in Japan. Going to the great Shiba temple, I saw a forest of superb trees. At the carved gate leading to the temple were hundreds of stone and bronze lanterns, which alone were worth a fortune. On either side of the gate were gigantic carved images of ferocious aspect. They were covered with wads of chewed paper. When I remarked that the school children must make very free with the images, a gentleman explained that the Japanese believed if they chewed paper and threw it at these gods and it stuck their prayers would be answered, if not, their prayers would pass unheeded. A great many prayers must have been answered. At another gate I saw the most disreputable looking god. It had no nose. The Japanese believe if they have a pain or ache and they rub their hands over the face of that god, and then where the pain is located, they will straightway be cured. I can't say whether it cured them or not, but I know they rubbed away the nose of the god.

The Japanese are very progressive people. They cling to their religion and their modes of life, which in many ways are superior to ours, but they readily adopt any trade or habit that is an improvement upon their own. Finding the European male attire more serviceable than their native dress for some trades they promptly adopted it. The women tested the European dress, and finding it barbarously uncomfortable and inartistic went back to their exquisite kimonos, retaining the use of European underwear, which they found more healthful and comfortable than the utter absence of it, to which they had been accustomed. The best proof of the comfort of kimonos lies in the fact that the European residents have adopted them entirely for indoor wear. Only their long subjection to fashion prevents their wearing them in public. Japanese patriotism should serve as a model for us careless Americans. No foreigner can go to Japan and monopolize a trade. It is true that a little while ago they were totally ignorant of modern conveniences. They knew nothing of railroads, or street cars, or engines, or electric lighting. They were too clever though to waste their wits in efforts to rediscover inventions known to other nations, but they had to have them. Straightway they sent to other countries for men who understood the secret of such things, and at fabulous prices and under contracts of three, five and occasionally ten years duration, brought them to their land. They were set to work, the work they had been hired to do, and with them toiled steadily and watchfully the cleverest of Japanese. When the contract is up it is no longer necessary to fill the coffers of a foreigner. The employé was released, and their own man, fully qualified for the work, stepped into the position. And so in this way they command all business in their country.

Kimonos are made in three parts, each part an inch or so longer than the other. I saw a kimono a Japanese woman bought for the holidays. It was a suit, gray silk crepe, with pink peach blossoms dotting it here and there. The whole was lined with the softest pink silk, and the hem, which trails, was thickly padded with a delicate perfume sachet. The underclothing was of the flimsiest white silk. The whole thing cost sixty dollars, a dollar and a half of which paid for the making. Japanese clothing is sewed with what we call a basting stitch, but it is as durable as it could be if sewed with the smallest of stitches. Japanese women have mirrors in which they view their numerous charms. Their mirrors are round, highly polished steel plates, and they know nothing whatever of glass mirrors. All the women carry silk card cases in their long sleeves, in which are their own diminutive cards.

English is taught in the Japan schools and so is gracefulness. The girls are taught graceful movements, how to receive, entertain and part with visitors, how to serve tea and sweets gracefully, and the proper and graceful way to use chopsticks. It is a pretty sight to see a lovely woman use chopsticks. At a tea-house or at an ordinary dinner a long paper laid at one's place contains a pair of chopsticks, probably twelve inches in length, but no thicker than the thinner size of lead pencils. The sticks are usually whittled in one piece and split only half apart to prove that they have never been used. Every one breaks the sticks apart before eating, and after the meal they are destroyed.

An American resident of Japan told me of his going to see a cremation. The Japanese graveyard is a strange affair, with headstones set close together, leaving the space for the graves less than the size of a baby's grave in America. As soon as the breath has left a body it is undressed and doubled up, head to feet, and is made to go in a very small bamboo box built in imitation of a Japanese house. This house may cost a great deal of money. It is carried along the streets on two poles to the place where it is to be cremated where it is given in charge of the cremator, and the friends go back to their homes until the following day, when they return for the ashes, which are generally placed in an urn and buried. The American, of whom I spoke, made arrangements with a cremator, and, accompanied by a friend, walked to the place in the country and waited out of sight until the mourners had vanished before they dared to draw near enough to see the cremation. They had walked quite a distance, dinnerless, and said, naively, that the odor was like that of veal, and it made him ravenously hungry.

A small hole about three feet long is made in the earth and in it the fire is built. When it was the proper heat the box was set over it, and in an instant it was consumed. The body released from its doubled position straightened out. The lower half being over the fire was soon cremated, excepting the feet and knee joints. The man in charge carefully pulled the upper part of the body over the fire, and with the same large fork put the half-consumed feet and knee-joints under the arms. In less than an hour all that remained of the body was a few ashes in the bottom of the pit. While the cremator was explaining it all to the gentleman he repeatedly filled his little pipe and lit it with the fire from the burning body. At his urgent request the gentleman consented to take tea with him when his task was done. They entered his neat little home while he jumped into a boiling bath in the open garden, from which he emerged later as red as a lobster. Meanwhile his charming and pretty daughters were dispensing the hospitalities of their home to their guests, and the father, desirous of enjoying their society, came and stood in the doorway, talking to them and watching them eat while he wiped his naked body with a towel!

The prettiest sight in Japan, I think, is the native streets in the afternoons. Men, women and children turn out to play shuttle-cock and fly kites. Can you imagine what an enchanting sight it is to see pretty women with cherry lips, black bright eyes, ornamented, glistening hair, exquisitely graceful gowns, tidy white-stockinged feet thrust into wooden sandals, dimpled cheeks, dimpled arms, dimpled baby hands, lovely, innocent, artless, happy, playing shuttle-cock in the streets of Yokohama?

Japanese children are unlike any other children I ever saw at play. They always look happy and never seem to quarrel or cry. Little Japanese girls, elevated on wooden sandals and with babies almost as large as themselves tied on their backs, play shuttle-cock with an abandon that is terrifying until one grows confident of the fact that they move with as much agility as they could if their little backs were free from nursemaid burdens. Japanese babies are such comical little fellows. They wear such wonderfully padded clothing that they are as shapeless as a feather pillow. Others may think, as I did, that the funny little shaven spots on their heads was a queer style of ornamentation, but it is not. I am assured the spots are shaven to keep their baby heads cool.

The Japanese are not only pretty and artistic but most obliging. A friend of mine who guided us in Japan had a Kodak, and whenever we came upon an interesting group he was always taking snap shots. No one objected, and especially were the children pleasant about being photographed. When he placed them in position, or asked them to stand as they were, they would pose like little drum-majors until he gave them permission to move.

The only regret of my trip, and one I can never cease to deplore, was that in my hasty departure I forgot to take a Kodak. On every ship and at every port I met others—and envied them—with Kodaks. They could photograph everything that pleased them; the light in those lands is excellent, and many were the pleasant mementos of their acquaintances and themselves they carried home on their plates. I met a German who was spending two years going around the world and he carried two Kodaks, a large and a small size, and his collection of photographs was the most interesting I ever saw. At the different ports he had professional photographers develop his plates.

The Japanese thoughtfully reserve a trade for their blind. They are all taught massage bathing, and none but the blind are allowed to follow this calling. These people go through the streets uttering to a plaintive melody these words:

"I'll give you a bath from head to toe for two cents."

At Uyeno park, where they point out a tree planted by General Grant when on his tour around the world, I saw a most amusing monkey which belonged to the very interesting menagerie. It was very large and had a scarlet face and gray fur. It was chained to the fence, and when one of the young men in our party went up and talked to him the monkey looked very sagacious and wise. In the little crowd that gathered around, quite out of the monkey's reach, was a young Jap, who, in a spirit of mischief, tossed a pebble at the red-faced mystery, who turned with a grieved and inquiring air to my friend.

"Go for him," my friend responded, sympathetically, to the look, and the monkey turned and with its utmost strength endeavored to free itself so it could obey the bidding. The Jap made his escape and the monkey quieted down, looking expressively at the place where the Jap had stood and then at my friend for approval, which he obtained.

The keeper gave the monkey its dinner, which consisted of two large boiled sweet potatoes. My friend broke one in two and the monkey greedily ate the inside, placing the remainder with the other potato on the fence between his feet. Suddenly he looked up, and as quick as a flash he flung, with his entire force, which was something terrific, the remaining potato at the head of some one in the crowd. There was some loud screaming and a scattering, but the potato missing all heads, went crashing with such force against a board fence that every particle of it remained sticking there in one shapeless splotch. The Jap who had tossed the pebble at the monkey, and so earned his enmity, quietly shrunk away with a whitened face. He had returned unnoticed by all except the monkey, who tried to revenge himself with the potato. I admired the monkey's cleverness so much that I would have tried to buy him if I had not already owned one.

In Yokohama, I went to Hundred Steps, at the top of which lives a Japanese belle, Oyuchisan, who is the theme for artist and poet, and the admiration of tourists. One of the pleasant events of my stay was the luncheon given for me on the Omaha, the American war vessel lying at Yokohama. I took several drives, enjoying the novelty of having a Japanese running by the horses' heads all the while. I ate rice and eel. I visited the curio shops, one of which is built in imitation of a Japanese house, and was charmed with the exquisite art I saw there; in short, I found nothing but what delighted the finer senses while in Japan.

THE GOBI DESERT

Mildred Cable and Francesca French

Mildred Cable (1878–1952) and **Francesca French** (1871–1960) and Francesca's sister, Evangeline, joined forces as Christian missionaries in Shanxi province, China. After many years there, the pioneering trio turned their attentions to Gansu province, where they spent 13 years crisscrossing the Gobi Desert via the ancient trade routes. You get to know a place in that time, and as it turned out there was more to Mildred and Francesca than missionary zeal – they were excellent writers, too. *The Gobi Desert: The Account of Three Women Travelling Across the Gobi Desert in the 1920s* emerged as an outstanding travel guide despite its rather pedantic title.

On the Threshold of the Desert

First Impressions

A ray of the rising sun touched the scalloped ridge of ice-fields in the Tibetan Alps and threw a veil of pink over their snowy slopes, but the great mass of the mountain range was still in the grip of that death-like hue which marks the last resistance of night to the coming day. The morning star was still visible, but it was grey dawn on the plain below, and light was gaining rapidly. There was a strange sense of vibration in the air, for the world was awakening and all nature responded to the call of a new day.

At the foot of the mountain range lay the old travel road, wide and deeply marked, literally cut to bits by the sharp nail-studded wheels of countless caravan carts. The ruts parted and merged, then spread again, as the eddies of a current mark the face of a river. Over this road myriads of travellers had journeyed for thousands of years, making of it a ceaselessly flowing stream of life, for it was the great highway of Asia, which connected the Far East with distant European lands.

That morning the road was deserted, save for two heavy carts covered with matting and drawn by mules. The beasts stood for a rest while two Chinese carters, dressed in blue cotton, squatted on their heels and each one stuffed the bowl of his long-stemmed pipe with a pinch of tobacco from the leather pouch hanging at his waist.

The land around was arid and the scene desolate but, toward the west, the outline of a mighty fortress and a long line of battlemented wall was silhouetted against the morning sky.

"Another ten *li*[1] and we shall be at the fortress of Kiayükwan," said the head carter, looking toward it. "Let us push on."

The cart bumped mercilessly over the loose stones of the dismal plain, and each slow mile brought the outline of the fort into clearer relief. It was an impressive structure. To the north of the central arch was a turreted watch-tower, and from it the long line of the wall dipped into a valley, climbed a hill and vanished over its summit. Then a few poplar trees came in sight, and it was evident from the shade of green at the foot of the wall that here was grass and water. Farther on a patch of wild irises spread a carpet of blue by the roadside, just where the cart passed under an ornamental memorial arch and lurched across a rickety bridge over a bubbling stream.

The massive monument now towered overhead, and, impressive as it was by its own dignity, it made a yet further appeal to the imagination, for this was Kiayükwan (Barrier of the Pleasant Valley), the barrier which marks the western end of that amazing and absurd structure known as the Great Wall of China, dating back to 214 B.C., and built as a protection against Tatar enemy tribes. The length of wall which outlined the crest of the hill to the north would continue, irrespective of difficulties caused by mountains and valleys, rivers and deserts, until it reached the sea 1400 miles away.

Were this a clumsy, grotesque structure it would be a blot on north-west China, but its beauty and dignity redeem it from criticism, and

1 *li*—a Chinese mile, and equivalent to one-third of an English mile.

since, in her unique way, China has ordained that her great western outlet should be controlled by a single door, she has made of that door such a striking portal as to be one of the impressive sights of the East. This fortification China calls her "mouth," and in colloquial speech those who have passed beyond it are "outside the mouth," while those still within are "inside the mouth." She thus makes the shame of compulsory exile doubly bitter by the offensive suggestion that an unwanted son has been ejected from her mouth.

The heavy cart shook the loose planks of the unsafe bridge, and the carter with a final shout turned the mules toward the stone-paved approach to the main entrance. The last pull up the ramp was an effort to man and beast. Both were weary with the long night stage, but each carter urged on his team with yells, lashing the air with his whip and cutting circles over his head. One sharp turn to the right, another pull through a further arch, and the carts were in the street of the inns, which was built against the fortress wall.

Then the innkeepers came out to secure custom.

"Turn in, turn in," each man called, and the carter questioned them as he went past: "Have you grass enough for our beasts?"

"Plenty," was the answer.

"What price?"

"A fair price, and no more."

So the caravan swept through the wide portal of the Inn of Harmonious Brotherhood. It took all the drivers' skill to bring the carts round till they stood with shafts facing the entrance. Then the mules were unhitched, the carts unladen, the tired men gathered to a drink of boiling water, and the street relapsed once more into its atmosphere of stagnation.

It was thus that I and my two companions first came to the western portal of the Great Wall of China, now called Kiayükwan (Barrier of the Pleasant Valley), but known to men of a former generation as Kweimenkwan (Gate of the Demons).

The old citadel had three gates, one facing north, one south and another west. Each was symbolic of the particular class of inhabitant whose life demanded its constant use. One was the low Door of Necessity through which the old residents passed each day carrying water from the spring at the foot of the hill. Occasionally they took a longer journey when three families joined together to drive a dozen donkeys to the coal-mines hidden in the foot-hills, and bring them back laden with fuel.

There was also the larger gate made of heavy wood and studded with nails. Each night that gate was locked and the great iron key deposited at the *yamen.*[2] It looked toward the distant green oasis of Suchow (Spring of Wine), and every day soldiers were galloping through the gate and over the plain to fetch supplies of pleasant food for the Governor and his ladies. Their horses clattered through the little crooked street, but the old residents, sitting at their counters, exchanged not a word with the youthful riders. News of matters outside their own gates meant nothing to them, nor had they any requirements which were not met by their own meagre supplies. Even the opium from the poppy patch by the side of the stream was sufficient for their dope.

The most important door was on the farther side of the fortress, and it might be called Traveller's Gate, though some spoke of it as the Gate of Sighs. It was a deep archway tunnelled in the thickness of the wall, where footsteps echoed and re-echoed. Every traveller toward the north-west passed through this gate, and it opened out on that great and always mysterious waste called the Desert of Gobi.

The long archway was covered with writings, and anyone with sufficient knowledge to appreciate Chinese penmanship could see at once that these were the work of men of scholarship, who had fallen on an hour of deep distress. There were lines quoted from the Book of Odes, poems composed in the pure tradition of classic literature, and verses inspired by sorrow too heavy for the careful balance of literary values, yet unbearable unless expressed in words.

Who then were the writers of this Anthology of Grief? Some were heavy-hearted exiles, others were disgraced officials, and some were criminals no longer tolerated within China's borders. Torn from all they loved on earth and banished with dishonoured name to the dreary

2 *yamen*—official residence of the City Magistrate.

regions outside, they stood awhile within the tomb-like vault, to add their moan to the pitiful dirge of the Gate of Sighs.

The men of the garrison shunned that gate, and the old inhabitants never used it. It was only the traveller who must needs pass the grim portal, and he always did so with some dread, for this was a door leading to the unknown, and to man the unknown is ever the fearful.

Unlike those who never looked beyond the gate until they must, I wished to prepare myself for the great adventure, so I set out on foot to view the land. Two men of the patrol joined me, forcing their way, as I did, against the head-wind which fiercely resisted us. Just outside the gate was a high stony mound which blocked the view. It had been thrown up to act as a barrier against the elemental and inimical spirits of the Gobi, for the simple-minded men of the garrison would never credit the goblins with sense enough to find their way round the mound and into the fortress.

We climbed it, and from the summit came into full view of the plain. Stretching as far as eye could see was the arid plateau from which the driving winds had swept away all the finer sand and left nothing but dull, grey grit.

"A place of desolation," murmured one of my companions.

I was fully aware of the acute terror with which the Chinese regard the Gobi regions, and I determined to get a better understanding of their outlook from these men who lived on the very edge of the desert yet always turned away from it with a shudder, and hurried toward the noisy clatter of the drill-ground and the barrack-room.

"It is desolate," I said, "but in the silence and solitude God is still there."

The youth stared, then shook his head. "Demons," he said, "they are the ones who inhabit the Gobi. This place is full of them, and many have heard their voices calling."

"How do they call?" I asked.

"From among the sand-mounds," he answered. "They call out just as a man would shout if he wanted help, but those who turn away from the track to answer them never find anyone, and the next call is always a little farther from the true path, for those voices will lead a man on, but they will never call him back to the right way."

"Do many get lost in this desert?" I enquired.

"Very many," he said. "Some miss their way and die of thirst, and others are frozen to death in winter blizzards. You do not yet know, Lady, the terrors of that journey. Must you go out into the Gobi? You have come from Suchow. That is a good place with many people and plenty to eat, but out yonder... Must you go?"

"Yes," I said, "I must, for I seek the lost, and some of them are out there."

"Ah!" he said. "You seek the lost; now I understand. There are many like you who go across the Gobi to seek a lost relative. Boys leave home to go out there, and never even send a word back to say where they are. Then the old parents are always unhappy until a second son goes in search of the first. Very often he comes back without finding that lost brother. Perhaps you have some clue as to where the lost ones are, and where you should go to look for them?"

"I have a clue and I know that I shall surely find them, even though the demons of the Gobi try to keep me from reaching them. God Who is their Father and mine will lead me to where they are."

The young soldier stared, dimly feeling that I was speaking of things which concerned the gods, and were outside his ken: "People like you are not in peril as we are," he concluded, "for the spirits cannot hurt them. When there is danger you know how to pray to your God."

We turned back to the great gate and, sordid as the fortress enclosure was, I felt glad to be safe within its walls again, for the howling gale blew grit and sand into my face, and when I reached my tumbledown room at the Inn of Harmonious Brotherhood I was thankful for its shelter. Before another week has passed, I thought, that great gate will have closed behind our caravan. We shall be out on the Gobi, and once we have started on that journey there can be no turning back.

Life in the Fortress

Inside the fortress, life was divided into three distinct sections, each of which had an existence quite different from the others. All the inns and shops were in the suburb. The people who owned them were descendants of a long line of old residents who took pride in the very exclusiveness which was imposed by their isolation. Few of them ever left the place, and many had never even seen the neighbouring town of Suchow. Business could not be made an excuse for always staying at home; the takings were too paltry to count. For the night's lodging a traveller would give two pence, and for that small sum have room enough to stretch himself on the *kang*,[3] get his dinner cooked for him at the kitchen fire, and have unlimited boiling water to drink. Custom required, however, that where the innkeeper could supply it, the traveller should buy the flour or millet needed for his dinner from him, even if the price were high. In the shops he could purchase tobacco, cigarettes, matches and rough paper made from the pulped leaf of the dwarf iris, small screws of red pepper mixed with coarse salt as condiment to the tasteless inn food, strong hand-woven braid for tying a man's trousers round his waist and ankles, and leather thongs for mending harness. Nothing else was regarded as a necessity or worth stocking, except sticks of incense to burn at the shrine so that the traveller might seek the favour of the gods as he journeyed on.

The only really busy place was the blacksmith's shop, which was always lively. In front of it a strong construction of wooden posts, ropes and pulleys looked like a mediaeval instrument of torture, but it was only a contrivance used for slinging difficult beasts who would not be quiet during the process of shoeing. With some mules it was sufficient to tie the hair of the tail to the tongue in order to quell the rebellious spirit, but others had to be lifted from the ground and thoroughly incapacitated before they would stop kicking.

The blacksmith was, incidentally, the veterinary surgeon of the place, and there was constant entertainment for carters in watching the dosing of desert-tried beasts, the ramming of needles into the tongue of a sick mule, and the more delicate operation of cutting the cartilage of the nostrils to cure spasms.

An inner gate led to the military section of the fortress, where life was entirely different. The *yamen*, built in traditional Chinese style,

3 *kang*—a mud bed warmed by a fire.

was the centre of garrison life, and here the General and his family lived, guarded day and night by sentries. Officers marched in and out, and much official business was done, for this was an important military centre and the officer in command held a high rank.

Unlike the old residents, the military hated the place and seized every chance of being away from it, bitterly resenting the appointment to such a lonely outpost, and longing to be transferred elsewhere. Nothing would have induced them to walk outside the North-West Gate where that fateful Gobi Desert stretched, and their eyes always turned longingly to the city where, twenty miles away, there was solace, gaiety and life.

If the men disliked Kiayükwan, the women hated it. "There is nothing to do here all day but sit and listen to that howling wind," they would say fretfully.

The ladies of the *yamen* would gather in each other's rooms, play *ma-jong* for small stakes, sip tea and gossip. Often the game was prolonged until midnight, with interludes for drawing on the opium pipe, but the next morning's reaction brought a fierce hatred of this place where desert demons hid themselves in dust-clouds and whistled through every crevice of the crazy buildings. The little slave girls learnt to dread the days of blizzard when their mistresses' nerves were taut and blows were dealt out irritably for the slightest offence.

Each festival of the year was the occasion for a welcome social function, and during the summer months life was made brighter by the frequent exchange of visits with the officials from Suchow. Twice each year a theatrical troupe visited the fortress, and for the three days of its performance all the inhabitants enjoyed themselves and made merry. But it was soon over, and when the properties were packed and carts carried both actors and their belongings elsewhere, life in the fortress relapsed into desolating stagnation.

The third category of human beings to be met in Kiayükwan were the travellers who came, lodged for a night or two at the inns, and forthwith went their way. Every sunset and every sunrise they arrived, some taking night stages and some travelling by day, but all were travel-worn and weary. They hailed from every part of China's dominion and were bound for her remotest frontiers. For one day or one night they used the place like masters, commanded the innkeeper's time and resources, fed their beasts in his stable and visited the shops, turning over the poor goods, always looking for something new though never finding it, till in disgust they would take a packet of cigarettes or a box of matches, fling down a few coppers and go their way.

These formed the stream of living men and women who moved up and down the great road, acquainted with life and full of knowledge about distant places. They were familiar with the large cities and the great waterways of China, and had traversed her wide plains by the "iron track" at a speed which seemed fabulous to the owners of these little shops. The static inhabitants saw them come, heard them talk, watched them go, but failed to understand the matters of which they spoke, for, to them, everything which they had never seen was unreal, vague, remote and seemed to bear no relation to daily life. Enough for them that today they had sold three boxes of matches, two packets of cigarettes and a handful of salt. They cared little for travellers' tales and probably believed none of them, and I was scarcely more advanced in my outlook than they were, for while all which lay behind was real and tangible, the new life across the desert seemed weird and illusory. With many of the travellers we shared past experience, for we, as they, had crossed China on her broad waterways and far-flung railroads, but we, too, were baffled by strange ultra-Gobi tales. Some told of rushing rivers cutting their way through sand, of an unfathomable lake hidden among the dunes, of sand-hills with a voice like thunder, of water which could be clearly seen and yet was a deception. We listened incredulously and, equally with the rough boys of the garrison town, found ourselves giving credence only to that which was confirmed by our own experience.

The restless soldiers of the garrison rushed to and from the large town, but the old inhabitants cared for none of these things, and when the fortress gates were closed each night they put up the shutters of the little shops and crept under miserable coverlets to lie on the mud *kangs*, fill their opium pipes and escape into the land of illusion and dreams, which was the only wider horizon that they knew.

We were in no hurry to leave the Barrier of the Pleasant Valley, for the days spent there were full of interest. We often walked out through the small gate and took the sharp downward path to where the springs bubbled up. The stretch of grass down there was always cool and damp, from the water which welled up and filtered through it in tiny rivulets. These formed a cheerful brook, which in turn joined the larger stream at the foot of the fortress. Here we met most of the "odd-and-end" boys from the inns, for all the drinking-water of the citadel was carried from here in wooden boxes laid across the backs of small donkeys. The "odd-and-ender's" job is the first rung of the ladder which leads to any post of oasis dignity. His work is exactly described by his title. He leads the overheated horse to and fro on a patient stroll until it is safe to water it, he runs about with kettles of boiling water, he wields the guillotine knife which chops sorghum[4] leaves for fodder, he fetches and carries for carters, and is the rich man's servant's servant. He works the box-bellows which fan the coal-dust fire, and wipes out the big iron food pot while his master eats its scrapings. There is little he does not see and he is proverbially communicative. Through listening to their chatter we came to know all about the different households in Kiayükwan.

They told how Merchant Chang's son had stolen sixty dollars of his father's savings and had joined the famous robber chief White Wolf, how Liu the miller had beaten his young wife and how she had killed herself by eating a whole box of matches, how Li the blacksmith's son was so profligate that his father took a sledge-hammer and crushed his head as he lay asleep. The gossip of that sleepy township was one long string of tragic happenings.

We often sat on the customer's bench at the shop doors and talked with the old residents, who liked to recount the past glories of the fortress, and many hours were spent with all sorts and conditions of women, sometimes in hovels, sometimes in hack-shops or in private houses, as well as in official residences. Such talk was always interesting and we learnt a great deal from it; we all enjoyed each other's company so that when the time came to move on there was already a root let down which it hurt to tear up. On the last days there were

4 sorghum—cereal plant known also as Indian millet, Guinea corn, durra.

many good-byes to be said, and an exchange of small presents left us provided with a variety of road necessities such as candles, sugar, cakes, crisp sun-dried rusks, and even a handful of fresh green vegetable from someone's little cabbage plot.

One evening before sunset our carts clattered noisily through the echoing arch, plunged through the awkward double gates, swung aside to avoid the spirit mound, pulled up a short steep ascent and drew up on the level plain just where the great stone tablet stood which bore the inscription: "Earth's Greatest Barrier."

The two friendly soldiers were there to see us off. "Look here, Lady," one of them said excitedly, "you cannot start without throwing a stone at our old wall."

They led us to where a portion of the brick facing of the fortress wall had been broken away, leaving a rough hollow, and near by lay a large heap of small stones.

"It is the custom that every traveller as he goes outside the wall, should throw a stone at the fortress. If the stone rebounds he will come back safe and sound, but if not..." he left the doom unuttered.

We each picked up a few small stones and threw them. Rebounding from the wall they skipped back with a sharp sound, and the two boys grinned with pleasure.

"What a strange noise!" I said. "It is like the cheeping of chicks."

"That is the echo of this spot," they said proudly. "It is lucky to have heard it. Your journey will be prosperous."

As the sun was now nearing the horizon the carter shouted, "We must be off," and the soldier boys saluted and said, "We shall meet again." Then they quickly turned and re-entered the fortress, for the trumpet was calling all men to barracks. The gate swung to, and we heard them shoot the heavy bar. We were irrevocably launched on the long trek.

We had all lived for many years in the East and were used to the leisurely pace of Oriental life. We had followed many of the trunk roads of China and were familiar with the varied life of the Chinese people. We knew their language, were at home with their customs and habits, and in matters of food and dress had become one of themselves. We had no nostalgia left for Western life and had long been detached from European lands. The Far East had become our home, and our thoughts, occupations and interests were focussed there. In so knowing the Chinese people we had learnt to love them, and it was perhaps this very understanding of them which imparted the dread we all felt in facing this desert isolation. The carter's burdened sigh found an echo in my own heart.

Life in China is always unhurried, and I, for one, had outgrown the hasty impatience which makes the Westerner such a trial to the Easterner. I had even developed the art of concentrating into the faculty of observation the whole mental activity of travel days, when for twelve hours, almost motionless, I watched the passing scene slowly unroll itself, observing every feature of the landscape and seeking to fathom each aspect of human life that we met and passed on the long road. Although the journeys which lay behind had often seemed long, slow and tedious, yet they always led to a kindly shelter for the night, toward a goal which lay within measurable distance, and gave certain promise of a return to a welcoming home. In China the wayside inn had had its unfailing atmosphere of cordiality and pleasant intercourse, but this place had none of these amenities. The life of China's main roads was one of stirring activity, with something happening every moment to interest or to amuse. What faced me here might be the burden of boundless monotony. Should I ever distinguish one stage from the other? Might I not even die, not, as some had done, of thirst or fatigue, but of boredom? In the end, should I make good my quest, or would the desert prove too much for me ? Where would it all end? How would it end? Anything might happen and it might end anywhere.

All this went through my mind as I walked ahead of the carts for a few miles of that first Gobi journey. The loose stones hurt my feet and cut them through my Chinese cotton shoes. Soon the landscape faded in the falling night and I could no longer distinguish the detail of the road. I began to stumble among the stones, and fearful of losing my way I climbed up on the cart beside my companions, trusting the beasts, who could see in the dark, to find the track.

The wind had dropped, all was still, and darkness soon spread over the plain. The evening star appeared, then one by one the stars came out and hung like golden lights in the velvety depths of the sky. I watched the expanse of the heavens throughout the whole night and the glory of it amazed me. The polar star unerringly pointed the way, and the constellations swung slowly overhead. The only sound was the steady quiet tramp of the animals' feet and the soft tread of the carter's cloth shoes. We were all conscious of passing through a great silence and instinctively interrupted it as little as might be.

At midnight a light haze on the horizon showed that moonrise was near. Soon the scene was bathed in clear soft light. The stillness intensified. I had previously known great silences, but in comparison with this it seemed that they were noisy. There was not even a blade of grass to rustle, a leaf to move, a bird to stir in its nest, nor an insect on the wing to fly past. No one spoke, we only listened intently and it seemed as though every vibration was stilled. When the moon rode high in the heavens and the hour was nearing three in the morning, the carter spoke once: "That, yonder, is Gold Washer's Halt," he said.

I stared among the undulating gravel-ridges and detected the sharper outline of a man-made structure and then a wall such as might enclose a village. Now that the spell was broken I wanted to speak and ask what this strange place was, and whether it held human inhabitants behind that sheltering wall. The carts came up slowly, and then stood still. Chilled and cramped, I alighted to stretch my limbs. I found a breach in the wall, and walking through it saw in the bright moonlight an old street with ruined buildings, and the remains of what had once been human homes. It was a city of the dead, yet it was impossible to throw off the feeling that the place was still used during the night hours by some ghostly inhabitants, and that I was being watched by vigilant eyes though I could not see them. I felt that I was an intruder.

This was all I saw that night, but later, when the desert road had become familiar by reason of many journeys, I was able to locate the deep well now choked with sand where the long-dead inhabitants had once drawn water. Slowly but surely the level of that water had sunk until the people had fled lest they should die of thirst. The shell of a temple was still standing where vanished gods of mud and stone had once guarded the tank in which gold-washers had carefully scanned the grains of sand, in their search for fragments of the precious metal.

At a certain season of the year a small quantity of evil-coloured water collected in a hole near by, and then an old man would come to stay in a hovel he had built from débris. He sold an infusion of desert herbs which he called "tea," and it sometimes happened that a gang of men bent on plunder joined the old man, so that every traveller was happier when, as now, there was neither water nor human inhabitant.

The gold-dust washers were not the first settlers in this place, for long before their day primitive man had made his abode here. Anyone who climbed the gravel ridges and searched among the stones which littered the ground would be likely to pick up a scraper or other stone implement made, used and discarded by prehistoric man. How strange it seemed that human beings should have used this place for so long and yet allowed the desert to reconquer it. With all his ingenuity man had not been able to hold his own against the all-devouring sands.

I was called back to the immediate by a summons from the carter: "On!" he said. "Let us be off! This is no place for delay."

"Let us get on!" I echoed.

The place was terrifying and even more inimical than I had feared.

A Wayside Halt

At sunrise the dreary stage came to an end, and we drove into the short street of a village where already there were signs of life. We met a few people fresh from sleep who were taking on the normal occupations of the day. During the hours of darkness they had been steeped in unconsciousness, and now they faced a new day, restored and vigorous. The weary beasts, the tired carters and the jaded travellers moved wraithlike among them, for all through the night they had been as living creatures who walked among the dead and surprised their secrets, and now they in turn felt like ghosts in this clear bright world, which was the inheritance of those who were refreshed and renewed. They had no part in the life of the new day, since for them it must be turned into night.

We all welcomed the windowless rooms of the dingy inn. Its doors were dilapidated, but a boulder rolled across the opening would prevent intrusion by these lusty, noisy, daylight people, so we spread coverlets on the mud bed, flung ourselves down and fell into deep sleep. I was awakened by flies alighting on my face, and looking upwards saw in the centre of the mat roof the *tunuk*[5] through which the midday sun directed a vertical ray which had reached my cheek. On the roof near the hole there was a large flat stone with which to close it, and, had I shouted, the fodder boy would have scrambled up and pushed it over the *tunuk*, excluding both light and air, and leaving only one small crack sufficient for the flies to use in making their exit to a brighter world. But I was now awake and even a few hours of sleep had reinvigorated me, so that I wished to take my part again in the world of men.

I walked out into the village street to look around. A clear stream somehow found its way here from distant snow-mountains and ran through the village, so dividing it that everyone must needs constantly cross and recross it on stepping-stones. A little general shop faced me, and on its small counter stood the inevitable heap of tobacco, the few boxes of cigarettes and matches, the bundles of incense sticks, the half-dozen screws of red pepper mixed with coarse salt and, hanging from a nail, were twists of hand-woven braid, home-made string and leather thongs.

There was something different here, however, for, in addition to the dull stock of the oasis shopkeeper, this man had a variety of articles made from a fine-grained, light-grey stone which was found near at hand. There were slabs on which to rub down the hard sticks of Chinese ink, and little pots to hold water with which to moisten them. The chief demand, however, was for small pieces to be used as whetstones for knives, razors or scissors, and many a carter passing that way added a hone to his small outfit of traveller's necessities.

In order to encourage business I bought a few stone articles, one of the small screws of red pepper and a box of matches, then sat down and talked with the owner of the shop. After answering all his

5 *tunuk*—a circular hole in the roof which admits light and air.

enquiries concerning myself, my age, my journey and my relatives, I took the lead and, in turn, questioned him about himself, his home and this village where he lived.

Concerning the oasis he had much to tell me. "This place," he said, "is famous for two things. One is its sweet, clear water which flows direct from the snow-fields. When you have been farther among the salt-water stages you will often long for a drink from our stream; but let me warn you, that when the sun is high and you water your beasts, the carter must either stand the pails in the sun, or pour a little hot water into them. The stream is rapid and the bed stony, so the water has no time to become sun-warmed, and many a horse goes sick in this place through drinking a draught of such chilly water. You too must be careful, but for sweetness there is no water like ours."

"Thank you for telling me," I said; "I will take your advice and be careful. But you spoke of some other things for which this place is renowned. What are they?"

"Our great tomb," he said. "This is the village of the Moslem Tomb (Huei-huei-pu), which is famous everywhere. Surely you have heard of it. Go and see it. A few steps beyond the temple is a wall, and behind the wall lies the Tomb of the great Moslem pilgrim."

I turned to go, and just as I was leaving I noticed on his counter a jar of coarse grey sand. Taking some of it in my hand I rubbed it between my fingers testing the quality of the grains, and as I did so I felt there was something unusual about it. "What do you keep sand for?" I asked. "Is there not enough of it by the roadside?"

"This is special sand, Lady," he said. "It comes from near here, but is not found elsewhere in the Gobi. It is so heavy that the wind does not blow it about, and it is the only sand which can be used for one process in the polishing of jade. Though it is hard enough to use even on jade, yet it never scratches the surface. It is very highly valued, and jade polishers send here to get it."

"Does each oasis have some special product?" I asked.

"More or less," he replied. "If you go straight across there," pointing to the north, "you come to the village of Tien-tsin-wei, and in summer you can find your way there by the melon skins on the sand. The melons are sweeter and more juicy there than elsewhere, and every traveller buys them and eats them as he goes. If you travel one stage farther on the main road, you will see all the houses surrounded with stacks of liquorice root. Traders from "within the mouth" all go there to buy it, and nowhere else is the quality so fine."

"Liquorice and melons are both good things," I said, "but Moslem Tomb supplies sand for the rare beauty of polished jade, and inkslabs for the writer's art, so it counts second to none for its products."

Parting from the friendly merchant with the customary "*tsai chien*" ("we shall meet again"), and joined by my companions, I walked into the little village in search of the pilgrim's tomb, and found it almost immediately. It was enclosed with an outer mud wall, the door through which was locked, but the man in charge saw me try the bolt and came over to open it and take us in. The plot of land held one building only, and this stood in the very centre of the ground: a small, square, mud-built tomb, with domed roof and a crenated border. As we walked round it the old Moslem fitted the key to the heavy lock and we followed him inside.

It was an empty room, but in the centre of the floor was a slightly raised opening covered over with a red satin pall, embroidered in Arabic characters. We were struck by the cleanliness, the order and the tidiness which the Moslem shows in regard to his sacred places. This mud-built tomb was many centuries old, but, thanks to the dry climate and constant attention to repairs, it stood intact.

We questioned the guardian concerning the pilgrim whose body lay buried there, and learnt from him that he was one of three companions who journeyed toward China from distant lands in the west. They overcame all difficulties until they reached the rocky ravine called Hsing-hsing-hsia (Ravine of Baboons), which is at present the frontier of Chinese Turkestan. There one of them died, and only ten stages farther his companion also died and was buried here, leaving the third to travel on alone.

"I suppose that the body of this pilgrim lies in a vault," I said. "Is there any stone slab under that satin pall?"

"No, indeed," was the indignant reply, "for when the angel calls the dead man of Islam by his name, he must sit upright and respond. How could he do that if he were held down by coffin-boards or by stone slabs? When you reach Hsing-hsing-hsia," he continued, "you will find the tomb where the body of the first holy man lies. It is a deep rock sepulchre and you must be sure to see it."

"What happened to the third pilgrim?" I asked.

"He travelled on right through China, and in the end died in Canton. His tomb is there and these graves are always spoken of as 'The Graves of the Three Pilgrims,' but," he added with some pride, "this is the only tomb which gives its name to a locality."

Many legends have grown up round the tradition of the three renowned pilgrims, and later we were assured that the body of the first one had already risen from the cave tomb in Hsing-hsing-hsia. Miracles are also freely quoted in connection with the other burying-sites, but through all the legendary lore the basic fact persists, of three companion pilgrims whose bodies are buried respectively at Hsing-hsing-hsia, at Huei-huei-pu and in Canton.

From the Moslem burying-place we walked on a few steps to the temple which overlooked it. An old Chinese priest lived there, who received us with kindliness, and we sat talking for a long time. To all that we said he nodded approval, murmuring, "Those are true words," and before leaving we handed him a scroll of paper on which the fundamental commands of God were printed in clear ideographs. He read them through, expressed his approbation and immediately rose to fix the paper to the door of the central shrine, well pleased that the people who entered it should read "good words," from whatever source they came.

Gobi Merrymakers

All through the hot afternoon of the day on which we left Moslem Tomb Halt I was aware of a reiterated phrase woven by the carter into a lilting tune, and sung in a nasal falsetto as he went about the business of overhauling harness and trappings.

"Eighteen hills ahead I see,
Eighteen hills to climb they'll be;

Mules will sweat, and men waste strength,
All because of the steep hills' length."

The terse monosyllabic Chinese phrases subconsciously arrested my attention and I began to wonder what were these eighteen hills about which he was lilting so insistently. Without addressing me he had captured my attention and without a single direct word he was telling me what he wished me to know. Great people these Chinese carters! Finally I could no longer ignore his tale and he had it his own way, for I was questioning him.

"Carter Li," I said, "what is tonight's stage like?"

"A stage to be remembered," he said. "Eighteen hills between here and Pure Gold Hollow."

I had pictured the Gobi as a flat expanse, but that night showed me how it varied from place to place, and before morning we had gone over eighteen steep hills in succession. I do not know which the animals found harder, the pull up or the jog down; uphill was heavier for the beasts in the traces, but the descent was cruel on the shaft mule, for the cart was brakeless and its whole weight fell on the creature's haunches, as, step by step, he resisted its downward course.

As we left the last slope of the eighteenth hill behind us the carter's quavering falsetto was raised again, and this time he sang about the village just ahead:

"Pure Gold Pond tonight we'll see,
At Pure Gold Rise then soon we'll be;
South we'll turn to Pure Gold Fort,
And round we'll come to Pure Gold Halt."

This opened up a new subject of conversation, and we found that the district of Chihkin (Pure Gold), to which we were coming, was surprisingly extensive and included all the localities of which the carter sang. It spread over the whole area reaching from the bare volcanic hills on the south to three separate stages on the main road which were fully twenty miles apart. The ideographs which composed the name Chihkin stood for Pure Gold and connected the oasis with many other places in the South Mountains which bore this character *kin* (gold) incorporated in their names. We were evidently entering the land of gold dust.

It was a wide basin almost surrounded by hills and fertilised by the water which ran down from them. This basin, like every Gobi oasis, was cultivated to capacity, and besides a large number of isolated farmsteads it held many small hamlets. The farms were rich, and fortified with high crenellated walls, on which stones suitable for throwing at invaders were stored, and below there was a runway for the stone-throwers. A heavy wooden door, strengthened with iron nails, closed the one and only entrance to each farm, and this door was guarded by fierce Tibetan mastiffs, ready to tear a man to pieces if he attempted to force his way past them.

Standing alone on this plain was one small fortified town called the Citadel. About five hundred families lived there permanently, but when an enemy swept down on the fruitful plain all the farmers crowded into the fort for shelter. Secret stocks of provisions were carefully laid up and the people believed themselves able to sustain a long siege.

The outside world scarcely existed for the people of Pure Gold. They married within their own area, they seldom travelled outside it, and decisions of the clan on any point were never questioned within the community. Men and women born and bred in such conditions of monotony and isolation inevitably develop intensified characteristics of exclusiveness, distrust and rigidity. They are unable to mix with any circle other than the one into which they were born, or to have intercourse with any people who think differently from themselves. Should any daring spirit venture to question a local habit, or to suggest that in other places, things were done otherwise, the answer with which he was silenced was brief and conclusive: "It is our custom." No discussion which might open the door to another view-point was tolerated. The people of Chihkin were so convinced that their way was the only right one, that their minds were barricaded as effectively by prejudice as their citadel was by stone walls. The opening of a fissure through which a new thought might find entrance to the mind would be more terrifying than a sudden crack and collapse of the stone battlement which safeguarded them from the enemy.

We wandered for long among this group of oases and tapped its resources in food and in other commodities. We found these sufficient, but absolutely limited to local products, yet Pure Gold, like Moslem Tomb Halt, boasted one special product which was not to be found elsewhere. This was a thick crude mineral oil, drawn from local wells. The oiling of axles on hot desert sands is a great care to carters, and the linseed-oil bottle, generally in use both for cooking and greasing purposes, is a source of perpetual contention between master and man. The oil is bought in order to grease the axle, but the carter covets it as a condiment. The axle is dry and thirsty and requires constant lubrication, but the man's food is tasteless, unless he can flavour it with garlic crushed in oil. The mineral oil of Pure Gold was both inexpensive and totally unsuitable for food, therefore in that area peace reigned in the caravan as the carter was never tempted to add it to his bowl of *mien*.[6]

A few buyers of mineral oil came regularly to the wells from other oases. We talked with one of them whose donkey, saddled with two five-gallon tins stamped with the mark of the Standard Oil Company, spent the whole of its life walking to and fro between Pure Gold and another oasis. The journey took eight days and the net profit made on each trip was the sum of one dollar, at that time worth one shilling and eightpence.

The people's clothes were made of stout, hand-woven cotton cloth, and were very clumsy and old-fashioned, but the contents of the pawnshops, which are the best indication of a district's riches, revealed big stocks of silk, satin and fur garments. These handsome clothes were most carefully stored by the pawnbrokers and were only redeemed by their owners on such occasions as weddings, funerals and the New Year festivities. After being worn for a few days they were returned to the safe shelves of the pawnbroker's shop until they should be needed again.

Sometimes we stayed in the homes of the people and sometimes we camped on their threshing-floors. They were all immensely proud of the locality where they were born, and considered Pure Gold to be

6 *mien*—home-made macaroni, often called dough-strips.

a prime oasis of the desert. They still boasted of the gold-mines once very plentiful there, but built great hopes on the oil-wells because rumour had it that these might yet be of more value than even the gold had been. There was yet another unusual product found in the mountains, described vaguely as a substance which could go into the fire and come out unburnt. We talked about it a good deal and I came to the conclusion that what they spoke of might be asbestos.

It was at the Temple of Pure Gold that we first saw some gay side to the desert dweller's life. It was a boisterous but pathetic attempt at hilarity, and its occasion was the celebration of the fifth day of the fifth moon, a very old festival connected with the historical annals of the Chinese people. Such commemorations date from very ancient times and some recurring feasts, such as the Spring Festival and the Feast of the Moon, have an origin which is lost in the dimmest antiquity.

All over China there is a special and traditional way of celebrating each festival, and even in far-away Gobi oases the pasteboard cow is dragged forth at the birth of spring, and each time his anniversary comes round the old dragon curls and twirls through the sandy streets of dusty villages. Moon cakes appear at the full moon of the eighth month, and on the correct day the Boat Festival is remembered.

This fifth day of the fifth moon demands special recognition. In happier climes it is the Dragon-boat Festival, but Gobi folk have never seen a boat, so must find some other way of merry-making than sailing small river craft, and therefore celebrate the event with a theatrical performance.

The historic incident which is commemorated on that day dates back to the third century B.C. There was at that time a virtuous and loyal Minister of State named Chu-yüan. So long as his counsel was sought and followed by the Prince all was well, but the time came when the machinations of a jealous rival prevailed and Chu-yüan was dismissed from office. Knowing that under the new conditions the ruin of the country must ensue, he wandered out to the bank of the Mi-lo River with the intention of ending his life. There he met a fisherman and the following conversation took place: "Are you not His Excellency the Minister?" asked this man. "Why then should you weary of life?"

"The world," replied Chu-yüan, "is foul and I alone am clean, men are drunk and I alone am sober, therefore I am dismissed from office."

To this the fisherman replied: "The true sage does not quarrel with his environment, but adapts himself to it. If, as you say, the world is foul, why not leap into the tide and make it clean? If all men are drunk, why not drink with them, yet by example teach them to avoid excess?"

Having said this the fisherman moved away, and Chu-yüan, clasping a large stone in his arms, plunged into the river and was seen no more. The Dragon-boat Festival commemorates the search made by the people for the body of this virtuous and courageous Minister of State who preferred death to compromise.

The Chinese are a laughter-loving people and regard the theatre as one of the best forms of entertainment, therefore troupes of actors move up and down the trade-routes of the Gobi giving performances as they go, and the Temple of Pure Gold had engaged one of them for a gala performance on the fifth day of the fifth moon. To see the actors arrive was an entertainment in itself. First of all two bullock carts appeared laden with roughly made stage properties and some simple scenery, and with the carts came thirty men dressed in shabby clothes. They walked with a light springy step and carried large wooden boxes slung from a pole between each two men. These boxes held their precious costumes—faded, ragged, embroidered dresses, elaborate tinsel headgear, flowing beards made from the soft white tail of the Tibetan yak, and the mock implements of war which take a large place in Chinese historic drama. The stage was part of the temple structure and only needed the addition of mat roofing for an immediate performance. In a very short while after arrival the players and musicians appeared dressed for their parts, and the musicians' band of cymbals, pipes, flutes and drums crashed out the most hideous din that mortal ears ever heard.

The effect on the oasis dwellers was almost hypnotic, and the noise and show held them spellbound. They had come in their bullock carts from every oasis within reach of the temple, and the crowd was composed of men and women, old and young, and children of every age. The men stood massed in front of the stage, the women, dressed in clothes of the brightest colours, sat in their carts which formed a semicircle a little farther back, while the children ran to and fro indefatigably. The performance was soon in full swing. Each time an actor left the stage and returned he explained to the audience what he was going to do and what he was supposed to have done during his absence. The play was continuous and, though there was no clapping or other expression of appreciation, the rapt attention of the audience evidenced its enjoyment.

There was no admission fee, for the richer people had provided the entertainment and were satisfied to have gained prestige with both gods and men by their generosity. Each performance lasted eighteen hours out of the twenty-four, and during that time was only suspended for the brief space needed for actors and audience to cook a meal and eat it. Immediately after, the play was resumed and continued by torchlight until after midnight.

At Pure Gold Temple there was an unusual and picturesque crowd. The most important person present was an old abbot named Li. He was eighty years old and had entered on his novitiate as a child, when he was dedicated by his parents to a priestly life. Since boyhood his hair had been neither cut nor combed. It now formed a matted rope which he proudly compared with the tail of a cow. This "cow's tail" was, in some way, symbolic of virtue. He wore it twisted round his head, but when let down it reached his knees.

Several priests from neighbouring temples had come to help, as there were many shrines and a priest was required to read the rituals in each. Everyone who came to the theatre visited all the shrines, and at each altar took a few sticks of incense, lighted them at a vegetable-oil lamp which burned perpetually before the god, and then stood them upright in the ash of the large incense-burner. As each worshipper did so the priest's voice rose to a higher pitch, and he beat rhythmic strokes on the crab-shaped wooden clapper at his side. The worshipper prostrated himself in a profound obeisance, then threw down a few coppers and passed out.

While the theatre supplied the prime entertainment, and incense-burning was a good diversion, there were still those who derived their chief enjoyment from the food-market. It was no easy business to supply this hungry crowd with seasonable dainties, yet in spite of all difficulties there were pork dumplings, both boiled and fried according to taste, and cauldrons of chitterling broth in which to soak the dry bread which was brought from home. Substantial doughnuts had the advantage of being very filling at small cost, and steamed rolls of bread with their little centre of black sugar were a nice change.

The special dish connected with the Dragon-boat Festival, however, is made of rice. In old times rice was cast into the river on the anniversary of Chu-yüan's death, but now the revellers eat cakes made of the rice. These cakes are made of sticky, glutinous rice and are stuffed with the fruit of the jujube[7] tree, then wrapped in reeds and steamed.

In the large oases which lie in deep declivities there are often wide ponds where reeds grow abundantly. These reeds are picked and carried all over the Gobi by itinerant cooks who use them in making the three-cornered rice cake for the fifth of the fifth moon. The floor space round the open-air stage is always littered with reed wrappings, stripped from the sticky sweetmeat and flung around.

At dark the children refused to stay awake any longer and there was a general spreading out of wadded quilts. Each family secured a corner of a temple verandah and made itself at home there for the three days of the performance. The men folk stood till after midnight watching the play, but tired women, on foot since dawn, were glad to make their children the excuse for an early bed.

Even the voracious appetite of the Chinese for crowds, din and display must have been satisfied by the time the third day was over and the actors brought their long and exhausting performance to a close. Food vendors abandoned the mud fireplaces, actors packed their properties and tramped off to the next fair, and the desert dwellers drove their bullock carts back to their poor farms, where each would take up again the round of his monotonous and dreary existence.

It was then that Abbot Wang, visiting priest from a famous rock temple, asked us to visit the cave shrines of which he was guardian.

"Few travellers ever come our way," he said, "but the shrines are

7 The common jujube—*zizyphus vulgaris*.

very ancient and belong to the line of Thousand Buddha Temples which lies along the base of the South Mountains."

"Abbot," we said, "before many moons have passed we hope to pitch our tent in the shade of your temple walls. You will be more leisured then, and you shall tell us all you know of the Thousand Buddha Shrines, and we will tell you all we know of the Way of man's approach to God."

"I shall see you again," he said, then bowed and left us.

A TRAVELLER ON HORSEBACK

Christina Dodwell

Christina Dodwell (1951–present), born in Nigeria to British parents, has spent her life demonstrating that there are far more exciting forms of transport available than cars – horse, canoe, elephant, camel and microlight to name but a few. As a dedicated explorer of the world's remotest corners her choices may also have been driven by necessity. She's made radio documentaries, TV films, won awards, written travel books such as *A Traveller on Horseback* and established the Dodwell Trust, a charity to support the poverty-stricken of Madagascar.

Riding to Persepolis

The Royal Road from Sardis to Susa (which branched to Persepolis) had post stations at intervals of one day's ride. Royal messages, with changes of horse and rider, could cover 2,500 kilometres in a week. Fragments of stone-paved surface are still visible near Bibahan but in this stretch my route relied on an ancient map and local advice.

When I met some village boys with horses I asked if I could hire one to ride to Naksh-i-Rustam and on to Persepolis. The idea proved acceptable and they squabbled over whose horse would earn the money. I interrupted and chose a leggy strawberry roan, whereupon the youngest boy, a ten-year-old, assured me the horse was his responsibility and he handled our negotiations with practised shrewdness. After fitting my saddlebags on its back I mounted and tried to set out but the horse didn't want to leave and my urging made him buck. Determined not to fall off I clamped my knees to the saddle, and let him buck his fill as we cantered. At least we were moving forward and the bucking wasn't the jack-knifing kind of a bronco.

As our road led away from the greenness into an arid stretch, the horse calmed down and settled into an easy lope. I was just beginning to relax when I heard galloping hooves behind me and saw a loose horse following us, pursued by four boys on two other horses. Without too much fuss they recaptured the loose horse and one of the boys led it home. The others decided to accompany me for a while.

The land became more fertile again and the track led through wheatfields and across a main road. At midday I turned west along a path beside a stream. Its greenness of reeds and waterweeds was cool to my eyes.

One of the boys brought his horse alongside mine but there wasn't room for us both on the path, my horse was pushed on to the edge of the stream cliff, so I reined in. Soon the other boy was jostling me so I kicked my horse into a canter and outpaced them. But this didn't last, the boys were continually nudging me, though when I yelled at them they behaved better.

We forded that stream, then through a second stream, wading it where a small barrage had formed a shallow pool. The far bank was a steep scramble and I kept well to the side of my plunging horse. A small gallant one, its mottled red coat was soon generously splashed with mud and water. The three boys were riding two horses, and the smallest boy who had rented me my horse kept asking if he could ride pillion behind me, to which I said no.

At 1 p.m. we stopped by the stream to let the horses rest. I sat watching an enamel-blue kingfisher diving in the water; the boys sat too close to me for comfort, then pulled out a long knife and tried to frighten me.

But I had just begun a bout of hay fever and I couldn't pay attention to anything while sneezing almost continuously. The sneezing kept the boys at bay. And when it seemed to subside I walked over to my horse and secretly rubbed some of his dust under my nose. That produced another paroxysm of sneezes, and the boys eventually decided to saddle up again, though not without a final argument, in which the youngest boy ranged on my side and I said he could ride pillion with me if he made the other boys and their horses go home.

So the youngster vaulted up on to my horse's back behind the saddle, and yelled abuse at the older boys until they left. We loped away in the opposite direction, with my young ally sitting behind me easily on the horse's rump. The boys' behaviour wasn't out of character if one considers that many of the heroes and warriors of ancient Persia were bandits and robbers, which was not a disreputable profession. Travellers took such risks carrying money that, by the ninth century, credit notes and cheques were introduced. Our word cheque is of Persian origin.

We crossed another small river and came on to a plain where nomads had set up their black goats'-hair tents in the stony golden sand. Behind them a line of tall cliffs rose and sagged. The boy pointed to the end tip of the cliffs and shouted, 'Naksh-i-Rustam.'

I urged the horse into a canter, which the boy hadn't been expecting, and he nearly fell off backwards.

My pillion passenger was not giving much trouble, although he had again brought out the knife and waved it around until I told him to put it away. It was easy to get my revenge on him by making the horse trot, a most uncomfortable pace if you're sitting on its rump, and the boy soon learned to do as I said.

Approaching Naksh-i-Rustam, we could see bold cross-shaped tombs cut into the cliffs. These are the royal tombs of Darius, who followed Cyrus in an even more brilliant way; of Xerxes, intoxicated with power, who succeeded him; of Artaxerxes, a mild man who made a peace pact with Greece; and Darius II, the last in the weakening line. These were the Achaemenians, the first Persians. The tombs' cliff-face entrances are set high in rock polished and sculpted to show kings being respected by their peoples and blessed by their gods.

This point in the cliffs had previously been a sacred place of the Elamites, and later of the Parthians and Sassanians. The latter, whom I'd encountered civilised in north-east Iran, had here recorded their central power with great stone-carved pictures on panels of polished rock.

These magnificent panels portray men jousting on horseback, tilting with lances, and wearing thick robes and pointed helmets. One huge panel (10 metres by 5 metres) shows King Shapur receiving homage from a cringing Roman Emperor Valerian, who was captured in AD 260. Other relief panels depict royal investitures, triumphs, and the king surrounded by court finery. When I rode closer to them I could see how some are far more weather-worn than others, representing the rock art of over twenty centuries.

There are yet more panels further along the rocky bluff: two figures on horseback, one a god handing a crown to a king, who has a curious hair-bubble atop his head, while the god wears long curly hair and a crown. Their horses are trampling their enemies, the god's tramples Ahriman, synonymous with the forces of darkness. One should be able to identify the kings by matching their distinctive crowns to their coinage. As we rode past a carving of jousting my horse suddenly reared up. The boy slid off the back. Luckily only his pride was wounded, so I gave him my camera and asked him to take some pictures, which made him very happy. Grandiose stuff, the static dignity of the eastern heraldic style, but it doesn't have much artistic merit. Early Sassanian groups are set in single-file with the king the tallest man present. During Shapur's reign the artists introduced a new way of moulding drapery, learning from the Roman style of decorative relief how to make stone clothes on a curved body, and to compose scenes with groups.

The purpose of some panels seems to be a show of might to deter any further challenges, as at Bisitun where, in gory detail, nineteen rebellions are being squashed. Not artistic, but it doesn't lack effect. This was a vast and rich empire; the friezes weren't an understatement.

A square white marble building stands in front of the tombs, its base nearly six metres below ground level, an excavated trench showing a three-tiered plinth and a broken flight of marble steps. A water channel had run around the base. The windows are black marble and blind, unseeing, though the door is open, but the steps to reach it are missing. There has been much debate over the purpose of this building, though to me it looked like a fire temple. The fire-worshipping cult of Manes had been given official status by Shapur because the religion was a unifying factor within his empire and it supported the state's struggle against Christian Rome. This building would have been an ideal repository for sacred fire, kept alight by a priest, with blind windows so that no draught would kill the flame.

Around the bluff, invisible from the tombs, are two small fire altars, square with raised rounded corners, standing as tall as myself, so I had to climb the mountain slope behind to see down into them where the fire bowls lay empty. While on the hillside I found two sets of what seemed to be water channels, cut with deep sheer sides and spreading into a handful of channels. The only explanation I could think of was that they were channels for the blood of the animal sacrifices recorded by Xenophon.

From there I rode back on to the course of the Royal Road, following it along the base of the cliffs to a nomad camp. Some Qashgai girls were shepherding sheep, their faces rounded with high cheekbones, their hair growing low over the forehead, parted centrally and pulled forward in bangs threaded under red and pink tinsel-woven scarves. Their multi-skirted dresses were fluorescent colours with gold and silver embroidery.

A man on a white donkey galloped past, I was amused by the way its ears flapped as it ran. Another man rode by on a motorbike carrying a protesting goat with one hand, by the scruff of its neck. I reached down into my saddlebags and found the smelly cheese balls. The boy and I munched a few, he thought they were delicious.

About three kilometres from Naksh-i-Rustam where the valley narrows between craggy ranges we passed through the site of a ruined town. It would have been easy to miss, marked only by one pillar with a double capital of bulls' heads. But nearby are many pillars fallen from sight, and the foundations of buildings that had stretched extensively. There is also the more modern ruin of a caravanserai with fragments of one big mud wall still standing.

We rode on around the base of the eastern mountain range, crossing the stubble of harvested wheatfields where herds of sheep and goats were guzzling any fallen grain.

To cut across an unharvested field, my horse walked in a dry irrigation ditch. From that level the wheat was taller than the horse, and mixed with wild hollyhocks, blue-ball flowers and giant purple thistles. We crossed a river on a rickety iron bridge, below which men were picnicking and swimming in two pools. I pulled my headscarf forward so they couldn't tell I wasn't just a local woman.

We passed Naksh-i-Rajab, the site of more rock engravings. Plots of gold wheat were interspersed with green lucerne and sugar beet. I put the horse into a canter aiming to jump the next irrigation ditch. The boy held on tight, I had forgotten he was there.

Over two earthen ridges, we came down on to an asphalt road along the base of another mountain ridge. A brush-fire filled the air with clouds of smoke, but when the wind blew the smoke aside I could see in the very far distance the raised columns of Persepolis. My heart soared.

For the last stretch I cut back to the road, now a wide asphalt drive broad enough for six lanes. Being empty, I rode down the middle, and from an ambling trot the horse broke into a gallop. I would not normally gallop on tarmac, it's too jarring for a horse's legs, but the boy was whooping encouragement.

Persepolis' columns grew larger, they had to be over twenty metres tall, and I could see archways and the winged bullgods of the main gate, all raised above the surrounding plain on a high stone platform.

In a clump of flowering trees near the ruins was a small guest lodge. The owner gave me a jug of iced water; ah, there's nothing as good as cold water, then tea; and although he had no room for me he arranged for one of the management to move out of his room so that I could stay. Later, having said goodbye to the boy and his horse, I went out to look at the ruins.

The king who followed soon after Cyrus was Darius; he wanted his own personal capital so he built Persepolis, and the city was added to by Xerxes and Artaxerxes. But it was Darius who was the real genius; a benevolent and progressive imperialist. Once he had firmed up his empire in a military way he turned to its administration, taking Cyrus' improvised schemes and perfecting them.

At Persepolis Darius claimed the apron of a sacred limestone mountain and had a massive platform built extending from it, above the level of the plain. The platform merges into the shoulder of the mountain, joining man and nature.

Winged bulls over five metres tall flank the entrance, the pair facing outward across the plain have animals' heads, while those facing the city have human faces. This, the Gate of Xerxes, leads into an open area big enough for small armies to camp. Beyond, massive stone double staircases go up to palaces and the Apadana, or Audience Hall, with pillars almost twenty metres high; their tops had borne double capitals of sculpted animal heads.

The nearby Hall of 100 Pillars used to have a ceiling of cedar from Lebanon, with the Zoroastrian scriptures written in gold and silver on 12,000 tanned oxhides. The columns had originally been covered in painted plaster that glittered with jewels.

Darius' Palace had massive stone trilithon doorways, of monolithic slab lintels on two uprights, their interior surfaces carved with lifesize men fighting griffins, and lions giving allegiance. Eighteen trilithons are still standing, their themes of attendants and godly blessings. The palace is made of darker rock than the rest of Persepolis, its good state of preservation and high-polished finish due to it being formerly covered in mud. Achaemenian monumental art had reached its peak in Darius' reign; Xerxes continued by translating into stone his own megalomania.

But it is the staircases themselves that command attention. Sloping shallowly enough to allow horses up at a walk or canter, the massive eastern stairway of the Apadana has a carved stone frieze showing a procession of subjects from over twenty nations, being ushered into court by Medes, recognisable by their rounded hats. The subjects bring gifts and tribute as diverse and exotic as the peoples: weapons, jewels, dishes, textiles, specialities of their lands including livestock, two-humped Bactrian camels being brought from near China and dromedaries from Arabia; by the end of Darius' reign, twenty-nine races were pledged to him in allegiance.

Then I paid attention to what I had really come to Persepolis for, to see if there are any miniature Caspian horses in these lines of people and their livestock. Many horses are shown, in correct proportion to everything else on the frieze; some of the breeds are as tall as men's shoulders, others smaller with long manes; cobs with hogged manes and steppe horse noses, bulging foreheads, different conformation and characteristics; and the men who brought the horses came from various tribes, as illustrated by their clothes and helmets.

The sight planted the thought in my mind that I'd like to go and look at the Kurdish Arabs in their native land. But Kurdistan is remote and I doubted there would be time for a visit since I also wanted to see the Assassins' Valley area.

Then I spotted a pair of miniature Caspians, pulling a chariot with a cloaked charioteer, and on another staircase Caspians are again shown, this time pulling a cart with a delegation of bearded men carrying jars and urns. The Caspians are unmistakable; donkeys have donkeys' ears, and Caspians have tiny curved ears.

On the final step of that staircase is an African tribe from Ethiopia, men with frizzy hair bringing a large elephant's tusk and leading a strange animal that looks like an outsize hyena; it was probably a giraffe, long-necked with a sloping back.

The architecture of Persepolis is something that hits you face on with its impact of strength, but there is nothing subtle about it. Gone is the restraint of Pasargad, this was designed to make mortals feel awed and humbled. The detail and technical skill are repetitious and regimented, their purpose to highlight power not beauty.

Leaving the palace I followed the contour of the hillside and explored tombs cut in a black polished rock face veined with white quartz. The cool interiors were a relief from the heat, and one contained a massive stone sarcophagus carved with attendant figures. I arrived back at the main ruins as the sun set in a cloudless orange sky, and a mullah began his call to prayer in a distant village. I listened as the sun's colours faded from the walls the Achaemenians had built 1,200 years before the arrival of Islam.

At the guest house people were chanting prayers in the corridor. My supper was rice and kebab; someone was singing outside, a traditional Persian ballad.

The next morning I went up to the ruins again. The only other tourists there were a few Iranian families, their raven-shaped women stood out starkly against the blinding glare of sun on pale stone. Some of the *chadoors* were lighter colours but always sober. While sitting in the shade of Darius' Palace I talked to one group from Tehran, and when we took some photographs they laughed because I pushed back my headscarf. Two of their women then pushed theirs back and shook out their hair. They said the *chadoor* makes their hair feel limp and smell bad. Afterwards I left my scarf pushed off my face but was ticked off by the curator for not being properly covered.

THE PASSIONATE NOMAD

Isabelle Eberhardt

Isabelle Eberhardt (1877–1904) was born in Geneva, the illegitimate daughter of Russian anarchists. In 1897 Eberhardt left Europe and moved to Algeria where she became deeply involved in politics and converted to Islam. Before her drowning at 27 in a freak desert flood, she lived her short life dressed as a man, travelling around North Africa and writing stories. She was also a heavy smoker, drinker and consumer of a hash-derivative called kef and she had many lovers. She was one of the few women allowed to join the Fantasia – a traditional Imazighen Horsemanship exhibition that involves racing horses in synch before stopping abruptly and shooting bullets at the ground. Isabelle fought the police in early Algerian uprisings, threw her large amounts of inherited money out of her windows and chose to live in destitution.

Friday 20 July 10 p.m. in Marseilles

Everything is finished, packed and closed... The only thing left here is my camp bed, which must wait till morning.

At one in the afternoon tomorrow I leave for Algiers.

The fact is that I did not really quite believe I would actually be leaving for Ouargla. So many things had stood in the way of my carrying out my daring plan.

My chances of success are good, for I leave well equipped. As for my mood, I feel great sadness, as I now do every time I leave this house, even though I am no more than a passing stranger in it.

Yet I also feel a glimmer of hope. I know my present mood will pass as soon as I am with my friend Eugène[1] in Algiers, when there

1 Eugène Letord.

will be new impressions for me to take in.

In any event I must work, and write, over there... My God, if I could only muster the energy to buckle down and finish part at least of all I have got to do! Would it not be a better idea to start my description of my trip through Algeria with Bône rather than Algiers? If I came across any impressions that warrant recording, I could present them as recollections from another period. That would give me the opportunity to produce some splendidly melancholy pages, in the vein of African perspectives.

That trip will give me the material for a book, a good one I can write quickly and that can perhaps be published before *Rakhil.*

I sometimes feel so pessimistic I look at the future with a feeling of irrational terror, as if it can only be bad and terrifying, even though many of those dark clouds have in fact gone from my horizon.

Isabelle quits Marseilles and returns to North Africa, arriving in Algiers on 22 July.

Algiers, 22 July 1900, 11 p.m.

It was hot yesterday afternoon when I boarded the same ship I took last September.[2] I kept staring at Augustin's silhouette till it disappeared from view when the ship tacked. I then studied the view. The harbour was full of the powerful red and black shapes of transatlantic steamers.

Then came the city... to begin with, when the ship was in the middle of the harbour, Marseilles looked like a delicate palette of grisailles: the grey of the smoky sky, the blue tones of the mountains, the pinkish-grey ones of the rooftops... the lilac hues of the sea, while the hardy vegetation growing among the rocks provided so many dots of a greenish-brown... The green foliage of the plane trees, the cathedral's gilded cupolas and statue of the Virgin Mary were the only things to stand out in sharp and lively contrast.

2 Isabelle left Marseilles on 21 July 1900, on board the *SS Eugène Pereire*. She arrived in Algiers at 3 p.m. the next day.

Yet once the ship was at some distance, everything looked quite different: it was all a monochrome gold, so intense one could hardly believe one's eyes.

Spent a peaceful night on the sternside bench. Felt truly well; woke up by about 2.45 a.m.

Saw the sun come up while sailors were putting up the canvas. First there was a rosy dawn, then a crimson disc appeared, clear-cut in outline. Slightly above it were the lacy shapes of pink clouds outlined in gold.

All night long I had the feeling of mysterious well-being I always get when peacefully asleep with the ship's lights shining over my head.

I will continue this report tomorrow.

Algiers, the 23rd

Oh, the sense of bliss I had this evening, knowing that I am *back* inside solemn mosques and in the ancient hustle and bustle of the Arab quarter in the Rue Jénina!

Oh that extraordinary feeling of intoxication I had tonight, in the peaceful shadows of the great al-Jadid Mosque during the icha prayer!

I feel I am coming back to life again… ☽ *Lead us along the straight path, the one taken by those to whom you have been generous!*

For a long, long time all you could see of the Algerian coast was Matifou steeped in vapours…

Next one could see the Algiers triangle, with the old part of town looking like an avalanche of snow… this was followed by a splendid view of the entire panorama in full daylight.

After a very brief moment spent in my room with Eugène, he left and I went exploring by myself. My hat bothered me, though, for it set me apart from Muslims.

I went back to don my fez, and went out again with Ahmed, the manservant, to go to the al-Kabir Mosque. It was so cool and peaceful there underneath those white arcades. Went to greet the mosque's wakil, a venerable old man who sat in a side niche writing on his knee.

Nothing surprises him any longer. No undue curiosity, no indiscretion. I then went to that charming blue-tinted zawyia of Sidi-Abd-al-Rahman.

Stood for a while in the cool shade facing the mihrab upon those thick rugs. Drank some jasmine-flavoured water from the earthenware pitcher on the windowsill.

The zawyia is one of great beauty, and I will certainly go back there before I leave Algiers.

Dashes of an unvarnished bluish-white among the greenery in the Jardin Marengo.

Smelled a sweet and heady fragrance I could not place as I walked through it, of flowers I could not identify.

Had supper at Al-Haj-Muhammad, on the corner of the Rue Jénina. Felt *intensely* happy to be here again, on this African soil to which I feel tied not only by memories but also by that strange appeal it has always had for me, even before I had ever seen it, when I was still living in that boring *Villa* of ours.

I felt so happy sitting at that table, a feeling impossible to describe, one I have never felt anywhere but in Africa.

How much Arabs resemble each other!

At Haj-Muhammad's yesterday I saw men come in whom I thought I had known in earlier days, in Bône, Batna, or in the South... but not in Tunisia, where they look very different.

After dinner this evening, went to say the icha prayer in the al-Jadid Mosque which is less beautiful than the two others, but the soaring sense of Islam was superb.

The place was cool and dark as I went in, and a handful of oil-lamps were the only source of light.

A feeling of ancient Islam, tranquil and mysterious.

Stood for a long time near the mihrab. Somewhere far behind us a clear, high voice went up, a dreamlike voice that took turns with that of the elderly Imam standing in the mihrab where he recited the *fatiha*.

Standing next to each other, we all prayed as we listened to the exhilarating yet solemn exchange between those two voices. The one in front of us sounded old and hoarse, but gradually grew louder and louder till it was strong and powerful, while the other one seemed to come from somewhere high up in the mosque's dark reaches as it sang triumphantly in regular intervals of its unshakable, radiant faith in Allah and His Prophet... I was in ecstasy as my heart soared up towards the celestial sphere from whence the second voice poured forth in sweet and confident bliss.

Oh, to lie upon the rugs of some silent mosque, far from the noise of wanton city life, and, eyes closed, gaze turned heavenwards, listen to Islam's song for ever!

I remember the time I wandered around till daybreak one night last year. I ended up by the Morkad ruins at the foot of the minaret, where the windows were all lit up. In the dead silence of the night I heard the muezzin's voice, which sounded infinitely mysterious as it sang ☾ *Prayer is better than sleep!* Those rhythmical notes still echo in my ears.

After the icha prayer, which is a lovely moment of the day, I went out for an aimless stroll.

Upon my return around ten o'clock, I spent some time in front of a small shop in a narrow street. The place was lit by an oil lamp. A guitar, pipestems and decoration in the form of paper cutouts.

The shopkeeper was stretched out on an oval mat in front, a dark, handsome indifferent-looking man whose gestures were very slow, as though his mind were elsewhere. Might that have been due to kif?

Bought a small pipe and some kif.

That more or less sums up what I did yesterday.

The day of my arrival has turned out to be an incomparably happy one.

Isabelle now begins her journey southward to the Souf region, where she sets up house in El Oued.

El-Merayer, 30 July 1900

Left Algiers on 27 July, eight o'clock in the morning.

Frame of mind fairly good, but spoiled by the presence of Lieutenant Lagrange's mistress, a horrible revolting creature.

At Sidi-Amram, I lay down near some burning dried djerid, next to a French soldier who had turned up out of the blue; drank some coffee, felt weak, slightly feverish. The fire's flames cast a strange red light upon the mud walls, underneath the stars.

*

Tuggurt, 31 July 1900, Tuesday noon

I am sitting in the obscurity of the dining room, to get away from the innumerable flies in my own room.

I am pleased to see the desert's torrid heat does not bother me too much, even though I am not feeling altogether normal because I am worn out by my journey and recent late nights. I can work and think. In fact, it is only today that I am beginning to recover. I will not really feel well, though, until the day I have settled in El Oued and all is quiet around me.

I am also beginning to find out about thrift and the willpower it takes to avoid squandering the little money I have left.

I must also remember that I have come to the desert, not to indulge in last year's dolce far niente, but to work, and that this journey of mine can either mean disaster for the rest of my life, or prove a prelude to salvation for both body and soul, depending on how well I manage.

I have an altogether charming memory of Algiers, from the first night to the last in particular.

The last evening I went with Mokhtar and Abd-el-Kaim Oulid-Issa to a tobacconist's on the Plateau Saulières. We had a rather lively conversation, and then went for a melancholy stroll along the quays. Ben Elimaur, Mokhtar and Zarrouk, the medical student, softly sang wistful Algerian songs.

I had several moments of great and altogether Oriental intensity at Algiers.

The long journey I made in third class, alone with someone as young as Mokhtar, also had its charm.

I have said farewell to the big Blue Sea, perhaps for a long time to come.

I travelled through wild Kabyle territory and a landscape of jagged rocks. Then, after the hills of the Portes de Fer, came the desolate plateaux gilded by fields cultivated by Arabs – long dots of a tawny-silvery hue upon the landscape's oranges and ochres.

The plains at Borj-bou-Arérij offer a desperately sad and dreary spectacle.

Saint Arnaud is a large village lost among the high plateaux of

Cheonïya country. Yet Saint Arnaud, *Elelma* in Arabic, is a verdant spot. Its gardens are like those of the Randon column at Bône.

The Cadi is a noble and serene old man, who belongs to another age.

In ten, twenty years' time, will today's young Algerians resemble their fathers and be as steeped as they are in the solemn serenity of their Islamic faith? His son Si Ali seems at first sight to be sleepy and heavy. Yet he is an intelligent man who does care about the public interest. Si Ihsan, who is of Turkish origin, is a man whose charm lies in his candour.

Had an intense and ever so pleasant sense of old Africa and Bedouin country the first night at Elelma: there was the distant sound of dogs barking all night long, and the crowing of the rooster.

Crossed the Ourlana oasis around two in the morning last night: vast gardens enclosed by walls made of clay, segniyas reeking of salt-petre, humidity and fever.

The houses built of ochre-coloured mud all seemed to be in a state of slumber.

At Sidi Amram I stretched out on the ground by a fire that was burning dried djerids. The sand felt warm and the sky was ablaze with countless stars.[3]

Oh Sahara, Sahara so full of perils, you hide your soul in bleak inhospitable solitudes!

I love this country of sand and stone, inhabited by camels and primitive men, and dotted with treacherous shotts and sebhkas.

Between Mraïer and El Berd last night I saw bizarre, fetishistic forms garbed in red and white rags, at the exact spot where a Muslim was assassinated a few years ago. It is a forlorn monument put up in memory of the man who lies buried at Tuggurt.

Borj Terjen, 1 August, 7 a.m.

Set off from Taïbet at 4.45 yesterday afternoon on N'Tardjallah's mule with Muhammad al-Haj. Reached Mguetla by nine o'clock.

3 Isabelle noted in the margin: 'There was a French soldier there who had turned up from nowhere.'

In spite of slight fatigue, had excellent impression of first encampment.

A wind that was almost cold during the night, and in the dunes a murmur like that of the sea. A feeling of desolation, for no reason at all.

Magnificent sunrise. Arose at 4 a.m. A pristine sky, cool and rather strong north-easterly wind.

Set off at five o'clock. Struck camp and made coffee in the dunes. The mailcoach caught up with us. Rode a camel till Terjen. Arrived at eight.

Excellent frame of mind. State of health, *ditto*.

How wise I have been to leave Europe and decide to make my home in El Oued, which is what I did yesterday. Provided my health holds up, I must stay at El Oued as long as I can.

Above all, I hope this is not a waste of time, especially vis à vis my intellectual and spiritual development and my literary endeavours. ☺ *Please Allah!*

El Oued, 4 August 1900, 7 a.m.

As I finished writing in my diary at Terjen, I sat down on my bed, facing the door.

Had an indescribable sense of well-being and profound bliss at being there... Siesta interrupted by children and goats.

Left with the mailcoach around 2.30 p.m. Intense heat. Did not feel well. Mounted the camel once more. Reached Mouïet-el-Caïd by maghreb [6 p.m.].

By 4 a.m. off to Ourmes, where we arrived by half-past seven. Crossed the biggest dune and came upon several dead camels, one of which was a recent casualty.

Ourmes. Siesta in the park. An enchanted sight. Did not sleep well because of inevitable flies and hot burnous. Was at El Oued around maghreb.

Went to see a house that belongs to a Caïd, on the town square opposite the Borj. Rented it. Have started moving in.

The evening of my arrival, beautiful ride on mules. A night that looked transparent on the white sand. A deep garden, fast asleep in darkness. Nothing but things cool and mellow all around.

Have now reached my goal at long last; now I must get to work with all the energy I can muster. As soon as I receive the money from Eugène, I must pay the rent, Habib, and buy basic necessities.

My luggage is to arrive today. As soon as I am living in less of a makeshift situation, I shall have to start writing the book about my journey, the first chapter of which will deal with Marseilles.

I am far from society, far from civilisation. I am by myself, on Muslim soil, out in the desert, free and in the best of circumstances, except for my health and even that is not too bad. The outcome of my undertaking is therefore up to me...

4 August 1900, 3.30 p.m.

I am beginning to feel bored, for my luggage has not turned up and I cannot get on with my house and life...

Habib's house. A square building of unbleached toub, in one of the winding streets paved with fine sand, not far from the dune.

Off in a corner is a small dark goat with an amulet around its neck. Habib's many brothers come and go. The old man's wife, tall and slim, dressed in long white veils, a veritable mountain on top of her head: braids of black hair, braids and tassels made of red wool, and in her ears heavy iron rings held up by cords tied to the hairdo. To go out, she throws a blue veil over it all. A strange, ageless figure with a sunburnt skin and doleful black eyes.

Temperatures will soon start going down. There is already a little gust of wind from time to time.

To sum things up, I have not yet embarked upon my new way of life. Too much of it is still unsettled.

El Oued, Thursday 9 August 7.30 p.m.

For the time being there is nothing durable about this Arab lifestyle of mine, which is indolent but in no way dangerous for I know it will not last. My little household is beginning to look like one. I am still short of money though.

I must avoid borrowing any from the bach-adel, for he is clearly no altruist.

A few days from now I expect to change my lifestyle altogether.

Every evening we go to Bir Arby. We go across the snow-white sands translucent in the moonlight. We pass the gloomy-looking silhouettes of the Christian cemetery: high grey walls with a black cross on top… The impression is a lugubrious one. From there we go up a low hill, and in a deep and narrow valley we see the garden, which is no different from any other Souafa garden. At the bottom stand the highest palm trees, the smaller ones grow near the wells.

In the bluish-green light of the moon they look diaphanous, like delicate feathery plumes. Between their handsome chiselled trunks lies the odd verdant stretch of melons, water-melons and fragrant basil.

The water is clear and cool. The well's primitive iron frame made a squeaking noise and the goatskin fell in and made lapping noises in the well's dark interior before surfacing again, dripping wet. I threw my chechiya down on the sand, soaked my head in the oumara and took a few greedy gulps of water. It was refreshing and cool, and gave me the sort of shiver that a drink of water always does down here. After that we stretched out on the sand for a moment.

Slowly and laboriously, we headed back for the sleeping town and that white house that is now my home, God knows for how long…

Isabelle meets Slimène Ehnni, and begins to frequent the Kadrya confraternity to which he belongs.

A few nights ago I spent a night in a large garden that belongs to the Hacheich Caidat, west of El Oued, together with Slimène.[4]

Not a soul was breathing in the palm trees' shadows. We sat down near a well where I had unsuccessfully tried to draw water with a torn

4 This is Isabelle's first mention of Slimène Ehnni, a quartermaster of the Spahis, whose acquaintance she made one evening in the cool garden at Bir Arbi, and who was to become her husband. She refers to him as 'Rouh', 'Zouizou', and 'Ouïha Kahla'.

oumara. We both felt sad, in my case because of the trouble owing to local indiscretions which loomed large in my mind.

My soul has aged, alas. It has ceased to delude itself and I can only smile at Slimène's dreams. He does not believe in eternity but thinks that earthly love goes on for ever. He also wonders what will happen in a year's, in seven years' time.[5]

Yet what would be the use of telling him, of making him sad and hurting him. That will happen soon enough, the day we go our separate ways.

After an hour spent talking, with tears in our eyes, about the truly awful possibilities ahead, we went to sleep under the palm trees on top of our burnous, using a thickness of sand for a pillow.

Slept till about 2.30 a.m. In the rising pre-dawn chill, we laboriously retraced our steps up the path through the dunes. A maze of tiny alleyways reeking heavily of saltpetre, rather like the Oued Rir oases. Crossed the marketplace which was deserted except for a few camels and their drivers, asleep by the great well's iron frame.

Rode the bad white horse last night, taking the road to Kouïnine through El Oued's tiny suburbs, where black and white goats graze on top of the roofs of zéribas made of djérid.

To the west, in the direction of Kouïnine and Tuggurt, the sun was a ball of blood sinking in a blaze of gold and crimson. The slopes of the dunes seemed to be on fire below the ridges, in hues that deepened from one moment to the next.

This morning the sky looked dark and cloudy, a most unexpected sight in this land of implacably blue skies and perennial sunshine.

The fact is that at the moment my time is not being put to good use. The siesta hour has a lot to do with that.

I would like to start working. That would mean getting up for reveille, at the very least, and not going back to bed after Slimène has left… I do, alas, from sheer boredom and from the fact that I have nothing else to do.

I must go out right after reveille, for the occasional morning ride, on whatever horse happens to be available.

5 Isabelle noted in the margin: 'A year's span! A year has gone by, and my life is linked to his for ever!'

Spent a quarter of an hour taking measures against the swarms of flies in my two rooms. The day will come when I will cherish the memory of such tiny chores in this very simple lifestyle of mine.

Oh, if my present way of life could last, if Slimène could continue to be the good friend and brother he is right now. And if only I could share more in the local side of life and get to work as soon as the weather starts to cool!

When a girl gets married over here she is taken to her husband on a man's back. To see his wife, the husband must hide for seven nights, come after the maghreb and leave before the morning.

Obviously a vestige of the abductions of earlier days.

18 August 1900, 3.30 p.m.

Went riding by myself last night, through the little townships all along the road to Tuggurt. Went through Teksebet. A melancholy, derelict-looking place, virtually deserted, where ruins crumble with every step.

Headed back for El Oued by sundown. Watched the sand pour down the greyish dunes in a constant stream.

Getting in the saddle yesterday I heard nearby wails, the Arab way of broadcasting someone's death. The daughter of Salah the Spahi, young Abd-el-Kader's sister, had died.

The little girl was buried in the hot sand yesterday at maghreb... she was swallowed up for all time by eternal night, like one of those meteors one sees flashing through this land's infinite sky.

Isabelle travels around the area on her horse 'Souf', named after the region.

Monday 9 October 1900, 9 a.m.

Shortly after the maghreb last night, rode Souf by the back of the café through the white sandy streets along houses that are half in ruin.

A few moments earlier, just as the sun had been about to set and

El Oued had been ablaze in gold, I had spotted the silhouettes of two Arabs garbed in white standing on top of the little dune where the lime kiln is; they looked as if set against a heavenly light. The impression was a biblical one, and I suddenly felt as if transported back to the ancient days of primitive humanity, when the great light-giving bodies in the sky had been the object of veneration...

At that frontier between town and desert, I was reminded of those autumn and winter sunsets in the land of exile, when the great snow-capped Jura mountains seemed to come closer in an expanse of pale bluish hues.

It is chilly in the morning now. The light has changed colour. We no longer have the flat glare of stifling summer days. The sky is now a violent shade of blue, pure and invigorating.

Everything has come to life again, and so has my soul. Yet, as always, I feel a boundless sadness, an inarticulate longing for something I cannot describe, a nostalgia for a *place* for which I have no name.

For several days now, intellectual endeavour has seemed less repellent to me than it did this summer, and I think I shall go on writing. The wellspring does not seem to have run dry.

For the moment I do not feel up to taking off and parting from Slimène for ever, even if I could afford to do so. And why should I?

I feel a tranquil heart is mine at last; the same cannot be said for any peace of mind, alas!

Isabelle gets to know the two sons of the Grand Sheikh of the Kadrya, Sidi-el-Hussein and Si Lachmi.

El Oued, 27 October 1900, 9 p.m.

Went to Amiche on the 17th, to look for Sidi-el-Hussein.[6]

It was chilly when we left around six that morning. Arrived in

6 Sidi Hussein ben Brahim, mokkadem of the zawyia of Guemar, and one of the sons of the venerated marabout and grand sheikh of the Kadrya confraternity, the late Sidi Brahim. Isabelle received her initiation into the sect through Sidi Hussein, who was impressed with her devotion, but who also thought that she might prove useful to him with the French authorities, with whom he believed she was affiliated.

no time at all at Sheikh Blanc's great zawyia, which seemed quite deserted, near those vast and gloomy cemeteries. Set off again with two menservants, and passed houses and gardens which looked quite picturesque.

Found Sidi-el-Hussein at long last at the far end of Ras-el-Amiche, facing the infinite stretches of sand that lead to the distant Sudan.

Spent the siesta hour with the sheikh in a narrow primitive room with no windows. It was vaulted and had sand on the floor, and it constituted the whole interior of the house, which stands all by itself.[7]

A strange figure showed up, an almost black Southerner with burning eyes who suffers from a form of epilepsy that makes him strike at anyone who touches or frightens him... Yet he is also very congenial. Left at about three o'clock with the sheikh for the Chaambas colony. Set off again by myself around 3.15. Reached the cemeteries located to the right of Amiche by sundown. At the maghreb hour, stopped on the dune that overlooks the Ouled-Touati.

On my left the plains looked pink, and in the village I saw a few women in blue rags and an oddly shaped red dromedary. Utter peace and silence all around... Came back home around 5.15 p.m.

I have now reached a state of destitution foreseen for some time. Yet, in bringing me to El Oued, Providence seems to have wanted to spare me worse suffering in other places.

Who knows, it may be that all these strokes of bad luck will merely serve to forge my character and pull me out of the indolent *indifference* that often comes over me when the future is at stake.

May God help me succeed! So far I have always survived even the worst and most perilous of pitfalls unscathed. Fate will not quite forsake me just yet, perhaps. + *The ways of the Lord are inscrutable.*

7 Isabelle noted in the margin on 22 December 1900: 'A few days later, the house where we had that siesta was ravaged by typhus, which killed five people.'

OMAN

Catherine Fairweather

Catherine Fairweather's (1963–present) itinerant childhood as the daughter of a British diplomat and a Greek-Russian interpreter and author mother, living and being educated in countries as diverse as Italy, Angola and Laos, shaped her 22-year career as a travel writer and editor (for *Porter* magazine and previously, *Harper's Bazaar*). She satiates her continuing desire for movement with frequent travels to far-flung places – most recently Armenia and Nagorno Karabakh on a personal mission to trace her forgotten forebears – and shuttles between her 'landing pads' in Greece, a London office and Somerset where she lives with her photographer husband, Don McCullin, and her 16-year-old son in an old cottage which remains blissfully removed from any known mobile-phone network.

On the Sands of Time

Cradled between the grapefruits and the lemons in the fruit bowl of my Somerset kitchen are the geodes that my son looted from an Omani sand dune when he was ten years old. He pocketed them as they lay scattered around our desert camp, knobbly and uninteresting as small cauliflowers. But crack one open and there is a surprise: a fistful of sparkling quartz, a bit of geological, millennia-old magic; a perfect schoolboy memento of a journey to Rub'al-Khali, the 'Empty Quarter', the world's largest, driest and most inhospitable sand desert, whose shifting borders stretch deep into Saudi Arabia, Yemen, UAE and Oman.

We had travelled into this desert within a desert, Wilfred Thesiger's beloved Arabian Sands, during one half-term break. Reading this adventure classic as a navel-gazing adolescent, I was drawn to the idea of deserts as hostile 'blanks in time' with 'no intelligible history', the ultimate introspective empty space or canvas onto which you can paint your own narrative. But it's a measure of how we travel now, that even this most remote and harsh area of the globe, which fifty years ago was unreachable and reviled, seemed to be a perfectly acceptable escape for a nearly middle-aged woman to camp with a ten year old (and a retinue of support vehicles and staff) in tow.

We acclimatised first in the city of Salalah in Southern Oman, a balmy coastal city wrapped in banana, papaya and mango and coconut groves, the historical gateway of the incense trade route that reached to Mesopotamia, Zanzibar and beyond from its ancient port of Khor Rori, where the Queen of Sheba shipped her precious cargo of frankincense back to her Yemeni strongholds. There was no one there when I visited the ruins from which the sea has now been divided, only the roped off paraphernalia left behind by absent archaeologists. Beyond the site, the white-sand beaches unroll, broad and long as highways, bordered by the pale jade of the Arabian Sea. Dolphins rock in and out of the swell, and dark smudges in the water turn out to be great shoals of sardines hauled in by the netful by fishermen along the shores. These are destined, not, as I discover, for our table, but as fodder for the herds of camels who pad soundlessly across the shores as though they were walking on water and not on firm-packed sand, and who maintain an aura of regal sanctity despite the manic flapping of the hungry seagulls.

Stretching out the days in this charming city set between ocean and the edge of the lush mountainous hinterland of the Jebel Qara, a city which as the only corner of Arabia to catch the tail of monsoon or khareef, is invariably and incongruously cloaked in mist, it is easy to be dazzled by the green abundance, easy to be lulled by soporific effect of soft rain pattering on the tent canvas for successive days, so that we can only guess at the grim realities of the great explorer Wilfred Thesiger's experience of the interior: 'a bitter, desiccated land that knows nothing of gentleness or ease'.

But soon we were leaving the city, its minarets disappearing in the cloak of fog that drapes over the wadis shiny with a volcanic glass they call desert varnish. Tarmac gives way to gravel and then sand and out on the endless plains, the scattered thousand year old geodes crunch like Malteasers beneath the tyres of the 4x4 on the spine-jarring drive into nowhere. The hypnotic monotony and featureless horizons are alleviated only occasionally by the sight of a nodding donkey, signs of the oil production that has yanked Oman out of the Middle Ages, given it political independence and a strong economy. In the five decades since the current Sultan Qaboos bin Said al Said came to power and reversed the extreme conservatism of his father's regime that also banned sunglasses or Coca Cola as being 'Western' and corrupting, he has modernised the country, built schools and hospitals, given women the vote and made it one of the safest countries to travel in the Middle East. And so it is that with shades firmly clamped to eyes against the sun and Cokes in hand, our modern day caravanserai of one lone woman and a child including one support vehicle, makes air-conditioned tracks across the desert crust. Hours pass, the temperature gauge flashes 39 degrees outside. What can I see outside the window? It makes for a challenging game of I-Spy. A cloudless sky, the odd group of lolloping flabby-lipped camels. Ah! there, a pyramid-shaped hill, a granite boulder, and suddenly, to spice things up a bit, a tree. We screech to a halt. We pile out of the cars. No ordinary tree this, for burnt and twisted though it seems to be, this, the Boswellia Sacra is the source of the precious crystallised resin, frankincense; the amber-coloured sap still valued as a digestif, an aphrodisiac, air-sweetener and a medicine, that we had bought bagsful of in the former slave markets in Salalah. Growing only in Southern Arabia and the Horn of Africa, in pre-bible times it was more revered and valued than gold for the part it played in pagan rituals. It is one of the gifts the Magi presented to the Baby Jesus in the manger in Bethlehem, I remind my son who remains underwhelmed, as we toast Boswellia Sacra with a ceremonial cup of tea in its puny shade.

But here in the desert, where there is no gentle transition between day and night, we know we must make camp before dusk. We release the air in the tyres in order to surf the sea of undulating dunes that soon rise up to meet us. In the fading light they glow every colour of vanilla, caramel and butterscotch, as soft and innocuous as Angel Delight whipped and scooped into giant peaks and troughs by wind over the millennia. The ten year old whoops and claps as he races down the windward side of the towering dunes, some of them 500 foot high, on a black bin liner. In the traditional black goat-skin majlis oriental rugs and cushions are strewn. I settle in. A line of camels in single file, crosses my line of vision as if in slow motion, a distant twister on the rising horizon, a djinn or genie as the Bedouins would have them be, sends up spirals of sand and dust. In the magic hour between day and night the sense of time unfurls. Mint tea pours slowly from a silver spout held aloft and warm pitta bread enveloping juicy yoghurt-and-saffron marinated lamb is served. Then there is silence: no evening birdsong, no ambient night insect's buzz, no rustle of vegetation, no bars on my mobile phone, just the sound of our breath and the steady beat of my pulse.

Back in Somerset, I chuck another handful of my frankincense on the hearth fire. Its earthy, resin smell brings back some memories; the driver guide Mussalim rustling around the camp in incense-scented robes, the apparently featureless landscapes with gnarled and stumpy sap trees growing out of the barren rock, the power of nothing in this great empty space that forces an existential sense of peace and calm.

Rather less of a benediction, is the imprint of the journey in the shape of a huge crescent-shape scar on my ankle, a skin graft that is the result of an insect bite (the notorious desert-spider) incurred after days walking over the dune and the sepsis that followed after foolish soaking of the ankle in a camel-contaminated oasis reservoir that almost lost me my leg.

The experience left a less-physical but lasting impression on my son, who has since grown out of the charmed age when his imagination was sparked by the treasures and tales from the lands of Sinbad and Scheherazade. The remaining geodes still remain, un-cracked and intact, and the camel's jawbone that he discovered beside the oasis, polished by the sun and sand still sits amidst a collection of fossils, flintstones and 'desert varnish', adorning our garden's dry-stone wall.

FORBIDDEN ROAD

Rosita Forbes

Rosita Forbes (1890–1967) was a rebel. At 27, she dumped her husband, pawned her wedding ring and tried to return from South Africa to England alone on horseback before detouring on a trip around Asia with a female friend, visiting 30 countries along the way. She was the first European woman to see the Kufra Oasis in Libya, disguising herself as an Arab in order to do so, and she later courted controversy by documenting a walk through a flower garden with Adolf Hitler. In Afghanistan, she drove from Kabul to Samarkand in a chauffeured lorry and wrote about it in *Forbidden Road*. Forbes also made an early travel film, *From Red Sea to Blue Nile* and was a fellow of the Royal Geographical Society.

Midnight on the Mazar Pass

We left Doab soon after it was light, but the camels had already gone. While I was trying to wash, in a chased silver basin rather larger than a breakfast cup, I heard them grunting as the bales were adjusted. Then they swelled past the window, their loads tossing in the half light like timber on a flood.

While Kuli Khan drooped about the lorry, and the driver fussed because he had lost a tool he couldn't describe, we walked beside the river. It was an ugly maroon colour. The rocks towered into immense pipes, violently red and yellow. Later on, they were a curiously hot purple powdered with snow.

The gorge continued for twenty-three miles to Talla, after which we came out of the mountains and found ourselves in a waste of crumpled hills. They were utterly arid and of a strange greyish gold. We left the lorry, to take photographs, and when it was out of sight we might as well have been on some lunar tableland. Nothing grew.

There were no birds, no sign of animal life. Far away on the horizon lay the snows of the second range we had to cross, but in between there was nothing but dead hills indescribably bleak, more frozen in their ashen yellow than if they had been covered with rime.

After traversing this silent land reft from the moon, we entered a narrow valley, pleasantly cultivated. It grew wider. Grass spread beside the stream and we saw the first yurts, precursors of Turkestan. These round, mushroom-like structures cluster in circles on the plains of Central Asia. They are the dwellings of Mongol nomads, of Usbegs, Tartars and Tadjiks, of the shepherds and the herdsmen who pack their belongings on bullock-back and move with the change of seasons.

These yurts are the equivalent of the black camel-hair tents which do not change between Jerusalem and Kabul, but they are made of reed matting mounted on curved poles. They are lined with strips of felt and covered with a goat's-hair cloth, bound down with ropes of hide.

In Central Asia every country begins before its authorised frontier. Peshawar is much more Afghan than Indian, and now, between the two ranges of the Kush, we found ourselves in the Steppes. Pathans had disappeared with their fortified villages. Here were unarmed riders, with smooth, round faces and short legs. Their horses were small and well bred. The loose, long-ended turbans had gone with the bearded men of the South. Apple cheeks bloomed under fair hair and neatly wound headgear. The riders wore knee-length coats (chapans) of cotton heavily wadded and of the brightest colours. Their legs were encased in knee-boots and their stirrups shaped like coal shovels.

Forty-two miles beyond Talla, we came upon the first caraculi sheep. They were black, brown and grey, with closely curled fleeces, and in this distant valley, shut away among the hills, inhabited by nomads who have never seen a town or heard of a railway, they represented trade born of fashion. For these sheepskins acquire a dozen different names before, as the best broadtail, they sell for fabulous prices in Bond Street and the Rue de la Paix. In Northern Afghanistan a ram is worth about 1500 Afghanis, and a ewe 80 to 100. The unborn lamb, called tagher, fetches 120 to 140 Afghanis according to its colour—grey and brown are more valuable than black—but the ewe has to be killed to get the best skin.

Two rams serve some five hundred ewes. The small farmers possess flocks of about this size. The big men may have fifteen or sixteen flocks, each numbering a thousand head. The poorest of all have a few caraculi sheep running with their goats. They keep any ewe lambs born and sell the males, or use their skins as currency on a journey. North of the Kush caraculi are liable to take the place of petty cash. The big men send their skins in bulk to Russia, but there are always shepherds who will sell uncured skins, still raw and bleeding, for the price of a few meals or some bitter green tobacco.

Two hundred and fifteen miles from Kabul, we came to Dowshi, which is a real Turkoman serai on the edge of the Steppes. There is no village. Booths made of straw matting had been set up at the confluence of the Andarab and Surkhab rivers. In front of them were collected a number of riders. Their horses were tethered within arm's reach. The wind of the Steppes played with the dust and tossed manes and tails into the air. A baker sat in the open surrounded by breads. He was making them one after another in a hole scooped out of the earth. He had only a handful of charcoal, but the cakes of bread which he whisked out of his primitive oven and spread round him, flat as pancakes, were excellent and very hot. We bought some and settled down on the pushtins in the shelter of a wall. In front of us a bridge that looked as if it were made of nothing but straw spanned the main river. The road had disappeared, but where it should have been there was a general impression of tea-pots and painted straw tents.

The crowd soon left their tea-drinking for the more unusual amusement provided by the sight of strangers eating out of pots. An enormous goat established himself beside us, and George used him as a waste-paper basket. For his appetite was voracious and unquestioning.

When we were at our stickiest and silted over with dust, a commotion on the other side of the bridge indicated the arrival of a personage. It turned out to be no less than the Foreign Minister, who had been shooting in a neighbouring valley. A lorry full of soldiers preceded him. A headman materialised out of the dust.

George went to meet the procession. In some remarkable way he had ceased to look smeared with butter, crumby, or dust-stained. With becoming gravity, the two men conversed. Together they walked across the flimsy bridge. In another moment, to the awed amusement of the spectators, the Foreign Minister had seated himself amidst the fragments of lunch upon the pushtin. He had just returned from England. Doubtless he remembered that even dukes sat in ditches to eat in a maximum of discomfort the indigestible food considered essential to shooters. So he carried off the unusual situation with the ease of manner habitual to his countrymen.

Kuli Khan was impressed. He produced coffee with an air of other concessions to follow. The crowd thickened. The goat indicated that he was still hungry. Several soldiers in tin helmets became officious. With a few sentences the Foreign Minister dispersed our mutual admirers. "I've sent them to pray," he said, "so they will be better occupied. It is mid-day."

The goat, being a heathen, remained with us.

While we drank green tea, which tasted less realistic than Kuli Khan's coffee, we enquired about the state of the road.

"We want to reach Haibak to-night."

"Haibak?" exclaimed the Minister, as if he doubted the very existence of the town. He continued to look disconcerted while he murmured: "Well—providing it does not rain——"

We all looked at the sky. Then, spurred by the evident distance of Haibak, we began our farewells. The Minister pressed upon us pheasants and a duck. With another startled glance at the sun, he begged us to hurry. We did so, with the result that half the bridge fell down—fortunately behind us.

For a few miles we kept to the valley, which was little more than the river bed. Then we came to the grass lands, in which the road as such ceased to exist. Vague ruts ran across a green desert. The lorry bucked over hillocks of every shape and size. Its action reminded me of many a good day's hunting with plenty of fences and deep plough between them.

After several hours, in which we had made negligible progress, George said, "Intelligent fellow, the Foreign Minister." It was becoming evident to both of us that we should not arrive at Haibak. Later, we wondered if we should ever arrive anywhere.

But the plains were beautiful. It was the first time I'd seen such an expanse of green, smooth, rolling green, lush as silk and with the sheen and shadows of silk. In all that world, there was no other colour but green, until, emerging from the great, verdant dunes, we saw, far off, a blue-white snow-line. Near at hand was a nomad encampment. The yurts were dark growths among the grass and towards them, slowly, there came from every side a black tide of sheep.

The afternoon waned, and we drove westwards straight into the sun.

"It's the wrong direction," I said helplessly.

"Yes," said George. "We'll probably find ourselves back at Kabul."

The green continued, but it was fecund with young animals. Camels and their foals stood knee-deep in what appeared to be pools of lilac water—but they were flowers. Herds of wild horses galloped by with their tails streaming in the wind. A gentle dusk fell upon the plain and fires began to glimmer among the scattered encampments. Riders hurried past us. The hoofs of their small, sturdy horses made no sound. Their rifle-barrels gleamed in the pale clarity that belonged neither to the day nor the night. While this half-light continued we came to a large and straggling village, whose houses seemed to have been transported from another country. Nothing could have been more alien to the Steppes. For, within an outer ring of yurts and straw hovels huddled a collection of the square mud dwellings familiar to the Punjab. They were indescribably dirty and forlorn. From them came people equally waif-like, who spoke to us in a tongue that was neither Persian nor Pushtu. Patiently George questioned, and they answered, "Aa-oh." Changing his tactics, he indulged in a slow and cheerful monologue. Gradually, a few distinctive sounds punctuated the repetition of "Aa-oh."

"That's better," said George. "They're getting used to us."

By this time Kuli Khan must have been considerably shaken, for since lunch he had bounced continually between the roof of the lorry and the baggage which now rolled about inside it, but he leaned cautiously above us and produced an entirely new speech. The Ishmaels who stood round us, wild, dark and terrified, began to show signs of understanding.

"You can't hurry them," said George. "You've got to give them time to gape at us and decide we're human." He began to talk about the places we'd come from and the state of the road. "No use asking a question—they won't answer."

But Kuli Khan was still crooning in clipped syllables and eventually one of the tattered men said, "Ghori—Aaoh."

Kuli Khan looked perplexed. "I think," he said, "this place must be Ghori—unless, of course, it's Aaoh—but why it's here at all I can't imagine."

He asked for information on this point, and the men's heads sunk suddenly between their shoulder-blades. Not another word came from them.

Defeated, we bumped past the disreputable village. It sprawled like a disease upon the lovely plain which still contrived to look untrodden and immune. Sombre men, in type neither Pathan nor Mongol, shambled past us, their coats bulging with young animals. From between the torn wadding peered the delicious, intelligent faces of kids and the less responsive ones of newly-born lambs. Beyond the last houses was a tea-khané of the roughest description. The owner had faded to the colour of clay, but he still had the use of his tongue. While we drank a muddy liquid that bore little resemblance to tea, and George, who liked feeding things, attempted to ruin the digestion of a wild white horse with yeastless bread, he told us that the dumb people, who still looked as if they were exiles, had been transported from the neighbourhood of Kabul forty years ago. They were Chinzais and they had proved too turbulent for the local authorities, so, bag and baggage, they had been moved north of the Kush, and they hadn't yet got used to it!

While we talked, a gaily-painted lorry blundered through the mud, to disgorge a mass of passengers in front of the tea-house. Among them Kuli Khan found an acquaintance from whom he had separated at Dowshi. With hands clasped, they gazed ecstatically at each other and at the wild grass country, shadowed now and formless.

"Come with us," urged Kuli Khan, for friendship to him was like food. It was also very beautiful. He could not bear to be parted again from this new, this satisfactory friend.

The other protested, "You cannot go over the pass to-night, and you cannot go to-morrow or for many days, because it will snow—yes, within a few hours, it will snow." That decided us. Kuli Khan was reft from his friend, who immediately began to argue with the driver of the painted lorry. He paused to call after us, "God will look after you, but fear not, for I myself will assuredly be behind you."

That was the last we saw of him.

Dusk fell and the Steppes had no end. For ever, it seemed to us, we should jolt across the yielding dunes that were grass instead of sand. Camp-fires outnumbered the stars. It seemed to me that heaven and earth were confused, so that the planets burned at our feet and the sky was full of sparks.

Shortly after leaving Ghori things began to happen. They happened mostly to the engine, and the driver spent his time bent over it or lying under it. In a cloud of perfume "Deadly Nightshade" leaped about the lorry searching for tools. Kuli Khan, less mournful than usual, produced a lamp.

In darkness I sat upon a mud-heap and wondered how soon it would begin to snow. "The radiator's leaking," said George, "and there's a choke in the feed-pipe. I think one wheel's a bit loose. It won't take long."

After an hour or so we started again. Strange noises went with us. Our lamps were less effective than the stars. When there wasn't even a yurt within sight, they went out. I suggested camping for the night. It seemed to me impossible to negotiate an unknown pass, probably deep in snow, without lights, but we had no tent, we were averse to clearing the lorry, and the temperature was Arctic. The deciding factor, of course, was the storm. We must get over the Mazar Pass while it was still open.

Slowly we progressed across invisible country. Sometimes Kuli Khan walked ahead. His exhaustion had disappeared. Even his voice changed. He was quite willing now to instruct the driver, advise George, put up beds, conjure food, lamps, extra clothing, from the welter of baggage with which he alone seemed able to cope. But we would not wait for him to display his talents.

I don't remember how many breakdowns we had before we reached the serai at Robatak, but by then it must have been about ten. The radiator had acquired the habits of a sponge. The brakes were slipping.

At Robatak, therefore, we woke the keeper of the serai and asked how far it was to the Pass. "Far, no," he said. "But high! So high it goes, it must reach heaven." He looked at the outline of the khaki beast couchant beneath the walls. "Your lorry may do it," he said, "but no other would." And at that moment a frightened man panted towards us, crying that a truck had gone over the edge of the Pass, the driver had been killed, everybody had been killed except the driver who could be heard screaming. He paused for breath. Perhaps, as there were so many screams, nobody had been entirely killed, but——

The keeper of the serai asked where the accident had happened—on the Haibak side? Yes. He drew a long breath of relief. No effort would be required from him. Fat and shapeless, he abhorred activity. While we asked him if we could sleep in the serai, we saw his features dissolve in the light of the hurricane lamp he carried. They wavered into a patchwork of uncertainty and the man himself drifted away from us, a jelly-fish into the darkness of the sea. Bereft of a guide, we pushed past a door-keeper and through the great arch into the serai. It was a huge open square surrounded by mud walls and in the thickness of these were windowless cubicles inhabited by men and animals.

Blundering about in the darkness, it was as if we looked into the cells of a man's brain and saw his thoughts as well as the actions to which they gave rise. For when we'd negotiated the mass of camels, bales and wadded drivers huddled about the yard, George opened the door of one room after another. In the first a man who had taken off his turban and looked, therefore, strangely naked in spite of his coats and knee-boots, stood with a knife in his hand. He was alone. His eyes glittered and he didn't move when we appeared.

Next door, a mare kicked at us and a small, hairless person twisted into the corner and lay with his head on his arms.

Further on, a husband made love to his wife. Both stared at us unblushing and said nothing.

In the last cubicle, three men sat round a pan of charcoal. Their heads were bent together. They talked in low voices. As soon as they saw us, they made a move towards the rifles stacked in the corner. There was a smell of sweat, dung, tobacco and something else. The presence of a solitary camel saddle—the padding can so easily be stuffed with charras—suggested smuggling, but we saw only the men's fear.

In the opposite cubicle, which we imagined empty, we fell over a lump of something living. I think it was composed of sheep and shepherd sleeping together for warmth.

Under the arch, within reach of the huge metal-studded door, there was a better room with rugs on the floor. But it was inhabited by a large and evil-smelling family who had already made the most intimate preparations for the night. Abashed, we backed out, and stepped immediately into the supper of some Kochis. A dish upset. A man cursed while he scrambled on all fours among the food. The camel which he was using as a pillow reared to its knees. In the subsequent confusion we fled.

"Better sleep in the lorry," I suggested. "There'll be some air."

"Too much," expostulated George.

"Not enough to ventilate 'Deadly Nightshade.'"

But Kuli Khan came to meet us. "The engine is going," he said. "I will sit on the mudguard with a lamp. The pass is near—in an hour we shall be over it." His tone implied that we were making a great fuss about nothing.

Supported by the driver, he had his way. We started. We stopped. We tinkered. Eventually we reached the foot of the Mazar Pass. In a series of hairpin bends the road shot out of sight. We crawled after it. Snow and frozen mud had drifted into twin breakers. Between these we could see the ruts made by the lorry that had gone over the edge. But we could see little else. A yard to the right the drop was invisible, but occasionally we heard a stone fall.

On bottom gear we crept along the base of the cliff. Its solidity was reassuring. Every hundred yards or so we had to stop, for the engine was overheating and in spite of chains the wheels could not grip. They spun helpless in the slime, and when we skidded only a rim of ice-bound scarlet mud separated us from the precipice. It was a curious situation, for we could do nothing to minimise the risk. From the front bench, with the greaser breathing heavily over my shoulder, I saw Kuli Khan crouched upon the outer mudguard and beyond him the snow breakers rearing up against a wall of darkness. George walked behind, putting stones under the wheels whenever we showed signs of going backwards instead of forwards. Occasionally he said, "We can't be far from the top." But it was too cold to talk.

On the steepest slope, the lorry settled down with a bump. After a hurried application of stones, the driver buried himself under the bonnet. Kuli Khan produced a scrag-end of meat. From it we tore strips and ate them in our fingers. If possible, it grew colder.

By this time, hours had ceased to exist. The night had become an indefinite period. I saw no reason why it should ever end. We got out and pushed. The engine made noises. We pushed harder. The mud spat into our faces.

Then the pump burst and clouds of smoke poured from the engine. At this moment the moon chose to sail out of the clouds and we saw the pass which we'd imagined close at hand suspended far above us like a cable between two posts.

Till then the driver had been silent. But when the pump had been mended and the whole lorry ransacked to find new plugs, he made his first remark. "Had I known," he said, "we should not have come——" But Kuli Khan interrupted with a reminder of Ali waiting at Mazar-i-Sherif.

"If Allah wills, we shall greet the Sherif in heaven!" retorted the driver.

For another immeasurable period we crawled upwards. Like a mule, the lorry seemed to prefer the outside edge. With two wheels on the border of eternity we slithered and twisted with the track until it seemed to us a living thing which we pursued into the darkness. To keep warm, we took turns with the stones which in moments of doubt—and they were frequent—had to be forced under the wheels.

I don't think any of us knew when we crossed the pass. The moon had gone. So had the fan belt. But the darkness was slipping away from us and the figure of Kuli Khan humped on the mudguard acquired a new perspective. "There is no more top," he called to us. The lorry began to buck like a hard-held colt.

At a terrifying pace we went downwards. George had become an image. The driver was clamped about the wheel. Kuli Khan lay flat upon the bonnet, but he still held the light. "What's happened?"

I asked, but nobody spoke. We were roaring down like a canoe caught in the rapids. Corners rushed at us and were gone. In a welter of stones and mud, with a screech of gears and a long-drawn hiss from the engine, we rocked over obstacles that we could not see. Below us lay wave after wave of hills. There appeared to be no end to them. Frozen and still, their crests filled an immensity of space that reached beyond our vision. The world had never seemed so large and so uninhabited.

An upheaval flung me against George. The lorry heeled and hesitated. "It's all right," said my British companion. "The hand-brake's gone."

Somewhere a dog barked. The road straightened. It acquired shape and purpose. "A village! There must be a village——" muttered the greaser, who had been exuding fear. But it was a long time before the succeeding hills gave way.

At last, when we'd given up all hope of arriving anywhere at any time, we saw a ghostly castle reared upon a mound. Its walls had crumbled. Its towers looked like decayed molars. "Haibak," came in a tenuous whisper from Kuli Khan, but the streets were deserted. On either side gaped empty houses. The doors were gone and the holes that had been windows peered with the effect of eyeless sockets.

Through this scarecrow town we went, searching for somebody alive, but there wasn't a sound or a movement. Kuli Khan left his post on the mudguard. I understood that he objected to ghosts and indeed, in the shivering grey light precursor of the dawn, I felt we might quite well meet something headless or otherwise odd.

Even George was affected by the spectral effect of a town without a single inhabitant. He said, "D'you think it was an earthquake, or no water?" but his voice became more normal when we saw a light.

Kuli Khan, with teeth chattering, leaped from the lorry and pursued it, although, as he afterwards explained, he felt "in his stomach" that it might be a ghoul if not one of those luminous serpents which lure travellers into a waterless desert, or a swamp according to the amenities of the latitude.

The light turned out to be a lantern held in the shaky hand of an old man who, hearing our shouts and fearing robbers, had decided to hide himself and his few pieces of silver in the well. Assured of his quarry's human origin, Kuli Khan soon frustrated this purpose. With one leg over the well and the Indian's hands half throttling him, the man choked and argued. George came to the rescue. "What has happened to Haibak?" he asked.

"Nothing."

For a moment the two of them glared at each other. Then it transpired that we had come to the wrong Haibak. The other, the new town, which was very fine—the old man registered awe—lay in a different direction.

"Will you show us the way?" We offered money, but our victim, who wore only a long cotton night-shirt and a skull-cap, said he was too old. He shook as if he had an ague, but we wouldn't let him go until he dragged from a bed of rags and straw in the corner of a mud hovel a grandson, who appeared to be half-witted.

In spite of Kuli Khan's reassurances, uttered in the voice of a mother to her first child, the boy would not put on any clothes, nor would he get into the lorry, which no doubt seemed to him a monster. While we backed and turned, the boy ran bare-footed into the country, his cotton slip blowing behind him, his knees so bowed that he looked like a fat, white frog hopping frenziedly in front of us.

"We can't let him go on like this," I protested. "He'll burst——"

But Kuli Khan was ruthless. "We must find some place to sleep, although it is long after to-morrow when we must immediately go on." The confusion of thought indicated exhaustion, for Kuli Khan's pessimism was usually presented in the fewest and most destructive words.

The boy continued to run until we instructed "Deadly Nightshade" to catch him and force him into the lorry. There followed a sharp struggle on the step. Prayers rocketed to Heaven. I held a very dirty handkerchief to my nose. Fortunately the boy escaped, leaving his night-shirt behind him; he slid like an eel into some bushes.

A little later, we found Haibak. The road ran suddenly into a modern bazaar with a rest-house at the end of it. Under its adequate roof, Kuli Khan's pessimism returned. "There is no furniture but beds," he said.

"What else d'you want?" I asked.

Words failed the Indian. He set a bucket on one bed, the lamp on another, and went out, trailing his gloom as a garment.

GRANDMOTHER'S FOOTSTEPS

Imogen Lycett Green

Imogen Lycett Green (1967–present) is an English author, journalist – and granddaughter of the writers John Betjeman and Penelope Chetwode. In 1985, the year before Chetwode's death, the teenaged Imogen accompanied her grandmother on a memorable expedition through India. Seven years later, she retraced their steps, starting with a three-day trek in the Kullu Valley to lay a memorial stone at the place where her grandmother had died. *Grandmother's Footsteps* is her account of that trip.

The Stone goes over the Mountain

'I love the companionship of animals. My idea of heaven is trekking alone on a pony through beautiful country; I feel I really get in touch with God.'

Paddy arrived in his jeep to pick us up at 7.30 a.m. on Saturday morning (we had not expected him to be on time at all and were still enjoying a breakfast of bananas and *dahi* when he arrived). Panchok, a small, wiry Tibetan, was ready and squatting beside my rucksack, smoking a *bidi* and guarding the stone.

With serene reverence the night before, Boura Singh had wrapped the stone in newspaper, straw and hessian, and tied it up with string. He was morose in the morning. He wanted to come with us, he said, in fact he didn't think we could possibly manage the trek without him. Watch those clouds, he said, as he gloomily stirred the tea in his godown.

Like a concerned parent, he instructed Panchok to look after me.

And don't put too much chilli in the *dahl*, he told him. Then he waved us off furiously, until our jeep had rounded the corner along the road back into Manali.

The bazaar in Manali was just beginning to show the first signs of waking. Wisps of grey smoke were rising from the Tibetan huts clustered round their Buddhist *gompa*, and the stallholders in the main street were sweeping the steps in front of their stores. Buses sat purring in the bus stand, and against a bill-covered wall beside the bus stand squatted Manbadur, our second man.

Panchok, the Tibetan, was short (he barely came to my shoulder) but Manbadur, a Nepali, was shorter. He looked like a leprechaun, with pointed ears and bandy legs. His smooth, tough, brown face folded into even creases when he smiled, and he leapt nimbly into the back of the jeep. He was shy and couldn't quite meet my eye.

The drive to Banjar, which is only twenty miles down the Kulu valley, took a good two and a half hours, as Paddy found it necessary to wave at every passing notable. Several times he stopped to conduct a shouted conversation with two engines' worth of clamour, after which he would accelerate off violently (so that Manbadur and Panchok and I lurched backwards), slapping his horn jovially in salute.

We also stopped halfway for provisions at a bustling market town called Bajaura. Panchok and Manbadur had a whispered conference and then disappeared into the market. I could not see them for apples and mounds of lentils and the dust raised by laden carts and straw in the packing boxes. Their tiny little fingers were lost between huge-bottomed housewives in lurid purple saris.

Not that that made them any the less skilled at efficient shopping. The pair of them returned half an hour later and handed me a list of thirty-four 'items', neatly drafted in Hindi on a piece of cardboard. I was baffled by the number of different things, as I knew that Panchok only cooked rice and *dahl* and sometimes cauliflower. I added tea to that and sugar, powdered milk, coffee, flour for chapattis and oil and still I counted only nine 'items' at the most. He began to go through the list in Hindi, but I was flummoxed after four names and could only hope that he had brought a whole spice rack with which to flavour his *dahl*. I anticipated a wide variety of mountain-top culinary delights.

My grandmother always complained about what she called DDD (damned dull dahl), the thick and nourishing lentil soup which provides the only protein in most Pahari diets. She used to stock her own supply of tinned sardines and chocolate bars and pistachio nuts. Rice and lentils are the staple diet of all the hill people, because vegetables are hard to grow high on the hills, and eggs are rare and precious. Rice and lentils are also the cheapest commodities available. You can dine out in a roadside eating-house on such a menu for 5 rupees a head, which is about 14p, and the restaurateur will go on filling your plate until you are sated – a case of 'have as much as you can eat'.

I bought simply a bag of dried apricots in Bajaura for emergencies and trusted the rest to Panchok. I thought he ought to be able to conjure up something tasty from thirty-four different ingredients.

We trundled on down the main valley and then turned off left into a side valley up beside the Tirthan river (a tributary of the Beas). We halted for toilets at the rest-house at Larji where my grandmother had had a memorable egg curry in 1964 (so she wrote in her book). I doubt if the same *chowkidar* was still in residence, but whoever it was he gave us a strong *chai* (tea) each and told us that he had a party of Indian civil servants arriving that day for a weekend fishing trip – there's a good stock of trout on the river.

All over the lower Himalaya is a series of Public Works Department (PWD) rest-houses built by the British in the last century to accommodate the commissioners and engineers who walked all over those mountains inspecting their appointed regions. The Victorian bungalows crop up at ten-mile stages on all the old routes in and out of the valleys, and are now meant for use by Indian government officials. Each rest-house has a *chowkidar* who protects his particular property fiercely. A *ferhingi* (foreigner) is only permitted to stay after a certain amount of persuasion and on one condition – that if an Indian dignitary arrives in the middle of the night, that *ferhingi* will disappear quickly. It's a risk you have to take. Panchok seemed on speaking terms with all the *chowkidars* we encountered, and it became his job to negotiate the deal at each rest-house. I doled out packets of *bidis* where and when it was required.

The deal usually meant that we could use the kitchen (always a smoke-filled clay-built outhouse with an open wood fire or *chula*) and that when Panchok cooked our supper, it was understood that he'd cook enough for the *chowkidar* as well. I began to see why we needed thirty-four items on our shopping list when the *chowkidar* so often produced a friend or a son and his son's friend too.

We didn't stay to fish with the civil servants but climbed up a thousand feet to Banjar, where we all hoped Paddy's plan of operation would come into effect. Our first task was to raise Mensingh, the local Thakur, out of bed. Which might not have been difficult had not the Thakur built his farmhouse five hundred feet up a precipitous slope on the outskirts of the village. It was raining hard now, and Paddy and I stood under a black umbrella shouting up the mountain, while poor Panchok was detailed to race up the zigzagging goat track leading to the house to see where Mensingh had got to. Paddy had written to tell him we were coining, but it was impossible to tell whether he had received the missive or not.

He hadn't, it transpired, and he was most surprised to see us. He came bounding down the mountain after Panchok, in his pyjamas of all things and his eyes were stuck together and puffy. He had the pale skin and brown hair of a Kashmiri, and an air of relaxed confidence about him (which Paddy said came of his having been to Europe). Paddy gave him a cigarette to wake him up – which seemed to do the trick – and then we got down to business. However, at every suggestion Paddy made – to find a mason, to buy two bags of cement – Mensingh shook his head vigorously. I despaired.

Mensingh spoke English and he had been to France, but he was still an Indian, and for an Indian a shake of the head does not always mean no. It sometimes means no, but more often it signals assent. It is easy to forget this common Indian habit, and as Mensingh shook his head at every turn, I thought that we would never reach Khanag and lay the stone, for it seemed that he thought it was impossible to go to Khanag, impossible to get cement, impossible to carry the stone and impossible to find a mason. I was furious with Paddy for having built up our hopes for nothing.

In fact, of course, as Paddy explained to me after I had simmered down, it was possible to do all these things. We arranged that while

Panchok, Manbadur and I would walk up and over the Jalori Pass to Khanag, reaching the rest-house there in three days' time, Mensingh would see to the mason. Then, somehow, Paddy would get the mason, the stone, Mensingh and himself to Khanag in time to build a plinth for the stone.

The rest-house at Bajaura was lavish. A blue and white Victorian bungalow, it stood in its own lawns, terraced especially for it on the side of the mountain. Running along the front of the house there was a great glass enclosed veranda which was furnished with a three-piece suite in black leather. You could hear the water rushing in the river below. Paddy left me there and wished me luck.

Dinner was delicious. Panchok appeared at 6.30 p.m. looking flushed and pleased with a huge tray heavy with potato curry and fried cabbage and chapattis and rice and *dahl* and lime pickle and set it down before me. I had never been cooked for alone and I felt silly and spoiled when the monumental meal materialized, but I learnt that first night that my porters were eating the same food at the same time and that Panchok actually liked to cook and took pride in what he produced. If I left so much as a chapatti on my plate he would be disappointed. So I tucked in nightly to a series of varied vegetarian feasts and had no more say on the subject.

It rained hard in the night on to the corrugated iron roof over my head and the mosquitoes were persistent and aggressive, so I was up and out of that room at six sharp. I'd bought a smart black umbrella in the Banjar bazaar and I used that as my early morning walking stick. On my way down to the Tirthan river I came upon a smiley Sadhu, who was shrouded in the morning mist and swathes of orange cloth, and swung an umbrella, just like mine, on his arm.

Sadhus are Hindus who have rejected the material world for a nomadic life of prayer and pilgrimage. But there are many Sadhus in India who are not really Sadhus at all and Mytannion was one of those. He let down his tied-up dreadlocks especially for me and they tumbled, thick and dark and matted, to the back of his knees. He spoke perfect English.

'Will you come and see my ashram beside this heavenly river?' he asked. I followed him down the goat path, and with energetic swings of his dreadlocks, he turned his head to tell me about his German girlfriend.

'She has gone back to Germany, you see. We have two sons who are called Rama and Krishna but only in her homeland will they get the schooling they need.' He went on: 'And now I am so lonely.'

Then he showed me his beehives.

'You would enjoy to stay here at the ashram? It would be no more than 300 rupees for one night,' he said. 'I will teach you how to make honey and also to meditate.' Persuasive though he was, I explained I had my own mission to accomplish.

'I am leaving today for Khanag,' I said.

'And I must meditate all day and tend to my cabbages,' he said, dolefully. 'Would you come to the *chaikhana* [teahouse] for a glass of tea?'

I imagined him sitting there all day, gossiping and accepting handouts and tempting every passing stranger with lures of honey and heaven at his well-appointed ashram, and I declined. I hurried hack up hill to gobble down a chapatti with a banana rolled up inside it before Panchok, Manbadur and I put our packs on our backs to walk to the bus stop.

I like walking, and I wanted to walk all the way over the mountain, but Panchok and Manbadur and all Indians as well (sensibly, I suppose), think you are potty to walk when you might take a bus instead. I could not persuade Panchok that I would prefer to walk the whole way. There was a bus at 8.30 to Gaggi, five miles higher than Banjar, and we three were going to be on it. We were at the bus stop well in time, but the bus didn't come.

We made a place for ourselves on the sloping forecourt of the bus stand, which seemed to double as the market square and the town's meeting place. We waited there while a pan-wallah with red teeth set up his stall. He took some popcorn out of a dirty tin box and pushed it in fresh plastic bags to sell.

As we waited a madman asked me for a cup of tea. He wore a khaki uniform and a coloured pillbox Kulu cap into which he'd stuck a bunch of wild flowers as he marched up and down the market-place shouting military commands to the village at large. Nobody took any notice of him except me.

We waited as I listened to a woman vomiting in an upstairs room above a vegetable shop and I hoped it was a pregnant mother with nothing but morning sickness as three stubby (and grubby) children then came down the stairs. They stood giggling and shy and dared each other to cross the street to say hello to me, but then their attention was taken by three little boys in matching stiff prickly shirts and brown dungarees. The little boys marched in unison up the hill with their hair parted in the middle and oiled down each side, and their mother, trussed up in yellow chiffon, walked with mincing steps behind them, treading carefully through the market-place in her pink plastic sandals, as if she could not bear to touch such filthy ground. She glanced down with disdain at my three grubby friends as she passed. My stubby three with the vomiting mother followed the glowing family unit, all dressed in their Sunday best, and stared after them with wistful longing in their eyes.

We waited while a wiry man with a jeep, and a twitch on the left side of his face, told us the bus was cancelled and offered us a taxi service at an inflated price. But Panchok knew best and we waited on, for one and a half hours until our bus arrived. Perhaps the timetable was changed on Sundays.

When we got down at Gaggi, we had left densely populated bazaars worlds away. Gaggi was one short street with five or ten one-storey wooden houses on the left and five or ten one-storey wooden houses on the right. The track up which the bus had hauled us ended here. The bus turned round and went back down again and then the valley was quiet.

Panchok decided it was time for a cup of tea and a smoke, so I bent my head to enter one of the wooden houses on the right and we all sat down in line on a warped wooden bench. Tea is *chai* in India and this was a *chaikhana* or teahouse. But *chai* is not tea as you know it. It is brewed in a special way and you have to grow to like it because that is the only way it comes. There was no coffee up there in the hills.

Tea powder and milk powder and sugar and water are boiled up all at the same time in a saucepan on an open clay *chula* until the liquid is of syrupy consistency. It is poured from a height into small glasses and then poured from one glass to another for cooling purposes before it is set before you. It is warm and sugary and comforting.

So we had a cup of tea and a smoke. Panchok and Manbadur spoke the same language as each other which was slightly different from what the Paharis spoke, but they could all understand one another. Though I could not understand their tongue, we established a vague sign language and we always knew what each of us was on about. We sat together and walked alongside each other mostly in true companionable silence.

My two tiny pixies of protectors would not let me carry a thing. I sensed that Boura Singh must have had a word with them about that. I pleaded to be allowed, at least, to carry my rucksack with all its special straps and buckles that I loved to adjust so much, but Manbadur was firm. And then he ignored all my orthopaedically correct backstraps and strapped my pack instead to his shoulders with rope which he also wound round his head.

It would take three or four hours to walk up through the deodar forests to Shoja, our next stop, with a rest-house perched on a promontory just a mile below the pass. Now, after the bus rides were over, and the crowds were left in the valleys below, our trek would properly begin. We expected not to come across a single soul except for the odd herdsman with his flock of mountain goats or a woman gathering brushwood for her fire.

We expected too much. Not five minutes after our departure from Gaggi, a young man ran to catch up with us from behind, and introduced himself as Anul Kumar Arora. He was the only doctor in this wild region and he was walking that day to the civil dispensary at Kothi.

'Would it be of any inconvenience to you if I accompany your party for part of the way?' he asked, hopefully. We were so jolly and buoyed up with the mountain air that we didn't mind if he walked with us at all, but as the climb progressed through the thick ferns and the iris leaves of the forest floor, the magic of the woods enveloped us all and the doctor's remarks and comments and jokes began to pop up and irritate like uninvited guests at our private reverie. Our murky, dripping woodland atmosphere was crowded with his inane conversation. And I suffered most because he spoke English and directed his remarks at me.

'Actually, I do not like my mountain posting but it is necessary for a young doctor to do service in a remote area first of all... Actually I am bored by nature and I do not have any persons of interest to converse with... Actually, it is good to talk with you... Actually, I am perspiring because I come originally from the plains.'

Panchok was leading a fast march at this point up a steep and narrow goat track. He'd taken a short cut through the woods, and when Panchok veers off you follow, up however steep a goat path he happens to lead you.

Dr Arora continued: 'Actually, most of the diseases I attend to are respiratory and gastronomic. There are few casualties here... Actually I do not believe in these Gods... Actually with some bribery I may be able to take a better posting in the city.'

Uncharitably, I expect, I wished he'd bribed his official already for a distant posting. He was just the sort of handsome, charming young Indian that my grandmother tended to adore, and the sort of man she would have considered just right for me. One of her hobbies was fixing up her granddaughter with the right sort of Indian husband. Of course high-caste Indians would rarely take a Christian bride from abroad so we were usually quite safe, but that didn't stop her from making the preliminary arrangements.

This time, I wasn't in the mood. I had anticipated with relish our peaceful climb with not a word uttered in the still air, and with that prospect dashed I was even more distraught when the doctor came all the way to the rest-house and stayed for another two hours to talk incessantly and share my lunch. A proper monsoon thunderstorm then erupted across the skies and as he didn't have a coat or an umbrella it would have been mean to send the doctor off, so we had another discordant couple of hours together before I feigned exhaustion and sloped off 'for a rest'. He went then.

I sat on the yellow sofa in candlelight wrapped up in my Kulu shawl with a cold nose and cold toes. Panchok surpassed himself and arrived from the outside kitchen bearing delicious *dahl* and fried cabbage and rice and while I ate I read the myth about the Hindu demon goddess Durga killing the buffalo demon, to make myself brave and fearless.

Then I read the passage in my grandmother's book *Külu* which describes her preparations for bed on the night she spent there at Shoja rest-house in 1964:

> Went to bed in my pink silk and wool combinations, nightdress and jersey, with a tepid hot water bottle and my heavy hunting mac over the blanket which covered my sleeping bag. Even then I was cold and had to keep moving about to keep warm so I slept very little.

I went to bed in my thermal underwear, three shirts, pyjama trousers and slipper socks. I draped my Kulu shawl over my mountain sleeping bag, but still I fared little better than she had. There was deathly quiet that night in the Victorian rest-house, but it was not a companionable kind of silence.

The first thing I did in the morning was to wash my 'smalls' like my grandmother had always taught us. Then I climbed out of my various layers and had a cold bucket bath. Penelope had loved chucking jugs of cold water from a bucket over her body, so I steeled myself to perform this ritual daily. There was not exactly any alternative. After chapattis and *chai* with Panchok I felt washed and nourished and bold enough to venture out.

The grassy bank on which the rest-house sits in its commanding position at the head of the valley is covered in the leaves of irises. In May and June, the grassy bank is blue. But I just had to imagine that. I walked down on sheep paths to the village which hugs the steep side of the valley supported by terraces of crops. There were wild roses and horse chestnuts growing between the houses. There was meadow sweet and meadow crane's bill, ragwort, mint and sweet pea. There were whole fields of white sweet peas. I longed to try the fresh wild apricots that my grandmother had written about, but I didn't find any. And the apple trees and pears were fruitless too. There had been no rain that summer and the monsoons were only coming now, late, in September, so most of the high crops (unlike the valley crops) had failed.

The houses in the village and all the true Pahari villages in those hills are built in alternate courses of dry stone and deodar (Himalayan cedar) beams. On the ground floor the animals are often kept – a few cows or sheep and goats – and above them hay and corn may be stored. Round the top storey there is usually a veranda where the old men will sit and the toddlers will play and covering them is a chalet-style roof made with huge grey slates. There is no plumbing inside the house, and the villagers will wash their pots and themselves at the well or pump in the middle of the village. They go to the loo wherever they think is best.

Up and down the vertical village, the farmers who lived there stared briefly at me as I passed and then ignored me and went back to their work. In a flash of forwardness I showed a picture of my grandmother riding a pony up one of the mountain roads, to a man who was smoking a hookah on his veranda. He shook his head knowingly and said in his best English, 'Yes, I have seen her.' I supposed he meant five years ago, but I hoped he meant he had seen her spirit riding about more recently.

I poached a lot of peas and took great trouble shelling them and making sure there were enough for three and then I found some good strong mint, because I thought peas and fresh mint would be a welcome vegetable on the supper menu. When I showed my gatherings to Panchok he smiled in a sympathetic way.

'Good food,' I said and offered the mint for him to smell but he just looked knowledgeable and took it from me and threw it away.

'Not good food,' he scoffed. 'Not food.' He did the same with my preciously picked peas, threw them away and we had *dahl* and rice and fried cabbage for supper as usual.

The track which climbs the last stretch to the Jalori Pass is at first banked by irises, then ferns and lichen and then, near the top, lone tall fir trees and scraggy grass. There is no snow there in September but each time we climbed a few feet higher, our panorama of the far-off snows of the Great Himalaya grew wider. Every twenty minutes, Panchok would look round at me:

'*Bidi?*' he would say. 'Mmm, *bidi*,' I would answer, and we three would squat there on our haunches and smoke a *bidi* and survey the wondrous scene before us.

'Bot sunda! Bot sunda!' I could not help exclaiming at every turn. Panchok taught me this phrase which means 'very beautiful', and each time I said it he would nod in solemn agreement.

Then after a while spent gazing in silence he would turn and nudge us, '*Chelo*?' (Let's go), and on we marched.

We took tea in one of the three wooden shacks that are eating-houses at the 10,570 foot Jalori Pass, and huddled close in the biting wind. The cooks in their godowns were stirring lentil stew in anticipation of the needs of hungry travellers. The familiar smell of frying onions was a strange one to encounter at the top of a mountain pass. We ate only a stale and crumbly Marie biscuit or two with our tea and we did not linger.

Panchok led the way through the woods eastward along the top of the ridge to the holy Lake Saryalsar. The original route from Kulu to Saraj passed not where the rough motor road now crosses Jalori, where we had stopped for tea, but to the east at Lake Saryalsar. When my grandmother first entered the Kulu valley on horseback in 1931 with her mother, she must have come by the lake. She would have seen the view that we now saw, and she would, most probably, have been overcome by the magnitude of the mountains, as we were overcome.

She had probably slipped about in the mud as I was now slipping about. Panchok and Manbadur made a sandwich of me along the path to prevent me from falling but without fail I fell again and again on to my bottom, which they thought was very funny.

So we stumbled and I tumbled for those three high miles and we were in need of more hot beverages on arrival at the lakeside. Beside the small lake, which is fifty yards across and said to be full of live worms, is a shrine to Kali, the demon goddess, and wrapped in a blanket by the door was a very gloomy *pujari* (temple priest). His expression grew gloomier as I approached to have a look. Fog had descended and the outlook was grim, so in sympathy with his gloom, and to appease the goddess Kali and allow us smooth passage, I gave him eleven rupees. He looked gloomier still.

But there was a smiling *chai* wallah who cheered our hearts a little. He sat in a warm cave and he seemed glad to see us, and brewed up a saucepan of tea in our honour. He and the *pujari,* the only inhabitants of this spooky, raven-watched place, apparently were not on speaking terms.

Panchok found the atmosphere oppressive too and shortly uttered our moving off signal – *'Chelo?'* It was more of a command than a question, so Manbadur and I slipped in line for the last leg to Khanag. The euphorious morning's climb to the pass was overshadowed now, by the swirling mists of Lake Saryalsar, and we trudged down the sheep track, deep in thought. I was thinking about my grandmother, but I have absolutely no idea what they were thinking about.

We passed a Pahari woman who was watching her herd of cows with one eye and sewing a pair of *pulis* (string shoes) with a big needle. She had nine earrings in one ear and three black teeth. The Kului women wear a large, often checked, tweed shawl (a *pattu*) wrapped round them in such a way that it makes a long warm dress to the ground which is fastened on one shoulder by a sort of kilt pin. They tie a cotton scarf round their head like a gypsy. Since we had now come over the pass and out of the actual Kulu valley and into Inner Saraj, I could not call this woman a Kului, but her dress was still the same as we had seen on the other side. She beckoned us on past her and down to Khanag.

We could see the village now and the whole valley lay green and deep before us. We reached the village – a rough, ramshackle huddle of wooden and stone houses – and a group of perhaps ten boys and men were washing and fooling about by the pump. They wore skimpy trousers and their bodies were wet and glistening with soapy lather. The women on their verandas were knitting and the old men in the open-fronted tea shop abandoned their card game to follow us with their beady dark eyes as we pressed on down the main street. The rest-house sits alone, below the village, and it seemed we dragged our feet along the final last few hundred yards.

The rest-house itself is a brick-built bungalow with a corrugated iron roof and a wooden gabled open veranda which looks away from the mountainside over a round stage of a lawn. The lawn was edged with a tall and blooming border of mauve and white cosmos flowers. They were just the mauve and white of the checked shirts Penelope always wore and of her pinafores. Mauve was her favourite colour and I was absolutely sure that she must have seen to it that they grew there.

I collapsed on the veranda steps and I read what she had written about her arrival there in 1964:

> A more wonderful situation could hardly be imagined. In the foreground lay a little ledge of clover lawn with sweet-scented carmine, cabbage roses growing close to the bungalow veranda and beyond the lawn the *khud* fell steeply down the valley where you could see the torrent a long way below dashing in and out among the spurs of the mountain, while to the North West there was a great amphitheatre of deodars going round to the Jalori Pass, which was hidden by a fold in the hills.

It was heaven there, on the edge of the world. It was not India or Switzerland or England but a sort of magic land suspended between nations which might just as well have been Heaven. I minded so badly that my grandmother was not there in person but I was glad that she had died in the most wonderful situation she could imagine. I had no doubt that she was riding about there, still inspecting temples.

Just as I was feeling like the last person in the world, a short man with swept back hair, horn-rimmed glasses, a Kulu cap full of flowers and a long, smart, brown tweed coat appeared, leaping about like a dotty professor and gesticulating in a jerky way to his companion. His companion was a smiling, spacy looking young Sadhu in nothing but an orange sarong, slung so loosely around his narrow hips it seemed about to fall. The Sadhu kept kissing his mad master's knees. I thought, for a minute, that I was having an apparition.

The man in the brown tweed coat told me that he was the roads engineer of the district and that he lived in the cottage behind the rest-house with his personal Sadhu. The villagers later told me that he attended more to the Sadhu than to the roads and that he had a perfectly nice wife and ten children whom he kept in another village.

I invited the engineer to lunch, but it appeared he was fasting on some religious account, so it was just Panchok, Manbadur and I who sat down to sweet fried potatoes. (They would eat with me at lunchtime, but never at 'dinner'.) The plan had been for Paddy Singh and Mensingh to arrive here at Khanag with the mason and the memorial stone the next day. We would build a plinth and set the stone in plaster strong enough to weather the monsoon rains. Of course, the plan had now changed.

The communication system in the mountains was extraordinary. Panchok told me over lunch that now we were to walk back up to the Jalori Pass the next day by the motor road to meet Paddy at ten o'clock, because the jeep would be unable to manage the road any further down to Khanag, devastated as it was by landslides and as yet unrepaired by the recalcitrant engineer.

The *chowkidar*, whom we had met on our arrival at Khanag, had given this message to Panchok. How Paddy knew in advance from forty miles away up the Kulu valley at Manali that the last three miles of the mountain road had fallen into the *khud*, and how he had relayed his instructions to the *chowkidar* at Khanag so that we might be told of the new arrangements when we arrived, I had no way of knowing.

I was so excited about laying the stone at last that I woke very early and went to sit on the lawn. The mauve and white flowers were a firm reminder of Penelope. Vaguely, I had hoped that her ghost would visit me in the night, but I was never so lucky and I did not even dream of her. We walked back up the shoulder of the mountain, round the amphitheatre of deodars to the Jalori Pass in a couple of hours and met Mensingh and Paddy Singh and a very neatly dressed and precisely mustachioed mason whom they had hired for the day. It felt like a proper pilgrimage as the six of us struggled back to the rest-house carrying 40 lb of cement and the heavy slate that Boura Singh had wrapped in straw and hessian and bound with twine a week ago.

We chose a site at the entrance to the rest-house so that the stone might be seen by travellers passing – a flat plateau of ground where we could plant a garden of irises and more mauve and white cosmos. We all began to gather stones.

Manbadur was selected as cement mixer and with gentle care and almost reverence he mixed the sand with the dry cement. A gleaming brass pail of water was brought by the *chowkidar* and a hole made in the round mound. For half an hour we all watched mesmerized as little by little the water was poured into the hole and allowed to seep right through from the middle to the outside, and Manbadur's delicate spadework held the soaking mound together. Our skilled mason did not touch it – he gave orders as to how it should be done, and was treated with respect by the other men. For now a small crowd had gathered.

Men who had gathered wood for my grandmother's funeral pyre five years before, now gathered stones for a monument in her memory. Mensingh told them all that I was the *putri* (daughter's daughter) of Lady Penelope, the lady who used to ride on a pony there. Mensingh told me they all had known her for many years and loved her and that they all remembered the night she died. We gathered more stones.

The mason began to build a plinth and the afternoon came and the children were out of school. We'd heard them repeat their lessons in the open barn behind the rest-house, and now they delayed their separate journeys home to watch our proceedings. They stood clutching their slates to their chests in awed rows, and watched in wonder at the skill of the mason from Banjar. The mason knocked each stone we brought into shape, making corner stones and bricks to fit. He always knew exactly what shape was required and with extreme dexterity he manoeuvred his manicured hands about the rocks, feeling for just the right one. Every slick but careful movement of his trowel bewitched us all.

It was dusk in an instant it seemed and I worried that we wouldn't finish by dark. But the mason began to quicken and we handed him stones to fit the gaps and then each man would place his own stone on the plinth himself, so that though the mason was the architect of the building it seemed we had all helped it grow. And the chatter ceased and we worked silently and then, just before dark, the mason fitted the wide flat engraved stone on top and smoothed the cement round its corners and the job was done before night came. The crowd dispersed and Mensingh took the mason and Manbadur home, and I stood there in the heavenly place on top of the world and said as many Hail Marys as I could and fumbled my way through the Lord's Prayer and we all hoped that my grandmother might have been pleased with what we had done.

THROUGH PERSIA IN DISGUISE

Sarah Hobson

Sarah Hobson (1947–present) is an English author, film-maker, philanthropist and a fellow of California's Oakland Institute – a progressive think tank addressing social, economic and environmental issues. When she was 23 years old, she visited Iran where the Shah's grip on power was loosening, revolution was brewing and the fundamentalist Mullahs were in the ascendency. This was dangerous territory, particularly for an unaccompanied woman, so Hobson, like many female explorers before her, took to the road disguised as a man and fought off excitable suitors of both sexes to tell the tale in *Through Persia in Disguise.*

Tehran—Secular Beginnings

We passed through land carved up by an earthquake, where cultivated patches were cracked and strewn with boulders. Black lumps of earth were scattered among maize and sunflowers and grey rocks balanced on the hill above, waiting for spring when thawing snows would dislodge them. Houses were glued to the face, optimistic that the next set of boulders would again spring over them. They were small houses, light in construction to lessen the damage of earth tremors. To our right stretched a range of volcanic peaks.

Water was more frequent here than in the dry plains of Eastern Turkey. Streams diverged into channels to irrigate fields of beans and vines, and a gathering of people worked every well. A line of trees accompanied the conduits—poplars, willows and almond trees.

Villages were numerous, tucked into hollows and guarded by mud walls and orchards. But beyond the cultivation, the hills and gorges were parched, varying only in their height and colour, from beige through cinnamon to russet.

It was late in the afternoon when most of us were dozing that one of the passengers called out:

'Stop, stop, *qanat*.'

The bus drew up and we bustled out. The Iranian men ran forward past a line of mounds in the ground until they came to a place where cold, clear water flowed into the open. Scooping it into their hands, they drank noisily and then poured handfuls over their heads. They washed out their eyes, spat, and started the process again.

Qanat—the oldest system of irrigation in Iran, first recorded by a Greek in the second century, B.C. They are man-made, underground channels which carry water from foothills to cultivable land, even as far as fifty miles. And if the spring water fails, or the *qanat* collapses, the village and fields die.

The water had excited the Iranians, and one of them decided to demonstrate how a *qanat* was made. He took off his shoes, rolled up his trousers, and walked along the watercourse to the opening. Crouching, he pretended to shovel earth.

'*Muqanni*, digger, very clever,' he said. 'Knows what slope to make. Just like that. Allah must help him.'

But vertical shafts, dug down to the depth of the channel, help keep him on course, provide ventilation and allow the removal of earth; and their mouths, like miniature volcanoes, are a characteristic blemish on the landscape.

I looked at the man pretending to dig, and thought of the *muqanni* in a small black tunnel, harassed by falling earth and the shortage of air.

'Worse than mining coal,' I said.

'Better than digging for gold,' said the Hajji, and quoted from the Quran:

> *'It is He who sent down out of heaven water, and thereby*
> *We have brought forth the shoot of every plant,*

and then We have brought forth the green leaf of it, bringing forth from it close-compounded grain.'[1]

The effect of the *qanat* was stronger than a visit to a pub. Perhaps it was merely a symbol of our arrival in Iran; but for the next two hours, the men danced and sang in the bus, beating time with their hands and feet. A youth drew out a small wooden pipe and accompanied another who wiggled his way up and down the gangway. Even the Hajji gave an enlivened recital of poetry.

Merely travelling on the main road to Tehran, I began to understand the contradictions which exist in Iran, the old and new, the attempted efficiency and its subversion. There were the 'Hiway' police who sat in glass and metal boxes estimating the speed between towns. But the system broke down either because of unmanned checkpoints, or because the drivers sped along, then stopped at a tea-house for half an hour to reduce their average speed.

There were the roads themselves, with impressive wide tarmac crossed by twisting dust tracks and corrugated access roads. Buses overtook motor-bicycles which overtook donkeys. Even the cars and lorries were a paradox. A shining Mercedes, its aerial flowing, its new tyres flashing, was crammed with the male driver, two veiled women, possibly wives, five children, four hens and a tea urn. On the roof, the suitcases and bundles were protected not by polythene but a Persian carpet.

The lorries carried the agricultural wealth of Iran—grain, cotton, timber, sheep—or a load of manufactured goods. But they were dilapidated lorries resembling cattle trucks, their wooden frames painted extravagantly in scarlets and sapphire. The drivers were carefree, chewing tobacco as they swung across the road, acknowledging a lorry in the ditch with a wave, and perhaps a grin to Allah for protecting them.

I was unnerved once when a bus overtook us. Its windows were

1 Quran, 6 'Cattle'.

broken and the red curtains flapped angrily against the jagged glass. The left wing was missing, and blood coated the radiator. Contorted bundles were heaped in the gangway, and two men bounced in the driver's seat, their teeth bared in a wild grin, their heads turbanned in red curtain. It seemed more eerie than the skeleton ship in 'The Ancient Mariner', but unperturbed, our driver accelerated and pursued the wreck, overtaking and being overtaken in a cacophony of horns.

As we approached Tehran, the Elburz mountains rose to the left, like up-turned sponge cakes baked in a fluted tin. Their main peak Damavand, almost as high as Kilimanjaro, was obliterated by the haze of heat and industry. Ahead, growing out of a brown, scarcely vegetated plain, was the city, a sprawl of cube houses and blocks of flats.

Tehran has boomed in the last twenty years and carries the flag of materialism. But it has only been a capital since the nineteenth century, when the Qajars promoted it because of its proximity to their native province. Then it was a small town, dingy according to the British Missions, though they were often greeted riotously—Sir John Malcolm was met on the plain by six hundred horsemen at full gallop, tossing and shooting at hundreds of lemons.

As we crossed the suburbs, lemons were still plentiful, piled beside the gutter. Factories also were plentiful, with black smoke ballooning from chimneys, and men standing near the gates hopelessly waiting for work. I found it depressing, for Persian expression, especially detail, seemed submerged in industrial expansion. Not even the walls of old Tehran existed, walls which had been extended in the 1870's on the lines of the fortifications of Paris. According to Lord Curzon,[2] and typically of that period, most of the funds sent out from England for the Persian famine were spent on this extension.

I was staying the first few days at the British Institute of Persian Studies, a sedate building protected by high walls and iron gates. And as I was registered as a female member, everyone soon knew me as a girl. Each morning we sat down to breakfast of eggs, toast and

2 *Persia and the Persian Question*, London 1892.

marmalade, with yesterday's English papers. Conversation was minimal and specialised—an economist explained with a mouthful the problems of rural-urban migration, or an anthropologist graphed on his napkin the structure of sub-tribes. One or two advised me how to look after myself: I should never go out without a stick to protect me; it was silly to eat in local restaurants; and everyone agreed that whether as a boy or girl, I should not travel by myself.

After breakfast, I went out in my boy's clothes to explore the city. I was disappointed at first for it seemed like any other modern capital with its featureless blocks of skyscrapers and wide tarmac boulevards. Though I knew it to be a commercial city, at least in architecture, I had hoped the Persian sensitivity would inspire exciting buildings which blended Eastern harmony with Western practicality. But according to Sadiq Hidayat, a leading writer of Iran, 'The [Iranian] architects of today despite all facilities at their disposal have apparently lost good taste as well as the sense of fitness.'[3]

However I soon found reminders of old ways. Only a few yards from the skyscrapers, along the edge of the pavements, were open channels of water for drainage and irrigation. The water was murky and people drank from metal cups fixed to overhanging poles. Along the pavements, merchants spread out their newly-made carpets which swirled and shouted with chemical colours. They invited pedestrians to walk over this garden of flowers, praising themselves for saving people's shoes, but probably calculating that in four months' time, they could sell the carpet as an old and rare one.

Next to a delicatessen, I found a sunken room from which came the smell of hot bread. Three men pulled pats of dough from a large tub, slapped them into oblongs and shovelled them onto hot pebbles in a furnace. A few minutes later, the bread was removed: it was weighed, still stuck with some pebbles, and wrapped in newspaper.

In one narrow street, I noticed a boy combing his hair in front of a shop window, and staring at my reflection. He was wearing tight trousers, and a cream shirt casually unbuttoned to his ribs. Glancing along the street, he walked over to me and touched my arm.

3 H. Kamshad, *Modern Persian Prose Literature*, Cambridge 1966.

'Hello,' he said, lowering his long eyelashes.

'Hello,' I answered, flattered that he should pay attention to me as a girl in such unappealing clothes.

'You want to come with me?' he asked.

'Where?' I asked guardedly.

'To my home. Don't worry, we won't be disturbed there.' And he ran his fingers along my shoulder.

'No, no I'm not interested,' I said, and began to walk away.

'But Mister,' he called. I turned to look at him quickly. 'Hey Mister, what's wrong?'

It was a wry development. I had forgotten, or at least had never considered, that if I succeeded as a boy I would have to cope with homosexuality; and though it was illegal in Iran, I had heard it was commonplace.

It seemed that most people I met accepted me as a boy. Perhaps I had grown more masculine, but probably they took me at face-value, and put down any doubts to the difference of culture and habits. Nonetheless I was surprised one morning to be picked up by two girls. I was looking for the Ethnographical Museum, and they offered to help; when we could not find it they asked me to lunch. With a girl either side of me, we walked along the street passing more and more eating-places, and I began to wonder nervously where they were taking me. Perhaps they were prostitutes, though I could gauge nothing from their appearance. One wore a lilac dacron dress and giggled, the skin wrinkling between her nose and plump cheeks; the other, in a short white skirt and printed blouse, had a spotty chin and dirty fingernails.

They queued at a bus-stop, and I had just decided to make some excuse and slip away when a bus drew up and they pushed me on. We sat until the terminus in the eastern suburbs, and then walked along some dusty streets which were flanked by small brick houses. We jumped over an open drain and the fat girl knocked on a door set in a high wall, calling as she knocked. It was opened immediately and six children in faded clothes jumped up and down in the entrance, greeting us simultaneously:

'Salaam, peace. Welcome to our house. Mother, come quickly, a guest. Please, come in. Are you tired? What's your name? Welcome.'

They jostled and pushed to gaze at me shyly from behind one another; they laughed and whispered until an old woman in a long veil came and pushed them away. Clasping my hand she took me into a room, and offered me a plastic armchair with lime-coloured antimacassars.

'No it's all right, I'll sit on the floor with you,' I said, and we both sat down cross-legged. As people entered the room, she introduced them to me.

'This is my daughter-in-law, Fatima, and four of her children. This is Shirin, oh look, what a beautiful dress. How's the child, Shirin? She's got three, but the baby's sick. And this is my son, he's at school. He's very clever. Yes, you know these two.' They were the girls who had brought me. 'Both my daughters.' She pointed to the plump one. 'Zuhreh is getting married soon. She'll live with her husband's family of course.' Then she pulled the other towards her. 'And this one's Farah. Pretty isn't she? She'll make a good wife, don't you think?'

The girl covered her spotty chin with the veil she had put on, and blushed with embarrassment—there seemed no doubt of my masculinity.

Zuhreh spread a plastic cloth on the floor beside me, and she, the old lady and Fatima sat round it. The children brought in the food — fresh green herbs, bowls of yoghourt, warm unleavened bread wrapped in a rag, a dish heaped with saffron rice and chunks of meat, and a separate plateful of rice and kebab.

'Please, that's for you,' said the old lady and gave me the plate with a spoon and fork. The three women dug into the central dish using pieces of bread as scoops, or wrapped a few herbs in the bread which they chewed for a moment before adding rice.

'Don't you like kebab?' asked the old lady suddenly.

'Very much,' I said.

'But you eat so slowly.'

I gulped down the food, and when I had finished, she piled up my plate again.

'No honestly, I couldn't eat any more,' I protested.

'Isn't it good?' asked Zuhreh, her eyes widening in dismay, so that I felt I had to eat it.

The meal was cleared away and we settled down for the afternoon, sipping tea. With the help of the dictionary I always carried, I practised my Persian and they their English. The old lady dozed against the wall, her open mouth showing blackened gums. The skin of her face was cracked with lines like the veins of a leaf when held up to the fight, and her bumpy nose was spotted with blackheads. Once her veil fell from her head to show wisps of orange hair dyed with henna, but she woke with a jerk and hastily pulled it about her again.

The daughters were not so particular when their veils fell open, even if I was looking at them, and they made no effort to cover their bare legs. Shirin came and sat beside me. Her hair was bleached with peroxide, and black roots showed at the parting. The pink varnish on her toenails was chipped, and her thumbnails were bitten right down so that the skin overlapped.

'You must come and visit us often,' she said.

'Thank you, I'd like to.'

'My sister's very pretty, you know.'

'You're all very pretty,' I said, refusing to acknowledge her reference to Farah.

'And you're not married yet?'

'Oh no. I'm not getting married for years yet.'

She shrugged, and turned on the television. The family moved closer to giggle and stare at a production of *Swan Lake*. I looked round the room as clouds floated behind the pirouetting swans. The walls were bare except for an unframed photograph of the Shah, and a sunset picture in coloured tinsel. On a mock mahogany table, plastic flowers gushed from a vase which was moulded in the shape of a naked lady, her hair streaming down to her buttocks. The doors of a built-in cupboard were pasted with pictures of laughing women, their faces coated with make-up. The carpet seemed the only thing untouched by kitsch, for it was patterned with arabesque and had faded to soft blue.

The news came on. The Shah had opened a new factory. Another school had been built in Tehran. Oil production was up on the previous month. The Shah was to visit Isfahan. A jet had been hijacked.

The son turned to me.

'You are Catholic or Protestant?'

'Well, neither particularly.'

'Oh.' There was a pause. 'So you haven't been fighting?'

'Fighting? Where?'

'In Ireland.'

'Oh, of course. No, I'm not a fighting man.'

'But why are they fighting? Surely no-one fights any more about religion in England?'

'They seem to in Ireland. But it goes much deeper.' I reflected a moment. 'I'd hate to kill anyone though, whatever the reason.' That seemed unmanly, so I added: 'I mean, not my neighbours.'

Towards five o'clock, I said I must go, and they asked why. I had no reason, except that I could not throw off my London habit of continuous and organised activity. It took me some time to realise that the best way for me to see Iran was to do nothing until something happened, for such was the way of the Iranians. And within weeks I was happy to spend whole days just sitting cross-legged, sipping tea and talking.

I shook hands with the family, and the son said he would take me to the bus.

'You were wise not to take my sister,' he said as we walked along the street.

'Wise? How?'

'Can't you have just as much fun in England without getting married? You have less troubles that way.'

'Maybe. But it might be quite fun to have a wife.'

We both laughed, and when I got on the bus, I felt like embracing him as a man, for he had given me confidence at last in my disguise.

I set out to study the art of the nineteenth-century Qajars,[4] for I felt they were an essential part of Tehran, indeed of Iran. True, they were greedy and cruel: Aga Mohammad, the first of the dynasty, ordered 20,000 pairs of his enemies' eyes to be brought to him on a silver

4 Aga Mohammad was crowned Shah in 1796; Ahmad Shah left for Europe in 1923, ending the Qajar succession. He had been Shah more in name than effect.

tray. But for me, they excelled in the traditions of Iranian sovereignty, its display and aloofness, and represented a secularity not found in the rest of the country. Not that the rulers separated themselves from religion, but they seemed more concerned with kingship.

I spent much of my time studying Qajar pieces—papier-mâché pen boxes, mirror frames and snuff boxes decorated in lacquer. Some depicted traditional scenes of battles or gardens filled with kneeling men, but others had realistic street scenes with carriages and gutters, or figures of upturned women dancing on their hands, their skirts and trousers alive with folds. Still others had floral patterns, some glowing with natural flowers in amber, copper and faded cinnabar colours. There were roses, camelias, tulips, and small flowers resembling primroses and forget-me-nots—all the favourite flowers of a contemporary English chintz. Perhaps it was no coincidence, for English fabric was coveted by members of the court, who made it into long quilted vests or tied it round their tabard-type coats.

In most of these pieces, there was a richness of colour and form which seemed to express the sensuality and ostentation of the Qajars. And it seemed that the style had moved away from the strict traditions of Persian miniatures, to incorporate Western concepts of perspective in depth and delineation. This was particularly so in the larger paintings where figures were set against blank windows, or velvet-textured drapes, more in the style of Italian Renaissance painting. There was even a madonna and child in pyramidal da Vinci pose.

I was also struck by the resemblance to Byzantine facial features. Both men and women had wide heavy eyes, long straight noses, rosebud lips, thick black eyebrows which usually met in the middle, and hair neatly arranged in curves of recurring lines. It seemed odd that the artists of such a secular dynasty might have derived their inspiration from a religious art—though perhaps it gave them the excuse of disregarding the Islamic ban on human representation. But it certainly seemed that both Russian and European influence, so strong politically in Persia in the nineteenth century, had also penetrated the country's art.

The portraits were mainly of princes or courtiers, but a few girls balanced upside-down on knives. There was strong use of black which set off the splashes of subdued scarlet and pale mustard, and highlighted the creamy white of jewels—for jewels hung in their hair, on belts and daggers, and were sewn in solid formation along borders, collars and cuffs.

The more I looked at this Qajar art, the more I felt that the contact with Europe had revived an art which had become degenerate, even if its revival was secular and outside the tradition of Islam. Certainly the effects of Nasir ud-Din Shah's three visits to Europe[5] stimulated bizarre innovations in Tehran: the theatre in his palace complex was given a dome like the Albert Hall; Victorian gas-lamps lit up his rose-garden; and so delighted had he been with the Parisian ballet that he insisted his harem wear the *tutu*, and soon all fashionable women were doing the same.

Later I went to see the crown jewels in the Central Bank of Iran, for many of the pieces are Qajar. I found them spectacular, but overpoweringly opulent. Fath 'Ali Shah's coronation crown shone with hundreds of rubies and pearls, surmounted by a soft plume of diamonds. Candlesticks and platters of gold glistened with emeralds; belts and daggers were impossibly heavy with so many jewels studding their surface. There was a throne encrusted with over 27,000 stones, and handfuls of pearls and rubies strewn on shelves. A globe was on a gold stand, its oceans made of emeralds, the continents of rubies, with Iran, France and England highlighted in diamonds.

Yet these jewels are not just typical of the Qajars, but rather form part of the heritage of kingship which stretches back over two thousand years. And I felt that though such spectacle opposed Islamic principles, yet nonetheless they formed part of Iran, were an intrinsic part of its character. For with many of its rulers, right back to the Achaemenians, there had been a love of display for its own sake which bore little relation to the lives and beliefs of the people.

I often wandered round Tehran in the afternoon, for it seemed to lose its officiousness and relax into the heat of the day. I found in one dark shop a man idly stirring yoghourt in a huge cauldron which was heated from beneath by a wood fire. He was dressed in green pyjama

5 In 1873, 1878 and 1889.

bottoms and his chin was black with stubble. As the white liquid thickened, he ladled it into tough pottery bowls which he set on a wooden plank to cool. Then he filled a small cup, and blowing on it and stirring it with his finger, he handed it to me.

'Try it,' he said. 'It's only a poor man's work.'

I squatted on the floor and sipped it. It was good, slightly sour and clean-tasting.

'How much do you make a day?' I asked.

'If God gives me the milk, then about forty bowls.'

'And you sell them all?'

'God willing. He is good to me most days.'

'So you earn enough to live on?'

'With six children? We live, we live. And my youngest son comes to help some days. He's at school, you know,' said the man proudly.

'And your other children?'

He frowned slightly. 'They're looking for work. They don't like the idea of making yoghourt. Still, God will guide them.'

He sighed and turned back to the cauldron, scraping the solidified milk from its sides.

Further along the street, I went into a tea-house. The owner was sprawled on a table, asleep, and in one corner, a youth contemplated the floor.

I sat down quietly and waited. The room was hot and still smelt of the meat the man had been frying for lunch. Chipped cups lay by a bowl of cold water and a blackened kettle simmered on the stove. A torn page of calligraphy hung on the wall and below on the floor was a rolled-up prayer mat.

The man grunted, and turned over, slightly opening one eye. He caught sight of me, and with surprise, tried to wake up and get off the table. He stumbled and fell.

'Forgive me, forgive me,' he said. 'I'm worse than all the donkeys of the world.'

'But a donkey does lots of work,' I laughed.

'Oh well, I can't be so bad then.' And he brushed the dust off his clothes, and buttoned up his flies. Then he looked at me curiously. 'Don't you want some tea? Why didn't you wake me?'

I shrugged. 'I didn't mind waiting.'

'Well as you've waited so long, you must have some tea as my guest.' He made the tea and began to cook some meat.

'Please, don't do anything extra for me,' I said.

'It's no trouble, not for a guest.'

'But you can't treat everyone as guests.'

'Why not? I charge some, and if ever I'm in need, then I can always go to a friend. God will look after us.'

I felt such an attitude was unusual in Tehran, but perhaps in this quarter the influence of Islam was still strong—it was the first time since my arrival that I had encountered an implicit faith in the ways of God. And it made me realise that so long as I stayed in Tehran I would be unlikely to learn from what roots this faith stemmed.

THE ENGLISH GOVERNESS AT THE SIAMESE COURT

Anna Leonowens

Anna Leonowens (1834–1914) was a travel writer, educator and activist, who featured in Margaret Landon's biographical novel *Anna and the King of Siam*. She was portrayed far more frivolously on the big screen by Deborah Kerr in *The King and I,* most memorably dancing the polka with Yul Brynner to 'Shall We Dance?' Fortunately, her first-hand account of her experiences as teacher to the children of King Mongkut of Siam (Thailand), *The English Governess at the Siamese Court*, is equally entertaining.

The King and the Governess

In 1825 a royal prince of Siam (his birthright wrested from him, and his life imperilled) took refuge in a Buddhist monastery and assumed the yellow garb of a priest. His father, commonly known as Phen-den-Klang, first or supreme king of Siam, had just died, leaving this prince, Chowfa Mongkut, at the age of twenty, lawful heir to the crown; for he was the eldest son of the acknowledged queen, and therefore by courtesy and honored custom, if not by absolute right, the legitimate successor to the throne of the P'hra-batts. [Footnote: The Golden-footed.] But he had an elder half-brother, who, through the intrigues of his mother, had already obtained control of the royal treasury, and now, with the connivance, if not by the authority, of the Senabawdee, the Grand Council of the kingdom, proclaimed himself king. He had the grace, however, to promise his plundered brother—such royal promises being a cheap form of propitiation in Siam—to hold the reins of government only until Chowfa Mongkut should be of years and strength and skill to manage them. But, once firmly seated on the throne, the usurper saw in his patient but proud and astute kinsman only a hindrance and a peril in the path of his own cruder and fiercer aspirations. Hence the forewarning and the flight, the cloister and the yellow robes. And so the usurper continued to reign, unchallenged by any claim from the king that should be, until March, 1851, when, a mortal illness having overtaken him, he convoked the Grand Council of princes and nobles around his couch, and proposed his favorite son as his successor. Then the safe asses of the court kicked the dying lion with seven words of sententious scorn,—"The crown has already its rightful owner"; whereupon the king literally cursed himself to death, for it was almost in the convulsion, of his chagrin and rage that he came to his end, on the 3d of April.

In Siam there is no such personage as an heir-apparent to the throne, in the definite meaning and positive value which attaches to that phrase in Europe,—no prince with an absolute and exclusive title, by birth, adoption, or nomination, to succeed to the crown. And while it is true that the eldest living son of a Siamese sovereign by his queen or queen consort is recognized by all custom, ancient and modern, as the *probable* successor to the high seat of his royal sire, he cannot be said to have a clear and indefeasible right to it, because the question of his accession has yet to be decided by the electing voice of the Senabawdee, in whose judgment he may be ineligible, by reason of certain physical, mental, or moral disabilities,—as extreme youth, effeminacy, imbecility, intemperance, profligacy. Nevertheless, the election is popularly expected to result in the choice of the eldest son of the queen, though an interregnum or a regency is a contingency by no means unusual.

It was in view of this jurisdiction of the Senabawdee, exercised in deference to a just and honored usage, that the voice of the oracle fell upon the ear of the dying monarch with a disappointing and offensive significance; for he well knew who was meant by the "rightful owner" of the crown. Hardly had he breathed his last when, in spite of the busy intrigues of his eldest son (whom we find described in the *Bangkok Recorder* of July 26, 1866, as "most honorable and promising"), in spite of the bitter vexation of his lordship Chow Phya Sri Sury Wongse, so soon to be premier, the prince Chowfa Mongkut doffed his sacerdotal robes, emerged from his cloister, and was crowned, with the title of Somdetch Phra Paramendr Maha Mongkut. [Footnote: Duke, and royal bearer of the great crown.]

For twenty-five years had the true heir to the throne of the P'hrabatts, patiently biding his time, lain *perdu* in his monastery, diligently devoting himself to the study of Sanskrit, Pali, theology, history, geology, chemistry, and especially astronomy. He had been a familiar visitor at the houses of the American missionaries, two of whom (Dr. House and Mr. Mattoon) were, throughout his reign and life, gratefully revered by him for that pleasant and profitable converse which helped to unlock to him the secrets of European vigor and advancement, and to make straight and easy the paths of knowledge he had started upon. Not even the essential arrogance of his Siamese nature could prevent him from accepting cordially the happy influences these good and true men inspired; and doubtless he would have gone more than half-way to meet them, but for the dazzle of the golden throne in the distance which arrested him midway between Christianity and Buddhism, between truth and delusion, between light and darkness, between life and death.

In the Oriental tongues this progressive king was eminently proficient; and toward priests, preachers, and teachers, of all creeds, sects, and sciences, an enlightened exemplar of tolerance. It was likewise his peculiar vanity to pass for an accomplished English scholar, and to this end he maintained in his palace at Bangkok a private printing establishment, with fonts of English type, which, as may be perceived presently, he was at no loss to keep in "copy." Perhaps it was the printing-office which suggested, quite naturally, an English governess for the *élite* of his wives and concubines, and their offspring,—in number amply adequate to the constitution of a royal school, and in material most attractively fresh and romantic. Happy thought! Wherefore, behold me, just after sunset on a pleasant day in April, 1862, on the threshold of the outer court of the Grand Palace, accompanied by my own brave little boy, and escorted by a compatriot.

A flood of light sweeping through the spacious Hall of Audience displayed a throng of noblemen in waiting. None turned a glance, or seemingly a thought, on us, and, my child being tired and hungry, I urged Captain B—— to present us without delay. At once we mounted the marble steps, and entered the brilliant hall unannounced. Ranged on the carpet were many prostrate, mute, and motionless forms, over whose heads to step was a temptation as drolly natural as it was dangerous. His Majesty spied us quickly, and advanced abruptly, petulantly screaming, "Who? who? who?"

Captain B—— (who, by the by, is a titled nobleman of Siam) introduced me as the English governess, engaged for the royal family. The king shook hands with us, and immediately proceeded to march up and down in quick step, putting one foot before the other with mathematical precision, as if under drill. "Forewarned, forearmed!" my friend whispered that I should prepare myself for a sharp cross-questioning as to my age, my husband, children, and other strictly personal concerns. Suddenly his Majesty, having cogitated sufficiently in his peculiar manner, with one long final stride halted in front of us, and pointing straight at me with his forefinger, asked, "How old shall you be?"

Scarcely able to repress a smile at a proceeding so absurd, and with my sex's distaste for so serious a question, I demurely replied, "One hundred and fifty years old."

Had I made myself much younger, he might have ridiculed or assailed me; but now he stood surprised and embarrassed for a few moments, then resumed his queer march; and at last, beginning to perceive the jest, coughed, laughed, coughed again, and in a high, sharp key asked, "In what year were you borned?"

Instantly I struck a mental balance, and answered, as gravely as I could, "In 1788."

At this point the expression of his Majesty's face was indescribably comical. Captain B—— slipped behind a pillar to laugh; but the king only coughed, with a significant emphasis that startled me, and addressed a few words to his prostrate courtiers, who smiled at the carpet,—all except the prime minister, who turned to look at me. But his Majesty was not to be baffled so: again he marched with vigor, and then returned to the attack with *élan*.

"How many years shall you be married?"

"For several years, your Majesty."

He fell into a brown study; then, laughing, rushed at me, and demanded triumphantly:—

"Ha! How many grandchildren shall you now have? Ha, ha! How many? How many? Ha, ha, ha!"

Of course we all laughed with him; but the general hilarity admitted of a variety of constructions.

Then suddenly he seized my hand, and dragged me, *nolens volens*, my little Louis holding fast by my skirt, through several sombre passages, along which crouched duennas, shrivelled and grotesque, and many youthful women, covering their faces, as if blinded by the splendor of the passing Majesty. At length he stopped before one of the many-curtained recesses, and, drawing aside the hangings, disclosed a lovely, childlike form. He stooped and took her hand, (she naively hiding her face), and placing it in mine, said, "This is my wife, the Lady Tâlâp. She desires to be educated in English. She is as pleasing for her talents as for her beauty, and it is our pleasure to make her a good English scholar. You shall educate her for me."

I replied that the office would give me much pleasure; for nothing could be more eloquently winning than the modest, timid bearing of that tender young creature in the presence of her lord. She laughed low and pleasantly as he translated my sympathetic words to her, and seemed so enraptured with the graciousness of his act that I took my leave of her with a sentiment of profound pity.

He led me back by the way we had come; and now we met many children, who put my patient boy to much childish torture for the gratification of their startled curiosity.

"I have sixty-seven children," said his Majesty, when we had returned to the Audience Hall. "You shall educate them, and as many of my wives, likewise, as may wish to learn English. And I have much correspondence in which you must assist me. And, moreover, I have much difficulty for reading and translating French letters; for French are fond of using gloomily deceiving terms. You must undertake; and you shall make all their murky sentences and gloomily deceiving propositions clear to me. And, furthermore, I have by every mail foreign letters whose writing is not easily read by me. You shall copy on round hand, for my readily perusal thereof."

Nil desperandum, but I began by despairing of my ability to accomplish tasks so multifarious. I simply bowed, however, and so dismissed myself for that evening.

One tempting morning, when the air was cool, my boy and I ventured some distance beyond the bounds of our usual cautious promenade, close to the palace of the premier. Some forty or fifty carpenters, building boats under a long low shed, attracted the child's attention. We tarried awhile, watching their work, and then strolled to a stone bridge hard by, where we found a gang of repulsive wretches, all men, coupled by means of iron collars and short but heavy fetters, in which they moved with difficulty, if not with positive pain. They were carrying stone from the canal to the bridge, and as they stopped to deposit their burdens, I observed that most of them had hard, defiant faces, though here and there were sad and gentle eyes that bespoke sympathy. One of them approached us, holding out his hand, into which Boy dropped the few coins he had. Instantly, with a greedy shout, the whole gang were upon us, crowding us on all sides, wrangling, yelling. I was exceedingly alarmed, and having no more money there, knew not what to do, except to take my child in my arms, and strive again and again to break through the press; but still I fell back baffled, and sickened by the insufferable odors that emanated from their disgusting persons; and still they pressed and scrambled and screamed, and clanked their horrid chains. But behold! suddenly, as if struck by lightning, every man of them fell on his face, and officers flew among them pell-mell, swingeing with hard, heavy thongs the naked wincing backs.

It was with a sense of infinite relief that we found ourselves safe in our rooms at last; but the breakfast tasted earthy and the atmosphere was choking, and our very hearts were parched. At night Boy lay burning on his little bed, moaning for *aiyer sujok* (cold water), while I fainted for a breath of fresh, sweet air. But God blesses these Eastern prison-houses not at all; the air that visits them is no better than the life within,—heavy, stifling, stupefying. For relief I betook me to the study of the Siamese language, an occupation I had found very pleasant and inspiring. As for Boy, who spoke Malay fluently, it was wonderful with what aptness he acquired it.

When next I "interviewed" the king, I was accompanied by the premier's sister, a fair and friendly woman, whose whole stock of English was, "Good morning, sir"; and with this somewhat irrelevant greeting, a dozen times in an hour, though the hour were night, she relieved her pent-up feelings, and gave expression to her sympathy and regard for me.

Mr. Hunter, private secretary to the premier, had informed me, speaking for his Excellency, that I should prepare to enter upon my duties at the royal palace without delay. Accordingly, next morning, the elder sister of the Kralahome came for us. She led the way to the river, followed by slave-girls bearing a gold teapot, a pretty gold tray containing two tiny porcelain cups with covers, her betel-box, also of gold, and two large fans. When we were seated in the closely covered basket-boat, she took up one of the books I had brought with me, and, turning over the leaves, came upon the alphabet; whereat, with a look of pleased surprise, she began repeating the letters. I helped her, and for a while she seemed amused and gratified; but presently, growing weary of it, she abruptly closed the book, and, offering me her hand, said, "Good morning, sir!" I replied with equal cordiality, and I think we bade each other good morning at least a dozen times before we reached the palace.

We landed at a showy pavilion, and after traversing several covered passages came to a barrier guarded by Amazons, to whom the old lady was evidently well known, for they threw open the gate for us, and "squatted" till we passed. A hot walk of twenty minutes brought us to a curious oval door of polished brass, which opened and shut noiselessly in a highly ornate frame. This admitted us to a cool retreat, on one side of which were several temples or chapels in antique styles, and on the other a long dim gallery. On the marble floor of this pavilion a number of interesting children sat or sprawled, and quaint babies slept or frolicked in their nurses' arms. It was, indeed, a grateful change from the oppressive, irritating heat and glare through which we had just passed.

The loungers started up to greet our motherly guide, who humbly prostrated herself before them; and then refreshments were brought in on large silver trays, with covers of scarlet silk in the form of a bee-hive. As no knife or fork or spoon was visible, Boy and I were fain to content ourselves with oranges, wherewith we made ourselves an unexpected but cheerful show for the entertainment and edification of those juvenile spectators of the royal family of Siam. I smiled and held out my hand to them, for they were, almost without exception, attractive children; but they shyly shrank from me.

Meanwhile the "child-wife," to whom his Majesty had presented me at my first audience, appeared, and after saluting profoundly the sister of the Kralahome, and conversing with her for some minutes, lay down on the cool floor, and, using her betel-box for a pillow, beckoned to me. As I approached, and seated myself beside her, she said: "I am very glad to see you. It is long time I not see. Why you come so late?" to all of which she evidently expected no reply. I tried baby-talk, in the hope of making my amiable sentiments intelligible to so infantile a creature, but in vain. Seeing me disappointed and embarrassed, she oddly sang a scrap of the Sunday-school hymn, "There is a Happy Land, far, far away"; and then said, "I think of you very often. In the beginning, God created the heavens and the earth."

This meritorious but disjointed performance was followed by a protracted and trying silence, I sitting patient, and Boy wondering in my lap. At last she half rose, and, looking around, cautiously whispered, "Dear Mam Mattoon! I love you. I think of you. Your boy dead, you come to palace; you cry—I love you"; and laying her finger on her lips, and her head on the betel-box again, again she sang, "There is a Happy Land, far, far away!"

Mrs. Mattoon is the wife of that good and true American apostle who has nobly served the cause of missions in Siam as a co-laborer with the excellent Dr. Samuel House. While the wife of the latter devoted herself indefatigably to the improvement of schools for the native children whom the mission had gathered round it, Mrs. Mattoon shared her labors by occasionally teaching in the palace, which was for some time thrown open to the ladies of her faithful sisterhood. Here, as elsewhere, the blended force and gentleness of her character wrought marvels in the impressible and grateful minds to which she had access.

So spontaneous and ingenuous a tribute of reverence and affection from a pagan to a Christian lady was inexpressibly charming to me.

Thus the better part of the day passed. The longer I rested dreaming there, the more enchanted seemed the world within those walls. I was aroused by a slight noise proceeding from the covered gallery, whence an old lady appeared bearing a candlestick of gold, with branches supporting four lighted candles. I afterward learned that these were daily offerings, which the king, on awakening from his forenoon slumber, sent to the Watt P'hra Keau. This apparition was the signal for much stir. The Lady Tâlâp started to her feet and fled, and we were left alone with the premier's sister and the slaves in waiting. The entire household seemed to awake on the instant, as in the "Sleeping Palace" of Tennyson, at the kiss of the Fairy Prince,—

> "The maid and page renewed their strife;
> The palace banged, and buzzed, and clackt;
> And all the long-pent stream of life
> Dashed downward in a cataract."

A various procession of women and children—some pale and downcast, others bright and blooming, more moody and hardened—moved in the one direction; none tarried to chat, none loitered or looked back; the lord was awake.

> "And last with these the king awoke,
> And in his chair himself upreared,
> And yawned, and rubbed his face, and spoke."

Presently the child-wife reappeared,—arrayed now in dark blue silk, which contrasted well with the soft olive of her complexion,—and quickly followed the others, with a certain anxious alacrity expressed in her baby face. I readily guessed that his Majesty was the awful cause of all this careful bustle, and began to feel uneasy myself, as my ordeal approached. For an hour I stood on thorns. Then there was a general frantic rush. Attendants, nurses, slaves, vanished through doors, around corners, behind pillars, under stairways; and at last, preceded by a sharp, "cross" cough, behold the king!

We found his Majesty in a less genial mood than at my first

reception. He approached us coughing loudly and repeatedly, a sufficiently ominous fashion of announcing himself, which greatly discouraged my darling boy, who clung to me anxiously. He was followed by a numerous "tail" of women and children, who formally prostrated themselves around him. Shaking hands with me coldly, but remarking upon the beauty of the child's hair, half buried in the folds of my dress, he turned to the premier's sister, and conversed at some length with her, she apparently acquiescing in all that he had to say. He then approached me, and said, in a loud and domineering tone:—

"It is our pleasure that you shall reside within this palace with our family."

I replied that it would be quite impossible for me to do so; that, being as yet unable to speak the language, and the gates being shut every evening, I should feel like an unhappy prisoner in the palace.

"Where do you go every evening?" he demanded.

"Not anywhere, your Majesty. I am a stranger here."

"Then why you shall object to the gates being shut?"

"I do not clearly know," I replied, with a secret shudder at the idea of sleeping within those walls; "but I am afraid I could not do it. I beg your Majesty will remember that in your gracious letter you promised me 'a residence adjoining the royal palace,' not within it."

He turned and looked at me, his face growing almost purple with rage. "I do not know I have promised. I do not know former condition. I do not know anything but you are our servant; and it is our pleasure that you must live in this palace, and—*you shall obey*." Those last three words he fairly screamed.

I trembled in every limb, and for some time knew not how to reply. At length I ventured to say, "I am prepared to obey all your Majesty's commands within the obligation of my duty to your family, but beyond that I can promise no obedience."

"You *shall* live in palace," he roared,—"you _shall _live in palace! I will give woman slaves to wait on you. You shall commence royal school in this pavilion on Thursday next. That is the best day for such undertaking, in the estimation of our astrologers."

With that, he addressed, in a frantic manner, commands, unintelligible to me, to some of the old women about the pavilion. My boy began to cry; tears filled my own eyes; and the premier's sister, so kind but an hour before, cast fierce glances at us both. I turned and led my child toward the oval brass door. We heard voices behind us crying. "Mam! Mam!" I turned again, and saw the king beckoning and calling to me. I bowed to him profoundly, but passed on through the brass door. The prime minister's sister bounced after us in a distraction of excitement, tugging at my cloak, shaking her finger in my face, and crying, "*My di! my di!*" [Footnote: "Bad, bad!"] All the way back, in the boat, and on the street, to the very door of my apartments, instead of her jocund "Good morning, sir," I had nothing but *my di.*

But kings, who are not mad, have their sober second-thoughts like other rational people. His Golden-footed Majesty presently repented him of his arbitrary "cantankerousness," and in due time my ultimatum was accepted.

Marble Halls and Fish-Stalls

Well! by this time I was awake to the realities of time, place, and circumstance. The palace and its spells, the impracticable despot, the impassible premier, were not the phantasms of a witching night, but the hard facts of noonday. Here were the very Apollyons of paganry in the way, and only the Great Hearts of a lonely woman and a loving child to challenge them.

With a heart heavy with regret for the comparatively happy home I had left in Malacca, I sought an interview with the Kralahome, and told him (through his secretary, Mr. Hunter) how impossible it would be for me and my child to lodge within the walls of the Grand Palace; and that he was bound in honor to make good the conditions on which I had been induced to leave Singapore. At last I succeeded in interesting him, and he accorded me a gracious hearing. My objection to the palace, as a place of residence as well as of business, seemed to strike him as reasonable enough; and he promised to plead my cause with his Majesty, bidding me kindly "give myself no further trouble about the matter, for he would make it right."

Thus passed a few days more, while I waited monotonously under the roof of the premier, teaching Boy, studying Siamese, paying stated visits to the good Koon Ying Phan, and suffering tumultuous invasions from my "intimate enemies" of the harem, who came upon us like a flight of locusts, and rarely left without booty, in the shape of trifles they had begged of me. But things get themselves done, after a fashion, even in Siam; and so, one morning, came the slow but welcome news that the king was reconciled to the idea of my living outside the palace, that a house had been selected for me, and a messenger waited to conduct me to it.

Hastily donning our walking-gear, we found an elderly man, of somewhat sinister aspect, in a dingy red coat with faded facings of yellow, impatient to guide us to our unimaginable quarters. As we passed out, we met the premier, whose countenance wore a quizzing expression, which I afterward understood; but at the moment I saw in it only the characteristic conundrum that I had neither the time nor the talent to guess. It was with a lively sense of relief that I followed our conductor, in whom, by a desperate exploit of imagination, I discovered a promise of privacy and "home."

In a long, slender boat, with a high, uneven covering of wood, we stowed ourselves in the Oriental manner, my dress and appearance affording infinite amusement to the ten rowers as they plied their paddles, while our escort stood in the entrance chewing betel, and looking more ill-omened than ever. We alighted at the king's pavilion facing the river, and were led, by a long, circuitous, and unpleasant road, through two tall gates, into a street which, from the offensive odors that assailed us, I took to be a fish-market. The sun burned, the air stifled, the dust choked us, the ground blistered our feet; we were parching and suffocating, when our guide stopped at the end of this most execrable lane, and signed to us to follow him up three broken steps of brick. From a pouch in his dingy coat he produced a key, applied it to a door, and opened to us two small rooms, without a window in either, without a leaf to shade, without bath-closet or kitchen. And this was the residence sumptuously appointed for the English governess to the royal family of Siam!

And furnished! and garnished! In one room, on a remnant of filthy matting, stood the wreck of a table, superannuated, and maimed of a leg, but propped by two chairs that with broken arms sympathized with each other. In the other, a cheap excess of Chinese bedstead, that took the whole room to itself; and a mattress!—a mutilated epitome of a Lazarine hospital.

My stock of Siamese words was small, but strong. I gratefully recalled the emphatic monosyllables wherewith the premier's sister had so berated me; and turning upon the king's messenger with her tremendous *my di! my di!* dashed the key from his hand, as, inanely grinning, he held it out to me, caught my boy up in my arms, cleared the steps in a bound, and fled anywhere, anywhere, until I was stopped by the crowd of men, women, and children, half naked, who gathered around me, wondering. Then, remembering my adventure with the chain-gang, I was glad to accept the protection of my insulted escort, and escape from that suburb of disgust. All the way back to the premier's our guide grinned at us fiendishly, whether in token of apology or ridicule I knew not; and landing us safely, he departed to our great relief, still grinning.

Straight went I to the Kralahome, whose shy, inquisitive smile was more and more provoking. In a few sharp words I told him, through the interpreter, what I thought of the lodging provided for me, and that nothing should induce me to live in such a slum. To which, with cool, deliberate audacity, he replied that nothing prevented me from living where I was. I started from the low seat I had taken (in order to converse with him at my ease, he sitting on the floor), and not without difficulty found voice to say that neither his palace nor the den in the fish-market would suit me, and that I demanded suitable and independent accommodations, in a respectable neighborhood, for myself and my child. My rage only amused him. Smiling insolently, he rose, bade me, "Never mind: it will be all right by and by," and retired to an inner chamber.

My head throbbed with pain, my pulse bounded, my throat burned. I staggered to my rooms, exhausted and despairing, there to lie, for almost a week, prostrated with fever, and tortured day and night with frightful fancies and dreams. Beebe and the gentle Koon Ying Phan nursed me tenderly, bringing me water, deliciously cool, in which the fragrant flower of the jessamine had been steeped, both to drink and to bathe my temples. As soon as I began to recover, I caressed the soft hand of the dear pagan lady, and implored her, partly in Siamese, partly in English, to intercede for me with her husband, that a decent home might be provided for us. She assured me, while she smoothed my hair and patted my cheek as though I were a helpless child, that she would do her best with him, begging me meanwhile to be patient. But that I could not be; and I spared no opportunity to expostulate with the premier on the subject of my future abode and duties, telling him that the life I was leading under his roof was insupportable to me; though, indeed, I was not ungrateful for the many offices of affection I received from the ladies of his harem, who in my trouble were sympathetic and tender. From that time forth the imperturbable Kralahome was ever courteous to me. Nevertheless, when from time to time I grew warm again on the irrepressible topic, he would smile slyly, tap the ashes from his pipe, and say, "Yes, sir! Never mind, sir! You not like, you can live in fish-market, sir!" The apathy and supineness of these people oppressed me intolerably. Never well practised in patience, I chafed at the *sang-froid* of the deliberate premier. Without compromising my dignity, I did much to enrage him; but he bore all with a *nonchalance* that was the more irritating because it was not put on.

Thus more than two months passed, and I had desperately settled down to my Oriental studies, content to snub the Kralahome with his own indifference, whilst he, on the other hand, blandly ignored our existence, when, to my surprise, he paid me a visit one afternoon, complimented me on my progress in the language, and on my "great heart,"—or *chi yai*, as he called it,—and told me his Majesty was highly incensed at my conduct in the affair of the fish-market, and that he had found me something to do. I thanked him so cordially that he expressed his surprise, saying, "Siamese lady no like work; love play, love sleep. Why you no love play?"

I assured him that I liked play well enough when I was in the humor for play; but that at present I was not disposed to disport myself, being weary of my life in his palace, and sick of Siam altogether. He received my candor with his characteristic smile and a good-humored "Good by, sir!"

Next morning ten Siamese lads and a little girl came to my room. The former were the half-brothers, nephews, and other "encumbrances" of the Kralahome; the latter their sister, a simple child of nine or ten. Surely it was with no snobbery of condescension that I received these poor children, but rather gratefully, as a comfort and a wholesome discipline.

And so another month went by, and still I heard nothing from his Majesty. But the premier began to interest me. The more I saw of him the more he puzzled me. It was plain that all who came in contact with him both feared and loved him. He displayed a kind of passive amiability of which he seemed always conscious, which he made his *forte*. By what means he exacted such prompt obedience, and so completely controlled a people whom he seemed to drive with reins so loose and careless, was a mystery to me. But that his influence and the prestige of his name penetrated to every nook of that vast yet undeveloped kingdom was the phenomenon which slowly but surely impressed me. I was but a passing traveller, surveying from a distance and at large that vast plain of humanity; but I could see that it was systematically tilled by one master mind.

Our Home in Bangkok

Rebuked and saddened, I abandoned my long-cherished hope of a home, and resigned myself with no good grace to my routine of study and instruction. Where were all the romantic fancies and proud anticipations with which I had accepted the position of governess to the royal family of Siam? Alas! in two squalid rooms at the end of a Bangkok fish-market. I failed to find the fresh strength and courage that lay in the hope of improving the interesting children whose education had been intrusted to me, and day by day grew more and more desponding, less and less equal to the simple task my "mission" had set me. I was fairly sick at heart and ready to surrender that morning when the good Koon Ying Phan came unannounced into our rooms to tell us that a tolerable house was found for us at last. I cannot describe with what an access of joy I heard the glad tidings, nor how I thanked the messenger, nor how in a moment I forgot all my chagrin and repining, and hugged my boy and covered him with kisses. It was not until that "order for release" arrived, that I truly felt how offensive and galling had been the life I had led in the premier's palace. It was with unutterable gladness that I followed a half-brother of the Kralahome, Moonshee leading Boy by the hand, to our new house. Passing several streets, we entered a walled enclosure, abounding in broken bricks, stone, lime, mortar, and various rubbish.

A tall, dingy storehouse occupied one side of the wall; in the other, a low door opened toward the river; and at the farther end stood the house, sheltered by a few fine trees, that, drooping over the piazza, made the place almost picturesque. On entering, however, we found ourselves face to face with overpowering filth. Poor Moonshee stood aghast. "It must be a paradise," he had said when we set out, "since the great Vizier bestows it upon the Mem Sahib, whom he delights to honor." Now he cursed his fate, and reviled all viziers. I turned to see to whom his lamentations were addressed, and beheld another Mohammedan seated on the floor, and attending with an attitude and air of devout respect. The scene reminded Boy and me of our old home, and we laughed heartily. On making a tour of inspection, we found nine rooms, some of them pleasant and airy, and with every "modern convenience" (though somewhat Oriental as to style) of bath, kitchen, etc. It was clear that soap and water without stint would do much here toward the making of a home for us. Beebe and Boy were hopeful, and promptly put a full stop to the rhetorical outcry of Moonshee by requesting him to enlist the services of his admiring friend and two China coolies to fetch water. But there were no buckets. With a few dollars that I gave him, Moonshee, with all a Moslem's resignation to any new turn in his fate, departed to explore for the required utensils, while the brother of the awful Kralahome, perched on the piazza railing, adjusted his anatomy for a comfortable oversight of the proceedings. Boy, with his "pinny" on, ran off in glee to make himself promiscuously useful, and I sat down to plan an attack.

Where to begin?—that was the question. It was such filthy filth, so monstrous in quantity and kind,—dirt to be stared at, defied, savagely assaulted with rage and havoc. Suddenly I arose, shook my head dangerously at the prime minister's brother,—who, fascinated, had advanced into the room,—marched through a broken door, hung my hat and mantle on a rusty nail, doffed my neat half-mourning, slipped on an old wrapper, dashed at the vile matting that in ulcerous patches afflicted the floor, and began fiercely tearing it up.

In good time Moonshee and his new friend returned with half a dozen buckets, but no coolies; in place of the latter came a neat and pleasant Siamese lady, Mrs. Hunter, wife of the premier's secretary, bringing her slaves to help, and some rolls of fresh, sweet China matting for the floor. How quickly the general foulness was purified, the general raggedness repaired, the general shabbiness made "good as new"! The floors, that had been buried under immemorial dust, arose again under the excavating labors of the sweepers; and the walls, that had been gory with expectorations of betel, hid their "damnéd spots" under innocent veils of whitewash.

Moonshee, who had evidently been beguiled by a cheap and spurious variety of the wine of Shiraz, and now sat maudlin on the steps, weeping for his home in Singapore, I despatched peremptorily in search of Beebe, bedsteads, and boxes. But the Kralahome's brother had vanished, doubtless routed by the brooms.

Bright, fresh, fragrant matting; a table neither too low to be pretty nor too high to be useful; a couple of armchairs, hospitably embracing; a pair of silver candlesticks, quaint and homely; a goodly company of pleasant books; a piano, just escaping from its travelling-cage, with all its pent-up music in its bosom; a cosey little cot clinging to its ampler mother; a stream of generous sunlight from the window gilding and gladdening all,—behold our home in Siam!

I worked exultingly till the setting sun slanted his long shadows across the piazza. Then came comfortable Beebe with the soup and dainties she had prepared with the help of a "Bombay man." Boy slept soundly in an empty room, overcome by the spell of its sudden sweetness, his hands and face as dirty as a healthy, well-regulated boy could desire. Triumphantly I bore him to his own pretty couch, adjusted my hair, resumed my royal robes of mauve muslin, and prepared to queen it in my own palace.

And even as I stood, smiling at my own small grandeur, came tender memories crowding thick upon me,—of a soft, warm lap, in which I had once loved to lay my head; of a face, fair, pensive, loving, lovely; of eyes whose deep and quiet light a shadow of unkindness never crossed; of lips that sweetly crooned the songs of a far-off, happy land; of a presence full of comfort, hope, strength, courage, victory, peace, that perfect harmony that comes of perfect faith,—a child's trust in its mother.

Passionately I clasped my child in my arms, and awoke him with pious promises that took the form of kisses. Beebe, soup, teapot, candlesticks, teacups, and dear faithful Bessy, looked on and smiled.

Hardly had we finished this, our first and finest feast, in celebration of our glorious independence, when our late guide of fish-market fame, he of the seedy red coat and faded yellow facings, appeared on the piazza, saluted us with that vacant chuckle and grin wherefrom no inference could be drawn, and delivered his Majesty's order that I should now come to the school.

Unterrified and deliberate, we lingered yet a little over that famous breakfast, then rose, and prepared to follow the mechanical old ape. Boy hugged Bessy fondly by way of good-by, and, leaving Beebe on guard, we went forth. The same long, narrow, tall, and very crank boat received us. The sun was hot enough to daunt a sepoy; down the bare backs of the oarsmen flowed miniature Meinams of sweat, as they tugged, grunting, against the strong current. We landed at the familiar (king's) pavilion, the front of which projects into the river by a low portico. The roof, rising in several tiers, half shelters, half bridges the detached and dilapidated parts of the structure, which presents throughout a very ancient aspect, parts of the roof having evidently been renewed, and the gables showing traces of recent repairs, while the rickety pillars seem to protest with groans against the architectural anachronism that has piled so many young heads upon their timeworn shoulders.

THE CRUEL WAY

Ella Maillart

Ella Maillart (1903–1997) was an intrepid Swiss adventurer, travel writer and photographer who chose her career, she said, so that her life could be a perpetual holiday. With this in mind, we might question her choice of destinations – a 3,500-mile trek across hostile regions of China simply to learn about an unstable political situation, for example – but her writings provide a valuable historical record. *The Cruel Way* describes her journey by car from Geneva to Kabul, and it's debatable whether it was the checkpoints, poor roads, petty officials and vast deserts that were cruel, or the fact that, after enduring all this, the trip was truncated by the outbreak of the Second World War.

Band-i-Amir

"Theory of true civilisation. It is not in gas or in steam or in table-tapping. But in lessening of the traces of original sin.

Nomads, shepherds, hunters, farmers, even cannibals, all may be superior, by their energy, by their personal dignity, to our peoples of the West. Who perhaps will be destroyed."

Baudelaire (*Mon cœur mis à nu*, XV.)

We now had to cover forty-eight miles of mountain tracks leading to the Band-i-Amir in the direction of Herat. To the west of Bamian we followed the pleasant ravine where we had often fished trout with the Hackins. Once out of it, there was not a rock, not a trace of cliff to remind us of what we had left behind us. We were in a splendid world where barren hills of yellow earth shadowed with mauve succeeded each other to the distant horizon.

Plaques of snow covered the misty blueness of the Koh-i-Baba that barred the south.

From far away the earth looked goose-fleshed; near at hand one saw that the small asperities were thorny knobs of spare *buta*.

We rushed up the steep gradient to the Shahidan pass—much too steep for a heavily laden car. We grew anxious; we even thought we should have to give up our attempt. It was like a victory when, after many efforts, at last we crept to the top, beholding once more a sea of arid, treeless hills. The coldness of the whipping wind reminded us that we were at a height of ten thousand feet, some one thousand five hundred feet higher than Bamian.

We were in the heart of an old, a very old world. Was it not already old sixteenth centuries B.C. (young were the forests of Europe then) when Aryan tribes speaking vedic Sanskrit came from the North on their way to Kurdistan and India? In this great empty space there were now myself and the earth, a pair in good accord. Reduced to essentials, a skeleton of hills covered with the leanest flesh, for all the little it gave, the world pleased me as it was. Nothing too much. Almost nothing at all: sometimes among a succession of yellow shoulders, a small patch of lucerne in a lean armpit; ridges with their fading, fleeing lines that call us, draw us; tracks followed by our rushing ideas, rudiments of such simple landscapes that our imagination can make them resemble memories of the Issyk Kul or Kuen Lun. Attraction of an horizon we want to reach but push back with every step.

To be accepted by the earth. To understand its meaning. Then to feel how much it is one whole, to live the strength of that unity. Then only will it be time to love each part of that whole, freed at last from the blindness of partial love.

My meditation was interrupted by two successive punctures which forced us to deal with inner tubes. Just as we were beginning to worry about the possibility of a breakdown on this deserted track, a rider ambled towards us. Something in his long refined face made us think him an Arab and it was no surprise to hear him say he was a Sayid, a descendant of the Prophet. A bazaar rumour having announced the arrival of Englishmen from Kabul, we asked our Sayid to take a written message to the hotel. We gave our whereabouts, asking for a car to be sent to our rescue should we fail to reach the hotel by the evening of next day.

Greatly relieved, we bumped towards the Shibartu pass.

Dreamy camels on a slope; then a horse bolted in front of the car, its mane waving wildly. Soon afterwards we reached a little dale where two tents were caught in a web of ropes. Squatting on the earth, a woman was weaving at a tripod loom, some twenty yards of narrow warp firmly pegged down. These details were very like what I had seen in the T'ien Shan or among the shepherds of Sinkiang: I felt as if approaching old friends.

The women were reserved while we exchanged the usual questions. And how many camels did we have at home? Were we Russian? Or English? "Oh, then, please" said the chief woman smiling "you must share food with us!" Rice was brought in an enamelled basin: it might have meant that our new friends were well off, for as a rule nomads can only afford wheat-cakes. They are cooked either on an iron disk or wrapped round a cobble-stone near the embers. By counting the round stones of an abandoned camp one knows how strong the party was.

They were all very good-looking, the women in their black and red attire showing Roman features framed by tiny plaits neat and austere like metallic chains looped up to leave the forehead free; the girls with a coin dangling at the end of a short lock, in long dresses pinned up with amulets. The women moved easily and with commanding gestures, continually pulling up the great black cloth that fell loosely from the top of the head. The men were away with the herds.

They were a Mandozai tribe and would soon return, they told us, to the plains near Khanabad: the nights were beginning to be too cold.

We took leave (*Khoda hafiz!*), giving a red scarf to a boy and Russian sweets to the other children.

With the Hackins I had visited a similar camp. The tribesmen were hard hit by the new lorry-transport. Since no-one bought their camels they were trying to develop their sheep-breeding.

Without counting the few tens of thousand *powindahs* who go every autumn to India for trading purposes, there is still a part of the Afghan population, a tenth perhaps, which is almost or quite nomadic.

But, following the example of Iran and Turkey, the government was planning to change their habits.

Nomadic life is doomed even in Saudi Arabia or in Mongolia, and I think the main reasons for this disappearance are the same in all these countries. Nowadays frontiers are exactly delimited and they complicate nomadic life. The central power of every country wants to become strong, needs obedient soldiers and settled tax-paying subjects; to make his country independent, the Chief of State has to enforce these conditions at all costs; that this kind of independence is not the one wanted by nomads cannot be taken into consideration. People who obey only their tribal laws cannot be allowed in modern constitutional states.

Leaving aside those pests that live by banditry (like certain Turkomans), one can say that nomads have many good qualities: besides their handsome physique they have a greatly developed sense of honour while their laws of hospitality have become second nature to them. They are good fighters because they are not afraid of death, their customs and religions having given them an understanding of what it is. They are absolutely loyal to the tribe. It is exactly these qualities which are their undoing to-day, though so far they have helped them.

Because they are fully themselves, they can only with difficulty become peasants or artisans; not having known the old life, their children may be more adaptable. In the meantime this wonderful human material is wasted. The Kurds are in utter misery, their ways of living crushed, whether in Turkey, Iran or Iraq. Other nomads, some two hundred thousand of them, were sent away from the mountains of South Persia or fled to sun-scorched Mesopotamia where they all died within two years. In Turkestan, the Kazak-Kirghizes as well as the Turkomans have melted away by millions. The Mongols had to give away their pasture-land to innumerable Chinese settlers supported by the authorities; after a few years of hoeing, the thin soil was blown away and the land became a desert. In Arabia, King Ibn Saud knew he would obtain allegiance only from a settled people: he had to break their tribal system and their blood-feuds and turn them into peasants obeying God and King instead of their own chief.

Those who do not know the nomads may ask: Does it matter

whether one or two million more disappear from the face of Asia when so many are already killed by floods, famine or epidemics? Yes, it matters indeed, it is greatly to be deplored. For the nomads are a good leaven that could regenerate the tired Syrians, exhausted Persians, decimated Chinese. In the past, the period of devastation once ended, the nomads infused their boldness of conception into the conquered people. Grafted on to old trunks, they brought forth new blossoming in China, Persia, India, Turkey. From the Aryans long ago down to the Arabs, the Seljuks, the Mongols, how much poorer our world would have been without the impulse given by those who, like King David, were wandering shepherds?

"We are content with discord, alarms, blood, but we will never be content with a master" is a saying attributed to the Ghilzai tribesman; and if he remains unruly now, he will be broken. But it seems foolish forcibly to settle nomads who used to tend their flocks, since sheep will have to be looked after anyhow, whether in Arabia, Mongolia, Iran or Afghanistan. Why not leave this work to those who love it instead of destroying their life and skill?

I stopped the car with a jerk: straight ahead in a trough between steep slopes of rose-coloured earth, a tiny jewel of an incredible blue density dazzled in the silent solitude. It was our first glimpse of the King's Dam, the Band-i-Amir. Mountain wheat grew sparsely at our feet, short, stiff, solid, its ear like a broad blade.

Further on we found an amazing scene spread at our feet—a string of lakes caught between pink cliffs, their colours passing from apple-green, turquoise, gentian and Prussian blue to dark indigo. Shallow, the two first were set in a ring of bright white limestone. The last were linked by a wide sloping threshold dotted with round bushes, the only touch of vegetation in a barren world.

"I love it..." said Christina, her face lit with surprise. Not a soul nor a house in sight but for the small *ziarat* across the big lake. "You haven't seen all," I said; "but let us first follow the track down that cliff."

We slid down till we were actually forty feet below the level of the lake: slowly through the ages, these waters had built a beautifully curved rim at their southern end. Down this barrage came the overflowing ripples sparkling over gluey terraces; at one point spurting among its asperities, at another building a waterfall that was caught by the wheel of a mill.

We skirted the foot of the dam, our tyres splashing through clear rivulets, and climbed up to the small platform before the *ziarat* of Hazrat Ali. Steps led down to a little shore beyond which the lake was a dark-blue fjord meandering between mauve sandstone cliffs: it was astonishing to meet the radiance of these waters. Wavelets rocked a few blades of amphibian grass while big fish that no-one is allowed to catch soared up to look at us.

A bearded man in quilted rags, the keeper of the shrine, said the lake was bottomless. He led us to one of the three rooms of the *ziarat,* vaulted, blackened by smoke. There, in the heart of the dense silence, we camped.

While the lake became a mass of fretting molten metal, the sunset painted the hills with dahlia, lilac, hyacinth. And when we went to sleep there were two freezing Milky Ways, the one at our feet just as many millions of miles away as the one above our heads.

But the windless early morning gave the best spectacle. A crack in the steep bank led to the table-land above the shrine; from there we saw at our feet a huge surface of polished bronze, a gigantic curved mirror that reproduced every tint, slope, gully, stone and mood that existed in the upper world.

No sooner had it opened our eyes to the beauty of the earth than the enchanted mirror altered: a lively breeze changed it into an opaque arena of lapis lazuli hung half-way between a pale lowland and tall blushing cliffs. We walked through that ethereal atmosphere till we dominated the second barrage where green bushes grew between white rivulets. Every detail had the sharpness not only of something one sees for the first time but of a beauty that can be compared with nothing else.

At the shrine three witches wanted drugs. One was blind, her hand led over the car by her companion. The windscreen delayed them: I imagine it was difficult to convey the idea that a solid can be transparent. The tomb is supposed to contain the remains of Ali, son-in-law of the Prophet. Two men were worshipping in the clean, whitewashed sanctuary. Seeing once more with what devotion the shrines of Afghanistan are cared for, I realised that Islam is the main force that links together a population in which blood, language and customs differ so widely. I have seen Afghans praying not only in mosques, but in fields, in shops, on the road—till I came to understand that it means much to them. And I think he was an exception, my neighbour in the bus who when I had remarked that Europeans do sometimes pray but mostly when alone, retorted: "But what is the good of praying if you aren't seen doing it?" Reforms or plans for reconstruction will have to agree with the spirit of Islam if they are to stay for good. It is only because he had successfully reawakened the faith that Ibn Saud could draw to himself allegiances that formerly went to the tribes: thus he brought together in the army or in the fields men whose ancestors had for generations been at feud.

A legend explains the origin of the Band-i-Amir (I reproduce here the details given by Major Rupert Hay*). King Barbar, an infidel, was oppressing his subjects. A man who had been searching for Hazrat Ali and found him near Haibak, was ordered to bind that saint and bring him as a slave to the king. Ali was then asked to perform three tasks—kill the dragon of Bamian, build dams in a valley and lastly, save his own head. The dragon was killed. With mighty rage a rock was hurled down which built the Band-i-Haibat or Dam of Wrath; while with his sword he clove the Band-i-Zulfikar, the Dam of the Sword. Then Ali told Barbar to load him with chains. When he had rendered everybody senseless by reciting the Muhammadan profession of faith, he freed himself and converted King Barbar.

* Geographical Journal, April, 1936.

ON SLEDGE & HORSEBACK TO OUTCAST SIBERIAN LEPERS

Kate Marsden

Kate Marsden (1859–1931) was an English missionary, explorer and nurse, who spent most of 1891 trekking through the challenging terrain of Siberia in search of an elusive herb said to have healing properties for the treatment of leprosy; this was her pet project. After travelling some 18,000km by train, sledge, horseback and boat, she still hadn't found that all-important herb, but she didn't abandon the lepers of Siberia, devoting her time instead to raising money to build a hospital for them. She provides fascinating detail on what was deemed appropriate clothing back in the day for such a climatically challenging expedition and so much more in *On Sledge and Horseback to Outcast Siberian Lepers.*

Yakutsk—The Province—And the People

Area and population of Yakutsk—Native traits and habits—Poverty of the people partly caused by leprosy—Rules of etiquette—Laying up stores for twelve months—Visit to the Bishop—Kindness of the Bishop—Formation of a committee for the lepers—"A chiel amang us takin' notes"—Arrangements for forming the cavalcade to the lepers—My outfit—The start for the 2000 miles' ride on horseback.

The Yakutsk province, situated in the far north-east of Siberia, extends over three and a half million square versts (nearly two and a half million miles), and contains only 250,000 inhabitants. The population is made up of different tribes, the Yakuts, a people of Mongolian origin, forming more than three-quarters of the entire number. There are about 16,000 Russians, and the rest of the population consists of several small nomad tribes, such as the Toungus, the Tchuktes, the Lamouts, the Youkagirs, and the Tchuvantses.

For administrative purposes the province is divided into circuits, *oulousses* (a district including several villages), and *nasslegs* (village communities). There are five circuits in this province, namely, the Yakutsk, the Viluisk, the Olekminsk, the Verchoyansk, and the Kolimsk. The town of Yakutsk, with a population of about 7000, is the chief administrative centre of the province, and stands on the River Lena.

The Viluisk Circuit, which interests us the most under the present conditions, extends over 883,000 square versts (about 559,000 miles), and comprises four oulousses: the Viluisk, the Sredni Viluisk, the Marinsk, and the Suntarsky. Forests, marshes, and lakes abound; and along the shores of lakes and rivers there are patches of pasture land which the inhabitants utilise on a small scale for rearing cattle. As no arable land exists, the natives are not agriculturists, whilst fur trading, which is comparatively flourishing in other parts of the province, is here very fluctuating and small.

The natives, even now, are only in a semi-barbarous state, having but recently been brought under the influence of civilisation. In their original state they were idolaters, and at the present time, although considered Christians, they are addicted to many heathen practices. Their abodes are found on the margins of lakes and rivers, where small communities are formed at long distances from each other. This comparative isolation of the communities seems to be a desirable arrangement, owing to the quarrelling propensities of the people. They are also very distrustful, and, therefore, secretive and taciturn; but, nevertheless, they are always ready to give a hearty welcome to a stranger, who may, if he likes, help himself to the contents of the humble larder. Most of the inhabitants of the Viluisk Circuit are very poor, and how some of them continue to exist is little short of a mystery. The fur trade offers a fluctuating source of livelihood; and many of the people make odds and ends, such as baskets, vessels for food, drinking vessels, ornaments, and cradles out of the bark of trees. Some of these baskets are very pretty, being interlaced with fish scales, which radiate with all kinds of colours. The people live in *yourtas* (huts), of simple construction, for the most part extremely dirty, and devoid of the ordinary comforts of home life. The *yourta*, for winter habitation is usually made of light beams, well plastered externally with thick layers of clay and cow-dung.

The poverty of the people, in a measure, arises from the ravages of leprosy amongst the able-bodied. The Sredni Viluisk oulousse is the greatest sufferer in this respect; and thus the accumulation of arrears of taxes is constantly on the increase. Suntarsky, when compared with the other oulousses, is said to be wealthy, the people being able to build *yourtas* similar to the Russian peasants' *izbas*, and to provide themselves with at least one great domestic comfort—a good Russian stove.

The town of Yakutsk is not a pretty place, and has a dreary, dead appearance. At eight o'clock the houses are shut up, and there are no amusements or recreations. The winter temperature is about 45° of cold, and the air is then filled with mist or fog. The shawl which screens the face is soon covered with a sheet of ice, on account of respiration; the frost also covers the eyelashes, so that it is almost impossible to see at all. Sometimes the cold is so frightful that strong people cannot go out of their houses for days together. It is not light till ten or half-past, and is dark about two; and this state of things continues for nearly eight months out of the year.

The people play cards and smoke, sometimes six hours out of twelve. All the ladies smoke; and the first thing offered to a guest on his or her arrival is a cigarette. The samovar and tea follow, and, whilst smoking, tea-drinking, and talking are going on, the men walk up and down the room the whole time. Never mind how small the room, this constant walking, talking, and smoking all at once is an inveterate habit. The stranger, of necessity, gets somewhat bewildered, until he makes up his mind to feel at home. According to the rules of etiquette, the gentleman must be the first to give his hand to the visitor, who must take off in the hall his cloak, or *shouba*, and fur boots. On no account must the visitor enter the room in his outdoor costume; and if he declines the proffered tea he is guilty almost of a crime. The poorer people use sheets of ice three or four inches thick instead of glass windows, and how they keep themselves warm is almost incomprehensible. Stores come in once a year, and the people must buy for twelve months. There are doctors, but no chemists, and the doctors only buy drugs from Irkutsk once a year.

Soon after my arrival in the town of Yakutsk I went to see the Bishop. We drove in a vehicle called a *dolgushka*, which consists of a few boards, painted a dark colour, placed on wheels, forming a long centre back, the people sit sideways and back to back; it can hold six or eight people, and is considered a superior kind of vehicle. In passing through the broad streets, lined with dilapidated houses, we met a few Yakuts driving carts drawn by bullocks, and sitting on the animals' backs. Their tall hats, long, high-shouldered cloaks, high top-boots, and singularly plain faces looked altogether comical.

In the garden of the Bishop were three churches; and as I mounted the wooden stairs of his house, and entered the small plain hall, the unpretentious look of the place struck me. When His Grace came in, it was impossible not to be attracted by his noble, peaceful face. Devout, unruffled restfulness seemed to be imprinted there; and, as he welcomed me, that peacefulness seemed somehow to influence me. His blue robes, the blue furniture, and the blue paper on the walls, seemed to give him almost an ethereal look; but of course this was only a woman's fancy. He greeted me most kindly. He is very earnest in his work, and does not limit it to Yakutsk only, but sends missionaries thousands of versts up to the north, among the different tribes, to proclaim the glad tidings of Christ's love. His Christianity is practised in all his daily works.

I spoke about forming a committee in Yakutsk; and he at once promised to use every exertion to bring the leading people together, and to help the lepers, not only by relieving their material wants, but also by giving them an opportunity of receiving the consolations of religion. He gave me one of the rare copies of the complete New Testament in the Yakutsk tongue.

On my referring to the herb he said, much to my surprise and delight, that he had a few specimens, and before I left he placed some in my hands. He could give no definite information as to its curative or alleviating properties. It was, however, a source of some satisfaction that the reports I had heard were not altogether groundless. As I was leaving, he came forward and blessed me. Perhaps some friends may think it wrong of me (a Protestant) to receive the blessing of a dignitary of the Greek Church. I took it as a sign of oneness in Christ, notwithstanding wide divergences in creed, and as a mark of brotherhood amongst those working for Christ and in His name. I rejoice to believe that, with our Lord, there is no distinction of church or creed; we are all one in Him, and He in us. I must add that, during the time I spent in Yakutsk, the Bishop looked after me lovingly and tenderly, as if I had been his own daughter.

Not only from the Bishop, but also from a doctor in the town, I heard fearful accounts of the lepers in the forests and on the marshes, which were almost inaccessible. The doctor begged me to take tea and tobacco, luxuries unknown to them. I longed to get off, but had to wait for the committee to meet, whilst the preparations for so long and difficult a journey involved a great deal of thought. At last the committee met, consisting of the following members: His Eminence the Bishop of Yakutsk, Meletie; His Excellency the Vice-Governor, Mr. Ostashkin; the Medical Inspector, Smirnoff; the doctor of the district, Mons. Tschevinsky; the doctor of the Yakutsk Hospital, Mons. Nesmeloff; the assistant of the Viluisk police; the tchinovnick of the Governor; the Cossack, Jean Procopieff; and myself.

We discussed the state of the lepers, who had been visited by the Medical Inspector, whose report,* whilst corroborating what I had already heard, supplied additional details of terrible sufferings. Then the question of getting to the lepers came up; and various suggestions were made for my guidance. A plan was prepared of the route I ought to take. But I must refer, in passing, to some difficulties, which I thought were particularly serious for a woman to suffer. Notwithstanding my credentials, a suspicion existed that I was nothing better than a political

* See Appendix.

spy; and it is not always pleasant to find that there is "a chiel amang us takin' notes," which "notes" may be used against one at some future time. It seems to be one of the primary duties of some of the officials in Yakutsk to look out for suspects, and carry a note-book and pencil in their pockets for jotting down any matters which may appear to them of a compromising nature. After some delay, I began buying stores for the journey. I cannot enumerate everything, but only just a few to give an idea of what we thought it necessary to take. Dried bread (almost as hard as a stone, and which had to be soaked in tea before being eaten) packed in fish skins and boxes, covered with fish skin, and, for this reason, smelling and tasting for ever after of bad fish; tea, sugar, tobacco, tinned meats and fruits, biscuits, and an assortment of drugs and an *en-route* basket from Drew & Sons, Piccadilly. What became of most of these things the reader can easily imagine as we continue this narrative.

The Cossack, Jean Procopieff, knowing of my small pecuniary means, and being touched deeply by the sufferings of the lepers, offered, with expressions of sympathy, to lend me all the horses required for the journey as far as Viluisk. He further offered his services as leader of the cavalcade. It was useless to think of travelling by tarantass; such a conveyance would have got wedged fatally in the forest, or would have sunk in some treacherous morass before a single mile had been covered. It was therefore absolutely necessary to make the journey on horseback, and also necessary to employ a number of men not only for carrying stores, but also as a means of protection against the dangers to be encountered, not the least amongst them being the bears, with which the woods are infested. Our cavalcade was a curious one. It consisted of fifteen men and thirty horses. The photographer in the town tried to take our photographs, but the attempt was a failure, for some one moved during the operation. I rather shrink from giving a description of my costume, because it was so inelegant. I wore a jacket, with very long sleeves, and had the badge of the red cross on my left arm. Then I had to wear full trousers to the knees.

The hat was an ordinary deer-stalker, which I had bought in London. I carried a revolver, a whip, and a little travelling bag, slung over the shoulder. I was obliged to ride as a man for several reasons—

first, because the Yakutsk horses were so wild that it was impossible to ride safely sideways; second, because no woman could ride on a lady's saddle for three thousand versts; third, because, in the absence of roads, the horse has a nasty propensity of stumbling on the stones and amongst the roots of trees, which in these virgin forests make a perfect network, thus precipitating the unfortunate rider on to the ground; and, fourth, because the horse frequently sinks into the mud up to the rider's feet, and then, recovering its footing, rushes madly along amongst the shrubs and the branches of trees, utterly regardless of the fact that the lady-rider's dress (if she wore one) was being torn into fragments. For these reasons I think no one will blame me for adopting man's mode of riding, and for making adequate provisions by means of the thick leather boots against the probability of bruises, contusions, etc.

Before starting, the Bishop invited us all to his house for prayer. He held a special service, praying for God's blessing and protection on our work. It was a touching sight—this motley assemblage of men, and I the only woman amongst them, receiving the benediction of this servant of Christ on the eve of our perilous journey.

Our object being a very serious one, I took care that as little attention as possible should be attracted by our departure. All being ready, we set out on the journey of 2000 miles on June 22nd, 1891.

PASSENGER TO TEHERAN

Vita Sackville-West

Vita Sackville-West (1892–1962) was an English novelist, poet, diarist and journalist, known also for her unconventional marriage to Sir Harold Nicolson. Sackville-West loved her home county of Kent, but in the mid-1920s she travelled to Persia (Iran) to visit her diplomat husband, recording her experiences in *Passenger to Teheran*. She proved a fearless traveller, taking the opportunity to linger in Egypt and India en route and returning to the UK via post-Revolutionary Russia – perhaps not the safest of places for an aristocrat to be, but nothing compared to the bandit-ridden mountains she documents negotiating between Iraq and Iran.

Into Persia

Heaven knows Bagdad had seemed remote enough, at Victoria on a January morning; but now, looking towards the east, it appeared almost suburban, and the great spaces only on the point of opening out. This was the last train I should see; the last time I should be jolted with that familiar railway-clanking into the night.

A poor little train it was too, taking ten laborious hours to cover the hundred miles of its journey. It climbed from the plain into the hills, and a frosty dawn found it steaming and stationary at the railhead. Railheads are not commonly seen in Europe. In England we see them, because otherwise at certain points the train would have no choice but to run on into the sea; at Dover, at Brighton, we see them – though even at Brighton there is a branch line which goes, at a right angle, along the coast to Worthing. But in Europe we do not often see them, unless we go to Lisbon or Constantinople. Even Venice is a cheat, because the train after backing curves round again and goes merrily off through the Balkans. We are accustomed to see the rails shining away over fresh country, after we have got out and are left standing beside our luggage on the platform. But here, at Khaniquin, there was no geographical reason why the rails should leave off; why, instead of going on for a thousand, two thousand, ten thousand shining miles, they should end in a pair of blunt buffers.

Mountain air at five o'clock in the morning makes one hungry. I found the little canteen in occupation of a fellow-traveller. He was a stout man, dressed in complete riding-kit – breeches, leather gaiters, even to the hunting-crop. He recommended the porridge and we got into conversation. I said something about walking to the cars. "Walk?" he said, "I have just walked eleven thousand miles." I asked if this was the first time he had been to Persia. *"Been to Persia?"* he said, "I have been round the world seventeen times." From his accent I thought he was Scotch, but he gave me his name, told me he spoke twenty-five languages, and was a Belgian marquis. He had a secretary with him, a silent, downtrodden young man, hung with cameras, thermos bottles, and field-glasses. I never heard him speak, and I never discovered his nationality. He simply ate his breakfast as though he were not sure when he would next replenish his larder. In this he reminded me of the saluki, who, a true camp-follower, had a perfectly definite attitude towards life: eat when you can and sleep when you can, for you never know when your next meal and your next rest are coming.

There was a delay over starting, the usual delay, and meanwhile the sky turned pink behind the hills, and a long caravan of camels got up and lurched away across the plateau, their bells sounding more faintly and their extraordinary silhouettes growing blacker and more precise as they trailed out against the morning sky. Then the sun came up, the snow flushed on the distant hills, the grey morning had gone, the whole plateau was full of light. It elated me to see that the road led straight into the dawn. "The sun rises in the east," we are accustomed to say; and a new significance welled up into that empty maxim. The sun was leading the way. Indeed, to wander about the world is to become very intimately mixed up with astronomy. Familiar stars tilt, and even disappear; the Bear performs antics, Orion climbs. We become conscious of the path of the sun. At home, the heavenly phenomena pass and repass over our heads, without our troubling to lift our eyes to this display of punctual and stupendous mechanism. But the traveller notices.

Outside the station the cars were waiting, muddy, loaded, the legend TRANS-DESERT MAIL in white paint on their bonnets. They had come from Beyrout, and looked it. The marquis, smacking his gaiters with his crop, was fussing round, like the fly round the coach in the fable. Avoiding the marquis, I got the front seat in the other car, with Zurcha, who although as leggy as a colt, folded up into a surprisingly small space and immediately went to sleep. I was glad to see this, as I had not looked forward to restraining a struggling dog over five hundred miles of country, and had not been at all easy in my mind as to what a saluki straight out of the desert would make of a motor. That yellow nomad, however, accepted whatever life sent her with a perfect and even slightly irritating philosophy. Warmth and food she insisted on; shared my luncheon and crawled under my sheepskin, but otherwise gave no trouble. I was relieved, but felt it a little ungrateful of her not to notice that she was being taken into Persia.

I was myself very vividly aware of going into Persia. The nose of the motor pointed straight at the sun; this way had come Alexander, but not Marco Polo, not Mme. Dieulafoy, not M. de Gobineau, not even Lord Curzon. This road, which lay between the two wild provinces of Kurdistan and Luristan, had, until the war, existed only as a caravan route between Persia and Bagdad; no traveller dreamt of risking his property and possibly his life that way. True, Nasr-ed-Din Shah had made an expedition, summoning the tribal chiefs of the Kurds and Lurs to meet him, but, being informed that among these superstitious and ignorant brigands the Shah was commonly supposed to be a giant fifteen feet high, and being warned that the disappointment of seeing a man of mere ordinary stature might prove subversive to their loyalty, yet being determined to show himself to his predatory vassals, he hit upon an ingenious expedient. Having caused his tent to be pitched so that the rays of the rising sun should strike full upon it, he ordered the breast of his uniform to be sewn from collar to hem with every diamond in the Persian treasury. The chiefs assembled at dawn. Then, as the sun rose, the flap of the Shah's pavilion was thrown open, and in the sun's illumination appeared that motionless and resplendent figure. The chiefs prostrated themselves; but when they again raised their dazzled eyes, the Shah had vanished.

I asked my driver if he had ever been held up on the road. No, he said, he hadn't, but several of his mates had, because they were fools enough to stop when ordered. "Now if anybody comes at me," he added. "I drive straight at them." With that, he let in his gears, and we started. The first few miles were atrocious, and populous. We overtook the long string of camels, and innumerable donkeys loaded with petrol tins; waggons too, with drivers asleep; lorries full of grain, some advancing, others stuck askew in the mud. Streams crossed the track every hundred yards or so, and this meant mud up to the axles; in between the streams the road was less a road full of holes, than a series of holes connected by fragments of road. Our luggage truck bounded and bounced ahead of us. There was a great deal of shouting and of digging out of stranded lorries in progress, and mingled with the shouts of the men came the grave note of the camel bells, and the creaking of the overloaded waggons. They all seemed to be going east; we met no one coming the other way. They trailed across the rolling ground towards the frontier, a straggling concourse, in the clear morning.

The Iraq frontier consisted of a post-house, a crazy gate hung across the road, and a few strands of barbed wire. Inside the post-house we were given tea and cigarettes while our passports were being stamped, and admired the collection of visiting-cards with which the walls were papered. The marquis took a number of photographs with different kodaks. Three woolly puppies tumbled in the dust. Meanwhile the traffic accumulated into a block of waggons and animals, which we left behind us, jostling and abusive, as we swung into the No-man's land between Iraq and Persia. The Persian frontier lay about five miles ahead; here we were offered an escort of soldiers, which we declined; the pole that barred the road was raised; we moved forward; we were in Persia.

I discovered then that not one of the various intelligent people I had spoken with in England had been able to tell me anything about Persia at all – the truth being, I suppose, that different persons observe different things, and attribute to them a different degree of importance. Such a diversity of information I should not have resented; but here I was obliged to recognise that they had told me simply nothing. No one, for instance, had mentioned the beauty of the country, though they had dwelt at length, and with much exaggeration, on the discomforts of the way. It reminded me of nothing so much as the traditional reply of the negro, who, when asked, "How far is it to such-and-such a place?" replies, "Not too far." "Is the road steep?" I had asked, and had been told, "Not too steep," which was true enough of the road across the plains, but quite untrue of the road over the passes, which climbs to ten thousand feet in a seven-mile series of hairpin bends. No one had told me that I must take my own provisions for three or four days; but that, fortunately, I had found out in Bagdad. No one had told me that I might have to spend several nights in a mud hut by the roadside, held up by a fresh fall of snow, though that was constantly happening to travellers less lucky than I. No one, in fact, had made one single useful or illuminating remark. It had its advantages, and allowed me to enter Persia with an open mind. I had no idea whatever of what I was going to see.

I saw, as, with the sun, we swept onwards, a country unlike anything I had ever seen before. England, France, Germany, Poland have their points in common; a sense of care and cultivation; snug little villages; homesteads tiled and self-contained; evidences of husbandry, in ploughed fields, meadows, ricks; a trim landscape, a landscape ordered by man, and submissive to his needs. Italy and Spain have their points in common; a landscape again submissive to man, though compelling him to work on lines dictated by the rougher lie of the land: he has had to make terraces for his vines, his cities wear a rude mediæval aspect, the general wild beauty of the country has been conquered indeed, but only after a struggle; murder and pillage, Moors and tyrants, still stalk those slopes. Russia has the green rolling steppe; predominantly the face of the dry land is cultivated, it is used, it is forced to be of service to man and his creatures, it is green.

But Persia had been left as it was before man's advent. Here and there he had scraped a bit of the surface, and scattered a little grain; here and there, in an oasis of poplars and fruit trees outlining a stream, he had raised a village, and his black lambs skipped under the peach-blossom; but for miles there was no sign of him, nothing but the brown plains and the blue or white mountains, and the sense of space. The crowds of Europe suddenly rushed at me, overwhelmed me; I was drowning under the pressure, when they cleared away, and I was left, breathing, with space all round me, and a serenity that looked down from the peaks on to the great bowl of the plain. The motor, as it swept up and down the hills, might have been an eagle swooping; no sooner had it reached the top of an eminence than it swept down again and was off, eating up the long road, till the smooth monotony of our movement lulled me into a sort of hypnotic state, through which I perceived the landscape rushing past; the shadows of clouds bowling over the plain as though to race the car; the occasional dark patch made by a grazing flock. We were in Kurdistan. Such peasants as we met wore long blue coats with a broad, twisted sash; high, brimless hats of felt, their black hair curling out from underneath, in the mediæval fashion; their legs were bound in rags; they carried staves and drove animals before them. From their ragged, mediæval appearance they might have been stragglers from some routed army. They travelled on foot, on horseback, or in waggons; hooded waggons, going at a foot's pace, drawn by four little horses abreast; long strings of waggons, trailing along, heaped with rugs and household goods; a wretched, starved-looking procession. If the distances seemed great to us, sweeping along in a powerful motor, what must they have seemed to that crawling string, whose day's journey meant no change of scene, no appreciable lessening of the stretch between mountain-range and range?

We stopped to eat, that first day, by a brawling river at the foot of our first mountain-pass; then left the plain and climbed, round dizzy precipitous corners, squeezing past waggons and camels – for there is always more traffic on a pass than elsewhere: the horses cannot drag their loads, and have to be unharnessed and reharnessed as trace-horses, and started off again, scrambling and slipping on the stony surface. We met little donkeys, coming down, stepping delicately, and camels, swaying down on their soft padded feet. Looking up, we could see the whole road of the pass zigzagging up the cliff-side, populous with animals and shouting, thrashing men. Looking back, as we climbed, we could see the immense prospect of the plain stretching away behind us. A savage, desolating country! but one that filled me with extraordinary elation. I had never seen anything that pleased me so well as these Persian uplands, with their enormous views, clear light, and rocky grandeur. This was, in detail, in actuality, the region labelled 'Persia' on the maps. Let me be aware, I said; let me savour every mile of the way. But there were too many miles, and although I gazed, sitting in the front seat, the warm body of the dog pressed against me, the pungent smell of the sheepskin in my nostrils, it is only the general horizon that I remember, and not every unfolding of the way. This question of horizon, however; how important it is; how it alters the shape of the mind; how it expresses, essentially, one's ultimate sense of country! That is what can never be told in words: the exact size, proportion, contour; the new standard to which the mind must adjust itself.

After the top of the pass I expected to drop down again, to come down on the other side; the experience of remaining up, once one has climbed, had not yet become familiar to me. I was not yet accustomed to motoring along a level road, in the close company of mountain tops. But these were the high levels of Asia. All day we continued, until darkness fell, and the shapes of hills became like the shapes of crouching beasts, uncertain, disquieting. This country, which all the day had been flooded with light, and which now and then had softened from its austerity into the gentler swell of hills like English downs, rounded, and bathed in light like the pink light of sunset – even at midday – now reverted to its pristine secrecy; the secrecy of days when no traveller passed that way, but only the nomad Kurds driving their flocks to other pastures; the secrecy of darker days, when the armies of Alexander and Darius, making for Ecbatana, penetrated the unmapped, tumbled region, seizing a peasant to act as guide; captain and emperor surveying from a summit the unknown distances. The moon came up from behind a hill; the full moon, whose birth I had seen netted in the rigging, in an opalescent dawn on the

Indian Ocean. I watched, turning to human things, the blunt, young profile of the chauffeur under his peaked cap. I talked to him, as the air freshened and the moon climbed, and Zurcha settled closer into my arms with a contented sigh, as though I had not plucked her out of the Arabian desert, away from the life of tents and the weary sleep beside the camels' packs.

HONOURING HIGH PLACES

Junko Tabei

Junko Tabei (1939–2016) was a Japanese mountaineer. At 4 foot 11 (1.5m), she was diminutive in stature, but the same cannot be said of the mountains she climbed. Founding an all-female mountaineering club in 1969 she led its members on the first woman-only ascent of Annapurna III. In 1975, she became the first woman to reach the summit of Everest, again leading an all-female group, and in 1992 she was the first woman to conquer the 'Seven Summits', the highest peaks on seven continents. Junko's childhood love of mountains never faltered, as *Honouring High Places* illustrates, and it endured to the end. Just months before her death, at age 77, she led an expedition of young people affected by the 2011 Fukushima nuclear disaster up Mount Fuji.

The Summit: May 16

After two hours, I was awake, trying to convince myself that lying stationary was enough to provide the body rest. I checked my watch: 11:30 p.m. I closed my eyes but sleep evaded me. I checked my watch again: 1:20 a.m., 3:00, 3:50. I listened to the outdoors – silence. No wind. I woke Ang Tsering. Still embedded in my sleeping bag, I raised the front flap of the tent to a sea of stars that twinkled in the serene air high above the hovering 8000-metre peaks. It was almost eerily quiet as the mountains stared back at me. I knew the weather was good for a climb to the summit.

Slowly, I crawled from the warmth of my cocoon and began to pack things away. Every movement was sluggish. I had to rest after pulling up a sock. My brain was sending the message to hurry but my body found it impossible to cooperate. My actions were that of a slow-motion film. Sloth-like, I fired up the stove to melt the frozen chunk of concrete that had been hot water the night before. The thawing process allowed me enough time to put on my over-pants, leather climbing boots and nylon overboots, which had holes in them, mementoes from Annapurna III. When we eventually earned the morning's first mouthful of milk tea, the heat spread through me like life itself. "*Mitho*," said my companion. Tasty.

We had two more cups of coffee each and filled our Thermoses with black tea and our pockets with candies, and were out the tent at 5:50 a.m. It was dawn and neither wind nor a wisp of cloud was evident. In front of me lay the route to the summit, a long white ridge that we would follow. Every other peak – Makalu, Lhotse, Pumori – was vibrant in its presence. The scenery was one of crystal clearness, like the air we breathed.

I put on my crampons while staring at those beautiful mountains in full morning light. I thought of how unlike this day was to the Japanese harp concerts of my youth where I could calm myself with the assurance that no matter how poorly I performed, it would not kill me. Everest was different; performance was everything, the line between life and death. Nonetheless, to my own surprise, I felt at ease.

My pack was ready with two cameras, an 8-millimetre movie camera (the journalists asked us to bring two as a backup but we decided against it), one radio, a spare pair of gloves, food, drink and emergency kits. The two oxygen bottles I also carried, plus the regulator and mask I wore on my face, forced the straps of the pack to dig into my shoulders and accentuate the weight of the 20 kilograms on my back. Ang Tsering saw the problem and grabbed the movie camera, Thermoses and emergency kits, and buried them in his pack.

No sooner had we left camp than we were breaking trail in knee-deep snow, which, unbelievably, became waist deep. Essentially, we ploughed our way through in a whole-body tackle of the conditions. Five metres of climbing made my heart want to leap from my mouth; my mask was covered in snow from leaning into the steep slope. My breathing was so arduous that it erased the sound of the supplemental oxygen flow, which was usually a loud hiss in my head. In a persistent action of first padding down the snow with knees and then stamping feet, Ang Tsering and I alternated breaking trail.

Two hours of desperate work led to a ridge of steep rock and snow. Although very rugged and unstable, it was not technically difficult. We continued to climb, tied into the rope with 20 metres between us and alternating leads. Our only chance for rest was when we belayed one another. I suffered less than expected, likely a tribute to the supplemental oxygen, and mainly felt the weight of my pack and a screaming pain in my ankles from the steepness of the pitch.

"South Peak!" bellowed Ang Tsering, his face mask removed so he could speak. Although not the true summit of Everest, the South Peak marked significant progress. We arrived there at 9:40 a.m. Almost four hours had passed since we left Camp 6. We stomped out a spot in the snow, dropped our packs, and for the first time since dawn, sat down.

"We have just arrived at South Peak," we reported to Camp 2.

"You'll be at the summit in about an hour then? The radio will remain on. Have a good one," Hisano said, her voice cheerful.

"I don't think we can get to the summit in an hour due to the tremendous amount of snow. Please estimate two to three hours," I said. Then I took a moment to pour tea into a cup, soak three biscuits in the lukewarm liquid and eat them with a handful of chocolates.

I glanced in the direction that Ang Tsering pointed towards. "That's the summit," he said. From where we sat on the first peak, our route descended a sharp upside-down V-shaped ridge that abruptly dropped from our perch. After a bit, it trended upwards into a rocky gully with the crack pitch called Hillary's Chimney (now, the Hillary Step), and then onto the final snowy ridge above.

Even though I had read from the records of prior Everest climbers that the terrain between the South Peak and the summit was difficult and dangerous, I had not read a description of the sheer drop and knife-point ridge that we encountered. I immediately begrudged the lack of detail in previously written Everest reports but knew I had to accept the route in front of us. Simultaneously, I realized this was the section that Lhakpa Tenzing, our sirdar-turned-liaison-officer, had warned us about earlier.

We exchanged our used oxygen bottles (leaving them at the South Peak) for full ones, and began the final push to the summit at 10:10 a.m.

Carefully, I made my first downward step onto the two-pitched knife-point ridge, one side of which descended east into Tibet, and the other west into Nepal. The exposure was dizzying. My movement mimicked a sideways crawl, with my trunk on the Nepal side of the ridge and my arms swung over to Tibet. I kicked into the slope with the toe of my crampons and placed my weight on the platform of my boot, knowing that each time I relied entirely on a foot placement was the very moment I risked my life. Would the next kick be faultless? A minuscule sense of balance came from grabbing at the sharp ridgeline positioned at chest height in front me. It was all I could do to hold on. There was no option to use my ice axe for stability. It was more a matter of precisely shifting my body weight inch by inch in the direction of the summit.

Leaning over the ridgeline for a glimpse down the Tibetan side caused my body, chest to toes, to hang freely towards Nepal. I could see the slope run at least 3000 metres nonstop into the country below. Dropping my head and peeking at the Nepali side between my legs, I saw our bean-sized tents at Camp 2. Nonchalantly, clouds like cotton candy floated below me, as if I was looking out from an airplane.

It was surreal to be at such a high altitude, knowing there was no room for mistakes. Neither one of us could have stopped the other if we had slipped. A fall would mean death. My hair stood on end beneath my helmet, my scalp shook, and goose bumps crawled up my back. I felt on the verge of madness from the extreme tension of the situation. Yet we were able to continue.

Forty metres along the ridge was a spot where I could finally place my feet side by side instead of supporting myself on one foot at a time. Next was the freshly snow-covered rock gully that marked Hillary's Chimney. I cleaned the new snow away with my ice axe and over-mitts and readied myself to climb. The initial overhang required me to wedge my entire right leg into the crack as I reached both arms outwards and up diagonally to my left. With nothing but air between my backside and Camp 2, I managed to climb the chimney. How would we descend this on the return trip? As soon as that thought popped into my mind, I was driven to anxiety, knowing that 90 per cent of climbing accidents in the Himalayas occur on the descent.

Thirty-seven climbers before us had successfully summitted Mount Everest and safely descended. For now, my job was to climb. Later I would concern myself with the descent. As we continued, another 7 metres of the shallow crack deposited us on an upward ridge of solid snow.

Although the labour-intensive trail breaking in deep snow ended with Hillary's Chimney, the slope remained steep. It was critical to not be drawn too far to the right of the ridge where huge cornices crested on the Tibetan side. The blue sky was almost touchable, and I was baffled by how many times I thought we were at the summit, only to be mistaken. Repeatedly, the highest point of Everest seemed to grow taller as I pressed forward. I could barely lift my legs any more. The utmost I could raise my feet from the snow was the nail-length of my crampons' teeth. Basically, I dragged my body up the mountain.

I thought of the previous climbers who had succeeded on this face of Everest, among them the five Japanese mountaineers Teruo Matsuura, Naomi Uemura, Katsutoshi Hirabayashi, Hisashi Ishiguro and Yasuo Kato, all of whom I admired. As my mind travelled, my body fatigued. Again and again I had to rest, leaning onto my ice axe with my forehead slumped on top. Every step was agony, but I persuaded myself to continue; soon there would be a final uphill step. The view of the Tibetan landscape grew increasingly larger as I climbed. Then, Ang Tsering, who was a few paces ahead of me, stopped. The rope between us no longer pulled at my waist.

"Tabei-*san*, *tyojo dayo*," he said in Japanese. "It's the summit."

I lifted my feet up one by one, slowly wrapping the rope in a rough coil as I walked. Then, I took my last step to the summit of Mount Everest. It had been six and half hours since we had left camp earlier that day. I felt pure joy as my thoughts registered: "Here is the summit. I don't have to climb any more."

My crampons bit into the snow as I firmly stood beside Ang Tsering. He stretched out his big mitt and we shook hands. His sunglasses shone with the reflection of the sun, highlighting our success. The time was 12:30 p.m. on May 16, 1975.

The summit of Everest was narrow with snow thrusting up from both sides of the mountain to form its pinnacle. In ankle-deep snow, which was unpredictably soft, we stomped down a flat spot about .05 metres wide by 1.5 metres long. We secured ourselves by anchoring the ice axes through loops of the rope and driving them deep into the snow. The mild-featured mountains of Tibet spread vastly to the north, and the gentle curves of Rongbuk Glacier were easily identified. In contrast, the rugged slopes, rock and ice of Nepal filled the view to the south.

Since we had no room to offload our gear, I asked Ang Tsering to grab the radio from my pack. I embraced our success for a moment longer, not quite ready to share the news. Then I made contact with Advanced Base Camp, "ABC, ABC, we arrived at the summit at 12:30. Both of us are in good shape," I said.

We were met with the cheerful singing of the Sherpas, and our teammates and Ang Tsering laughed out loud listening to them. "*Otsukaresama deshita*!" they said in Japanese. Good job!

"The black and white contrast of the Tibetan mountains that we can see from here is of outstanding beauty. Please say a big thanks to all the Sherpas and team members," I said, trying to give justice to the view from the top of the world.

We readied the movie camera and began to film as I continued to speak on the radio. Spanning from the Nepali side of Everest to Tibet, there was Lhotse in front of us; Makalu, big and beautiful, to its left; and then in the distance, Kanchenjunga and the graceful Jannu. Layered beyond the sharp ridgeline of Lhotse and Nuptse were Thamserku and Kangtega; to their right stood Gaurishankar, Cho Oyu and Gyachung Kang, and below them was the brown basin of Namche Bazaar, home of the Sherpa people. Silvery clouds floated around the summits of the giant peaks, emphasizing the dramatic difference between Nepal's rugged Himalayas and the endless, mildly sloped mountains of Tibet. One could imagine the smell of the Tibetan soil it was so prevalent in the rolling landscape, while the precipitous environment of the Nepali side remained breathtaking.

When I looked through the camera lens to take a photograph of Ang Tsering and saw him standing there with flags from two nations in his hand, the reality of the Everest summit touched my heart for the first time. I was warmed by our success. There was no higher place in the world than where we stood, and the sensation was tremendous.

Time was short. In the background of Ang Tsering's stance, a misty cloud rose around the peak of Makalu and made me feel unsettled. We quickly snapped photographs of each other, me asking Ang Tsering to take several to ensure an in-focus shot. Fifty minutes passed in a second. Ang Tsering spoke again on the radio with the Sherpas, his voice song-like with excitement. I experimented with removing my oxygen mask for a while and was pleasantly surprised that I could do so without any immediate problem. Then came the time to descend. We had to return to the South Peak before our oxygen supply ran out. A moment of fear set in: could we climb down without trouble? I yearned to be in a spot where I could stand on both feet, in safety and without feeling anxiety. Fear aside, the clarity of knowing there was only one direction to go – down – offered me relief.

To mark our victory and embed the moment in our minds, we left a green Thermos on the summit along with the Nepali and Japanese flags thrust into the snowpack. Fifteen metres down from the top, I asked Ang Tsering to pick up souvenir stones for all my teammates. As I looked back at the summit once more, our flags proudly flapped in the wind, connecting earth and sky, and bidding us farewell.

We began our descent at 1:30 p.m., and it became obvious that going down would require far more nerve than climbing up. Humans were not made for this. Climbing, yes; descending, no. As I tucked my chin to see the security of each foot placement, the oxygen mask stopped short like a barrier. It nudged out of place, and cold air leaked in and fogged up my sunglasses, which immediately froze. Trying to clear the frost with my over-mitts made things worse. Ultimately, I pulled off my glasses for comfort and clearer vision, but Ang Tsering berated me, "Though it feels OK now, you'll be snow-blind by tomorrow if you continue without sunglasses."

"Heck, I know that! But I don't care," I thought. I was fixated on ending the relentless step after step of the descent. I was dying to stand on flat terrain. At the same time, my mind tried to gain control: "Stay calm, one slip could end your life. Bear with this tension; it's now or never." My fear was a safety net, and if kept in check by my inner voice, it enabled me to continue. The visible tracks from our ascent also provided encouragement. The much-anticipated knife-edge ridge that fed from the South Peak was easier to traverse on the way back, and that felt good. In almost the same amount of time it took us to reach the summit from the South Peak, we had returned there. The main hardship was over.

The oxygen bottles we had switched to at the South Peak on the ascent were almost empty upon our return so we dug them into the snow to leave behind. To our surprise, we found a couple of old bottles of an ancient type, and my heart raced with exhilaration, imagining them to be the ones left behind by Everest's first climbers, Sir Edmund Hillary and Tenzing Norgay. In admiration, we buried our empty bottles beside the old ones before switching to our other bottles for the remainder of the descent.

The cloud – more like fog – around Makalu was a growing concern. It forced us to continue, heads down, radio silent. When we arrived at the section where we had broken trail through deeper snow earlier that day, we knew we were close to Camp 6, and we eventually arrived at 4:30 p.m. Tired, we clambered into the tent with crampons still on, pulled off the oxygen masks and quickly fired up the stove. Hot coffee was in order, then a tin of pineapple, which was frozen solid – we had to thaw it directly over the flame. An exquisite after-summit meal!

Nervous about the weather and confident we had enough energy in reserve, Ang Tsering and I decided to descend as far as the South Col that evening. We reported our plan to Advanced Base Camp and asked them to inform the Sherpas so they would be ready for us later that night. It was 5:20 p.m. when we left Camp 6, and even though we had only stayed there one night on our way up the mountain, I felt regret leaving the pitched tent behind. Later in my fife, I would act on that regret.

The monotony of descending resumed. One saving grace was that my pack, despite the added weight of restocked personal equipment from Camp 6, was manageable. Unsure why, I felt no further distress from the extra load. As we worked our way down the route, darkness gradually filled the sky. The summits of Makalu and Cho Oyu were tinged a reddish brown from the reflection of the sunset, the last bit of colour bringing closure to the day.

Black dots moving on the ice below came into view. Ang Tsering shouted to Lhak-pa (Lama-*san*), his older brother, and Reenjee (Reen-*chan*). They were there to welcome us. Ang Tsering and I turned to each other and acknowledged our appreciation for such a gesture, then Ang Tsering quickly sped up and the rope between us became as taut as a cable. "No rush, no rush, make one firm step after the other," I told myself in order to stay in control of my footing. I had to remain careful on the descent of the steep rock and ice. This was no place to be complacent, but Ang Tsering was on a mission. My only choice was to follow.

Two lights swirled in the not-too-far distance, voices percolated into earshot, and then the two parties – us and them – became one. Lama-*san* and Reen-*chan* leapt at me and heartily shook my hands then patted my shoulder over and over, saying, "Good job, good job!" They were oblivious to the steepness of the slope on which I still stood, not entirely stable.

The 8000-metre peaks that were wrapped in twilight hours before were now transformed into a deep purple. The drape of night had gently settled upon them. Ang Tsering spoke incessantly in Nepali, surrounded by the magnificent mountains he called home. All the while, the summits maintained their whitish glow in the night sky. I sat heavily in the snow, immobile, and listened to his words, which danced around me.

In 1975 I had no idea that the equipment we left behind on Everest would be considered garbage in the future, partly because we were following suit of all the expeditions prior to ours. Discarded items like oxygen bottles and tents were not considered a wrong-doing, and I never gave it much thought. We had made what we presumed was a reasonable effort in asking the Sherpas to remove everything from Camp 5 and lower, leaving only fixed ropes on the mountain. Nevertheless, when I walked away from the tent at Camp 6, I felt an unidentified tug at my conscience.

In 1975 I was the thirty-eighth person to summit Mount Everest, twenty-two years after Sir Edmund Hillary made the first ascent. By May 1993, thirty-eight climbers reached the peak in a single day, part of the increasing rate of climbers that would ensure Everest was scattered with garbage in no time.

Interest led me to become passionate about the health of mountain environments. In 2000, I completed a master's course in social culture with my focus on the garbage problem in the Himalayas. I also acted as chairperson (until 2014) of the Japanese branch of the Himalayan Adventure Trust, an organization that was formed by Sir Hillary and stands under the umbrella of a larger international mountain ecology association whose motto is "Carry down everything you carry up."

Along with my commitment to the role of chairperson came regret for leaving the empty oxygen bottles at the South Peak and the tent at Camp 6. I cannot change those occurrences, but I am the first to admit they make my voice stronger in encouraging as many people as possible to keep mountains clean.

PART FOUR

AUSTRALIA

STATION LIFE IN NEW ZEALAND

Mary Barker

Mary Barker (1831–1911) was a journalist for *The Times* and a writer. She wrote a wonderful account of life in colonial New Zealand, where she and her second husband spent three 'supremely happy' years running a sheep farm – which ultimately failed but gave her a great story. Her book *Station Life in New Zealand*, a collection of the letters she wrote during her first Antipodean sojourn (she later lived in Australia), was published in 1870, the first of many written after the couple's return to London.

Letter XX: the New Zealand snowstorm of 1867

Broomielaw, August 1867. I have had my first experience of real hardships since I last wrote to you. Yes, we have all had to endure positive hunger and cold, and, what I found much harder to bear, great anxiety of mind. I think I mentioned that the weather towards the end of July had been unusually disagreeable, but not very cold. This wet fortnight had a great deal to do with our sufferings afterwards, for it came exactly at the time we were accustomed to send our dray down to Christchurch for supplies of flour and groceries, and to lay in a good stock of coals for the winter; these latter had been ordered, and were expected every day. Just the last few days of July the weather cleared up, and became like our usual most beautiful winter climate; so, after waiting a day or two, to allow the roads to dry a little, the dray was despatched to town, bearing a long list of orders, and with many injunctions to the driver to return as quickly as possible, for all the stores were at the lowest ebb. I am obliged to tell you these domestic details, in order that you may understand the reason of our privations. I acknowledge, humbly, that it was not good management, but sometimes accidents *will* occur. It was also necessary for F— to make a journey to Christchurch on business, and as he probably would be detained there for nearly a week, it was arranged that one of the young gentlemen from Rockwood should ride over and escort me back there, to remain during F—'s absence. I am going to give you all the exact dates, for this snowstorm will be a matter of history, during the present generation at all events: there is no tradition among the Maoris of such a severe one ever having occurred; and what made it more fatal in its financial consequences to every one was, that the lambing season had only just commenced or terminated on most of the runs. Only a few days before he left, F— had taken me for a ride in the sheltered valleys, that he might see the state of the lambs, and pronounced it most satisfactory; thousands of the pretty little creatures were skipping about by their mothers' side.

I find, by my Diary, July 29th marked, as the beginning of a "sou'-wester." F— had arranged to start that morning, and as his business was urgent, he did not like to delay his departure, though the day was most unpromising, a steady, fine drizzle, and raw atmosphere; however, we hurried breakfast, and he set off, determining to push on to town as quickly as possible. I never spent such a dismal day in my life: my mind was disturbed by secret anxieties about the possibility of the dray being detained by wet weather, and there was such an extraordinary weight in the air, the dense mist seemed pressing everything down to the ground; however, I drew the sofa to the fire, made up a good blaze (the last I saw for some time), and prepared to pass a lazy day with a book; but I felt so restless and miserable I did not know what was the matter with me. I wandered from window to window, and still the same unusual sight met my eyes; a long procession of ewes and lambs, all travelling steadily down from the hills towards the large flat in front of the house; the bleating was incessant, and added to the intense melancholy of the whole affair. When Mr. U— came in to dinner, at one o'clock, he agreed with me that it was most unusual weather, and said, that on the other ranges the sheep were drifting before the cold mist and rain just in the same way. Our only anxiety arose from the certainty that the dray would be delayed at least a day, and perhaps two; this was a dreadful idea: for some time past we had been economising our resources to make them last, and we knew that there was absolutely nothing at the home-station, nor at our nearest neighbour's, for they had sent to borrow tea and sugar from us. Just at dusk that evening, two gentlemen rode up, not knowing F— was from home, and asked if they might remain for the night. I knew them both very well; in fact, one was our cousin T—, and the other an old friend; so they put up their horses, and housed their dogs (for each had a valuable sheep-dog with him) in a barrel full of clean straw, and we all tried to spend a cheerful evening, but everybody confessed to the same extraordinary depression of spirits that I felt.

When I awoke the next morning, I was not much surprised to see the snow falling thick and fast: no sheep were now visible, there was a great silence, and the oppression in the atmosphere had if possible increased. We had a very poor breakfast,—no porridge, very little mutton (for in expectation of the house being nearly empty, the shepherd had not brought any over the preceding day), and *very* weak tea; coffee and cocoa all finished, and about an ounce of tea in the chest. I don't know how the gentlemen amused themselves that day; I believe they smoked a good deal; I could only afford a small fire in the drawing-room, over which I shivered. The snow continued to fall in dense fine clouds, quite unlike any snow I ever saw before, and towards night I fancied the garden fence was becoming very much dwarfed. Still the consolation was, "Oh, it won't last; New Zealand snow never does." However, on Wednesday morning things began to look very serious indeed: the snow covered the ground to a depth of four feet in the shallowest places, and still continued to fall steadily; the cows we knew *must* be in the paddock were not to be seen anywhere; the fowl-house and pig-styes which stood towards the weather quarter had entirely disappeared; every scrap of wood (and several logs were lying about at the back) was quite covered up; both the verandahs were impassable; in one the snow was six feet deep, and the only door which could be opened was the back-kitchen door, as that opened inwards; but here the snow was half-way over the roof, so it took a good deal of work with the kitchen-shovel, for no spades could be found, to dig out a passage. Indoors, we were approaching our last mouthful very rapidly, the tea at breakfast was merely coloured hot water, and we had some picnic biscuits with it. For dinner we had the last tin of sardines, the last pot of apricot jam, and a tin of ratifia biscuits a most extraordinary mixture, I admit, but there was nothing else. There were six people to be fed every day, and nothing to feed them with. Thursday's breakfast was a discovered crust of dry bread, very stale, and our dinner that day was rice and salt—the last rice in the storeroom. The snow still never ceased falling, and only one window in the house afforded us any light; every box was broken up and used for fuel. The gentlemen used to go all together and cut, or rather dig, a passage through the huge drift in front of the stable, and with much difficulty get some food for the seven starving horses outside, who were keeping a few yards clear by incessantly moving about, the snow making high walls all around them.

It was wonderful to see how completely the whole aspect of the surrounding scenery was changed; the gullies were all filled up, and nearly level with the downs; sharp-pointed cliffs were now round bluffs; there was no vestige of a fence or gate or shrub to be seen, and still the snow came down as if it had only just begun to fall; out of doors the silence was like death, I was told, for I could only peep down the tunnel dug every few hours at the back-kitchen door. My two maids now gave way, and sat clasped in each other's arms all day, crying piteously, and bewailing their fate, asking me whenever I came into the kitchen, which was about every half-hour, for there was no fire elsewhere, "And oh, when do you think we'll be found, mum?" Of course this only referred to the ultimate discovery of our bodies. There was a great search to-day for the cows, but it was useless, the gentlemen sank up to their shoulders in snow. Friday, the same state of things: a little flour had been discovered in a discarded flour-bag, and we had a sort of girdle-cake and water. The only thing remaining in the store-room was some blacklead, and I was considering seriously how that could be cooked, or whether it would be better raw: we were all more than half starved, and quite frozen: very little fire in the kitchen, and none in any other room. Of course, the constant thought was, “Where are the sheep?” Not a sign or sound could be heard. The dogs’ kennels were covered several feet deep; so we could not get at them at all. Saturday morning: the first good news I heard was that the cows had been found, and dragged by ropes down to the enclosure the horses had made for them-selves: they were half dead, poor beasts; but after struggling for four hours to and from a haystack two hundred yards off, one end of which was unburied, some oaten hay was procured for them. There was now not a particle of food in the house. The servants remained in their beds, declining to get up, and alleging that they might as well “die warm.” In the middle of the day a sort of forlorn-hope was organized by the gentlemen to try to find the fowl-house, but they could not get through the drift: however, they dug a passage to the wash-house, and returned in triumph with about a pound of very rusty bacon they had found hanging up there; this was useless without fuel, so they dug for a little gate leading to the garden, fortunately hit its whereabouts, and soon had it broken up and in the kitchen grate. By dint of taking all the lead out of the tea-chests, shaking it, and collecting every pinch of tea-dust, we got enough to make a teapot of the weakest tea, a cup of which I took to my poor crying maids in their beds, having first put a spoonful of the last bottle of whisky which the house possessed into it, for there was neither sugar nor milk to be had. At midnight the snow ceased for a few hours, and a hard sharp frost set in; this made our position worse, for they could now make no impression on the snow, and only broke the shovels in trying. I began to think seriously of following the maids example, in order to “die warm.” We could do nothing but wait patiently. I went up to a sort of attic where odds and ends were stowed away, in search of something to eat, but could find nothing more tempting than a supply of wax matches. We knew there was a cat under the house, for we heard her mewing; and it was suggested to take up the carpets first, then the boards, and have a hunt for the poor old pussy but we agreed to bear our hunger a little longer, chiefly, I am afraid, because she was known to be both thin and aged.

Towards noon on Sunday the weather suddenly changed, and rain began to come down heavily and steadily; this cheered us all immensely, as it would wash the snow away probably, and so it did to some degree; the highest drifts near the house lessened considerably in a few hours, and the gentlemen, who by this time were desperately hungry, made a final attempt in the direction of the fowl-house, found the roof, tore off some shingles, and returned with a few aged hens, which were mere bundles of feathers after their week's starvation. The servants consented to rise and pluck them, whilst the gentlemen sallied forth once more to the stock-yard, and with great difficulty got off two of the cap or top rails, so we had a splendid though transitory blaze, and some hot stewed fowl; it was more of a soup than anything else, but still we thought it delicious: and then everybody went to bed again, for the house was quite dark still, and the oil and candles were running very low. On Monday morning the snow was washed off the roof a good deal by the deluge of rain which had never ceased to come steadily down, and the windows were cleared a little, just at the top; but we were delighted with the improvement, and some cold weak fowl-soup for breakfast, which we thought excellent. On getting out of doors, the gentlemen reported the creeks to be much swollen and rushing in yellow streams down the sides of the hills over the snow, which was apparently as thick as ever; but it was now easier to get through at the surface, though quite solid for many feet from the ground. A window was scraped clear, through which I could see the desolate landscape out of doors, and some hay was carried with much trouble to the starving cows and horses, but this was a work of almost incredible difficulty. Some more fowls were procured to-day, nearly the last, for a large hole in the roof showed most of them dead of cold and hunger.

We were all in much better spirits on this night, for there were signs of the wind shifting from south to north-west; and, for the first time in our lives I suppose, we were anxiously watching and desiring this change, as it was the only chance of saving the thousands of sheep and lambs we now knew lay buried under the smooth white winding-sheet of snow. Before bedtime we heard the fitful gusts we knew so well, and had never before hailed with such deep joy and thankfulness. Every time I woke the same welcome sound of the roaring warm gale met my ears; and we were prepared for the pleasant sight, on Tuesday morning, of the highest rocks on the hill-tops standing out gaunt and bare once more. The wind was blowing the snow off the hills in clouds like spray, and melting it everywhere so rapidly that we began to have a new anxiety, for the creeks were rising fast, and running in wide, angry-looking rivers over the frozen snow on the banks. All immediate apprehension of starvation, however, was removed, for the gentlemen dug a pig out of his stye, where he had been warm and comfortable with plenty of straw, and slaughtered him; and in the loft of the stable was found a bag of Indian meal for fattening poultry, which made excellent cakes of bread. It was very nasty having only ice-cold water to drink at every meal. I especially missed my tea for breakfast; but felt ashamed to grumble, for my disagreeables were very light compared to those of the three gentlemen. From morning to night they were wet through, as the snow of course melted the moment they came indoors. All the first part of the last week they used to work out of doors, trying to get food and fuel, or feeding the horses, in the teeth of a bitter wind, with the snow driving like powdered glass against their smarting hands and faces; and they were as cheery and merry as possible through it all, trying hard to pretend they were neither hungry nor cold, when they must have been both. Going out of doors at this stage of affairs simply meant plunging up to their middle in a slush of half-melted snow which wet them thoroughly in a moment; and they never had dry clothes on again till they changed after dark, when there was no more possibility of outdoor work.

Wednesday morning broke bright and clear for the first time since Sunday week; we actually saw the sun. Although the “nor-wester” had done so much good for us, and a light wind still blew softly from that quarter, the snow was yet very deep; but I felt in such high spirits that I determined to venture out, and equipped myself in a huge pair of F—’s riding-boots made of kangaroo-skin, well greased with weka-oil to keep the wet out. These I put on over my own thick boots, but my precautions “did nought avail,” for the first step I took sank me deep in the snow over the tops of my enormous boots. They filled immediately, and then merely served to keep the snow securely packed round my ankles; however, I struggled bravely on, every now and then sinking up to my shoulders, and having to be hauled out by main force. The first thing done was to dig out the dogs, who assisted the process by vigorously scratching away inside and tunnelling towards us. Poor things! how thin they looked, but they were quite warm; and after indulging in a long drink at the nearest creek, they bounded about, like mad creatures. The only casualties in the kennels were two little puppies, who were lying cuddled up as if they were asleep, but proved to be stiff and cold; and a very old but still valuable collie called "Gipsy." She was enduring such agonies from rheumatism that it was terrible to hear her howls; and after trying to relieve her by rubbing, taking her into the stable—and in fact doing all we could for her—it seemed better and kinder to shoot her two days afterwards.

We now agreed to venture into the paddock and see what had happened to the bathing-place about three hundred yards from the house. I don't think I have told you that the creek had been here dammed up with a sod wall twelve feet high, and a fine deep and broad pond made, which was cleared of weeds and grass, and kept entirely for the gentlemen to have a plunge and swim at daylight of a summer's morning; there had been a wide trench cut about two feet from the top, so as to carry off the water, and hitherto this had answered perfectly. The first thing we had to do was to walk over the high five-barred gate leading into the paddock just the topmost bar was sticking up, but there was not a trace of the little garden-gate or of the fence, which was quite a low one. We were, however, rejoiced to see that on the ridges of the sunny downs there were patches, or rather streaks, of tussocks visible, and they spread in size every moment, for the sun was quite warm, and the "nor'-wester," had done much towards softening the snow. It took us a long time to get down to where the bathing-place *had been*, for the sod wall was quite carried away, and there was now only a heap of ruin, with a muddy torrent pouring through the large gap and washing it still more away. Close to this was a very sunny sheltered down, or rather hill; and as the snow was rapidly melting off its warm sloping sides we agreed to climb it and see if any sheep could be discovered, for up to this time there had been none seen or heard, though we knew several thousands must be on this flat and the adjoining ones.

As soon as we got to the top the first glance showed us a small dusky patch close to the edge of one of the deepest and widest creeks at the bottom of the paddock; experienced eyes saw they were sheep, but to me they had not the shape of animals at all, though they were quite near enough to be seen distinctly. I observed the gentlemen exchange looks of alarm, and they said to each other some low words, from which I gathered that they feared the worst. Before we went down to the flat we took a long, careful look round, and made out another patch, dark by comparison with the snow, some two hundred yards lower down the creek, but apparently in the water. On the other side of the little hill the snow seemed to have drifted even more deeply, for the long narrow valley which lay there presented, as far as we could see, one smooth, level snow-field. On the dazzling white surface the least fleck shows, and I can never forget how beautiful some swamp-hens, with their dark blue plumage, short, pert, white tails, and long bright legs, looked, as they searched slowly along the banks of the swollen creek for some traces of their former haunts; but every tuft of tohi-grass lay bent and buried deep beneath its heavy covering. The gentlemen wanted me to go home before they attempted to see the extent of the disaster, which we all felt must be very great; but I found it impossible to do anything but accompany them. I am half glad and half sorry now that I was obstinate; glad because I helped a little at a time when the least help was precious, and sorry because it was really such a horrible sight. Even the first glance showed us that, as soon as we got near the spot we had observed, we were walking on frozen sheep embedded in the snow one over the other; but at all events their misery had been over some time. It was more horrible to see the drowning, or just drowned, huddled-up "mob" (as sheep *en masse* are technically called) which had made the dusky patch we had noticed from the hill.

No one can ever tell how many hundred ewes and lambs had taken refuge under the high terrace which forms the bank of the creek. The snow had soon covered them up, but they probably were quite warm and dry at first. The terrible mischief was caused by the creek rising so rapidly, and, filtering through the snow which it gradually dissolved, drowned them as they stood huddled together. Those nearest the edge of the water of course went first, but we were fortunately in time to save a good many, though the living seemed as nothing compared to the heaps of dead. We did not waste a moment in regrets or idleness; the most experienced of the gentlemen said briefly what was to be done, and took his coat off; the other coats and my little Astrachan jacket were lying by its side in an instant, and we all set to work, sometimes up to our knees in icy water, digging at the bank of snow above us—if you can call it digging when we had nothing but our hands to dig, or rather scratch, with. Oh, how hot we were in five minutes! the sun beating on us, and the reflection from the snow making its rays almost blinding. It was of no use my attempting to rescue the sheep, for I could not move them, even when I had *scrattled* the snow away from one. A sheep, especially with its fleece full of snow, is beyond my small powers: even the lambs I found a tremendous weight, and it must have been very absurd, if an idler had been by, to see me, with a little lamb in my arms, tumbling down at every second step, but still struggling manfully towards the dry oasis where we put each animal as it was dug out. The dear doggies helped us beautifully, working so eagerly and yet so wisely under their master's eye, as patient and gentle with the poor stiffened creatures as if they could feel for them. I was astonished at the vitality of some of the survivors; if they had been very far back and not chilled by the water, they were quite lively. The strongest sheep were put across the stream by the dogs, who were obedient to their master's finger, and not to be induced on any terms to allow the sheep to land a yard to one side of the place on the opposite bank, but just where they were to go. A good many were swept away, but after six hours' work we counted 1,400 rescued ones slowly "trailing" up the low sunny hill I have mentioned, and nibbling at the tussocks as they went. The proportion of lambs was, of course, very small, but the only wonder to me is that there were any alive at all. If I had been able to stop my scratching but for a moment, I would have had what the servants call a "good cry" over one little group I laid bare. Two fine young ewes were standing leaning against each other in a sloping position, like a tent, frozen and immoveable: between them, quite dry, and as lively as a kitten, was a dear little lamb of about a month old belonging to one; the lamb of the other lay curled up at her feet, dead and cold; I really believe they had hit upon this way of keeping the other alive. A more pathetic sight I never beheld.

It is needless to say that we were all most dreadfully exhausted by the time the sun went down, and it began to freeze; nothing but the sheer impossibility of doing anything more in the hardening snow and approaching darkness made us leave off even then, though we had not tasted food all day. The gentlemen took an old ewe, who could not stand, though it was not actually dead, up to the stable and killed it, to give the poor dogs a good meal, and then they had to get some more rails off the stock-yard to cook our own supper of pork and maize.

The next morning was again bright with a warm wind; so the effect of the night's frost soon disappeared, and we were hard at work directly after breakfast. Nothing would induce me to stay at home, but I armed myself with a coal-scoop to dig, and we made our way to the other "mob;" but, alas! there was nothing to do in the way of saving life, for all the sheep were dead. There was a large island formed at a bend in the creek, where the water had swept with such fury round a point as to wash the snow and sheep all away together, till at some little obstacle they began to accumulate in a heap. I counted ninety-two dead ewes in one spot, but I did not stay to count the lambs. We returned to the place where we had been digging the day before, and set the dogs to hunt in the drifts; wherever they began to scratch we shovelled the snow away, and were sure to find sheep either dead or nearly so: however, we liberated a good many more. This sort of work continued till the following Saturday, when F— returned, having had a most dangerous journey, as the roads are still blocked up in places with snow-drifts; but he was anxious to get back, knowing I must have been going through "hard times." He was terribly shocked at the state of things among the sheep; in Christchurch no definite news had reached them from any quarter: all the coaches were stopped and the telegraph wires broken down by the snow. He arrived about mid-day, and, directly after the meal we still called dinner, started off over the hills to my "nest of Cockatoos," and brought back some of the men with him to help to search for the sheep, and to skin those that were dead as fast as possible. He worked himself all day at the skinning,—a horrible job; but the fleeces were worth something, and soon all the fences, as they began to emerge from the snow, were tapestried with these ghastly skins, and walking became most disagreeable, on account of the evil odours arising every few yards.

We forgot all our personal sufferings in anxiety about the surviving sheep, and when the long-expected dray arrived it seemed a small boon compared to the discovery of a nice little "mob" feeding tranquilly on a sunny spur. It is impossible to estimate our loss until the grand muster at shearing, but we may set it down at half our flock, and *all* our lambs, or at least 90 per cent, of them. Our neighbours are all as busy as we are, so no accurate accounts of their sufferings or losses have reached us; but, to judge by appearances, the distant "back-country" ranges must have felt the storm more severely even than we have; and although the snow did not drift to such a depth on the plains as with us, or lie so long on the ground, they suffered just as much,—for the sheep took shelter under the high river-banks, and the tragedy of the creeks was enacted on a still larger scale; or they drifted along before the first day's gale till they came to a wire fence, and there they were soon covered up, and trampled each other to death. Not only were sheep, but cattle, found dead in hundreds along the fences on the plains. The newspapers give half a million as a rough estimate of the loss among the flocks in this province alone. We have no reliable news from other parts of the island, only vague rumours of the storm having been still more severe in the Province of Otago, which lies to the south, and would be right in its track; the only thing which all are agreed in saying is, that there never has been such a storm before, for the Maories are strong in weather traditions, and though they prophesied this one, it is said they have no legend of anything like it ever having happened.

TRACKS

Robyn Davidson

Robyn Davidson (1950–present) is an Australian adventurer and author. In 1975, she embarked from Alice Springs on a 2,700km trek across the unforgiving desert to the west coast of Australia, recording the experience in her memoir *Tracks*. For the most part, she travelled alone (though an indigenous elder called Eddie accompanied her for a month or so, and a *National Geographic* photographer occasionally turned up) accompanied by four haughty, but useful camels and her faithful dog, Diggity, on this endurance test through the outback.

All I remember of that first day alone was a feeling of release; a sustained, buoyant confidence as I strolled along, Bub's nose-line in my sweaty palm, the camels in a well-behaved line behind me and Goliath bringing up the rear. The muffled tinkling of their bells, the soft crunching of my feet in the sand and the faint twittering of the wood-swallows were the only sounds. The desert was otherwise still.

I had decided to follow an abandoned track that would eventually meet up with the main Areyonga road. Now, the definition of a track in Australia is a mark made across the landscape by the repeated passage of a vehicle or, if you are very lucky, initially by a bulldozer. These tracks vary in quality from a corrugated, bull-dust-covered, well-defined and well-used road to something which you can barely discern by climbing a hill and squinting in the general direction you think the said track may go. Sometimes you can see where a track is by the tell-tale blossoms of wildflowers. Those along the track will either be growing more thickly or be of a different type. Sometimes, you may be able to follow the trail by searching for the ridge left aeons ago by a bulldozer. The track may wind around or over hills and ridges and rocky outcroppings, straight into sand-dunes, get swallowed up by sandy creek-beds, get totally lost in stony creek-beds, or fray into a maze of animal pads. Following tracks is most often easy, sometimes frustrating, and occasionally downright terrifying.

When you are in cattle or sheep station country, the following of tracks can be especially puzzling, mainly because one always assumes that a track will lead somewhere. This is not necessarily so since station people just don't think like that. Also there is the problem of choice. When you are presented with half a dozen tracks all leading off in the general direction you want to go, all used within the last year, and none of them marked on the map, which one do you choose? If you choose the wrong one it may simply stop five miles ahead, so that you have to back-track, having lost half a day's travel. Or it may lead you to an abandoned, waterless windmill and bore, or slap-bang into a new fence-line, which, if followed, will begin leading you in exactly the opposite direction to where you thought you wanted to go, only now you're not quite sure because you've made so many turnings and weavings that you are beginning to lose confidence in your sense of direction. Or it might lead you to a gate made by some jackaroo who thought he was Charles Atlas and which you haven't got a hope in hell of opening, or if you can open it without suffering a rupture, then closing it is impossible without using the camels as a winch, which takes half an hour to do and you're already hot and bothered and dusty and all you really want in life is to get to the next watering place and have an aspirin and a cup of tea and a good lie down.

This is complicated further by the fact that whoever those people are who fly in planes and make maps of the area, they need glasses; or perhaps were drunk at the time; or perhaps just felt like breaking free of departmental rulings and added a few bits and pieces of imaginative topography, or even, in some cases, rubbed out a few features in a fit of solitary anarchic vice. One expects maps to be always but always 100 per cent correct, and most of the time they are. It's those other times that can set you into a real panic. Make you think that perhaps that sand-ridge you swore you sat on back there was a mirage. Make you entertain the notion that you are sun-struck. Make you gulp once or twice and titter nervously.

However, that first day held none of these problems. If the track petered out into dust bowls with drinking spots in the middle of them, it was relatively easy to find where it continued on the other side. The camels were going well and behaving like lambs. Life was good. The country I was travelling through held my undivided attention with its diversity. This particular area had had three bumper seasons in succession and was carpeted in green and dotted with white, yellow, red, blue wildflowers. Then I would find myself in a creek-bed where tall gums and delicate acacias cast deep cool shadow. And birds. Everywhere birds. Black cockatoos, sulphur-cresteds, swallows, Major Mitchells, willy-wagtails, quarrian, kestrels, budgerigar flocks, bronze-wings, finches. And there were kunga-berries and various solanums and mulga apples and eucalyptus manna to eat as I walked along. This searching for and picking wild food is one of the most pleasant, calming pastimes I know. Contrary to popular belief, the desert is bountiful and teeming with life in the good seasons. It is like a vast untended communal garden, the closest thing to earthly paradise I can imagine. Mind you, I wouldn't want to have to survive on bush-tucker during the drought. And even in the good season, I admit I would prefer my diet to be supplemented by the occasional tin of sardines, and a frequent cup of sweet billy tea.

I had learnt about wild foods from Aboriginal friends in Alice Springs, and from Peter Latz, an ethnobotanist whose passion was desert plant-foods. At first, I had not found it easy to remember and recognize plants after they had been pointed out to me, but eventually the scales fell from my eyes. The Solanaceae especially had me confused. This is a huge family, including such well knowns as potatoes, tomatoes, capsicums, datura and nightshades. The most interesting thing about the group is that many of them form a staple diet for Aboriginal people, while others which look almost identical are deadly poisonous. Peter had done some tests of various species and found that one tiny berry contained more vitamin C than an orange. Since these were eaten by the thousands when Aboriginal people were free to travel through their own country, it stands to reason that their modern-day diet, almost totally devoid of vitamin C, is just one more factor contributing to their crippling health problems.

I was a little nervous my first night out. Not because I was frightened of the dark (the desert is benign and beautiful at night, and except for the eight-inch-long, pink millipedes that sleep under the bottom of the swag and may wish to bite you when you roll it up at dawn, or the careless straying of a scorpion under your sleep-twitching hand, or the lonely slithering of a Joe Blake who may want to cuddle up and get warm under the bedclothes then fang you to death when you wake up, there is not much to worry about) but because I wondered if I would ever see the camels again. I hobbled them out at dusk, unclogged their bells and tied little Goliath to a tree. Would it work, I asked myself? The answer came back, 'She'll be right, mate,' the closest thing to a Zen statement to come out of Australia, and one I used frequently in the months ahead.

The process of unloading had been infinitely easier than putting the stuff on. It only took an hour. Then there was wood to be gathered, a fire and lamp to be lit, camels to be checked on, cooking utensils, food and cassette player to be got out, Diggity to be fed, camels to be checked on, food to be cooked and camels to be checked on. They were munching their heads off happily enough. Except Goliath. He was yelling piggishly for his mother, who, thank God, was taking no notice whatsoever.

I think I cooked a freeze-dried dish that night. A vastly overrated cardboard-like substitute for edible food. The fruit was OK, you could eat that straight like biscuit, but the meat and vegetable dishes were tasteless soggy tack. I fed all my packets to the camels later on, and stuck with what was to be my staple diet: brown rice, lentils, garlic, spices, oil, pancakes made with all manner of cereals and coconut and dried egg, various root vegetables cooked in the coals, cocoa, tea, sugar, honey, powdered milk, and every now and then, the ultimate in luxury, a can of sardines, some pepperoni and Kraft cheese, a tin of fruit, and an orange or lemon. I supplemented this with vitamin pills, various wild foods, and the occasional rabbit. Far from being deficient, this diet made me so healthy, I felt like a cast-iron amazon; cuts and gashes vanished in a day, I could see almost as well at night as I could in sunlight, and I grew muscles on my shit.

After that first lacklustre meal, I built the fire up, checked again on the camels, and put my Pitjantjara learning tapes into the cassette.

Nyuntu palya nyinanyi. Uwa, palyarna, palu nyuntu, I mumbled repeatedly at the night sky now thick and gorgeous with billions of stars. There was no moon that night.

I nodded off with Diggity snoring in my arms as usual. And from that first night, I developed a habit of waking once or twice to check on the bells. I would wait until I heard a chime, and if I didn't I would call to them so they turned their heads and chimed, and if that didn't work, I would get up and see where they were. They were usually no more than a hundred yards from camp. I would then fall instantly back to sleep and remember waking up only vaguely in the morning. When I woke well before dawn, one fear at least had diminished. The camels were huddled around my swag, as close as they could get without actually crushing me. They got up at the same time I did, that is, over an hour before sun-up, for their early-morning feed.

My camels were all still young and growing. Zeleika, the oldest, I thought was maybe four and a half or five. Dookie was going on for four and Bub was three – mere puppies, since camels can live until they're fifty. So they needed all the food they could get. My routine was built around their needs and never my own. They were carrying what I would consider a lot of weight for young animals though Sallay would have scoffed at such an idea. He had told me how a bull camel had stood up with a ton on its back and that up to half a ton was usually carrying capacity. Getting up and down was the hardest thing for them. Once they were up, carrying the weight was not so difficult. The weight, however, had to be evenly balanced or the saddle would rub, causing discomfort and eventually producing a saddle-sore, so at this stage the process of loading up was fastidiously checked and rechecked. On the second morning I got it down to just under two hours.

I never ate much in the mornings. I would build a cooking fire, boil one or two billies of tea, and fill a small Thermos with what was left. Sometimes I craved sugar and would pile two tablespoons into the billy then wolf down several tablespoons of cocoa or honey. I burnt it up quickly enough.

My main problem now seemed to be whether the gear would hold together, whether the saddles would rub, and how the camels handled the work. I was a little worried over Zeleika. Diggity was doing fine but occasionally got foot-sore. I felt great, if knock-kneed with exhaustion by the end of a day. I decided to cover approximately twenty miles a day, six days a week. (And on the seventh she rested.) Well, not always. I wanted to keep a fair distance covered in case something went wrong, and I had to sit somewhere for days or weeks. There was a slight pressure on me not to take it as easy as I would have liked. I didn't want to be travelling in summer and I had promised *Geographic* I would be at journey's end before the year was out. That gave me six months of comfortable travel, which I could stretch to eight if needs be.

So, by the time everything was packed away and the fire smothered, the camels would have had a couple of hours of feeding. I would then bring them in nose-line to tail, tie Bub with his halter to the tree and ask them to whoosh down please. The cloths and saddles went on first, front to back, the girths done up, by pushing them underneath the animal and behind the brisket. The nose-lines were taken off the tail and attached to the saddle. Next the loading, first one object, then its equivalent on the other side. It was all checked and checked again, then I asked them to stand up, and the girths were tightened and the holding ropes run through them. All set to go. One more check. Departure. Hey ho.

But wouldn't it be my luck that on the third day, when I was still a cub-scout in the ways of the bush, and still believing blindly that all maps were infallible and certainly more reliable than common sense, I found a road that wasn't meant to be there. While the road I wanted to be there was nowhere to be seen.

'You've lost a whole road,' I said to myself, incredulously. 'Not just a turning or a well or a ridge, but a whole bloody road.

'Take it easy, be calm, she'll be right, mate, settle down settle DOWN.'

My little heart felt like a macaw in a canary cage. I could feel the enormity of the desert in my belly and on the back of my neck. I was not in any real danger – I could easily have set a compass course for Areyonga. But I kept thinking, what if this happens when I'm two hundred miles from anywhere? What if, what if? And I felt very small and very alone suddenly in this great emptiness. I could climb a hill and look to where the horizon shimmered blue into the sky and see nothing. Absolutely nothing.

I re-read the map. No enlightenment there. I was only fifteen or so miles from the settlement, and here was this giant dirt highway where there should only be sandstone and roly-poly. Should I follow it or what? Where the hell did it lead? Was it a new mining road? I checked the map for mines but there was nothing marked.

I sat back and watched myself perform. 'OK. First of all, you are not lost, you are merely misplaced, no no, you know exactly where you are so stifle that impulse to scream at the camels and kick Diggity. Think clearly. Then, make camp for the night here, there is plenty of green feed, and spend the rest of the afternoon looking for that goddamn track. If you don't find it, cut across country. Easy enough. Above all, do not flap around like a winged pigeon. Where's your pride? Right.'

I did all that, then went off scouting, map in hand, Diggity at foot. I found an ancient trail that wound up through the mountains, not exactly where the map said it should be but close enough for a margin of credibility at least. It went for a couple of miles off course then came out to meet up with, yes, yet another major highway that had no right to exist. 'Shit and damnation.' This I followed for another half mile in the general direction of Areyonga, until I came across a bullet-ridden piece of tin bent over double and almost rusted away, but with an arrow that pointed at the ground and the letters A ON upon it. I skipped back to camp in the gathering twilight, apologized profusely to my poor dumb entourage, and fixed lesson one firmly in my brain for future reference. When in doubt, follow your nose, trust your instincts, and don't rely on maps.

I had been alone for three days in country that people seldom visited. Now I was crawling down a wide dusty deserted boring road, an occasional beer or Coke can winking at me from the bushes. The walking was beginning to take its toll on all of us. Diggity's feet were pincushioned with bindy-eye prickles, so I heaved her up on to Dookie's back. She hated it, and stared off into the distance, sighing dramatically, with that long-suffering look common to brainwashed dogs. My own feet were blistered and aching, and my legs cramped up as soon as I stopped walking. Zeleika had a large lump which distended her milk vein and her nose-peg was infected. Dookie's saddle was rubbing him slightly but he stepped high and seemed, unlike the others, to be thoroughly enjoying himself. I suspected he had always wanted to travel.

This worry over the camels was unrelenting. Without them I would be nowhere, and I treated them like porcelain. Camels, so everyone says, are tough, hardy creatures, but perhaps mine were so pampered that they had turned into hypochondriacs; they always seemed to have some little thing wrong with them, which, doubtless, I blew out of all proportion. But I had been burnt once with Kate, and I wasn't about to take risks with their health.

Areyonga is a tiny missionary settlement wedged between two sandstone mountain faces of the MacDonnell Ranges. As settlements go, it is a good one. It is laid out traditionally, that is, a small village of houses where the whites live, a general store which Aborigines are being trained to run themselves, a school, a clinic, and the Aboriginal camps sprawling around the outskirts looking like Third World refugee centres. All the whites, about ten I think, could speak the language fluently and were pro-Aboriginal.

After 160 years of undeclared war on Aboriginal people, during which time wholesale slaughter was carried out in the name of progress, and while the last massacre was taking place in the Northern Territory in 1930, the colonialist government set up this and other Aboriginal reserves on land neither the cattlemen nor anyone else wanted. Because everyone believed that the indigenous people would eventually die out, allowing them to keep small sections of their land was seen as a temporary measure which would make life safer for the settlers. The blacks were rounded up like cattle by police and citizens on horseback wielding guns. Often, different tribes were forced to live on one small area; as some of these groups were traditionally antagonistic, this created friction and planted the seeds of cultural decay. The government allowed missionaries to rule many of these reserves and to confine and control the people. Half-caste children were taken forcibly from their mothers and kept separate, as they were seen as having at least a chance of becoming human. (This was still happening in Western Australia until very recently.)

Even these pitifully inadequate reserves are now under threat, because large mining concerns, notably Conzinc Rio-Tinto, have their eyes on them for further exploitation. Already, many companies have been allowed to mine what was once Aboriginal territory, bulldozing it into a scarred dust-bowl and leaving the people destitute, their land destroyed. Many reserves have been closed down and the people sent to the towns where they cannot find work. Although this is called 'promoting assimilation', it is another method of transferring Aboriginal land to white ownership. However, Pitjantjara people are slightly better off than most other central desert and northern tribes, because uranium has not yet been mined in their country and because the area is so remote. Many of the old people do not speak English, and the people on the whole have managed to keep their cultural integrity intact. It also became apparent to me that the majority of whites now involved with the Aborigines are fighting alongside them to protect what is left of their lands and their rights, and eventually to reach the point where the blacks are autonomous. Whether this is possible, given the rural white backlash, the racist attitudes of Australians generally and the genocidal policies of the present government, and given that the rest of the world seems neither to know nor care what is happening to the oldest culture in the world, is a doubtful question. The Aborigines do not have much time. They are dying.

I arrived a mile outside the settlement by mid-afternoon to be met by hordes of excited children, giggling, shouting and raving Pitjantjara. God knows how they knew I was coming, but now, from Areyonga all the way down the line, the inexplicable communication network called 'bush telegraph', or 'keeping one's ear to the ground', would tell people I was on my way.

I had been hot, irritable and tired when I arrived, but now these delightful children lifted my spirits with their cacophony of laughter. How easy they were. I had always felt slightly uncomfortable around most children, but Aboriginal kids were different. They never whined, or demanded. They were direct and filled with *joie de vivre* and so loving and giving with one another that they melted me immediately. I tried out my Pitjantjara. Stunned silence, then hoots of laughter. I let them lead the camels. There were children on my back, children clinging to camel legs and camel saddles and children ten deep on every side. The camels had a very special attitude to them. They would let them do anything, so I didn't have to worry about anyone getting hurt. Bub especially adored them. I remember how, at Utopia, when he was tied to his tree during the day, he would see the kids bounding towards him after school, and would immediately sit down and start to doze off in pleasant expectation of being jumped on, bounced on, pulled, tugged, pushed and walked on by the small people. By the time I got to the village proper everyone was out to meet me, all asking questions in lingo because word had already spread that the *kungka rama-rama* (crazy woman) could speak it fluently. I could not. It didn't seem to matter.

I could not have picked a better way to travel through their country. Pitjantjara people had a special relationship with camels as they had been the one tribe to use them constantly for walkabout right up to the mid-1960s, when cars and trucks eventually took over. The whole of the first section of my trip would be through their tribal territory, or what was left of it, a large reserve controlled by white bureaucrats and dotted with mission and government settlements.

I stayed three days in Areyonga, talking to people and generally getting the feel of the place and living with a school teacher and his family. I would have dearly loved to stay down at camp but was too shy to force myself on to people who might not want a whitefella hanging around, poking her nose into their business. One thing I particularly noticed, on all the settlements and camps I saw, was that many of the old people were blind. Trachoma, a chronic form of conjunctivitis, diabetes, ear infections, heart trouble and syphilis are just some of the diseases which ravage Aboriginal populations, living without proper housing, medical facilities or correct diet. Infant mortality has been reported by some at 200 per 1,000, though official estimates are not so high. The figure is increasing. Professor Hollows, an eye specialist, organized a national survey of eye diseases amongst Aborigines. He stated, 'It is clear that Aborigines have the worst ethnic blindness rate in the world.'

Despite these facts, the present Fraser government has seen fit to cut back violently on the Aboriginal Affairs budget. These cut-backs have almost devastated the work of Aboriginal health and legal aid organizations.

It is equally extraordinary that the Australian Broadcasting Commission was asked by the Federal Director General of Health to cancel a film about Aboriginal blindness in the Northern Territory because it might damage the tourist trade there.

Or how's this: the Queensland premier, Mr Bjelke Peterson, asked the federal government to stop Professor Hollows's anti-trachoma team from working in that state, because two of the Aboriginal field workers were 'enrolling Aboriginal people to vote'.

The rest of the time I spent worrying over the camels. Zeleika's suspicious lump was suspiciously bigger. When I inspected her peg, I found the inner knob fractured. Oh no, not again. I tied her down, twisted her head round and inserted a new one. I could hardly hear myself think through her bellowing, and did not notice Bub sneaking up behind me. He nipped me on the back of the head, then galloped away behind Dookie, as startled as I was by his audacity. Camels stick together.

When we were all rested, and when I thought most of our problems were ironed out, we headed off for Tempe Downs station, forty-odd miles to the south, over an unused path through the ranges. I was a bit windy about my ability to navigate through these hills. The people at Areyonga had sapped my confidence by insisting that I call them on the two-way radio when I made it to the other side. No one had used the track for ten years and it would be invisible at times. The range itself was a series of mountains, chasms, canyons and valleys that ran all the way to Tempe, perpendicular to my direction of travel.

It is difficult to describe Australian desert ranges as their beauty is not just visual. They have an awesome grandeur that can fill you with exaltation or dread, and usually a combination of both.

I camped that first night in a washaway, near the ruin of a cottage. I awoke to the muttering of a single crow staring at me not ten feet away. The pre-dawn light, all misty blue and translucent, filtered through the leaves and created a fairy land. The character of such country changes wonderfully throughout the day, and each change has its effect on one's mood.

I set off clutching map and compass. Every hour or so, my shoulders would tighten and my stomach knot as I searched for the right path. I got lost only once, ending up in a box-canyon and having to back-track to where the path had been obliterated by a series of cattle and donkey tracks. But the constant tension was sapping my energy and I sweated and strained. This went on for two days.

One afternoon, after our midday break, something dropped off Bub's back and he flew into a panic. I now had Zeleika in the lead, because of her sore nose, and Bub at the rear. He bucked and he bucked and the more he bucked, the more bits of pack went flying and the more frenzied he became. By the time he stopped, the saddle was dangling under his quivering belly, and the goods were scattered everywhere. I switched into automatic. The other camels were ready to leap out of their skins and head for home. Goliath was galloping between them and generally causing havoc. There was not a tree in sight to tie them to. If I blew this, they might take off and I would never see them again. I couldn't get back to Bub so I whooshed the lead camel down and tied her nose-line to her foreleg, so that if she tried to get up, she would be pulled down. I did the same with Dook, clouted Goliath across the nose with a branch of mulga so that he took off in a cloud of dust, and then went back to Bub. His eyes had rolled with fear and I had to talk to him and pacify him until I knew he trusted me and wouldn't kick. Then I lifted the saddle with my knees and undid the girth on top of his back. Then I gently took it off and whooshed him down like the others. I found a tree a little further on, and beat the living daylights out of him. The whole operation had been quick, sure, steady and precise – like Austrian clockwork. But now, whatever toxins had been stirred up by the flow of adrenalin hit my bloodstream like the Cayahogan River. I lay by the tree, trembling as hard as Bub. I had been out of control when I beat him and began to recognize a certain Kurtishness in my behaviour. This weakness, my inability to be terrified with any dignity, came to the forefront often during the trip, and my animals took the brunt of it. If, as Hemingway suggested, 'courage is grace under pressure', then the trip proved once and for all that I was sadly lacking in the stuff. I felt ashamed.

I learnt a couple of other things from that incident. I learnt to conserve energy by allowing at least part of myself to believe I could cope with any emergency. And I realized that this trip was not a game. There is nothing so real as having to think about survival. Believing in omens is all right as long as you know exactly what you are doing. I was becoming very careful and I was coming right back down to earth, where the desert was larger than I could comprehend. And not only was space an ungraspable concept, but my understanding of time needed reassessment. I was treating the trip like a nine-to-five job. Up bright and early (oh, the guilt if I slept in), boil the billy, drink tea, hurry up it's getting late, nice place for lunch but I can't stay too long... I simply could not rid myself of this regimentation. I was furious with myself, but I let it run its course. Better watch it now, then fight it later when I was feeling stronger. I had a clock which I told myself was for navigation purposes only, but at which I stole furtive glances from time to time. It played tricks on me. In the heat of the afternoon, when I was tired, aching and miserable, hours lapsed between ticks and tocks. I recognized a need for these absurd arbitrary structures at that stage. I did not know why, but I knew I was afraid of something like chaos. It was as if it were waiting for me to let down my guard and then it would pounce.

On the third day, and to my great relief, I found the well-used station track to Tempe. I called Areyonga on my radio set, that unwanted baggage, that encumbrance, that infringement of my privacy, that big smudgy patch on the purity of my gesture. I screamed into it that I was all right and got nothing but static as a reply.

Arriving in Tempe, I had a pleasant lunch with the people who ran the station, then filled my canteen with precious sweet rainwater from their tanks and continued on my way.

LONG CLOUD RIDE

Josie Dew

Josie Dew (1966–present) is an enterprising English touring cyclist, author and cook. Enterprising, because she set up a catering business in her mid-teens to fund her cycling trips, with such success that it funded her first major expedition to Africa and back. By the time she turned 40, Dew had already cycled through 48 countries. *Long Cloud Ride* is an account of her 6,000-mile journey around New Zealand, being pursued by ostriches and dive-bombed by harriers. Fortunately, Dew has a great sense of humour which proved as invaluable as her bicycle.

Near Amodeo Bay, Coromandel Peninsula, 31 December

Well, that's Christmas done and dusted. And a good thing too. Saying that, I had a fine feast at Jacquie's uncle's house. I didn't so much have seconds as fifths. But then I was feeling a bit half starved after two months bobbing about on the ocean wave. Not that the food on the freighter was anything to cause a rumpus about; it just wasn't up to my usual cyclist quantities. Here, though, there was a quantity of food and a profusion of tastes that were hard to say no to.

A large crowd of people in buoyant Christmas spirit gathered around the long table at Jacquie's uncle's. I tried my best to be full of festive jollity, but my heart and head felt on another planet. Have done ever since I received the news on the ship that my nephews' nineteen-year-old cousin Jonnie was killed in a car crash six days before Christmas. I can't quite take in that the happy strapping lad I hugged merely days before I left home in October is now lying in a coffin in a cold wintry graveyard. His funeral was yesterday. I spoke to Mel, my sister-in-law (though she's a lot more sister than law), who is Jonnie's aunt. She said the church was packed, mostly with Jonnie's school friends. Mum and dad and my brother Dave, Mel's husband, were there too. It was a freezing cold dark and drizzly December day. Which makes it seem even more unreal when I'm sitting in dazzling light bombarded by sweltering sunshine and busy summer birdsong.

Because of this terrible happening, I don't feel I've been particularly good company for Jacquie. But we've still managed to have a laugh. Especially at the amount I eat. On my first day with Jacquie I was well behaved and politely ate my food off a plate with a knife and fork. By the second day I had taken over the cooking (Jacquie was more than happy about this) and was eating out of her largest pasta bowl with a spoon. Over the next few days I rapidly progressed from pasta bowl to small mixing bowl to medium mixing bowl to deep bread-making bowl. Jacquie likes to tuck into her food while watching telly (usually Corrie, as *Coronation Street* is known over here) on the sofa. As I'm more of an eating-while-reading-person I sit at the table directly behind the sofa. The moment I plonk myself down at the table with my giant mixing bowl of food, Jacquie swivels round and looks at me in a state of shock. It's always most amusing.

Last night as I was packing my panniers ready for an early getaway this morning, Jacquie, who was watching the 6 o'clock news, called me in to come quickly and watch: one of the main news items was about how touring cyclists were being targeted by motorists throwing bottles at them from passing vehicles. The latest to fall victim to this missile-hurling pastime were two Swiss cyclists. The boyfriend had a bottle thrown at him from a car travelling at speed, and fell off. Apart from being a bit shook up he was uninjured. But his girlfriend, who was also the recipient of an airborne bottle, suffered a slashed ankle and a badly broken leg. They said how they had just spent the past few months cycling 5,000 km across Europe and the USA, but by far the worst drivers in their experience were Kiwis.

Jacquie was a bit concerned for my welfare. She thought maybe I should delay my departure until well after the New Year, as drink-driving is a huge problem in New Zealand and it would only exacerbate this sport. 'There're enough maniacs on the road as it is,' she said. But I was ready and rearing to go, and when I've got my sight set on things I don't tend to like to back down. Dogged stubbornness, my mother calls it.

So at dawn this morning I rolled up my sleeping mat and compressed my sleeping bag into its stuff-sack (Jacquie had offered me a sofa bed, but I prefer sleeping on the floor). After polishing off a substantial breakfast I loaded up my steed, gave Jacquie a big hug and was off, rolling into a dazzling early morning sun.

My original plan for leaving Auckland was to cycle south out of the city through the sprawl of traffic-laden suburbs. But the more I looked at my map of mile upon mile of mangled roads, and the more I heard about the undesirable driving antics of New Zealand's motorists, the faster I went off this idea. One of the surprising things about Auckland is that, though the population stands at around the one million mark (precious few people by world city standards), in terms of area it ranks as one of the largest cities on earth – a low-rise urban sprawl, straddled by the harbours of Waitemata to the east and Manukau to the west.

With a city surrounded by so much water I decided there must be a boat that could cart me out to greener lands. So one morning last week I cycled up the short but steep twisting road to the top of North Head, one of Devonport's two volcanic cones. From here I had a view of the whole harbour with its constant flurry of boats. Across the way lay the docks and downtown Auckland, dominated by the giant hypodermic-syringe shape of the Sky Tower piercing the sky. Over in the Hauraki Gulf floated a wide assortment of green-carpeted islands. Beyond them, sketchily purple in the east, rose a range of mountains. Peering at my map, I worked out without too much trouble that these were the backbone of the Coromandel Peninsula, a fattish thumb of land that extends northwards from the Hauraki Plain. Although the mountains looked a bit worrying for the likes of my legs (two cycle-free months on board a ship was not the recommended training for tackling the undulating topography of New Zealand – a country that is 70 per cent mountain), the Coromandel looked like a perfect spot to reach by boat.

Back at Jacquie's, I asked her if she knew of a ferry service from Auckland over to the Coromandel. She didn't, but said that it would be worth asking down at the wharf. So I did. After several enquiries among the flotilla of ferry booths on the waterfront I came across Glenys, who was manning one of these booths. She told me of a passenger ferry service that operated only over Christmas and the New Year and Easter and only on sporadic days and at sporadic times. As it was New Year there was a boat running, so I handed over $40 for me, and $10 for my bike, and booked myself on the 9 a.m. Fullers *Kawau Kat* ferry on New Year's Eve.

On board the *Kawau Kat* I strapped my bike on to the back railings outside the toilets. As I did so a man in a baseball cap, aviator sunglasses, shorts and flip-flops (or 'jandals' as I overheard someone refer to them), leaning against a railing while nonchalantly dangling a bottle of beer between his fingers, looked at me and said, 'That's some shit load of gear you've got on there, mate. I'm guessing you're either going to end up fit or fucked. There're some bastard big hills over there.'

With these encouraging words ringing in my ears, I climbed up the steps to plant myself on the open top deck in the wind and the sun. The ferry's engines grumbled into action and we took off out of the harbour past islands bushed in green and a yacht called *Stamp Machine* heeling over in the wind. An American man called Hank sat down next to me. He told me he was from Jackson, Mississippi, and asked if I had ever been to America. I told him I had cycled down the west coast a couple of times and across the country. 'But I never got as far south as Mississippi.'

'Whoa!' he said. 'That's some ride. Have any problems?'

'Not really. The worst thing was riding across the Prairies in tornado season.'

'I can believe it,' he said. 'You know what we say in Mississippi? That divorces and tornadoes have one thing in common – somebody's gonna lose a trailer!'

*

We landed on the Coromandel at a place called Te Kouma. Te Kouma consisted of a wooden jetty. That was it. One or two of the passengers were met by friends or family and driven away in four-wheel drives. The majority were scooped up in a waiting air-conditioned bus for a day tour of the local delights. Before long I was the only one left, standing with my bike beside a couple of battered pick-ups parked up on the side. I presumed they belonged to fishermen. One had a tailgate sticker stating: FISHING IS FOR LIFE – THE REST IS JUST DETAIL. The other one's sticker suggested that:

IF YOU WANT TO BE HAPPY FOR:
A DAY – GET DRUNK
A WEEK – GET MARRIED
LIFE – GO FISHING

I set off bumping along a track that soon gave way to a sealed road not two cars wide. A cliff face of jungle full of exotically whooping birds reared up on one side. On the other a languorous sea flopped on to the rocks. Soon I passed a sign that said: SUGAR LOAF LANDING. But despite having a good look around, I couldn't see any sugar loaves landing. All a bit disappointing.

I had managed a good five minutes' cycle (exhausting it was too) when I came across a beach. At the near end, beneath a shady tree, sat a simple plank for a bench. A perfect spot for a picnic. I leant my bike against the plank before noticing a fat knotted rope hanging from a wide bough off a big old tree nearby. On the spur of the moment I took a running leap at the rope, swung out widely into an admirable arc before narrowly missing being knocked out cold when I was flung back at speed towards the trunk. What fun that would have been: five minutes into my tour of the Antipodes, only to kill myself by an ill-timed Tarzan-style lunge on a rope. I don't think mum would have been too impressed.

After this rush of blood to the head I decided to take things a little more calmly and sat down on the bench to eat a bag of food.

Moments later a big Toyota Land Cruiser pulled up with a bumper sticker that said:

EAT RIGHT
EXERCISE
DIE ANYWAY

Two men with two small boys clambered out of the vehicle. One boy chased after a football that his dad had kicked along the beach. The other boy made straight for the swinging rope. Both men made straight for me. One said, with a rising intonation that turned his declarative sentence into a question, 'Apologies for shattering your peace, mate! Looks like you were having a cruisy time before us buggers arrived!'

The other said, 'If you don't mind me saying, that's one fuck of a load you've got on that bike.'

They asked where I was going, so I told them I was heading around the peninsula.

'You be careful,' said the bloke who had a splotched face like a burger in a bucket of beer. 'The roads are a bloody madhouse this time of year. Not that I want to worry you, but you know this country's got the worst record for driving in the world. And being alone and all that too…'

His mate, who liked to start his sentences with 'If you don't mind me saying/asking', said, 'If you don't mind me asking, doesn't a girl like you have no boyfriend?'

'Yes.'

'So why's he not out here with you?'

'He might be by May.'

'May? Jesus! You'll have another one by then!'

'Or had another few!' laughed the burger-face bloke.

Soon after this promising encounter I hit State Highway 25, also marked on my map as a 'Heritage Trail'. Heritage of what? I wondered. Road-kill victims?

Rolling into the 'township' (as it seems quaintly to be called) of

Coromandel, I read a roadside sign informing me that: COROMANDEL LION CLUB WELCOMES CAREFUL DRIVERS. WE HAVE TWO CEMETERIES, NO HOSPITAL.

Coromandel looks a bit like something out of the Wild West. The sort of place where you could imagine a gun-slinging cowboy suddenly flying through the swinging doors of a bar to land in the gutter. This probably has something to do with it being an old gold-mining town. There was a lot of kauri milling round here too. The township took its name from the storeship HMS *Coromandel,* which sailed from the Bay of Islands into this harbour in 1820 to take on kauri spars for the Royal Navy. The tall, straight kauri pine trees were greatly valued by mariners and the densely forested hills around Coromandel made ripe pickings for the timber mills to plunder. Despite the kauri, the town really only became famous in the 1880s when gold was discovered and people flocked to the area, pushing a virtually non-existent population up to a soaring 10,000. Some of the old Victorian and colonial buildings still line the short and slightly ramshackle main street.

These days Coromandel doesn't so much attract people to gold as to an alternative lifestyle. The place was full of conservationists, galleries and craft stores, pottery shops, woodcarvers' studios, furniture workshops and bumper stickers proclaiming NUCLEAR-FREE NEW ZEALAND – MAKING A DIFFERENCE. There were a lot of crystals and spiritual healing and vegetarian cafes too. I took a short spin around the town, riding past places like Fowl and Fancy Art and Craft, Kowhai Watercolour Studio, Kapanga Krafts, Gold Diggers Liquor Store and Furey's Creek Motors. As I leant my bike against the wall of the small Four Square grocery, with its green and yellow fascia and fifties-style logo, an anxious-looking man came up to me to warn that it wasn't a good time of year to be on the roads because of the amount of drunk drivers, who apparently like to get 'as pissed as a Sheila on a glass of wine'.

'We've usually got about a thousand, say, two thousand people at most, living up around this way,' he said. 'But come Christmas and New Year that number swells to around forty thousand. It's the kids and the hoons you got to really watch out for.'

'Hoons?' I said, thinking it was the way he pronounced hounds. 'You mean dogs?'

The man laughed. 'No, I mean the hoons. The yobs, the louts, the delinquent boy-racers. They're the hoons. No respect for anyone.'

After buying a bagful of food at the Four Square I pushed my bike around the corner to a park and sat at a shady picnic table. Someone had left a local paper on the table so I flapped it open and read the headline:

> RECORD NUMBERS OF POLICE
> ON PENINSULA
>
> More police than ever before are patrolling the peninsula this summer and new legislation will allow them to better manage the crowds. Operation CoroMass kicked off this week and Acting Eastern Area Commander John Kelly says the new laws should make their job easier. New 'boy racer' legislation and the inaugural 24-hour liquor ban mean more police will be out during the day. 'What we're saying is, come and have a good time, drink your alcohol but don't be out on the streets with it.'
>
> The new 'boy racer' law allows police to impound cars for 28 days if drivers are charged with sustained loss of traction, more commonly known as doing 'burnouts' or 'donuts'.
>
> Mr Kelly says many of the police have been through refresher courses including practising with riot equipment. 'Touch wood we don't have to use it.'

Operation CoroMass and riot equipment were not quite what I was expecting of New Zealand. I was banking more on a surplus of sheep (a reputed 48 million of them in all, compared with 4 million people) than something akin to an inner city battleground.

While I was contemplating this thought a man in his fifties and a sunhat came up to my table and said, 'Glad to see you've got the right idea by sitting in the shade. You can't be too careful of our sun. Most dangerous in the world. See this...' and he rolled up his sleeve to point at a darkened speckled splotch mark on his forearm. 'The makings of melonoma. No doubt about it.'

A woman called across to him from beside the toilet block.

'That'll be my wife,' he said. 'She's always after me to rattle my dags!'

'Rattle your what?' I said.

'Dags. Means get a bloody move on! At least it does when you rattle them!'

Jandals, hoons and rattling dags. Not to mention another word I seem to have learnt: grundies – not a family in *The Archers,* but a pair of underpants. Men's, I believe.

I was pushing my bike across the grass and back on to Kapanga Road when a man stopped me in my tracks and said, 'Don't tell me you're going to ride that thing across the mountains?'

From where we stood in the street, you could see a huge mound of Coromandel's great catapulting hills rising up behind the town. A road was just visible snaking its tortured way up the side of one of the inclines. Occasionally a toy-sized vehicle could be seen crawling upwards, advancing in slow motion. This was the continuation of State Highway 25 and led across the hills to the east coast. On my map the road was marked as 'minor road unsealed'. After telling the man that yes, I was, but not quite yet, as I was heading north first, I asked him if he knew what the condition of the road was like.

'Good as gold,' he said. 'It was metalled only six to nine months ago. My son worked as a foreman on it. Doesn't mean to say the gradient has got any easier, though. Just the thought of driving up there exhausts me!'

The road north out of Coromandel Town towards Colville was busy with hoons in noisy cars with exhaust pipes the size of the Mersey Tunnel. There was also a whole procession of big four-wheel drives, most of them pulling a boat behind them containing fishing-rod holders in the cockpit. None of the drivers appeared to have any idea how to pass a cyclist, or else they just didn't care, overtaking me on blind corners of narrow uphill winding roads. This inevitably led to me having overly close encounters with the sides of their trailers as the owners erratically slewed their tail-ends in towards me when they met another vehicle travelling in the opposite direction, trapping me up tight against the steep and unforgiving hillsides.

Every campsite I passed was packed with tents and boats and 4WDs and motorhomes and rowdy clumps of guffawing lads. I didn't fancy spending New Year's Eve among such a hullabaloo so after riding through Papaaroha and Amodeo Bay I dived into the roadside jungle (or 'bush' as they call it in local tongue). Here I put up my tent among a forest of enormous tree ferns with feathery umbrellas at least two storeys high with fat trunks that looked as if they were made of giant pineapple skins. It was a top spot for slumber, surrounded by extravagant foliage and tropical-looking birds and jungle noises. And at the bottom of the cliff came the swash and slap of the sea as it collided with the shore.

THE GREAT AUSTRALIAN LONELINESS

Ernestine Hill

Ernestine Hill (1899–1972) was an Australian journalist, travel writer and novelist whose extensive travels around the vast country, often with her son, Robert, in tow, provided bountiful fodder for her books and newspaper articles. It didn't always go well – she once penned an exaggerated report on the discovery of gold, triggering a gold rush, a stock-market boom and financial ruin for many. *The Great Australian Loneliness*, however, is an evocative and uncontentious account of Hill's pilgrimage 'with swag and typewriter' to explore the outback.

Where the Streets are Paved with Pearl

A hundred miles west of Carnarvon, and only two days' boat journey north of Perth, yet so remote from the world that sometimes neither a stranger nor a daily paper is seen here in a period of years, lies the extraordinary little settlement of Shark Bay, whose streets, like the nigger heaven of old revivalist hymns, are literally paved with pearl.

A fishing village of 250 people, white and coloured, Shark Bay, in its quaintness and isolation—and happily in its aura of dead shellfish—is unique on the Continent. Away from the tracks of steamers and the main roads to the North-west, other than the telegraph, there is no link with civilisation beyond the passing of the West Australian Government coastal ship *Koolinda*, that once in the month anchors seven miles off-shore, a wisp of smoke in the daytime, a spangle of lights at night. An old-fashioned lighter with grey sails, manned by seven burly young half-castes, lumbers out to meet her, exchanging bags of pearl-shell, frozen fish and shell-grit for the necessities of life, and news of the world.

To visit the port I was swung overboard from the *Koolinda's* decks in a cargo-basket—the only human cargo at three in the morning, to shelter behind bags and cases of stores for a two-hours' journey of bitter wind and whipping spray. The waters of the bay are so shallow that two miles out we trans-shipped to a dinghy, and finished up by wading the last couple of hundred yards to the beach with our luggage on our backs. Then I found myself marooned for a month, awaiting the steamer's return.

This is why there are so few travellers. A politician before election time, a clergyman or a pearl-buyer once in two years, and one visiting governor in half a century—that is all Shark Bay knows of the world, and all it needs to know. They told me that the first newcomer in eight years walked overland 500 miles from Perth—and they put him in gaol when he got there.

Those tawny, scrawny sand-hills look back to the dawn of Australian history. Dampier named the shallow inlet when he searched its shores for water in 1692. Freycinet and Baudin followed him a century later. Twenty-two miles away lies the mauve and blue patchwork of Dirk Hartog Island, where the unknown South Land showed up under the arched white sails of the *Eendraght* in 1616. Dirk Hartog is a sheep station to-day, its musterers cooking their lobsters and turtle-steaks of the evening camp on the beaches where Dirk Hartog and Vlaming, a century between them, set up the famous tin plates that were the title deeds of a continent, and, luckily for Britain, lost them both.

The town is a half-circle of modest little homes, one street wide, built on the beach, with huts of Darktown huddled at both ends. Below the line of indentured labour this coloured community is descended from the Arabs, Malays, Chinese and Manilamen, who found it a profitable fishing-ground before the passing of the Aliens' Restrictions Act, and of aboriginal tribes now practically extinct there. In fifty years of seclusion there has been such interbreeding among the coloured races and intermarriage of the whites that to-day the population is variegated indeed, and mostly related—a Pitcairn in Australia.

Toilers of the sea to the third and fourth generations, the people live by gathering shell-grit, found in countless millions of tons on the shores of Hamelin Pool, chilling fish in a little tin refrigerating works, of which the engineer is a South Sea Islander, and, principally, by pearling. Here they fish, not the magnificent *margaritifera meleagrina* of Broome seas, 10 inches across and pounds in lustrous weight, but *margaritifera radiata*, the golden-lip, not more than three inches in diameter, that produces the little honey-coloured pearls beloved of Hindu and Chinese women.

I watched them securing their pearls and pearl shell by a method curious and very primitive. Pegging the shallow bay into leases from 500 to 1,000 acres, fenced off like poultry-yards, the pearlers travel across it a week at a time in tiny cutters, dragging the ocean bed with hand-dredges of wire, sails set to some three miles an hour. At the weekend they return with the haul, each ship bringing from ten to twelve bags, and carry it up on shoulders bent double beneath the weight, for half a mile and more through the shallows.

In tumble-down tin shacks known as pearling-pits it is opened, trimmed, packed and graded, mainly by women of the settlement. Only the first quality is eligible for auction in London. The residue is piled high in heaps, or splintered along the beaches, where in fifty years it has become a mosaic of sparkling beauty, paving the road with living moonlight, and turning the world to dark blue before the eyes.

To obtain the pearls, the oysters are placed in 'pogey-pots,' boilers and barrels that line the seashore, forever steeping the town in the odour of long-dead shell-fish. There they are left to putrefy into a vile and liqueous mass, and when putrefaction can go no further, are boiled to a seething and even more evil-smelling scum, in which the sediment of pearls sinks to the bottom.

Gold and buff-colour and deep green, these tiny stones have now an increasing value in Eastern markets, but where the white and rose-ate beauties of Broome have realised as much as £8,000 for a single stone in the good days, the jewels of Shark Bay, 26 grains at most, rarely touch the £100 level. Its pearl-shell brings from £14 to £35 a ton, as opposed to £180.

In the very heart of the town, with its wool-sheds and yards, is the station homestead of Peron, with 15,000 sheep in the shearing season running in the main street, frolicking along the hotel verandah, and rollicking round the bay in barges.

Pursuing its sleepy destiny for half a century unbroken in a world of cataclysmic change, Shark Bay still slumbers on. Never has it heard the ringing of a church bell. No picture show has disturbed its solemnity to laughter. The only aeroplane that ever passed over came seeking the lost *Köbenhavn* some years ago. At first its whirring was mistaken for a whale blowing off, then for the menace of a coming hurricane. When at last it dipped and roared above the clustered roofs with a horrifying swoop, the inhabitants of Shark Bay looked at each other with a wild surmise. They had read of such things.

Tongues were wagging with a local—a very local—scandal in the tiny township, which consisted of a broken-down store, a hotel and a beacon on the sand-hills for the fishermen at night. The half-caste, Helen, who earned her living cooking at the station, shampooed her pretty curly hair twice a day, and lent a dash of colour to her dusky charms with lip-stick, was suing her equally half-caste husband in divorce. A half-caste divorce is very rare—in affairs of the heart the coloured people do not bother with formalities—but the lady had prospects of becoming the wife of a white man, or imagined she had. When her husband retaliated with a counter-suit, naming three of the most respectable residents as co-respondents, the fishing-village was pleasantly electrified.

'Why don't you let her go, Oscar? Then you don't have to keep her,' one of the casual nor'-westers asked him.

'I'm paying a solicitor over in Carnarvon £25 to fix all this,' said Oscar, 'because he says, if she wins it, I have to give her the aluminium.'

South of Shark Bay, on the shores of Hamelin Pool, are eight or nine prosperous sheep stations set in a sandy waste. Several of the homesteads are built of the shell-grit that has silted up the beaches in a solid white speedway for 100 miles and more, a lagoon-drift deposit of millions of tiny molluscs of some prehistoric time, that below the level of the sands have set into a cement block, easily cut. White and cool and clean and comfortable, these shell-grit houses withstand the years in that stoneless, timberless sand country, and are probably unique. Bores that run a million gallons a day provide the water for this excellent, if apparently barren, sheep country, and stores are frequently carried across the mud-flats by a camel-string, to and from the lighters at anchor, where the ships of the desert meet the ships of the sea.

At the little settlement of Hamelin Pool at the head of the bay—three roofs in blankness—Mr. Paddy Knight, one of the loneliest postmasters in Australia, has been in residence for thirty years, each morning punctiliously taking his weather and calling head office at Perth to keep this quaint corner in touch, while at Fauré Island lives Mr. Tom Simpson, an exile from the Lakes District in England, with never a passer-by from year's end to year's end to bear him company.

For Tom Simpson, the Crusoe of Fauré, the world holds nothing but memories. Sitting on an upturned boat, he told me his life-story. In 'God's Own Corner' he was one of the idle rich, with a country home, a yacht on Windermere, the systematic pleasures of an assured life. An unlucky gamble on the Liverpool cotton market—and a rude waking up in middle age, with nothing in the ledger but a happy youth of lost opportunities. From £2,000 a year his income fell to 13s. 6d. a week, and that earned gipsying round the North Country as a mole-catcher, with moleskin pelts at a farthing apiece.

Then came a period as ferryman on one of the lakes, the Boer War, and nine years in Africa. Twenty years ago he crossed to Australia, and on outcamps of the Gascoyne stations, and pearling in a little dinghy in Shark Bay, 'knocked about for colonial experience.' Fauré Island is a sheep-run of 11,000 acres and 3,000 sheep. It belongs to a Shark Bay pearler, who has given the management to Simpson as the only white man who will live there in isolation. His predecessor on the island, an old Malay, left him a legacy of forty-eight cats. He shot all but seventeen, because they killed the natural history specimens.

For the hermit of Fauré is a nature-lover. Turtles build their nests in the sands there unafraid, and every shell that is washed up, every bird that alights, is noted. Two or three times a year he heaves up the sail of his cutter and, with a fair wind, makes the mainland 15 miles away, cheerfully walking the next 15 miles in to Shark Bay for stores. Until he goes to look for them, he sees none of his own human kind, but there is no trace of taciturnity about him.

'Lonely? Me! Never!' he laughed. 'I have some books, and I have my dog Bubble. There were three of us when we came over, Bubble and Squeak and I. Squeak died, leaving us two together. It's a good place for an old fellow, and why should I be lonely? Long ago I learned the lesson that a man can have too many friends.'

A smile in which there was no trace of bitterness, a whistle to Bubble, growing a little deaf with age, and the shepherd of Fauré tipped his hat to me and took the trail of the sand-hills to Monkeymia, where his little skiff waited to take him back to the silence.

A SNAPSHOT OF AFGHANISTAN

Bella Pollen

Bella Pollen (1961–present) is a writer and journalist who has tackled a wide variety of subjects from illegal immigration on the Mexican border, to the Cold War, to the decline of the British aristocracy. Author of five novels, including the critically acclaimed *The Summer of the Bear* and the best-selling *Hunting Unicorns*, Pollen's memoir *Meet Me in the In-Between* was published by Picador in 2018. She lives between London and a remote barn she restored in Colorado.

We're flying low over the Hindu Kush when the plane is struck by lightning. An old Afghan springs to his feet, and ignoring the entreaties of the air stewardesses begins shrieking "God will not let us die!" over and over and over again. Given the trembling fuselage, the black twists of tornado outside the window, this is not a popular mantra amongst fellow passengers. Across the aisle from us the pop idol types barely react. Fleshy and vulgar in animal print leggings – cooing over duty free Tommy Hilfiger, they're a horrible pair, if not sisters, still united in their spite and meanness. Behind them sit their bodyguards, humiliated and red-eyed from a vigorous tongue-lashing that's been going on since we left Dubai. Forget the storm, it's this topsy turvy balance of power that's held my attention given we're about to land in a country where to call women second class citizens is to grossly overstate their position in society. But then Afghanistan is already proving to be a country of bewildering contradictions.

A week earlier, I'd been sitting in the Afghan embassy in London. The young woman in the visa department was beautiful if surly. She looked up from my required letters of recommendation. "You're visiting a school." She stated flatly.

"Yes."

"Marefat High School."

"Yes."

"Does it educate girls?" She asked and the question hung in the air between us.

It was 1996 when the Taliban imposed its iron grip on the country, stripping women of their civic and social rights and banishing them from schools, universities and the workforce. If a decade of allied intervention has greatly improved life for women, the Taliban have nevertheless made it quite clear what happens to brave little girls who dare cry education for all. Over the last few years, pupils, teachers and schools have all been shamefully targeted, Marefat among them.

Does Marefat educate girls? You bet it does.

The embassy woman was wearing a short black dress, demure, yet close fitting enough to accentuate the curve of her breasts.

"Yes, it educates girls." I said and waited for a flicker of solidarity. Nothing. Only a piercing stare as she stamped my form.

It's hard to know what to expect of this proud and embittered country – this Babylonian land of fractured beliefs and landscapes. *Don't stay more than five days. Don't take the same route twice. Don't go at all.* Travel tips have not been in short supply.

"You've been a good wife." My husband said in a heavy hearted fashion as I left for the airport.

"Thanks." I replied solemnly, trying to hide my excitement. Finally, after months of date juggling my colleague Christa and I were finally going.

"*Salaam alaikum,*" the air stewardess says as we jolt onto the runway, "welcome to Kabul."

The airport bus is empty and stationary – clapped out with worn pink velvet seats and a bullet hole in the windscreen that has sent a spider's web of cracks across the glass. The doors are too warped to close. The soldier guarding them becomes fractious when asked whether, at some point, the bus might be expected to go anywhere. "Car parking C. I told you. Wait inside."

"All our security passes have been confiscated," our contact Nate texts us, "it's a giant pain in the ass."

After ten minutes or so, an old woman cranks her bad hip onto a seat.

"Where are you going?" She demands through her chadri. "Where are you staying?"

"With friends." We tell her.

"What street?"

We pretend we cannot remember.

She continues to regard us suspiciously until the driver finally gets on. Reddish lashes, eerily pale eyes. He asks 20$ for the supposedly free ride. We pay up. What do we know? We're just HTH's, "Happy To Helps." the worst kind of do-gooders – ignorant and eager.

Nate is waiting for us in the car park. His driver speaks no English. His head of security is called Umer. A convoy of armoured vehicles is holding up traffic as we head into Kabul. "The US military flexing their muscles." Nate says as I watch them roll slowly by. Time after time history has proved there is no conquering this country and yet, here we go again…

Nate's driver pulls the car sharply off the main road. Steel doors slice shut behind us and we're suddenly in a compound of sorts. Two stories washed with fluorescent lights and the smell of new carpet. Nate's dog, a boisterous mongrel with severe cabin fever boxes her master to the floor, rips into our suitcases, then dashes outside to chase flies around a courtyard encircled with barbed wire. It's afternoon but curtains are drawn across all windows. Behind them, the glass is daubed with thick black paint. In the days that follow, I become increasingly depressed by this window blindness. This is a country I've always wanted to see. Pinned to my office noticeboard is a picture of a beautiful, green Kabul. A Liberal arts student, long shiny hair uncovered, walks alongside two boys with drooping moustaches and John Lennon glasses. Here was an intellectual Kabul, a progressive, philosophical Kabul where women went to university in bell-bottom trousers and held hands. But that was the seventies. Today this city is a war zone, ravaged by thirty years of conflict and the only way I will see it in the days to follow will be through stolen glimpses from a car window.

Kabul's morning colors are Mondrian. Blocky buildings of orange, mint and lemon washed in mountain light. Women shrouded in indigo blue glide through the streets. How different are their snapshots of life to mine? The half destroyed scaffolding; goats eating trash by the roadside; telephone wires looping round each other like black snakes. In the market, bananas and eggplant are heaped on rickety barrows. An ANSF soldier, gun parked under his arm, counts out change for a bag of dates. All around motorbikes growl, exhausts rattle and engines belch out oily fumes. A symphony of pollution in the air while in the sky, a storm hangs over a city permanently holding its breath. It's April. The snows have melted. The spring offensive is as inevitable as the blossoming of the almond trees. There is a frisson on the wind; of energy, of defiance, of fear.

Our driver makes a U turn, then another. "If you weren't sure where the school was," Nate scolds them, "you should have scouted it."

Happy though we are to be in Nate's care, we're not entirely sure who he is. Ex US military for sure, eyes and ears on the ground, some sniffing out of Al Qaida cells, a vague reference to the years spent easing kidnapped Americans out of the Bolivian jungle. The biggest danger here, he tells us, is wrong place, wrong time stuff. Bombs. Bad luck. And then there's kidnapping. Westerners have always been the bread and butter of that particular trade. Though Christa and I are worth diddly squat – on paper we tick a few boxes. Both journalists of sorts and then Christa's mother, the indomitable Baroness de Souza who co-founded Marefat is currently speaker of the House of Lords. "Take Christa!" I have practiced saying, "she's so much better connected…" And Nate's kidnapping MO, we're mildly interested to hear? Straight to the ATM machine?

"Oh, it's not about the money." Nate replies cheerfully. "It's about making them understand they've taken the wrong people. It's about making them understand the shit that's gonna come down on their heads if they harm you, if they sell you on to another faction because that's the very last thing you want, believe me." We do believe him, we do and whoever Nate is, we resolve to do precisely as he says.

We're in the district of Dashte Barchi now, where the school is located. Faces in the street have changed. Wider eyes, flatter bone structure attesting to Mongolian ancestry of the Hazara. Anyone familiar with the Kite Runner will remember its doomed hero Hassan – the hare lipped servant of a wealthy Pashtun family. The Hazara are his people. Victims of appalling oppression and multi ethnic massacres, the Hazara have been forced to relocate from country to country where they have endured life beneath the lowest rung of every societal ladder. Dashte Barchi is one of the poorest areas of Kabul, but these Hazaras are lucky. Those who fled to Iraq, to Iran and Syria have not fared so well.

The Mercedes is crawling along a narrow rutted road and suddenly there it is; a sign above a blue doorway, "Marefat school for learning. The future starts here."

Marefat began as an ideal, the tenets of democracy taught in a mud hut in a refugee camp. It had thirty kids then and a young fiercely voluble young man, Aziz Royesh whose vision was to build a center of academic excellence rooted in the local community of his hometown. Ten years on, Aziz's impossible dream is not only a reality, it's something of a miracle. It's "break" as we arrive and the courtyard is jostling with kids. Marefat has almost 3,000 students and an academic record so excellent that virtually all progress on to University, many scooping up international scholarships.

Small problem though. The original school building, built mostly by the kids' parents was constructed on a fault line. Health and safety in Kabul is not a government directive but a matter of faith. The seismic proof foundations of a new building have been laid but work needs to resume now, before the winter snows freeze the city's construction fingers and the children's education along with it. On our return to London, Christa and I will face the humbling task of bowl-begging half a million dollars and if that isn't a frightening prospect, tell me what is.

We move through the classrooms, taking turns to make inspirational speeches: Education for all! How much we in England care! But even as the girls cheer, I'm wondering, do we really? Unless we can somehow bottle and take home this gratitude, this hunger for knowledge, how can we possibly make people care?

I have a sudden flash of the clichéd deprived inner city school, the sprawled legs, and chewing gum, the weapons checked at the school gate. I think of my own children, brought up in a country where we take democracy and education for granted who consider learning the worst kind of drag and it makes these Afghan kids' determination to belong to another, better world that much more poignant.

Aziz tells us we must choose one girl to host us for lunch. Diplomatically, democratically we insist on picking names out of a hat. Three sisters "win." Flanked by our men in black, we follow Sugra, and Neema and Anisa along the broken streets, Aziz, behind us, carrying trays of eggs and flat bread.

At the girls' house, we are met by a woman with a weathered face and calloused hands. I'm about to greet her as grandmother before realizing it is their mother. Neema's parents fled first the Russians then hard line Islamic rule to raise their eight children in a refugee camp. Their path home has not been easy. The eggs disappear into the kitchen. Soon, there is the smell of onions sweating in a frying pan. We eat lunch sitting cross-legged on a colorful plastic tablecloth. Aziz talks like a brilliantly articulate intellectual on speed. The girls pass round plates of half scrambled omelets filled with fried tomatoes and I eat like a starved person.

Later that afternoon we hold an impromptu debate on equal rights between seniors. "What happens when you're married to a girl who's earning good money?" We ask the boys, "as much money as you. You have a child. Who makes the supper? Who changes the diaper?" The boys exchange panicked looks. Their culture has taught them it is the nature of the Afghan woman to "accept the supreme man over their heads", but Marefat is teaching them that it is their social responsibility to help their sisters claim back their rights.

"We are as good as men," Anisa cries, "and we will prove it." These girls will have to prove more than that. They must prove that they can square the ideals of democracy and feminism with being a good Moslem. And maybe it's all too much too soon. A quiet bespectacled boy stands up. "Better to show respect." He says. "Go slowly. Be cautious." But the girls are on fire. Not for them the long arm of political change. They have watched their own mothers put up and shut up. Education and employment is the goal of their generation's revolution and as I watch them, hands stretching in the air, a line of Rosa Parks, waiting and willing their bus to come along, I fear for them.

For all those throughout history who have conspired to take away the rights of their fellow humans, there have been others who have paid in blood to live in a world of their choosing. What happens when Neema decides to burn her headscarf? When Sugra angers a cleric or Anisa nudges the line of tolerance too far? As allied withdrawal slides into view, the future of Afghanistan looks increasingly unstable. What will happen to the dreams of these girls should Marefat fall under the jubilant return of the Taliban?

It's dusk. We're on a rat run. A road made of built-up rubble with steep drops on either side of the car. Ruins of the old city rise out of the ground, the same color as the earth. Small kids hug the verge in a mish mash of polyester and traditional costume. On the walls of a whitewashed building, the long snouts of AK47's are silhouetted against the darkening sky. The atmosphere in the car is tense. The address for the evening, originally vetted by Umer, turned out to have been wrong. The correct address is in the no-go area of the mountains.

We'd been standing on the roof of the new school building with Aziz and Jawed, a Kabul born academic and our host for the evening. Below us, rinsed in the orange light of late afternoon, a group of boys were playing football, kicking up small puffs of dust with their shoes.

"Make your excuses. " Nate said curtly when informed of the mistake. "I'm pulling you out."

I handed the mobile back to Umer. Umer is Pashtun. He's a nice man, a thoughtful man, whose son was born with a foot facing backwards. Umer's son will probably never play football but Nate, whose special operations exterior masks something infinitely softer, is helping him to get the operation free in the US. Jawed, our academic friend is Hazara. It is his parents who are hosting us for the evening – his brother who is roasting lamb.

"The girl's safety is a question of honor for my family." He says.

"I do what Mr. Nate says." Umer declares and suddenly tribal horns lock. "They are under my protection." Umer insists.

"If the girls die," Jawed counters quietly, "it would bring great shame. My family could never let this happen."

Christa and I eyeball each other. Too ignorant to unravel the tensions, the degrees of religious or political extremism, the ethnic and cultural nuances of this country, we do, nevertheless, have a code of our own. As a nation, Britain can rival any other for moral and spiritual decline, but damned if we can stand the idea of someone's parents being put out.

"You entrusted your safety to *me*." Nate says grimly when we ring back to tell him we're going. "You promised to do what *I said*."

Talk at dinner is NGO led – gender mainstreaming, activism versus advocacy. The roast lamb appears, fat spitting and speared onto six foot blades. Toffees are washed down with hot sweet tea and it's late by the time we head home. The streets are curfew empty.

Torches flash at our windscreen. Our driver slows the car for Umer to show his pass and the police wave us on.

Nate is waiting up for us arms crossed. "Is this what it's gonna be like when my daughter starts dating?" He jokes, but it seems we are forgiven, if only for now.

In the night I wake to the sound of sirens. Kabul's soundtrack for the foreseeable future. We have only another day here but I want to stay. Places where you can get lost in the lives of others have always been catnip for me, and I'm beginning to feel Afghanistan's pull.

On our last night Nate takes us to his favorite restaurant, La Taverna where we eat Lebanese food and drink red wine hidden in chipped blue and white tea-pots. "What no baklava?" I complain as the owner, Kamul brings us a slice of his famous chocolate cake. On our next visit to Kabul, Nate, still mildly offended by my diva behavior, suggests an alternative restaurant. As we're getting ready to leave a blast shakes the compound. La Taverna has been targeted. We sit in the darkness listening to the tat tat tat of gunfire – comforted by the swift response of ANSF forces. It doesn't take long to realize that it had not been ANSF but Taliban, storming the dining room on the heels of the suicide bomb and shooting diners as they ate. Twenty-one people die in La Taverna that night including its owner, Kamul. We won't eat out again in Kabul, but we won't stop coming back either. I guess you sign up for what you sign up for.

There's no hugging out in the open of Car Parking C. A terse nod to thank Nate is all that's permitted. In the airport we shuffle slowly through security, secondary security, extra security. We're searched, x-rayed, scratch n sniffed, our faces, eyes and souls examined. The flight is delayed. We buy a 14-dollar bag of almonds and offer them round our fellow travellers.

"They're bad quality," says a contractor, "you've been ripped off." But the nuts buy us friends: A quiet UN guy from Nepal. A pharmaceutical rep who tells us Afghanistan's cache of onyx is being raped by the allies and the Chinese. The young Afghan whose uncle was publicly beheaded. "I'm dying to go into politics." He says, seemingly without irony. "Make this country great again."

And maybe that is to be Afghanistan's future. To be great, to be green, to be civilized and at peace. Many believe it. Maybe the Taliban really are less hard line, ready to talk. Maybe rights so fiercely fought for will not be easily relinquished. On the plane I fiddle around with I photo on my computer, changing the color of the Kabul sky from grey to blue, as though that might be all it takes. There's a guttural sound and I realize the man occupying the window seat is watching me. Mullah? Cleric? Talib? I have no way of knowing. He leans over the empty middle seat and stares without embarrassment.

"Kabul?" He says. I nod warily.

Street scenes suddenly give onto an image of the Marefat girls in their distinctive blue and white uniforms. The medievally beautiful Neema stares straight at the lens. Panicked I switch files; randomly landing on a recent visit to Saigon and the iconic photograph of a wounded US soldier falling from a helicopter. Appalled I stab at the keyboard, but the Mullah/Cleric/Talib stops me with his hand.

"Good." He says.

I look at him even more uncertainly. His beard is made up of a thousand wiry springs. "Good photo." He nods at the fallen American hero and smiles slyly.

PART FIVE

EUROPE

LOVE OF COUNTRY

Madeleine Bunting

Madeleine Bunting (1964–present) is an award-winning journalist and writer who worked for many years as an editor and columnist on the *Guardian* with a special interest in religion. The author of several prize-winning books, she most recently embarked on a series of journeys to the Hebrides, the remote group of islands off the north-western Scottish coast that have had a fierce magnetic pull on the creative and spiritual imagination throughout history. *Love of Country: A Hebridean Journey* is Bunting's exploration of nature, belonging and the evolution of the islands' influence on ideas of Britishness.

Scientists have described the Hebrides as a biological frontier between continent and ocean, between two great ecosystems of opposite character; to the east, Eurasia's land mass stretches six thousand miles to Kamchatka and the shores of the Bering Sea, and to the west lie the marine pastures which were historically prolific with vast stocks of fin fish and shellfish. The temperatures are relatively mild, but Iona's position on the rim of one of the world's great oceans exposes it to the full force of the storm belts of the North Atlantic. The Hebrides is one of the windiest places in Europe, with gales gathering enormous fetch across the ocean, arriving on the islands laden with sea salt. On an average of five days in every month, the winds reach gale force, and in the winter, it can be twelve days a month. The hydrography of the Hebrides is complex, with currents, waves and tides which can make the sea treacherous. The strong winds and heavy rain slow down plant growth on these islands, making agriculture on the poor acidic soils difficult. They also subject the human body to a damp chill whose cooling effect is much greater than the average temperature suggests. Life here for Colum Cille and the monks was very hard; it was cold and usually wet. The crops could be wiped out by flood, heavy rain or wind, and famine and malnutrition were not unknown. The sea journeys from island to island were fraught with risk. This edge of the known world was a place of danger. Yet despite its vulnerability to the Atlantic's weather systems, Iona became a centre of learning, power and wealth.

The Atlantic had been richly mythologized in Europe long before the small coracles of the Irish monks spread out from Ireland to explore the islands along this frontier. The Atlantic was named after the Greek god Atlas, who bore his heavy burden, holding the sky and heavens on his shoulders to keep them apart from the earth in the extreme far west, where the sun set. Here, heaven and earth were close to meeting. It was the dwelling place of the three Hesperides, daughters of Atlas and goddesses of the evening, bathed in the golden light of sunset, which had been a gift to celebrate the marriage of Zeus and Hera. There, they tended the trees of golden apples which gave immortality.

After a dull day of rain, there were moments on my travels when the clouds cracked open, and Zeus' bridal gift blazed a brief, brilliant light from a place far away in the west. Every one of those moments brought the suggestion of elusive splendour, a glorious realm beyond the horizon, tantalizingly just beyond human reach. It provoked a stab of intense yearning for a place which was richly wondrous, where all tedium, banality and suffering were banished. In Greek myth, one of Hercules' twelve labours was to fetch the golden apples of the Hesperides. According to the poet Hesiod, 'the islands of the blest by the deep eddying Ocean' were where the glorious dead 'untroubled in spirit dwell' and 'for whom the grain-giving fields bear rich honey-sweet fruit three times a year'.

There is a recurrent mythical theme of lands lost in the Atlantic. One lost island was known as Hy Brazil or Brazil Rock, and was only taken off maps of the west of Ireland in 1865. Atlantis was a lost continent, the preserve of Poseidon, where the people became wealthy and corrupt and sought to conquer the world. It was swallowed up by the sea after incurring the wrath of Zeus. The twelfth-century Arab geographer Al Idrisi referred to 30,000 islands in the Atlantic, but he warned that passage to the riches of these fabled lands was full of danger in the 'sea of perpetual gloom'. The Atlantic struck terror into Europeans over the course of centuries. The Greeks also referred to the Atlantic as Oceanus, a sea which they believed encircled the known world. In the fifth century BCE Pindar warned that 'what lies beyond cannot be trodden by the wise or the unwise... one cannot cross from Gadir (Cadiz) towards the dark west. Turn again the sails towards the dry land of Europe.' The ocean held terrifying monsters and demons, and huge tangles of seaweed which could entrap and devour the vessels which dared to sail out of sight of land. A hungry place, it consumed the lives of sailors. Pythagoras suspected that the earth might be round and that it might be possible to sail from Spain to India, but such theories were impossible to test because of the barrier of the ocean and its 'destitution and loneliness'. The emptiness of the ocean was the cause of terror as much as the physical danger. Archaeologist Barry Cunliffe in *Facing the Ocean*, his magisterial overview of the prehistory of the Atlantic coastline, writes: 'The domains of land and sea were conceived as separate systems subject to their own very different supernatural powers, the interface between them was a liminal place and as such, was dangerous.'

The Christian monks arrived on Iona steeped in the theological traditions of the early Christian ascetics of Europe and the Near East; in particular they were inspired by the Desert Fathers of Egypt. They saw this coast as their 'green desert,' a place of 'revelation' and 'science' (in the sense of knowledge). In the twelfth-century Irish text the *Book of Leinster,* a young man 'heard a sound in the wave, to wit, a chant of wailing and sadness'. He cast a spell on the wave 'that it might reveal to him what the matter was'. For the Christian monks on the islands scattered along the Hebrides and west Ireland, the ocean was a theatre of the cosmic struggle between the Creator God and evil. Removed from the distractions of a corrupted world, a monk could take his part in that battle for his own salvation. Psalm 107 told the monks that 'those who go down to the sea in ships, and have business in its many waters, see the works of the Lord and his great deeds in the deep'. The seventh-century hermit on Rum, Beccán mac Luigdech, wrote a poem which vividly captures the wildness of the seas the monks lived with: 'the wave-strewn wild region, foam-flecked, seal-filled/Savage bounding, seething, white-tipped' runs the translation from the Gaelic. Natural phenomena such as thunderstorms and lightning inspired utter terror, and there were monsters and dangers at every turn. Beyond brief, fragile human life lay the horrors of judgement and eternal hellfire. Few would be saved, Christian preachers warned. God was above all to be feared by the pious in a chaotic world full of evil. This was a place in which to recognize and confront fear, and to throw oneself, utterly dependent, upon the mercy of God.

Such profound pessimism elicited intense piety, with acts of constant supplication and propitiation. Colum Cille's biographer, Adomnán, recounted how the saint slept on bare rock, and stood exposed to the winds in the freezing sea of early morning to recite the psalms, his form so thin that his ribs could be seen. The monks saw themselves as *peregrinati,* and their concept of pilgrimage was a form of martyrdom in which they removed themselves from all that they loved, all that was *familiar*; from the family and community they knew, the rituals and traditions of their homeland, for the sake of God. Liberated from the requirements of family and tribe, and in particular from expectations to fight as warriors, these monks begged for God's mercy, poured forth their praise and confessed their sins of gluttony, lust and avarice. Their pilgrimage was to seek salvation. They had gone into exile for God and they were searching 'for the place of one's resurrection'.

This bleak picture is a far cry from Iona's pilgrimage industry of the last two centuries. On the short ferry trip across the Sound of Iona, we were surrounded by the crowds arriving for Easter celebrations. A young American talked volubly about meeting his beautiful Spanish girlfriend on Ibiza and how he 'practised healing' on her until he discovered that he was falling in love. Many were carrying musical instruments and backpacks, and were swathed in colourful scarves. Amongst the heterogeneous passengers, the conversation was animated; some sought company, music and relaxation; some were seeking salvation. On arriving at the jetty, their backpacks and guitars were loaded onto vans and they peeled off in groups to walk the final mile to their hostels, laughing and talking. The next morning, the ferries disgorged contingents of day trippers at frequent intervals, who filled the pubs, restaurants and tea shops. The hotels were teeming with guests; the shops were doing a brisk business in Celtic memorabilia, bookmarks, jewellery, music and books. The distinctive knotwork and interlacing of Celtic design has found its way into thousands of homes and churches across the British Isles embellishing furniture, church vessels and jewellery. The islanders might be a bit bemused by the pilgrims' enthusiasm ('They're a few feet off the ground,' was the wry comment of one), but it gives them a living.

The candles flickered on the ancient stones of the abbey late into the evening during Good Friday's vigil. It felt cool, the walls impregnated with the winter's storms, and in the sombre silence people sat for five minutes, an hour or longer. Two days later the first service on Easter Sunday was at dawn. It was still dark when I got up in the quiet bed and breakfast, sitting with a cup of tea to watch light break over Beinn Mhòr on Mull across the Sound as the stars slowly faded. Leaving my son sleeping, I slipped out to head to the abbey. The sky was stained a soft pink and over the island of Erraid to the south hung a pale yellow full moon, its light gently glittering on the calm sea. At this early hour of 5 a.m., the air vibrated with the magnificent sound of thousands of birds singing; amid the larksong erupted intermittently the distinctive sound of the corncrake, a harsh rasp echoing from the field. It was just as the Iona boatman had described the day before, like a finger dragged along a comb. A soft wind blew and I heard the murmur of millions of small movements of water against the rocks of the Sound, the tiny slaps and gurgles of a sea breathing quietly. 'The sigh of all the seas breaking in measure round the isles soothed them; the night wrapped them; nothing broke their sleep, until the birds beginning and the dawn weaving their thin voices into its whiteness,' wrote Virginia Woolf in *To the Lighthouse*, set on the Hebridean island of Skye.

As I neared the abbey, I saw other figures hunched over in the cold, hurrying in the same direction, silhouetted against the lightening sky. Around a hundred of us gathered in the dark outside the small tenth-century St Oran's chapel in the abbey grounds. The women were closest to the door, the men were asked to hang back as a reminder that after his resurrection Christ revealed himself first to two women. A young woman began to sing, her clear voice rising into the twilit sky overhead. Tapers were passed around as women whispered with excitement, 'Jesus has risen, Jesus has risen. The Light of the World.' Tears came to my eyes and I could feel intense sensations passing along my spine. For a moment, it was possible to glimpse the salvation dreamt of by those Irish *peregrinati* in their lonely vigils on remote headlands all those centuries before, inspired by the idea of an extraordinary event in which a man rose from the dead, a man who declared himself the Son of God and offered salvation. Something stirred deeply in me.

'The man is little to be envied whose piety would not grow warmer among the ruins of Iona,' declared Johnson after his visit, a comment which, for its time, was a remarkable acknowledgement of Britain's Catholic past. The intense moment I had experienced faded, but it left an uncomfortable reminder of lost faith, that reserve of belief and meaning beyond reach. As the sun rose above Beinn Mhòr and splashed bright sunshine on the daffodils, I walked back up the road to breakfast, listening to the larks and corncrakes in full voice.

Much of Iona's power lies in the place. Like Holy Isle off Arran, it is a small island off an island, and the ritual of departure and arrival is played out twice. We were removed from the world twice over, and even Oban, with its supermarkets, car parks and traffic lights, seemed very distant. Iona felt like the last outpost, a lighthouse without the elevation: a scrap of low-lying land in the ocean which could be swallowed up like one of those mythological islands if a fierce Atlantic storm unleashed a monstrous wave. Only three miles long by one and half miles wide, it can be walked in a few hours; it has beaches, a small hill, rocky foreshore and the distinctive machair of these Hebridean islands, the thin layer of cropped green turf over white shell sand which sustains a brilliant embroidery of flowers. With so little on the island, the eye is repeatedly drawn to the horizon. From the west shore the Atlantic spreads out, unbroken by land for thousands of miles until it reaches Newfoundland. From the long beaches at the northern tip I looked across the sea towards the string of the Treshnish Isles and the island known as Bac Mòr, or the Dutchman's Cap. Back on the busy east side in the grounds of the grey stone abbey, the coastline of Mull lies across the narrow Sound. The shoreline of Ardmeanach on Mull is made up of steep grey cliffs with wide rugged skirts of scree and no trace of crofts or trees. Closer to, the Ross of Mull offers a contour of low rounded granite outcrops whose masses seem to be crouching as if in fear of the sea. Boulders are scattered along its coastline, creating inlets and islets. The little ferry port of Fionnphort has the boldness to insist on street lamps, but they were an incongruous intrusion at night when they light up the dark sky, matched only by the blazing lights of the cruise ships which anchor in the Sound. Along the coast I can pick out a single-track road leading down to a cluster of houses perched uncertainly amongst the bare, scored rocks. Iona's abbey is built of this rock, dragged and heaved into boats, sailed across the Sound and carried up from the shore. In later centuries, the rock was blasted out of the hillsides and loaded onto ships to be transported first round the north of Scotland to Aberdeen for polishing, before circumnavigating the world. This rock was used to build the world's cities: Glasgow, Liverpool, Manchester and London. It built bridges, including Jamaica Bridge and Kirklees Bridge in Glasgow, and Blackfriars Bridge, Holborn Viaduct and Westminster Bridge in London. It has travelled as far as New Zealand, and blocks as big as five metres high made their way to America. Its popularity was due to its exceptional durability and its beauty. A pale reddish brown, the coarse-grained crystals are a riot of matter, caught colliding millions of years ago.

From Iona, my eye frequently landed on Mull and its ungiving character. It contrasts with the rolling green fields which surround Iona's abbey, the harbour's lanes and the cottage gardens, and the brave stunted trees which have survived the Atlantic storms. Easter was late this year, and unexpectedly warm. Lambs tottered onto their unsteady legs or lay comatose, stoned by the warmth, on the turf. The sheep-cropped machair was already green after the salty winds of winter, and as absurdly neat as an Oxbridge lawn, edging the beaches of brilliant white sand, which shot the sea with an implausible Caribbean turquoise. There was a softness and clarity in the air as leaves unfurled from sticky pink buds before our eyes, and daffodils lazily nodded their heads in the flower beds. Robert Louis Stevenson, who spent time as a boy on the neighbouring island of Erraid, wrote of 'the inimitable seaside brightness of the air'.

At such a time of year, the miracles attributed to Colum Cille on Iona by Adomnán appeared entirely credible; the place was indeed magical. 'By divine grace he had several times experienced a miraculous enlarging of the grasp of the mind so that he seemed to look at the whole world caught in one ray of sunlight,' wrote Adomnán of Colum Cille. When the saint prayed in his retreat hut on the island of Hinba, 'rays of brilliant light could be seen at night, escaping through the chinks of the doors and through the keyholes'. In particular, Adomnán wrote of Colum Cille's voice and how his fellow monks remembered its power resonating in their chapel or singing the psalms on the shore. He added that the Loch Ness monster only had to hear it to recoil in fear.

Colum Cille found his vocation at the age of forty-one, then regarded as late middle age, when he set sail from Ireland with twelve companions for Scotland. The hagiographies and mythologies which have accumulated around him make it hard to discern the historical record, but it is known that he was a scholar, a man who left the security of tribe and home in pursuit of learning; he was a poet and he illuminated manuscripts. He is also known for his kindly attentiveness to the problems of all those who came to him for advice. The monastery he founded on Iona was a centre of learning, a centre on Britain's furthest edge. Its monks travelled round the British Isles and to Europe, founding monasteries as far away as Belgium and Switzerland. In their coracles, they travelled deep into the continent, along rivers such as the Seine, Somme and Loire. Iona produced two of the leading cosmographers of their age: in 742 Fergil went to Austria, where, known as Virgil of Salzburg, he advanced the argument that there could be life on the other side of the world. He was threatened with excommunication for his novel ideas, and his writings were destroyed in mysterious circumstances. Later that century another monk, Dicuil, wrote a geography book, *De mensura Orbis terrae* (*On Measurement of the Earth*), which attempted to measure the surface of the earth, detailing the then-known world of Europe, Asia and Africa. He incorporated accounts of travellers to the Faroe Islands and Iceland, and produced a list of what was believed to be the world's five great rivers and six highest mountains. His grasp of distant geography was remarkable; he included the then canal between the Nile and the Red Sea.

The most powerful evidence of the scholarship on Iona lies in the illuminated manuscripts, of which the *Book of Kells,* now housed in Trinity College, Dublin, is the most astonishing. It is one of the greatest artworks ever accomplished in the British Isles and there has been much scholarly debate about how and where it came to be written. The consensus has settled on Iona. The illuminations are overpowering in their intense, complex patterning and vivid, riotous imagery of animals, saints and scenes from the life of Christ. In borders and around capital letters, animals chase and devour each other: cats and mice, an otter and a fish, a moth with a chrysalis, snakes, peacocks and lions. Its pages are a rich and faithful interpretation of the mythologies of the eastern Mediterranean, that confluence of classical civilizations, the Middle East and Africa out of which had emerged Christianity. Aspects of the design have been linked to places as various as Rome, Carolingian Europe, Byzantium and Armenia, but even life-long scholars admit to finding its range of pattern and image bewildering in its profusion and variety. Mathematicians and engineers have studied its complex geometry, marvelling at its exactitude. One scholar, Margaret Stokes, commented in 1869 on 'the intense concentration of mind necessary for the accomplishment of work so minute where the power of the brain would seem, as it were, drawn to a needle's point to fulfil its purpose'. Some of the spirals are on such a minute scale, only 0.1 mm wide, that it has proved impossible to copy them, even with modern compasses.

This vivid imagery is not just decorative, it is part of the communication of the text. The pictures of animals are a form of commentary. In his definitive study, Bernard Meehan shows how the imagery flows in tandem with the text, anticipating or underlining points. The patterns are symbolic: one of the most common abstract elements is the lozenge representing Logos, the Word of God. Its four corners represent the cosmos, the quadripartite world in which four angels stood at the four corners of the earth, holding the four winds; the four seasons; the four elements of earth, air, water, fire; the four properties of heat, cold, moisture and dryness; the four humours of the body. The lozenge was an imagined geography, an orderly representation of the unruly world the Iona monks experienced on this edge of the Atlantic. Logos, the Word, was the central symbol of their faith, and had a sacred power. Throughout the *Book of Kells* there are allusions to speaking and hearing; figures gesture to their mouths or ears, tongues are often extended or bear fruit. Words, spoken or written, were cherished for their transformational power. Blessings, incantations, recitation and curses, all carried the authority of an omnipotent God.

The sheer sophistication and scale of the achievement represented by the *Book of Kells* is remarkable. Its production required a well-organized community of craftsmen: cattle farmers, tanners to prepare the calf skin, traders to bring the rare and brilliant powdered colours, metalsmiths to make the sharp knives, not to mention farmers to cultivate the hard soil to ensure there was food for this community of skilled craftsmen. Above all, it required a huge body of knowledge from across the known world – from civilizations and cultures as diverse as central Asia, the Near East, the Mediterranean and Celtic Ireland – to be assembled on this Hebridean island, and with it the skill and flamboyant courage to illuminate the Word, God's revealed truth for the world.

TWO MIDDLE-AGED LADIES IN ANDALUSIA

Penelope Chetwode

Penelope Chetwode, Lady Betjeman (1910–1986) was an English travel writer and wife of the poet laureate John Betjeman, who tended to prefer animals to humans and was rarely photographed without a horse alongside. She spent part of her childhood in India, and returned often, but in 1961, by way of a change, she embarked on a month-long trek through rural Andalusia in southern Spain and published an account of her travels entitled *Two Middle-Aged Ladies in Andalusia*. La Marquesa, a mule not in the first flush of youth, was the other lady of the title!

Monday, November 13

I had arranged for Juan, my landlady's first cousin, to guide me out of the infernal regions as there were no roads leading to my next port of call: only a labyrinth of mule-tracks and I knew I would never find the right one to lead me over the pale grey sierras on the far side of the canyon. When Juan had first called at the *posada* two days previously to fix terms, he wore his working clothes and had three days' growth of beard on his chin. So I simply did not recognise him until he came up and told me we ought to start in half an hour. He wore a neat blue suit and a grey homburg hat and had evidently just emerged from the barber's. He was a smallholder and had a nice, stocky black 13 hands 2-in. pony which he rode in an *aparejo*, the mattress-like pack-saddle used for all pack-animals in Spain, and a headcollar with only a rope to guide it by.

I think the whole *pueblo* was there to see us off, including a great crowd of exceptionally beautiful and healthy-looking children. As usual my landlord had to fetch a chair before I could climb up onto the Marquesa and as usual everyone was too nice to laugh. I made my customary royal exit, this time enhanced by my mounted attendant Juan, and I shouted '*Adios! Adios!*' while Doña Encarna and all the children shouted back '*Vaya Usted con Dio-o-o-o-o.*'

We set off along the same track through the garden of paradise as that which led to my scene with the Marquesa, only Juan knew of an alternative path which led over a wide bridge. Further on we turned right across the valley, riding through peach plantations, then through wilder country with casuarina trees and bamboo and oleander, to the banks of the river Guadiana Menor which we forded easily in spite of Juan's fears that it might be too deep after the recent rains. I put my feet up on either side of the Marquesa's shoulders and reached the further bank without getting wet.

We then rode along a soft grey track which led up into the bare beautifully modelled clay hills of Giotto's frescoes. As we got higher there was an ever wider view of the river valley below and the interminable grey sierras beyond it. This sort of landscape gives you an insight into Eternity: it is so vast and so beautiful and so still that you would like it to go on for ever.

Once out of the infernal regions we rode across a plain where flocks of sheep grazed on invisible grass. We passed a boy about eight years old riding a nice grey pony with a black mane and tail in a string halter with just a blanket thrown over its back. He was carrying a large basket of cabbages and had the natural seat of the born horseman. Then we came to some low grey hills covered with small round towers which turned out to be the chimneys of another trog colony. When I looked closer I could see some very superior cave-dwellings with front rooms of whitewashed stone built against the hill with strings of red peppers hanging from them, and brightly coloured shirts and frocks drying on the bushes near the doors. The Marquesa was going very short and I found a stone lodged in her off-fore foot which neither Juan nor I could dislodge with our *navajas*, so I led her the remaining half-mile to the *posada* in Cuevas del Campo where a hammer and pincers had to be produced to remove it. The animals then went up a very steep step into the stable and were fed *cebada y paja* while I went to explore the *pueblo*.

There was one long main street with a church half-way up it. Most of the houses here were free-standing but some of them were built against the hill behind them with caves forming the back rooms. On either side of this main street there were grey hills riddled with troglodyte dwellings, far more than at Don Diego but in a less romantic setting. I spoke to the *cura* who was standing outside his little church and asked if he minded if I went into it in jodhpurs. Discovered that he spoke French rather better than I did Spanish so we conversed in that language. He very kindly took me into the church himself and explained that it was only thirty years old as Cuevas had grown to its present size of four thousand inhabitants during the past half century. The building was whitewashed both inside and out and had pointed windows and a nice little tower that blended well with its surroundings. To the right of the high altar a door led into his presbytery where there was a smart Hispano-Olivetti typewriter on the desk. He offered me a glass of brandy which I felt ungrateful at refusing but I just cannot swallow spirits unless pushed by acute pain. So I had a large glass of refreshing cold water while we talked of the coming Ecumenical Council and the problems connected with reunion. He offered me lunch but Juan was waiting to have it with me at the *posada* so back I went.

I had brought the remains of my Sunday chicken along in a small cardboard box and Juan and I set to at a cosy-table, for some inexplicable reason in a bedroom on the first floor. It was all quite proper because we were surrounded by the landlord and his family and several of their friends, including a poor little crippled boy who dragged himself about the floor on his hands because his legs were paralysed. Eating tough cockerel with nothing but a jack-knife and your fingers before an admiring audience is a typical ordeal to which you must get accustomed when touring in rural Spain. Our landlady provided bread, tomatoes, melon and pomegranates and having eaten all we wanted I settled the account, including Juan's keep for the night and extra *cebada* for the pony. He could perfectly well have returned to Don Diego that afternoon (a three-hour ride) but I had originally agreed to pay a night's keep at Cuevas for him; he had five children and a sick wife, so I was delighted to treat him to a night out.

At four o'clock I set off on my own, along the straight flat unmetalled road to Pozo Alcón, eleven kilometres away. Suddenly a young man with a coal-black bristly face galloped past me sitting sideways on a donkey, chasing his leading donkey which had gone on ahead towards home while its master had stopped to have a drink in Cuevas. Such an extraordinary feat of balance I have never seen outside a circus. When he finally drew halter rope (as opposed to rein) he shouted back at me that he would accompany me to Pozo, which was an appalling bore as I longed to be alone for a bit. So we rode along together while he ate his lunch: an enormous quantity of bread and *raw* fish which he slit open with his *navaja*, removing the guts with his little finger which seemed to me an unnecessary refinement. He of course offered to share his meal but I protested, as politely as I could, that I had only just had lunch at the *posada*: I was, however, delighted to accept some walnuts and dried figs which he next produced out of a grimy pocket.

As we rode along he told me he was a coal merchant and had just delivered some coal to Cuevas. As I was a traveller I probably did not want to buy any coal. But would I like to buy some of his excellent home-cured *jamón* to take with me? Or perhaps his leading donkey to carry my belongings? I said that everything fitted very well into my *alforjas* and that the Marquesa was well able to carry them as well as me. This was a social occasion on which I badly needed my lost *bota*: Juan had one and I had had to drink out of it repeatedly on our morning ride for the sake of etiquette.

The coal merchant now proceeded to cross-question me as to how much I had paid at this and that *posada*, how much I had paid Juan, etc. (I quoted lower figures all the time), till I got so bored that I asked him to sing in order to stop him talking.

'Give me a hundred *pesetas*.'

'No – ten.'

'A hundred.'

Exasperated, I started to sing myself and treated him to all three verses of the *Lorelei* in German, one of my set pieces. All I got for this was to be told how poor he was as he pointed to his knees sticking through his trousers. In self-defence I said I would give him twenty-five *pesetas* if he would sing to me for the rest of the journey.

'Give me a hundred *pesetas*!'

I handed him a twenty-five *peseta* piece which he could not resist and he started to sing *cante jondo* very well indeed. But not for long.

'*¡Me da cien peseta!*' he shouted threateningly, barring the Marquesa's path with his sweet little *burro*.

'I go alone to Pozo!' I shouted back as I dug the iron points of my Moorish stirrups into the Marquesa's sides so that we set off at a smart canter along the soft sandy side of the road, *alforjas* flapping madly. I could hear little tiny galloping feet pursuing me, but not for long: the Marquesa's long stride soon outdistanced the donkeys, though I kept her cantering for at least a mile to put a comfortable distance between me and the nearest thing I ever got to a bandit.

Up till now I had felt too self-conscious to say 'May you go with God!' to people I met or took leave of; but speed gave me courage and I shouted: '*¡Vaya usted con Dio-o-o-o-o!*' at the top of my voice to everyone we passed. It was very exhilarating.

Pozo Alcón is a large *pueblo* of 12,000 inhabitants with three doctors and three priests. It has a big cement factory and an olive oil refinery. About fifty men are at present employed in building a dam nine kilometres away which will be used for electricity and for irrigation.

The *posada* to which I was directed had a very grand-sounding name: '*Parador del Carmen. Camas y Comidas*' (beds and meals) 'GARAGE'. I led the Marquesa through the usual covered cobbled yard into the garage which was full of mules, but I was told that they were tied up there temporarily while their masters were drinking at the bar, and that the real stable was beyond. My landlord's eldest son, a smiling boy of sixteen, delightedly removed the saddle for me and fetched some *cebada*, and during the two days I spent in this inn he was the mare's constant attendant, taking her out to water, seeing she had a continual supply of *paja* and saddling and unsaddling her. The corn feeds I always gave myself.

I had a single bedroom with a narrow window facing north which actually had some glass in it. But as the top pane was half out and the shutters did not shut properly and the *pueblo* stood on a high plain at the foot of the Sierra del Pozo with an icy wind blowing off it, the room was extremely cold and draughty. I unpacked my saddle-bags to find that my nice Dayella pyjamas had been jolted out in my flight. So the coal boy had won after all – having picked up a prize worth at least three hundred *pesetas*! Perhaps he would wear the striped legs on his rounds in place of the torn pants with which he failed to arouse my pity?

Opposite my bedroom there was a loo with the most ingenious plan for embarrassing the occupant which I have yet come across: it was L-shaped and the door was too big for its frame to shut properly. In the upper half there should have been four panes of frosted glass but one of them was missing so that any passer-by could look right in. When you slammed the door from the inside it stuck to its jambs for half a minute then burst open with a triumphant squeak. Impossible to reach round the angle of the wall to shut it again.

Having had no time to myself on the road all day and supper not being for another four hours, I sat in my bed with two pairs of socks on, two jerseys and my overcoat and wrote some letters. But the snow-laden wind blew into my bones so I got up and went to evening devotions. Surprised to hear '*Dios te salve Maria*' coming through a loud-speaker onto the plaza outside the church. This was the priest speaking through a mike as he led the congregation in the recitation of the Rosary from the pulpit. Afterwards I asked him what time Mass would be as the *posada* was ten minutes' walk away and I might not hear the three bells. He said 'Eight-thirty, no eight forty-five, no nine o'clock *más seguro*.'

Back from evening devotions I went to the stable to give the Marquesa her supper but could not open the door for the sheep which were leaning against it. Eventually forced my way in and fell flat across a fat ewe. She smelt deliciously of lanoline. When I finally got to the Marquesa there was another ewe lying on the chopped straw in her manger. She looked so cosy that I could not bear to dislodge her, so I moved the mare down a peg. Besides the sheep there were several large pigs, a string of nine mules, five donkeys, seven goats, two ponies, two white turkeys and a lot of chickens in the stable, which resembled Noah's Ark. As I left I caught the naughty Marquesa directing a sly kick at one of the poor pigs.

When I went along to the dining-room for supper my nerve nearly failed me: there were no less than seven men sitting at an outsize cosy-table eating saffron-coloured fish soup. I got the same sort of sinking feeling as I did thirty years ago before going into a deb's dinner-party. But now, as then, I had to go through with it so I sat down between an electrician working on the dam with the face of a Byzantine Saint, and a jovial round-faced pig dealer who had been buying pigs at the market and had seen and greatly admired my mare.

'*Que buena jaca*' (What a good hack!) he said, little knowing that the Marquesa was doing her best to maim his purchases.

I asked him if he had any horses of his own. He told me he had a farm near Pozo and used to keep two horses on it but they ate so much he sold them. Now he only keeps mules for farm work.

Maria, the seventeen-year-old girl who waited on us, had flashing black eyes and flirted outrageously with the customers. Afterwards while sitting in the kitchen waiting to fill my hot-water bottle I met my host and hostess and their nine children. She did all the *posada* cooking while the children played in and out of the kitchen and the garage and the stables. Talked to a dam engineer and his wife who had not been at my supper table. They came from Madrid and she was lamenting her fate at being stuck in this remote provincial town. I suggested that she ought to buy a horse and explore the surrounding sierras but she did not seem to think it a good idea.

In this large *posada* the cooking is not done on an open fire but at a tiled charcoal stove all along one wall. But even here there was no oven, so that the menus were confined to fried foods and stews.

Pyjamaless, I went to bed in two sets of underclothes, including a lovely long pair of pants I bought at Malaga, my two jerseys and two extra blankets provided by Maria; with a very hot hot-water bottle and my overcoat on top of the lot, I really was warm at last.

Only the French know how to deal with St Antony so I dozed off reciting...

Saint Antoine de Padou
Grand cocain, grand voleur, grand filou
Qui connaissez tous les p'tits trous
Rendez nous c'qui n'est pas à vous!

which had made him cough up so much for me in the past. But in my heart of hearts I felt that there was nothing he could do about my Dayella pyjamas.

MY GREAT, WIDE, BEAUTIFUL WORLD

Juanita Harrison

Juanita Harrison (1891–unknown) was an African-American adventurer, born just 26 years after the abolition of slavery. She was raised in Mississippi and left school at the age of 10. She defeated the odds by going on to journey the globe, visiting 22 countries before penning her exuberant, life-affirming travel memoir *My Great, Wide, Beautiful World*. Her spelling isn't always perfect – but as *Time* magazine commented, it's 'sometimes better than right' and her eye for detail and myriad adventures make her book a total delight. She ended her travels in Hawaii whereupon she disappeared without trace, adding further to the enigma of this remarkable woman.

Santa Maria, II Via Balb, Rome, Italy

The trip was delightful along the Italian Riviera I had an afternoon until 12 P.M. at Milan didnt like the city to big and no river nor mountain but I meet a fellow that lived in the same street I had lived in N.Y. we had a very joly time He had a sad tale He came to Italy 15 yrs. ago to visit and try to get His Grandpa back to N.Y. but could not. He said if Columbus come back now He would be sorry He discounted America when they refuse to let them come in. He has two Brothers there they write him and tell him they would not take a chance on leaving N.Y. He is a conducter of the street car I stood outside and when he know I am from the U.S. he would not let me pay my fare. He were proud of his English he said to me. Look at me I am a conducter on this car see how little pay we get oh, its auful rotten I could be making so much money then he introduce me to a man on the platform and said This is my friend hes perfectly happy here in Italy because all he like is to eat thats all he think about this little friend looked so rosy and fat.

Then I went to the end of the line his work was over and I had supper with him it was a sort of American tea place and I had whipped cream we went round to see all the big buildings he went down to the train with me traveling were very heavy 3 women and 6 men in my compartment the 3 studients boys fell in love with a very pretty blond girl about 22 each wanted to sit by her it was so very funny the night passed away in no time I arrived at Venice at 7 A.M. get a nice room in the old part right on the canal every comfort 15 liros a day.

When I started out to look over Venice I came near steping into a canal I went all over by foot then took to the canal by gondola. Venice is so beautiful I could have spent two weeks there but went on as the living are very high there.

I arrived in Florence just in time to see a big proceson around the Cathedral I liked Florence but it is so dusty. The traveling to Rome many people had to stand for a long time but that never happen to me I know how to get about. It was raining and very muddy on arriving just as I liked it the Lady at the Y. were away. Cooks nor American Express do not know anything about good and cheap Hotels, they told me 35 liros would be the cheapest. I only laughed to myself. I found a nice room for 10 liros a day near the third largest Church. Yesterday I told them in the express office where I was staying and what I was paying, they were very much surprised. I just love Rome I read up the things in a Guide book I go to the place of interest and waite until I see a bunch with an English speaking Guide then I fall in line and get my lecture for nothing I dont believe half they say no way.

I love the old things they look so new. such wonderful Paintings and my the Churches I am in and out of them all day because you do not want to miss any. and I can never leave without praying I learned that in Cuba. I just must do something at night I went to a good Tradgey play last night. the Spanish make the best Tradgey actors. the cheapest seat was 6 liros and not quite 5 cents for taxes there were many swells up there with me. the Italian are much better cooks than the French. I take my coffee in a place where they serve it in a bowl that hold nearly a pint all rich milk and a little strong coffee you crumble the bread in the coffee. just once I got stung about ording I saw something on the list and thought I was getting a dish real Roman. it was two artichokes we all laughed he said he would change it I orded again expecting something more Roman and it was broiled liver. They know me now and take an interest bring big potions and they dont want me to tip. the plainest little resturant with oil cloth on the table always have nice clean table napkins. I got out and do a little shoping at the street markets and you can learn so many every day words. The people that I room with are lovely they have a beautiful Lady daughter with blond hair to her nees. most of the Italians are pretty and what I like best are the modest Girls and not many bobbed heads it is a great change from the American English they are nauty the Scotch very nauty but the French are really bad the worst at Nice I didnt want to believe my eyes. The Italian men are so very gentle and Gentlemen. yet they dont fail to make love to you but in a very nice way. they make good Parents.

Rome, June 14th

I know every spot about Rome. after I had seen everything I accepted the company of an Italian Proffesor and He took me about. I was studing my Guide book in the Borgese Garden and he began to talk. First he asked me if I were from Spain then he asked me if I would go to lunch with him I said No then he said may I see you at five. and I told him yes then I left to go to lunch and he followed me unbeknownst to me. I had orded my lunch in the little place I go when he came in and sat beside me. I never let any man go to the place I eat and so I were really sorry when I saw him because I had been going so quietly there and they took more interest thinking I were alone. I thought Now this is going to spoil everything. he was disgusted they didnt wait on me sooner it was just the two things I orded when he saw them he said that is nothing and then orded artichokes oranges and cheese. After that I had to change my place of eating. He took me to hear Aida.

Always he would meet me in frount of the church and leave me at the door of the Y. Then Sat. and Sun. another Gentleman that lived in N.Y.C. 25 yrs. took me about. He run a big shoe shop. I went into have heel plates put on my shoes. He took me round But I had seen everything and we went many places he had never seen. I enjoyed the lovely lunch he gave me. I make them think I am living at the Y.W.C.A. and always stop there then come home later.

I spend the whole half day at each Galery and study each picture with two very good Guide books. The Picture I like best is The Crucifixion Reni it was so real it made cold chills run up my back I thought I saw the lips move.

It is the crazest laid out city I was ever in I am always lost and more so when I start home so I never think of turning in that direction until I hafter. The Proffesor wanted to take me to the Catacombs I wouldnt let him because we wouldnt had time to have lunch He had to be at his school at 3.30. It only cost 5 liros return. to go to the Catacombs and a lunch like He gives cost 3 times that. So He took me to lunch instead.

I went through it twice with the Italian bunch and Guide when we came out I told the monk that I didnt understand He laughed and told me to wait for an English Bunch so I did. In the churches the man show me everything I offer a tip but they wont take it they say because I am alone but just when I go to step out the door they kiss me. the same thing has happen in every Town it is done so quick it make me laugh. Rome is very dusty its nice you dont hafter shine your shoes. then when it rains it is very muddy the other day I went to get on the street car and the conducter was teasing me and told me not to get on until I got some of the mud off my shoes.

Via 62, Napoli, Italy, June 20

The last day in Rome I was walking through their largest park I notice setting down on one of the lower Terices a colored nurce about 40 and weigh about 200 lbs. I went and ask her if she spoke English and laughed when she answered "I say I do" She was a joly old Girl

I spent the rest of the afternoon She think that the men are the most delightful of all men. She said it seem like a dream To her to have a Hansom Italian kissing Her hand. I hadnt give it much thought but when we got togather we sure did have a good time talking it over. Then I went home with them and had supper. the Family are from Albany, N.Y. the Gentleman are in Diplomatic service. they have 4 children she is so sweet and Gentle with them and they love her so.

I was down early and got a good seat on the trip from Rome most of the passagners had their lunch so it looked like a picnik party all had wine but me. To be socible I accepted a few swollows from a jug. I found a large room with a Family it has a nice view of a big Castle upon a hill. They have a nice clean old man servant and a boy of 14. am glad to have a rest from the maids asking me questions. I love the Bay and Vesuvius look so grand I wish it would spit up a little fire my love are all for Naples just now. Tomorrow I will go to all the places that are free on Sun. Its nice to be in gay Naples after Churchie Rome.

June 30th

I went up Vesuvius on horseback, it is much cheaper and more thrilling. We took the train to a town Bosco Trescasa that were destroyed in 1908 and then a very old rattling auto up to the white house where we get the horses. There were some German Ladies but all of them was poor Hosewoman. I had a dandy little Horse his name was Spiggitti and I am not saying this to bost, but I was the best rider of all the woman. I made my Horse galop as ofen as I could but sufered for it for 3 days. A Friend I met on the train an Italian he looked German very fair but spoke English. I was really afraid he made me stand over the edge and the lava was just boiling and jumping up. The only thing I didnt like about him he wanted me to eat so much when we stoped at a town for refreshments.

I had supper with my same Friend at San Martino you get a wonderful view of Naples & the Bay. they had very good musice. I had hiked up there before but did not let on. If I go out without a Hat the Italians do not take any notice of me and always talk right along with me But if I have on a Hat they call me a Chinese or Japenese. You can get along so good if you are not dressed up.

One day at noon time I was in a suburb town I went to a door and ask if there was a resturant they said no the Father ask me if I wanted Spagitti. I said yes. He said come right in and He would cook some He did not look any to clean but he sure did cook clean I watched him. The Son begin to sweep up the floor of the room we was to eat in the Father called one of the Fat Daughters and she got out of a chest a camofar ball smelling napkin. They had 10 loafs of bread for the family and it was hot. I never ate any spagitti that tasted so good. I hate to think of leaving Italy the people are the kind you can live very close to.

July 6, Dijon, France

I had a delightful trip from Naples on the beautiful steamer to Genor. I was laying down on a roll of ropes on the deck of the 3rd Classe and a Egyptian Gentleman from the 1st Classe came and spoke to me. He was very fine looking and dressed so well I think my nice suite caught his eye. and he said to himself She looks nice. He said wont you come over to our side and pulled out a nice steamer chair for me. He was traveling with a young Sudan Prince as tutor. the Prince wore a beautiful costume. He gave me his address in Egypt and ask me to come and see him. When we left the boat everybody got into buggies but I said to myself I'm not going to be spending my money to smooth it over by taking a carrage so I started right out and truged up the hill with my bag. I had half a day there and a plesant day at beautiful Turin and left with a Ticket to Geneva. A young Italian in my compartment wanted to talk and kept me awake so when I did go to sleep we got to the place I was to change I was so sleepy I couldnt pull myself out the seat was such a comfortable bed I did not wake up until an hour of Dijon.

I had to pay the difference to the conducter and he cheated me changing my swiss money to French franc. I got off at Dijon and was well paid for it is so very Grand looking. they have 3 wonderful old Churches and fine stores. I went to a movie to see Mary Pickford in Sparrow. The girl said the Programs was one Franc. So I did not buy one and she said if that was too much for me I could read it then give it back to Her so I did. just in frount of me sat a French Lady that spoke English they bought candys and gave me some and the time passed very plesant. I found a lovely Hotel and tomorrow I'll leave for Lausanne.

TURKISH REFLECTIONS

Mary Lee Settle

Mary Lee Settle (1918–2005) was an American author who for a while 'chose exile' in England, to which she was very attached, not least because two of her three husbands were English. She lived in Turkey in the early 1970s, apparently because it was cheap, and returned 14 years later, after completing her famous Beulah Quintet, to write *Turkish Reflections: A Biography of a Place*. But she wasn't finished yet – at the age 82, she explored Spain, alone.

The Lords and Ladies of Byzantium

The Turkish that I speak is direct, like a child's. I call it, honoring *Casablanca*, "such much" Turkish. So this language, with its echoes of nomads and emperors, pashas and *ghazis*, sultans and riches, and country matters, with its verbs of more than forty tenses, including the very useful one for innuendo that I wish we had, its oblique politenesses, this language with its own poetry of front- and back-rhyming vowels, this old tongue that contains within it all the past of Anatolia, is, for me, a shorthand. I get along, though. Turks are very polite people.

I stood on a street corner in İstanbul and held out my hand to a Turkish traffic policeman, who was directing crowded, fast, darting, manic traffic that ignored the level crossing as if it had been a dead animal in the road.

"Korkuyorum," I said. I am scared.

He held up one imperious hand and stopped the traffic. To the music of furious horns, he took my hand and led me slowly across the street called the *Divan Yolu*—the road to the palace that followed the Roman Mese, the great central artery of old Constantinople, the

Roman road that runs from the Hagia Sophia to the Theodosian walls and beyond, aimed straight at the heart of Europe. This was the road of the Janissaries, the Crusaders, the armies of Mehmet II, the Turkish conqueror of İstanbul.

We reached the other side. "*Çok teşekkür ederim*," I give you much thanks, I said, of course.

"*Bir şey değil, hanım efendi*," It is nothing, ma'am, he said. The traffic waited.

"*Allahaısmarladık*," the Turkish good-bye that means, "We are putting ourselves in the hands of God," I said, meaning it in the İstanbul traffic.

"*Güle, güle*," he said, go happily.

At last the traffic moved again.

At times like these, and there are so many, İstanbul turns in pace to a country town. There are long walks there, and afternoons, like towns in the country in summer. It is a city of nearly ten million people that spreads from Europe to Asia, up the Bosporus, along the Sea of Marmara, up the Golden Horn.

I had thought of going to Turkey on my own, as I had done so long ago, with what I look back on now, knowing what I do, as somewhat comic courage. I had forgotten Turkish manners. I was met at the airport by the colleague of a friend of a friend. Already I was being handed from *arkadaş* to *arkadaş*—that word for friendship, one of the most important words in the Turkish language. It is a way of living, a self-expectation as old as the nomads, although the people who are so hospitable must have long forgotten why they do it. They just do it. It is as natural as kindness or anger. My new, solicitous friend, Ziya, whose name means "luminous," was an elegant, young, English-speaking İstanbul University graduate.

He may never have read Ibn Battuta, the fourteenth-century traveler who was handed from *akhis* to *akhis*, an old Turkish word for the generous organizations of young men who followed the standards of *futawwa*—an ideal of nobility, honesty, loyalty, and courage—but he was following, without considering anything else, the same rules of hospitality.

Ibn Battuta wrote, "We found ourselves in a fine building, carpeted with beautiful Turkish carpets and lit by a large number of chandeliers of Iraqi glass. A number of young men stood in rows in the hall, wearing long shirts and boots, and each had a knife about two cubits long attached to a girdle around his waist. On their heads were white woolen bonnets, and attached to the peak of those bonnets was a piece of stuff a cubit long and two fingers in breadth. When they took their seats, every man removed his bonnet and set it down in front of him, and kept on his head another ornamental bonnet of silk or other material. When we took our places, they served up a great banquet followed by fruits and sweetmeats, after which they began to sing and dance. We were filled with admiration and were greatly astonished by their open-handedness and generosity."

Now the word is *arkadaş*, not *akhis*, but it has the same sense to it, and although my young friend was dressed in a beautifully tailored Western suit, the same sense of care was there, the same warm concern.

I had come, as we all do when we go to cities we have heard about so much, to find an İstanbul I already thought I knew—my city of presuppositions—whispers and memories of pashas and harems and sultans and girls with almond eyes, the Orient Express of Agatha Christie, the spies of Eric Ambler, the civilized letters of Lady Mary Wortley Montagu.

My favorite travel book is *Eothen*, by Alexander Kinglake, published in 1844. I expected the "Asiatic contentment" he found there, and the naive world of his pasha, whose ecstatic vision of European locomotives he had never seen was, "... their horses are flaming coals! —whirr! whirr! All by wheels! Whiz! whizz! all by steam!"

I found almost at once that I had been as naive as the pasha. I had forgotten, except intellectually, that shadowed behind it all, like a huge broken monument of memory, was Constantinople, the Byzantine Empire of Constantine the Great, Justinian and Theodora, Julian the Apostate. In the fifteenth century, Mehmet the Conqueror captured it, and moved the capital of the young Ottoman Empire from Bursa and called the ancient city İstanbul.

It has one of the most familiar skylines in the world, but it is still a mystery. That is partly because of age, and partly because it is a monument to four men who changed the faces of cities and of borders, and the way the eye sees, yet who have been almost forgotten.

There they are, standing out against the sky over İstanbul. The first, nearest the confluence of the Golden Horn, the Sea of Marmara, and the Bosporus, thrusts up against the sky, one of the oldest and most magic of buildings, Hagia Sophia, built by the Emperor Justinian, who, in his long reign—from A.D. 527 to 565—built buildings that stretched all over the Byzantine Empire, and changed it forever. The second, the Mosque of Süleyman, honors two men: Süleyman the Magnificent, and Sinan, the architectural genius who captured light and changed the way both the Middle East and Europe looked at buildings. The third is the mosque that is the monument to Mehmet the Conqueror, who rode into a nearly ruined and long neglected Constantinople, repaired it, rebuilt it, and changed its name to İstanbul.

We drove past the great walls of Theodosius, then along the walls that are all that is left, except for fragments, of the first palace of the Byzantine emperors. We turned through one of the ancient gates and up the narrow road toward the Sublime Porte. We entered a maze of uphill streets, a welter of turns and horns and tombs and mosques and markets and people.

İstanbul is not the only place to have great monuments and the memory of great men, a city pulse like no other, its own sense of excitement. It has all of these but, beyond them, it has wonderful neighborhoods and streets, streets full of people, streets used as markets, with snarls of traffic beyond anything I have seen in any other city, with drivers who are incredibly polite and pedestrians who obey no laws, not even those of survival. I saw a taxi driver patiently instructing two lost country people who were walking down the middle of the street while we waited in heavy traffic and a snarl of drivers honked like furious geese.

Ziya took me to a line of pastel-painted Ottoman houses on the cobblestoned Street of the Cold Fountain. The old houses there have all been restored and combined into an inn called, appropriately, Aya Sofya Pansiyonları, since it looks out on the building built by Justinian in the sixth century as the Church of the Hagia Sophia, the Holy Wisdom, and changed by Mehmet the Conqueror in 1532 into the mosque now called Aya Sofya. The houses use the great wall of Mehmet's palace of Topkapı as their back walls.

As soon as I got to my room I called home, to Virginia. Somehow it seemed, not new, but old and right, to call the person I love most from Byzantium.

If there is a heart of the city, I found it in that little walking street between its two greatest monuments. Between the Byzantine Empire and the Ottoman, in front of my Ottoman house, I strolled at the pace of the Turks, which all the tourists seem to catch. To hurry and scrabble seemed silly and rude.

At dawn, the first call to prayer came from the Blue Mosque, and was echoed, fainter and fainter in the distance, from minarets all over the city of mosques. The gulls rose up in clouds from their perches on the roofs of Hagia Sophia and flew toward the water just beyond Topkapı, where the Sea of Marmara meets the Bosporus and the Golden Horn. They came back to roost there and flew among the minarets; their wings turned pink in the spotlights that illuminate the mosque at night.

Hagia Sophia seems to float there, on the hill that was the ancient acropolis of Byzantium, above the meeting of the three waters: the Bosporus, the Sea of Marmara, the Golden Horn.

It has been the font of three empires. Here emperors and sultans were crowned, first the Byzantine Romans, and then the terrible Latins who decimated it in the Fourth Crusade and formed the short-lived Latin Empire. Here Mehmet II, child of the Osmanlı Turks, ordered the blood of the slain washed from the marble floor, and had his name read as sultan at the first prayer in the new mosque of Aya Sofya.

Aya Sofya is a museum now, a new monument to the secular leader Atatürk, whose personal hatred of the clergy has left a void in Turkey that threatens to be filled dangerously.

More than a museum, too—I have walked many times through its great doors, and I have never heard a voice raised. The first sight of its captured space of golden light and twilight is more than breathtaking. I can only use the overused word: awe, an experience of awe.

The building covers more than four acres. It is wider than a football field is long, and yet there is not the overpowering sense of diminishment and human frailty that I find in the great dark spaces of the Gothic cathedrals. It is like walking into a field that contains the last sunset, under a dome that is a reflection of the sky, in the golden light of an early evening after a sunny day; a dome that rises to the height of a fifteen-story building and yet seems to shelter and not to intimidate. Most of the gold is gone, and the earliest mosaics were destroyed by the Iconoclasts between A.D. 729 and 843. The wall mosaics you see today were inlaid in the tenth century, some so high they seem to fly above you, some as intimate as portraits at the level of your eyes. The Holy Virgin looks down from the crown of the apse, so gentle on her gold chair that she seems just to have paused there for a little while to rest. Over the middle door of the inner narthex, called the imperial door and larger than the others, a tenth-century Christ receives obeisance from the kneeling emperor, supposedly Leo the Wise, who, according to the street joke of the time, was asking forgiveness for his many marriages.

Inlaid designs of marble veneer still make the walls into a patterned play of color from all over what was then the Roman Empire.

Dark green marble columns hold up the balconies so that they seem to soar. Some of these tall columns are said to have come from the temple of Artemis at Ephesus, and if so they would link the Hagia Sophia to the temple of the Asian Mother Goddess, all the way back to the Amazons.

But the controversy among scholars is almost as old as the story. Justinian did send out orders that marble should be brought from all over the empire for his church, and much was brought from the earthquake-broken city of Ephesus. The best explanation of how the legend rose is found in Selwyn Lloyd's *Ancient Turkey.* He says that the Artemision, one of the Seven Wonders of the ancient world, had already long been so lost to earthquake and silt and the reuse of its marble by the sixth century, that it was thought that the gymnasium, the only large building left partly standing, was the temple. The columns may well have come from there.

Maybe so, but sometimes legends are truer than facts. From a prehistoric grove on the Aegean, where the Amazons clashed their shields and sang as the women do in *The Bacchae*, to the great temple of

Artemis that grew there, to the Church of Hagia Sophia, the mosque of Aya Sofya, the museum, and to the first morning I saw it, is only a step, a dream of a night in archetypal terms. To legend and to me, they are the columns that once were in the place sacred to the great Anatolian Mother Goddess, so old that for centuries she needed no name.

The walls of the church were once covered with mosaic portraits of Byzantine rulers, but few of them are left. One is the Empress Zoë who, having been a virgin until she inherited the purple in her fifties, took to marriage as if she had invented it, and when she changed consorts, only the head on the mosaic of her coruler was changed, so that her last husband looks a little like one of those pictures you can have taken at the fair, when you stick your head through a hole and become Garbo or Scarlett O'Hara or the latest pop star.

Vague bishops look down from high above the second row of columns, and on all four squinches that help hold up the great dome there are huge cherubim with their folded blue wings. They have never been covered over, not by the Iconoclasts, who in their puritan zeal destroyed so much of Byzantine imagery, nor the Muslims, who do not allow any replica of the human figure. They have been restored through the centuries. Perhaps they were too high for the early reformers to reach, and when the church was made into a mosque, the Muslims still believed in fields of angels.

Although thousands of people troop through the building day after day, believers and unbelievers, there is a quiet corner of Hagia Sophia left, a niche out of time. Up on the north balcony, gentle in the sun of one of the windows, there are fragments, faces, a part of a robe, a hand intact and lifted in blessing—a sacred icon of a tragic Christ with a mourning Virgin on one side and John the Baptist on the other.

Across from it on the floor is the tomb of the Venetian Doge, Enrico Dandolo, who, nearly ninety and blind, was the first Venetian ashore at the capture and sack of Constantinople by the Crusaders in 1204. When the Byzantines returned, after nearly sixty years, it is said they took the bones of Dandolo and threw them to the dogs in the street.

Once the colors were dazzling. Now in that vast and grand simplicity, there is the subtlety of age, a visual echo. Thousands of people from all over the world visit Aya Sofya every day, as they have done since it was built. But now, instead of the voices of Goths and Latins, and rough Galatians, and traders from Cathay, instead of the shaggy skin trousers of the Scythians, the togas of the Romans from the west, the white robes of the Arab tribes, the stiff gold-laden caftans of the Byzantines, the silk shifts of the traders from China, there are English voices, and German, and French, and Japanese, tourists dressed in clothes that seem in modern times to be all alike, a world of jeans and T-shirts, and the man-made textiles of traveling clothes in chemical colors. There is a sprinkling of women in black *yaşmaks* from the Arab countries, where ever since it was the Caliphate and the Ottoman Sultan was also the Caliph of Islam, İstanbul has been one of the centers of the Muslim world.

But there is a more surprising monument to Justinian, and it would certainly seem so to him. In 532 he ordered that columns that were still lying, unused, from the broken, abandoned pagan temples that had fallen to neglect and riot and earthquake, and the change of religion, be used to hold up the roof of an underground cistern. The columns were the flotsam of the past that littered Constantinople. It was an engineering job, part of the water system, no more. For years, since long before the Ottoman takeover of the city, the cistern was forgotten, which probably saved it from being used yet again as material for rebuilding.

There are 336 of these columns. The thousands of tons of silt that had nearly buried them have been cleared out; the long rows that are as near to being like a Roman temple as can be found anywhere are uncovered in the half darkness, and their presentation is one of the theatrical triumphs of the showing of ancient monuments. Theatrical—yes—but the light and sound captures its magic. Lights flirt and change from the distance, open vistas darken them again. It is totally romantic. I seemed to be, and I knew I was not, discovering it for myself.

The columns seem to go into an infinity of darkness. I passed one that was the twin of one I had seen up in the street where once the Forum of Augustus stood. They had been carved like tree trunks with the branches lopped; the lopped places looked like eyes. One upside down, one on her side, two sad Medusas, that had once guarded temples from the evil eye, had been underwater for centuries. They are now partially out of the water, and they are tinged with color from the long drowning. They lie there, looking out into the dark. The music is Beethoven, and it should be: Only that heroic sound could match the gaunt majesty of the marble forest that the Turks call the Underground Palace.

Within the crowded quietness of the first hill—the overwhelming mixture of Greek, Roman, Byzantine, Ottoman empires—the Sultan Ahmet Camii, called the Blue Mosque by Westerners, is directly across the park flanked by a classic courtyard. Over the hill to the left, to be hunted in the poor streets with their tumbling wooden houses is all that remains, according to ancient travelers, of the greatest imperial palace ever built on earth. It was so looted by the Christian Europeans of the Fourth Crusade that, three hundred years later, when Mehmet rode through it on his entry into Constantinople, it was already an abandoned ruin. I walked along nearly deserted streets in the sunny morning, and children with voices like doves, who know two words, "hello" and "good-bye," said them both, usually at the same time.

On the other side of the Blue Mosque there is a long park with three columns in a line down the middle. On one of them a stone emperor with a stone court watches a chariot race long gone. It is the old Hippodrome, where the great rivalries of the Blues and the Greens turned from the backing of chariot teams into politics and martyrdom, and where the Empress Theodora worked as a circus girl and whore.

This place is soaked with sanctity and blood. To go down below the end of the park is to pass by what is left of the huge Hippodrome wall, pierced with houses, and with gates that no longer go any place, with caves that once were rooms. I walked, or climbed, up the ruined wasteland of a hill, among the fragments and the gravelike mounds, and looked for ghosts of the palace of the Caesars.

It was an eerie search. Where once there were courtiers, a vagrant stared out from his shelter, an arch, nearly filled with earth, that had once been a high regal arch of the palace. Time had made it a cave for squatters. He watched from the darkness of the cave like a wild animal. It was the only time in İstanbul, in all the days and nights of walking, that I was afraid.

THE LIVING MOUNTAIN

Nan Shepherd

Nan Shepherd (1893–1981) was a Scottish novelist and poet who lived in the same house in Aberdeen for 87 years. Despite limiting her adventures to the Cairngorms, she was an explorer at heart and her quest to understand their 'essential nature' led her to write, in 1945, *The Living Mountain*, a meditation on the magnificence of mountains and our relationship with the natural world. The manuscript, today considered a masterpiece of nature writing, remained unpublished until 1977. Since 2016, Shepherd has been the very serene face of the Royal Bank of Scotland's £5 note.

Being

Here then may be lived a life of the senses so pure, so untouched by any mode of apprehension but their own, that the body may be said to think. Each sense heightened to its most exquisite awareness is in itself total experience. This is the innocence we have lost, living in one sense at a time to live all the way through.

So there I lie on the plateau, under me the central core of fire from which was thrust this grumbling grinding mass of plutonic rock, over me blue air, and between the fire of the rock and the fire of the sun, scree, soil and water, moss, grass, flower and tree, insect, bird and beast, wind, rain and snow – the total mountain. Slowly I have found my way in. If I had other senses, there are other things I should know. It is nonsense to suppose, when I have perceived the exquisite division of running water, or a flower, that my separate senses can make, that there would be nothing more to perceive were we but endowed with other modes of perception. How could we imagine flavour, or perfume, without the senses of taste and smell? They are completely unimaginable. There must be many exciting properties of matter that we cannot know because we have no way to know them. Yet, with what we have, what wealth! I add to it each time I go to the mountain – the eye sees what it didn't see before, or sees in a new way what it had already seen. So the ear, the other senses. It is an experience that grows; undistinguished days add their part, and now and then, unpredictable and unforgettable, come the hours when heaven and earth fall away and one sees a new creation. The many details – a stroke here, a stroke there – come for a moment into perfect focus, and one can read at last the word that has been from the beginning.

These moments come unpredictably, yet governed, it would seem, by a law whose working is dimly understood. They come to me most often, as I have indicated, waking out of outdoor sleep, gazing tranced at the running of water and listening to its song, and most of all after hours of steady walking, with the long rhythm of motion sustained until motion is felt, not merely known by the brain, as the 'still centre' of being. In some such way I suppose the controlled breathing of the Yogi must operate. Walking thus, hour after hour, the senses keyed, one walks the flesh transparent. But no metaphor, *transparent*, or *light as air*, is adequate. The body is not made negligible, but paramount. Flesh is not annihilated but fulfilled. One is not bodiless, but essential body.

It is therefore when the body is keyed to its highest potential and controlled to a profound harmony deepening into something that resembles trance, that I discover most nearly what it is *to be*. I have walked out of the body and into the mountain. I am a manifestation of its total life, as is the starry saxifrage or the white-winged ptarmigan.

So I have found what I set out to find. I set out on my journey in pure love. It began in childhood, when the stormy violet of a gully on the back of Sgoran Dubh, at which I used to gaze from a shoulder of the Monadhliaths, haunted my dreams. That gully, with its floating, its almost tangible ultramarine, *thirled* me for life to the mountain. Climbing Cairngorms was then for me a legendary task, which heroes, not men, accomplished. Certainly not children. It was still legendary on the October day, blue, cold and brilliant after heavy snow, when I climbed Creag Dhubh above Loch an Eilein, alone and expectant.

I climbed like a child stealing apples, with a fearful look behind. The Cairngorms were forbidden country – this was the nearest I had come to them; I was delectably excited. But how near to them I was coming I could not guess, as I toiled up the last slope and came out above Glen Einich. Then I gulped the frosty air – I could not contain myself, I jumped up and down, I laughed and shouted. There was the whole plateau, glittering white, within reach of my fingers, an immaculate vision, sun-struck, lifting against a sky of dazzling blue. I drank and drank. I have not yet done drinking that draught. From that hour I belonged to the Cairngorms, though – for several reasons – it was a number of years until I climbed them.

So my journey into an experience began. It was a journey always for fun, with no motive beyond that I wanted it. But at first I was seeking only sensuous gratification – the sensation of height, the sensation of movement, the sensation of speed, the sensation of distance, the sensation of effort, the sensation of ease: the lust of the flesh, the lust of the eyes, the pride of life. I was not interested in the mountain for itself, but for its effect upon me, as puss caresses not the man but herself against the man's trouser leg. But as I grew older, and less self-sufficient, I began to discover the mountain in itself. Everything became good to me, its contours, its colours, its waters and rock, flowers and birds. This process has taken many years, and is not yet complete. Knowing another is endless. And I have discovered that man's experience of them enlarges rock, flower and bird. The thing to be known grows with the knowing.

I believe that I now understand in some small measure why the Buddhist goes on pilgrimage to a mountain. The journey is itself part of the technique by which the god is sought. It is a journey into Being; for as I penetrate more deeply into the mountain's life, I penetrate also into my own. For an hour I am beyond desire. It is not ecstasy, that leap out of the self that makes man like a god. I am not out of myself, but in myself. I am. To know Being, this is the final grace accorded from the mountain.

THE LIFE AND LETTERS OF LADY HESTER STANHOPE

Lady Hester Stanhope

Lady Hester Stanhope (1776–1839) was an English socialite, adventurer and trailblazer. Striking-looking, charismatic and articulate, like so many female explorers she never married and left England, aged 33, after a scandalous love affair, never to return. Travelling to the Middle East, she adopted flamboyant male Ottoman dress and, to her glee, was mistaken for royalty. Her refusal to conform to local convention shocked and delighted in equal measure. The 'Queen of the Desert' became the first European woman to reach the ruins at Palmyra and conducted the first modern archaeological dig in the Holy Land. She eventually noticed that her coffers were empty and became a recluse, albeit one with 37 servants. *The Life and Letters of Lady Hester Stanhope* was compiled by her niece Catherine Cleveland.

Lady Hester to Mr. Murray
The Island of Rhodes, January 2nd, 1812

"Dear Sir,—Before this letter reaches you, you will have heard, in all probability, an account of my shipwreck from Mr. Coutts. That I am here to relate it is rather extraordinary, for I escaped not only a sinking ship, but put to sea in a boat when one could hardly have supposed it could have lived five minutes—the storm was so great. Unable to make the land, I got ashore, not on an island, but a bare rock which stuck up in the sea, and remained thirty hours without food or water. It becoming calmer the second night, I once more put to sea, and fortunately landed upon the island of Rhodes, but above three days' journey from the town, travelling at the rate of eight hours a day over mountains and dreadful rocks. Could the fashionables I once associated with believe that I could have sufficient composure of mind to have given my orders as distinctly and as positively as if I had been sitting in the midst of them, and that I slept for many hours very sound on the bare rock, covered with a pelisse, and was in a sweet sleep the second night, when I was awoke by the men, who seemed to dread that, as it was becoming calmer, and the wind changing (which would bring the sea in another direction), that we might be washed off the rock before morning. So away I went, putting my faith in that God who has never quite forsaken me in all my various misfortunes. The next place I slept in was a mill, upon sacks of corn; after that, in a hut, where I turned out a poor ass to make more room, and congratulated myself on having a bed of straw. When I arrived (after a day of tremendous fatigue) at a tolerable village, I found myself too ill to proceed the next day, and was fortunate enough to make the acquaintance of a kind-hearted, hospitable Greek gentleman, whom misfortune had sent into obscurity, and he insisted upon keeping me in his house till I was recovered. At the end of a few days I continued my journey, and arrived here, having suffered less than any other woman would have done whose health was as precarious as mine has been for so long a time. Everything I possessed I have lost; had I attempted to have saved anything, others would have done the same, and the boat would have been sunk. To collect clothes in this part of the world to dress as an Englishwoman would be next to impossible; at least, it would cost me two years' income. To dress as a Turkish woman would not do, because I must not be seen to speak to a man; therefore I have nothing left for it but to dress as a Turk—not like the Turks you are in the habit of seeing in England, but as an Asiatic Turk in a travelling dress—just a sort of silk and cotton shirt; next a striped silk and cotton waistcoat; over that another with sleeves, and over that a cloth short jacket without sleeves or half-sleeves, beautifully worked in coloured twist, a large pair of breeches, and Turkish boots, a sash into which goes a brace of pistols, a knife, and a sort of short sword, a belt for powder and shot made of variegated leather, which goes over the shoulder, the pouches the same, and a turban of several colours, put on in a particular way with a large bunch of natural flowers on one side. This is the dress of the common Asiatic; the great men are covered with gold and embroidery, and nothing can be more splendid and becoming than their dress. At this moment I am a wretched figure—half a Greek, half a Turk, but most of all like a blackguard (Gallongi), a Turkish sailor. As there is nothing interesting in the town of Rhodes, and the Bey being the only disagreeable Turk I ever met with, once a slave, and now a tyrant, but not of my sort—ignorant, sordid, and vulgar—I have left him and his city for a little habitation on the sea coast, about three miles distant from the town. The situation of this summer residence is enchanting, even at this season of the year. Let those who envied me in my greatness alike envy me in rags; let them envy that contented and contemplative mind which rises superior to all worldly misfortunes which are independent of the affections of the heart. Tell them I can feel happier in wandering over wilds, observing and admiring the beauties of Nature, than ever I did when surrounded by pomp, flatterers, and fools.... All my curiosities, all my discoveries, are gone to the bottom, and many valuable ones I have made with *so much trouble.* If I want a Turk, it is the Ramazan, it is the feast of the Bairam; he is either at prayers, asleep, or in the bath. If I want a Greek, his shop is shut—it is a saint's day. If I want an Armenian, it is the same thing. The Jews are less provoking; but, between them all and their different languages, it requires not a little patience and exertion to get through with anything out of the common way. I have never yet received one letter from you.... I cannot hardly suppose that you have never written to me, but I think you cannot have forwarded my letters through the channel I have so repeatedly directed. To be ignorant about poor dear Grandmama, and not to know what is become of poor Nash,* and if I have the means to assist her, is really very painful to me. William Hillier and Mr. Norman have alike disobeyed my orders. I desired they would be

* The old nurse at Chevening. My father always spoke of her with much affection, and paid her pension till, as he computed, she must have been more than 100 years old. He then made enquiries, and found she had been long dead and fraudulently represented.

sure to write to me about Nash, and never have I had one line from any one of them. This is gratitude; but such has been my fate—to be forgotten the moment I am no longer useful. I am never low, but when I think of England and the monsters it contains—when I put them out of my mind I am happy, for I have great reason to be so; but who do I owe my comforts to?—to strangers!"

LONDON JOURNAL 1840

Flora Tristan

Flora Tristan (1803–1844) was a French-Peruvian socialist, writer, feminist and activist. Circumstances made her a sort of working-class aristocrat, an unhappy position that motivated her life's work. She travelled extensively, including to Peru where she attempted to claim her inheritance from her late father's estate. There, she discovered she could either be rich, or poor and independent. She chose the latter and *London Journal* is a riveting outsider's view of life in the city in the 1830s.

On the Character of Londoners

There must be some flaw in the character, in the domestic organization, in the habits of the English; for they are not satisfied anywhere: they seem to be tormented by a need for locomotion which propels them from city to country, from their country to others, from the interior to the coast. Whether or not they will be better off is of no significance, provided that tomorrow they are no longer where they are today. The variety, the diversion that other peoples seek in their imagination, they seek in going from one place to another. When they can no longer think of anywhere to go on land, they shut themselves up in the narrow confines of a yacht, and there they are exposed to the discomfort, the dangers of the sea, sailing with no destination, no fixed limit, no prospect of present enjoyment, nothing which promises memories, with no pleasure other than seeing an end to the one they profess to be enjoying. This mania is not peculiar to individuals; it is shared by a large number of families of every class, of every station, of every degree of wealth.

Baron d'Haussez, *La Grande Bretagne*

There is such a great difference between the climate of England, particularly of London, and that of countries on the Continent located in the same lattitudes that, wishing to speak of the character of Londoners, I have no doubt noted those effects which properly belong to their climate. My intention is not to analyse the many and diverse influences which modify human individuality, to examine the degree of influence exercised by climate, education, diet, manners, religion, government, walks of life, wealth, poverty, the events of life, which cause one people to be serious, puffed up with heroism and pride, and another to be clownish, devoted to the arts and the enjoyment of life; which make the Parisian gay, sociable, open and brave, and the Londoner serious, unsociable, suspicious and timorous, flying like a rabbit before policemen armed with a little stick; why a certain wealthy Member of Parliament is venal, and a certain poet or artist possessing no property is incorruptible; why the rich are so insolent and the poor so humble, why some are so hardhearted and others so compassionate. Such a study would be a lengthy one, for which the lives of several German philosophers would not suffice. I shall limit myself therefore to a rough sketch of the general character of London's inhabitants, while making no claim to the universality of the type. Of necessity, there are many who do not conform to type. The man of genius is always an exception, who owes more to his own nature than to outside influences. Therefore I leave a wide margin for exceptions and sketch only the ordinary physiognomy with which the monster city stamps, as with its seal, those who dwell in its bosom.

The Londoner is not very hospitable. The high cost of living and the formal tone which regulates intercourse prevent his being so. Moreover, his business takes up too much of his time, he has too little left to entertain his friends; so he issues no invitation nor shows any courtesy except as his own interest dictates; he is punctual where his business is concerned: the great distances make it absolutely necessary. The Londoner would fear the loss of public esteem if he arrived two minutes late for an appointment. He is slow to make a decision because he weighs the alternatives. It is, on his part, prudence and not hesitation; for, even more than to Englishmen of other ports, business on a large scale appeals to him; one might even say that he is a gambler in business matters. When he has made his decision, he is open and expansive; his complacency and helpfulness are almost always greater than merely business considerations would lead one to expect. He carries steadfastness in his undertakings to the point of stubbornness; he makes a point of honour of finishing what he has started; and neither loss of money, time, nor any obstacle can deter him.* In his family relationships he is cold and formal, requiring a good deal of deference, respect and consideration, and scrupulously returns the same deference, respect and consideration. With his friends he is circumspect, even distrustful, and yet he goes out of his way to make himself agreeable to them; but he rarely carries friendship so far as to put his purse at their disposal. With strangers he feigns a modesty which he does not possess, or puts on airs, which is ridiculous, to say the least. Toward his superiors he is compliant, fawning, and carries adulation to the point of servility toward those from whom he hopes to gain. With his inferiors he is brutal, insolent, harsh, cruel.

The Londoner has no opinions, no taste of his own: his opinions are those of the fashionable majority, his tastes, those established by fashion.

The servile conformity to fashion is typical of the nation. Nowhere in Europe are fashion, etiquette and prejudices of all sorts so slavishly followed. Life, in England, is surrounded by a thousand childish, absurd regulations as in monasteries; they are troublesome in the extreme; if one happens to transgress them, Londoners are offended to a man! The offender is banished from society, excommunicated forever! The violent animosity against anyone who wishes to maintain his individuality inevitably suggests that envy, that mean passion of the human heart, is further developed in England than anywhere else. The vast majority are always far below mediocrity: they detest those who surpass them, who awaken them to their own nonentity; thus, one wounds English susceptibility whenever one deviates from the beaten path. A daguerreotype of a Regent Street or Hyde Park crowd would be remarkable for the artificial expressions, the slavish

* During the construction of Waterloo bridge, the shareholders responded to three appeals for funds, and dividends do not surpass 2 per cent on their investment. Nor did the accidents during construction of the tunnel discourage the shareholders.

bearing, which are also to be seen crudely represented in Chinese paintings.

The Londoner professes the greatest respect for tradition and religiously observes time-honoured customs; he also complies with all that the prejudice of society and sect requires, and even though it often happens that his reason rebels, he submits in silence, and lets himself be bound by shackles which he does not have the moral strength to break.

His feelings of hatred for foreigners, especially the French, carefully fostered among the masses by the aristocracy, are fading day by day in spite of the efforts of the Tories to keep them alive. It is also good form among Londoners to appear to be free of them, lest one be mistaken for a London John Bull; however, be it business competition or envy, they are jealous of the French. Their hatred is revealed in every word with an intensity which their efforts to conceal it do nothing to diminish.

The dominant passion of the Londoner is luxury: to be well dressed, well lodged, to live in a style which puts him on a footing of respectability is the dream of his life, the goal of his ambition. In addition to this passion, there is another one of gigantic proportions: pride! to which he sacrifices everything—affection, fortune, future.

The Londoner has little room for affairs of the heart, he gives too much to pride, vanity and ostentation. He is habitually sad, taciturn and dull. His business excites his interest only through the greatness of the risks and the results; he is continuously seeking distractions, whatever the cost, but is rarely successful. When his profession and his financial situation do not present an insurmountable obstacle, he travels ceaselessly, never escaping his profound ennui, which so rarely lets a ray of light reach his soul. However, it can happen that sometimes this creature, whose sole destiny, it would seem, is "to be the recorder of human distresses", emerges from his taciturnity; then he goes to the other extreme: loud guffaws, wild outbursts, comical songs, and it is by fits and starts that he displays his unwonted gaiety. This contrast produces a painful impression.

Seeing the elegant comfort which the rich Londoner enjoys, one could believe him happy; but if one takes the trouble to study the expression on his face, one realizes from his features, which bear the stamp of boredom and lassitude, from his eyes devoid of any spark and wherein physical suffering can be read, that not only is he not happy, but the conditions in which he finds himself forbid his aspiring to happiness.

A GIRL'S RIDE IN ICELAND

Ethel Tweedie

Ethel Tweedie (1862–1940), as she styled herself, was an English travel writer, photographer, biographer, historian, philanthropist and illustrator. In 1886, she went on a horseback expedition to Iceland with a woman friend, her brother and three other men, including her future husband. Such unchaperoned adventures raised eyebrows when her account, *A Girl's Ride in Iceland*, was published – not least because she championed the right of women to sit astride a horse rather than riding side-saddle in a ladylike fashion.

The Geysers

We had been told at Reykjavik it was necessary to carry tents, as there was no accommodation for travellers at the Geysers, but on arriving the wind was so strong that there was considerable difficulty in pitching them, and while our guides and gentlemen friends were making the attempt, we ladies tied up some tea in a muslin bag, and put it into a kettle, which we filled at the nearest hot spring. In a very few minutes it was infused, and with thick cream procured from the neighbouring farm, we enjoyed it much after our long dusty ride.

Just as the tent had been, as my brother thought, securely fixed, and while Vaughan and Mr Gordon were inside arranging the rugs and pack-boxes as seats, unfortunately a fresh gust of wind brought the whole affair down, burying them under the ruin. Our guides hastened to the rescue, and, more experienced in the weather forecasts than they were, advised their waiting till the wind had subsided before attempting to put up the tent again. To take our tea sitting on the pack-boxes was all we could do, encouraging each other to patience. We dare not open our boxes of eatables till the storm had subsided, or at least until we had some shelter to protect them from a deposit of dust.

After tea we proceeded to make our inspection of the Geysers. Our first need was, however, to wash our hands and faces, so, armed with towels, sponges, and soap, we knelt at the brink of the nearest pool, and stooping down performed our ablutions, with our faces towards the east, our persons being reflected in the clear green water. We could but liken ourselves to Mahommedans, when they turn their faces towards Kibla, at Mecca, or Parsees when they kneel facing the sun.

The immediate neighbourhood of the Geysers is not pretty; hills rise on one side, but otherwise they lie in a plain, which, when we saw it on our first arrival, was so thickly covered with sand from the storm that we could hardly discern any separate object. We hastened to examine the Great Geyser. Alas! it did not, and would not play; it had done so two days previously, and we were told it was expected to renew the exploit, but, to our great mortification, it failed to do so during our visit. One of the peculiarities of this natural phenomenon is that sometimes at intervals of only a few hours it will eject columns of boiling water to the height of 100 feet, at others it will remain silent for days together. In 1770 it is recorded that this Geyser spouted eleven times in one day. Disappointed at losing the sight we had come so far to see, we turned our attention to the 'Stroker,' which is situated about 90 feet from its bigger neighbour. This also seemed in a quiescent state, but as the 'Stroker' can always be made to play by filling up the opening with earth sods, until there is no hole for the steam to escape, and it vomits the whole mass with a gigantic spout, we requested our guides to arrange for this artificial display. The emetic was consequently administered. 'Stroker' was evidently sulky, for the process had to be gone through no less than four times, whilst we waited the result in patience for at least two hours; but the display was all the better when it came.

I said we waited in patience, which was hardly true, as we were all on the tiptoe of excitement. Continual false alarms, and we all rushed to the 'Stroker's' side, only to be again disappointed, so we unpacked our goods, and made preparations for our evening meal, examining the Great Geyser and the hot springs meanwhile, grumbled at the smell of sulphur, and nearly despaired of the eruption ever taking place, when a sudden start from our guides, who were standing on the edge of the crater, and a shriek from them, 'He comes!' and a huge column of water ascended straight into the air for about 60 feet, the spray being ejected to a considerable distance. The eruption was accompanied by a rumbling noise and a hissing sound, as the shafts of water ascended.

We stood and watched the effect a few feet distant merely from this boiling column, feeling the rumbling distinctly under our feet and as the wind blew the steam back, it fell like rain, quite cold, but with sufficient force to wet us uncomfortably.

This great fountain display continued in full force a quarter of an hour; then the column gradually got smaller, though steam and water issued from its mouth for a full half-hour before it quite subsided. It was a splendid spectacle, and one which left a great impression on our minds; the height of the column was fully 60 feet, and even after it had subsided, we remained some time in contemplation of its cause and effect.

Speaking of Geysers, Professor Geikie says,—

'Eruptive formations of hot water and steam, to which the general name of Geyser (*i.e.*, gusher) is given from the examples in Iceland, which were the first to be seen and described, mark a declining phase of volcanic activity.... It is from irregular tubelike excrescences that the eruptions take place. The term Geyser is restricted to active openings whence columns of hot water and steam are from time to time ejected; the non-eruptive pools are only hot springs. A true Geyser should thus possess an underground pipe or passage, terminating at the surface in an opening built round with deposits of sinter. At more or less regular intervals, rumblings and sharp detonations in the pipe are followed by an agitation of water in the basin, and then the violent expulsion of a column of water and steam to a considerable height in the air.'

Dr Samuel Kneeland, in his interesting book on Iceland, says, 125—

'There are two kinds of Geysers, one having jets of clear water, the other puffs of scalding vapour, coming up through a soft mud or clay of a reddish colour, probably from iron salts. In the water silica is held in solution by salts of soda, a silicate of soda being the chief ingredient. They are said to have great remediable powers; but, judging from the facility with which objects are encrusted by their silicates, it would seem as if their free use would soon turn a person to stone.... The geyserite, or the solid incrustations, is over 80° of silica, with 3° alumina, and a little magnesia, iron, potash, and soda.'

One thing I looked for in vain at these Geysers, namely, the pretty-coloured mud which is found at the Yellowstone Park of America, and which I had often heard my father and brother describe. In New Zealand the Geyser mud was formerly used by the Maoris as a kind of porridge, which they were very fond of. It is a pity the starving Icelanders cannot do likewise.

I wish our party could have been photographed as it stood round the 'Stroker,' waiting for the display, everybody's face a picture of expectation, which changed to disappointment at the long time we had to wait. As 'little things please little minds,' to pass the time, Miss T. and I were trundled about in the wheelbarrow in which the old men had brought the sods for the Geyser's emetic from the farm; an occasional upset made our ride all the more amusing. It was a ride worth noting, as it was performed in one of the very few wheeled conveyances in the Island.

By the time the exhibition of the Geyser was over, the wind had lulled, the sandstorm had ceased, and our tents had been successfully pitched. In the larger tent we dined, and for such an out-of-the-way place, it was so wonderful a meal that I must describe it. We were sitting on the pack-boxes inside the tent, waited on by two guides. First there was ox-tail soup quite hot, the tin having been placed in a neighbouring hot spring—the Blissa—for twenty minutes. We had no soup plates, but tumblers served the occasion, being afterwards washed by the guides, and made ready for further use.

Tinned meat-collops followed, splendidly hot, and to us hungry mortals appeared excellent. The third course was tongue, followed by tinned apricots and thick cream. Alas! we had no spoons, and how to eat our cream and apricots was a puzzle. Our guide, whom we had christened 'Johnny,' to his great delight, helped us out of this difficulty. He produced some horn spoons which he had carved during the long winter evenings, and which he offered to sell to us for a krone a-piece. It was quite high price enough, notwithstanding the carving, but the necessity of the occasion made us glad to close with his offer. Cheese, biscuit, and figs concluded our magnificent repast.

After dinner, another inspection of the Great Geyser, to see if it was more inclined to favour us with a display of its power, but a fruitless one; a walk amongst the hot springs, and then, as it was bitterly cold, we decided to turn in for the night. Our tents were pitched exactly half way between the Great Geyser and the 'Stroker.' The large tent was to serve for the three gentlemen and the two guides, and the smaller one for Miss T. and myself.

We had secured some bundles of hay for our beds, and our mackintosh sheets were used to cover over them. My brother undertook to make our beds, and arrange our tent for the night, and disappeared inside, carrying with him the rugs, air-pillows, etc., necessary for the purpose.

On his returning and telling us all was ready, Miss T. and myself bid the party good-night. We had not till then realised the height of our bedchamber, and how to enter it was a puzzle. It was not like the big tent, which would hold a dozen people standing erect, but a tiny gipsy tent, the opening so low, we literally had to crawl in on our hands and knees, whilst the whole community stood round watching us, and laughing heartily.

Once inside, our difficulties were not over, for we found the sides of the tent so low that we could only sit up straight in the middle. So we could do no more than partially undress and roll ourselves in our fur cloaks and rugs. With the exception of waking now and then to listen to the rumblings we had been told to expect before the eruption of the Great Geyser, we spent a tolerably comfortable night, notwithstanding we were surrounded by boiling, seething waters on every side, and were in hopeful expectation of the big Geyser's eruption. By the morning we had got quite accustomed to the sulphurous odours.

We had several visitors in the early morning, who thrust under our tent such articles as jewellery, saddle-cloths, carved spoons, etc., for sale. We bargained for some of these, and ultimately obtained them. The prices at first asked were absurdly high, but these simple-minded Icelanders have an idea that our nation's liberality is unbounded.

There is really little good old jewellery left in the Island, in consequence of the extreme poverty of the natives, who have sold to travellers the greater portion of that which they possessed.

How to dress in our three feet tent, was a problem which for some time our minds failed to solve, and still more, how and where to wash, until the gentlemen informed us that as they were going to the springs to bathe, their tent was at our disposal for as long as we wished. Here we found that their forethought had provided a large tub from the farm, which they had filled with warm water, so, after all, we had a luxurious bath.

When our only looking-glass was passed round, we each in turn exclaimed, 'How fearfully burnt I am!' and so indeed we were. Our yachting caps and deerstalkers had been shade enough on board ship, but not for a four days' ride across country in wind and a dust storm.

We had arrived at our journey's end, had seen the 'Stroker' at any rate play, and now if we wished to catch our steamer at Reykjavik, we had no time to lose in preparing for our return journey, so after breakfast, while our guides collected our steeds, packed the tents, etc., we started for a final look at the Geysers and the hot springs, which so abound in this neighbourhood. There are, I believe, no less than fifty within the circuit of half a mile. These springs lie at the base of a mountain of no great height, the tract in which these thermal waters is found being about 700 yards in length and 300 in width.

The Great Geyser lies to the north of this plain, its basin, 60 feet in diameter, is at the summit of a mound 20 feet in height, composed of silica, a mineral that the Geyser water holds in solution, and which from the constant overflowing of the water, deposits layers of beautiful enamel, which at the top is too hard to detach, although round the base soft and crumbly. The basin is nearly circular, and is generally, except after an eruption, full to the brim, and always steaming, the water at the bottom being about 228° Fahr.

The tube in the centre, from which the water spouts is about 10 feet across, and I read somewhere that on measuring down about 70 feet, the tube took a sudden turn which prevented further soundings. The water is ejected at a heat of 180° or 190° Fahr., and rises over 100 feet into the air.

These Geysers are nearly 400 feet above sea level.

The formation of the 'Stroker' differs from that of the Great Geyser in not having any basin round its well, the latter being in shape like a rough test-tube, about 8 feet in diameter and 36 feet deep, with two pipe-mouths. After the eruption witnessed by 'Burton,' he noticed that 'the level of the water in the tube was at a depth of 25 feet, where might be seen, partly submerged, the mouths of two pipes entering at different angles, close together on the side nearest the Great Geyser. From these pipes steam belched forth at intervals with considerable force, churning the water in the well round rapidly.'

It is strange that the eruptions of the 'Stroker' do not affect the water in the well of the Great Geyser, though it is not 100 yards off, while on the other hand, when the Geyser is in eruption, the water of the 'Stroker' subsides.

It really was very tantalising to have come so far, and be within a few hours' distance of Hecla, and yet have to return without having visited it. Besides, from what we gathered, we could well have exhausted another week in expeditions in the neighbourhood, but snow-capped Hecla, the ice-clad heights of the Jöklar, and the Red Crater, with innumerable other interesting excursions of Icelandic note, had to be left for a future visit, if ever we should make it, to the Island.

The name of Hecla means a mantle: its last eruption occurred in 1845. Where is Hecla? Who has not been asked that question at school? and little did I think, when learning geography, that I should ever see it, even at a distance. Alas! time would not allow us a nearer acquaintance. Visiting it meant either seventeen days round the Island in a Danish boat, or waiting six weeks for the *Camoens,* circumstances over which we had no control made both impossible, and we had reluctantly to give up the excursion. While these volcanoes and their adjuncts must ever remain, from their uncertain eruptions, a cause of terror to the inhabitants—boiling and bubbling for years, and then suddenly bursting forth, to the entire destruction of all around—they have, we know also, a beneficial effect in the world's domestic economy. What, for instance, would happen to Britain were it not for the Gulf Stream? It would be as cold as Labrador. The streams in the Gulf of Mexico are fed from equatorial currents and boiling springs, and rush in to the North Atlantic 25° or 30° warmer than the sea through which it passes, warming the air of Western Europe.

Again, hot springs (caused by subterranean fires), which, from their curative celebrity, attract visitors and invalids, mean business, and business means money to the inhabitants of the locality.

Taking our last farewell of these seething pools, which bubbled and boiled around us, I could not help wondering what kind of commotion could be going on beneath the earth's surface. A power that could thus eject 100 feet of boiling water into the air, and not burst asunder the surrounding ground, was indeed a marvellous phenomenon. The Iceland Geysers, which were the first discovered, as well as those of New Zealand (so soon to be destroyed), and those of the Yellowstone Park, must ever be of enormous interest to the traveller and geologist, and with regret we turned our backs upon them, having reached the turning-point of our journey and the limit of our time. Time waits on no man, so we tore ourselves away, feeling, however, we had seen in the Iceland Geysers one of the greatest marvels of Nature.

Various explanations of Geysers have been attempted by scientific men, and as some of my readers may take sufficient interest in these wonderful phenomena to wish to know something regarding the causes which originate them, I have got my father to write a short chapter on what he saw and thought of the great Geysers in the volcanic district of the Yellowstone Park, which I have appended at the end of my narrative.

LETTERS WRITTEN DURING A SHORT RESIDENCE IN SWEDEN, NORWAY, AND DENMARK

Mary Wollstonecraft

Mary Wollstonecraft (1759–1797) was a versatile English writer, philosopher and pioneering feminist. Her best-known work, *A Vindication on the Rights of Women*, called for equal education for women and men. She flouted convention by twice becoming pregnant out of wedlock, by two different men – and having married the second (William Godwin), gave birth to the future author of *Frankenstein*, and died a few days later. But before that unhappy day, she spent time in Paris witnessing the French Revolution and journeyed to the wild frontiers of Scandinavia. *Letters Written During a Short Residence in Sweden, Norway and Denmark* documented that trip and was her most popular book in her lifetime.

Letter X

I have once more, my friend, taken flight; for I left Tonsberg yesterday; but with an intention of returning, in my way back to Sweden.

The road to Laurvig is very fine, and the country the best cultivated in Norway. I never before admired the beech tree; and when I met stragglers here, they pleased me still less. Long and lank, they would have forced me to allow that the line of beauty requires some curves, if the stately pine, standing near, erect, throwing her vast arms around, had not looked beautiful, in opposition to such narrow rules.

In these respects my very reason obliges me to permit my feelings to be my criterion. Whatever excites emotion has charms for me; though

I insist that the cultivation of the mind, by warming, nay almost creating the imagination, produces taste, and an immense variety of sensations and emotions, partaking of the exquisite pleasure inspired by beauty and sublimity. As I know of no end to them, the word infinite, so often misapplied, might, on this occasion, be introduced with something like propriety.

But I have rambled away again. I intended to have remarked to you the effect produced by a grove of towering beech. The airy lightness of their foliage admitting a degree of sunshine, which, giving a transparency to the leaves, exhibited an appearance of freshness and elegance that I had never before remarked, I thought of descriptions of Italian scenery. But these evanescent graces seemed the effect of enchantment; and I imperceptibly breathed softly, lest I should destroy what was real, yet looked so like the creation of fancy. Dryden's fable of the flower and the leaf[1] was not a more poetical reverie.

Adieu, however, to fancy, and to all the sentiments which ennoble our nature. I arrived at Laurvig, and found myself in the midst of a group of lawyers, of different descriptions. My head turned round, my heart grew sick, as I regarded visages deformed by vice; and listened to accounts of chicanery that were continually embroiling the ignorant. These locusts will probably diminish, as the people become more enlightened. In this period of social life the commonalty are always cunningly attentive to their own interest; but their faculties, confined to a few objects, are so narrowed, that they cannot discover it in the general good.[2] The profession of the law renders a set of men still shrewder and more selfish than the rest; and it is these men, whose wits have been sharpened by knavery, who here undermine morality, confounding right and wrong.

1 *Dryden's fable of the flower and the leaf.* 'The Flower and the Leaf; or, The Lady in the Arbour', an allegory by Dryden in his *Fables Ancient and Modern* (1700), adapted from a poem formerly attributed to Chaucer. The fable contrasts the brief pleasures of the flower with the laurel leaf of virtuous labour.

2 *general good*: the central standard of value in most republican and utilitarian thought. In *Enquiry Concerning Political Justice* (2nd edn., 1796), 122, for instance, Godwin laid out the view that 'Morality is that system of conduct which is determined by a consideration of the greatest general good: he is entitled to the highest moral approbation, whose conduct is, in the greatest number of instances, governed by views of benevolence, and made subservient to public utility.'

The count of Bernstorff, who really appears to me, from all I can gather, to have the good of the people at heart, aware of this, has lately sent to the mayor of each district to name, according to the size of the place, four or six of the best-informed inhabitants, not men of the law, out of which the citizens were to elect two, who are to be termed *mediators*.[3] Their office is to endeavour to prevent litigious suits, and conciliate differences. And no suit is to be commenced before the parties have discussed the dispute at their weekly meeting. If a reconciliation should, in consequence, take place, it is to be registered, and the parties are not allowed to retract.

By these means ignorant people will be prevented from applying for advice to men who may justly be termed stirrers-up of strife. They have, for a long time, to use a significant vulgarism, set the people by the ears, and lived by the spoil they caught up in the scramble. There is some reason to hope that this regulation will diminish their number, and restrain their mischievous activity. But till trials by jury[4] are established, little justice can be expected in Norway. Judges who cannot be bribed are often timid, and afraid of offending bold knaves, lest they should raise a set of hornets about themselves. The fear of censure undermines all energy of character; and, labouring to be prudent, they lose sight of rectitude. Besides, nothing is left to their conscience, or sagacity; they must be governed by evidence, though internally convinced that it is false.

There is a considerable iron manufactory at Laurvig, for coarse work, and a lake near the town supplies the water necessary for working several mills belonging to it.

This establishment belongs to the count of Laurvig.[5] Without a fortune, and influence equal to his, such a work could not have been set

3 *mediators*: Clarke, 27, provides a more detailed account of the work of these mediators: 'there is also, in every parish, a Commission of Conciliation, before which every cause must be stated, previous to its going into a court of justice; and it is the office of the commissioners to mediate between the parties, and, if possible, to compromise matters. The party refusing to abide by the opinion of the commissioner is condemned to all the costs, if he do not afterwards appear upon trial that he was in the right.'

4 *trials by jury*: trial by jury was not introduced to Norway until the new constitution of 1814.

5 *count of Laurvig*: Frederik Ahlefeldt-Laurvig (1760–1832) inherited the county of Larvik in 1791. It was sold to the crown in 1805.

afloat; personal fortunes are not yet sufficient to support such undertakings; nevertheless the inhabitants of the town speak of the size of his estate as an evil, because it obstructs commerce. The occupiers of small farms are obliged to bring their wood to the neighbouring seaports, to be shipped; but he, wishing to increase the value of his, will not allow it to be thus gradually cut down; which turns the trade into another channel. Added to this, nature is against them, the bay being open and insecure. I could not help smiling when I was informed that in a hard gale a vessel had been wrecked in the main street. When there are such a number of excellent harbours on the coast, it is a pity that accident has made one of the largest towns grow up in a bad one.

The father of the present count was a distant relation of the family; he resided constantly in Denmark; and his son follows his example. They have not been in possession of the estate many years; and their predecessor lived near the town, introducing a degree of profligacy of manners which has been ruinous to the inhabitants in every respect, their fortunes not being equal to the prevailing extravagance.

What little I have seen of the manners of the people does not please me so well as those of Tonsberg. I am forewarned that I shall find them still more cunning and fraudulent as I advance towards the west-ward, in proportion as traffic takes place of agriculture; for their towns are built on naked rocks; the streets are narrow bridges; and the inhabitants are all seafaring men, or owners of ships, who keep shops.

The inn I was at in Laurvig, this journey, was not the same that I was at before. It is a good one; the people civil, and the accommodations decent. They seem to be better provided in Sweden; but in justice I ought to add, that they charge more extravagantly. My bill at Tonsberg was also much higher than I had paid in Sweden, and much higher than it ought to have been where provisions are so cheap. Indeed they seem to consider foreigners as strangers whom they should never see again, and might fairly pluck. And the inhabitants of the western coast, insulated, as it were, regard those of the east almost as strangers. Each town in that quarter seems to be a great family, suspicious of every other, allowing none to cheat them, but themselves; and, right or wrong, they support one another in the face of justice.

On this journey I was fortunate enough to have one companion with more enlarged views than the generality of his countrymen, who spoke English tolerably.

I was informed that we might still advance a mile and a quarter in our *cabrioles*; afterwards there was no choice, but of a single horse and wretched path, or a boat, the usual mode of travelling.

We therefore sent our baggage forward in the boat, and followed rather slowly, for the road was rocky and sandy. We passed, however, through several beech groves, which still delighted me by the freshness of their light green foliage, and the elegance of their assemblage, forming retreats to veil, without obscuring the sun.

I was surprised, at approaching the water, to find a little cluster of houses pleasantly situated, and an excellent inn. I could have wished to have remained there all night; but as the wind was fair, and the evening fine, I was afraid to trust to the wind, the uncertain wind of to-morrow. We therefore left Helgeraac[6] immediately, with the declining sun.

Though we were in the open sea, we sailed more amongst the rocks and islands than in my passage from Stromstad; and they often formed very picturesque combinations. Few of the high ridges were entirely bare; the seeds of some pines or firs had been wafted by the winds or waves, and they stood to brave the elements.

Sitting then in a little boat on the ocean, amidst strangers, with sorrow and care pressing hard on me,—buffeting me about from clime to clime,—I felt

> 'Like the lone shrub at random cast,
> That sighs and trembles at each blast!'[7]

6 *Helgeraac*: modern-day Helgeroa, a village on the coast a little way westwards from Larvik towards Risør.

7 *Like the lone shrub… each blast*: Oliver Goldsmith, *The Traveller; or, A Prospect of Society* (1764), ll.103–4, a celebrated poem which was widely anthologized in the 1790s. Wollstonecraft slightly misquotes the following lines from memory.

> Here for a while, my proper cares resign'd,
> Here let me sit in sorrow for mankind,
> Like yon neglected shrub, at random cast,
> That shades the steep, and sighs at every blast. (ll.102–4)

Goldsmith's exploration of the relationship between virtue and commerce obviously fits in with many of Wollstonecraft's reflections.

On some of the largest rocks there were actually groves, the retreat of foxes and hares, which, I suppose, had tript over the ice during the winter, without thinking to regain the main land before the thaw.

Several of the islands were inhabited by pilots; and the Norwegian pilots are allowed to be the best in the world; perfectly acquainted with their coast, and ever at hand to observe the first signal or sail. They pay a small tax to the king, and to the regulating officer, and enjoy the fruit of their indefatigable industry.

One of the islands, called Virgin Land,[8] is a flat, with some depth of earth, extending for half a Norwegian mile, with three farms on it, tolerably well cultivated.

On some of the bare rocks I saw straggling houses; they rose above the denomination of huts inhabited by fishermen. My companions assured me that they were very comfortable dwellings, and that they have not only the necessaries, but even what might be reckoned the superfluities of life. It was too late for me to go on shore, if you will allow me to give that name to shivering rocks, to ascertain the fact.

But rain coming on, and the night growing dark, the pilot declared that it would be dangerous for us to attempt to go to the place of our destination, *East Riisoer*,[9] a Norwegian mile and a half further; and we determined to stop for the night at a little haven; some half dozen houses scattered under the curve of a rock. Though it became darker and darker, our pilot avoided the blind rocks with great dexterity.

It was about ten o'clock when we arrived; and the old hostess quickly prepared me a comfortable bed—a little too soft, or so; but I was weary; and opening the window to admit the sweetest of breezes to fan me to sleep, I sunk into the most luxurious rest: it was more than refreshing. The hospitable sprites of the grots surely hovered round my pillow; and if I woke, it was to listen to the melodious whispering of the wind amongst them, or to feel the mild breath of morn. Light slumbers produced dreams, where Paradise was before

8 *Virgin Land*: modern Jomfruland, an elongated small island with its own distinctive flora and fauna, the outermost in the Kragerø archipelago, lying off the coast between Larvik and Risør.

9 *East Riisoer*: Risør, home town of Peder Ellefsen. Wollstonecraft confronted him there and extracted a partial confession.

me. My little cherub was again hiding her face in my bosom. I heard her sweet cooing beat on my heart from the cliffs, and saw her tiny footsteps on the sands. New-born hopes seemed, like the rainbow, to appear in the clouds of sorrow, faint, yet sufficient to amuse away despair.

Some refreshing but heavy showers have detained us; and here I am writing quite alone—something more than gay, for which I want a name.

I could almost fancy myself in Nootka Sound,[10] or on some of the islands on the north west coast of America. We entered by a narrow pass through the rocks, which from this abode appear more romantic than you can well imagine; and seal-skins, hanging at the door to dry, add to the illusion.

It is indeed a corner of the world; but you would be surprised to see the cleanliness and comfort of the dwelling. The shelves are not only shining with pewter and queen's ware,[11] but some articles in silver, more ponderous, it is true, than elegant. The linen is good, as well as white. All the females spin; and there is a loom in the kitchen. A sort of individual taste appeared in the arrangement of the furniture, (this is not the place for imitation) and a kindness in their desire to oblige—how superior to the apish politeness of the towns! where the people, affecting to be well bred, fatigue with their endless ceremony.

The mistress is a widow; her daughter is married to a pilot, and has three cows. They have a little patch of land at about the distance of two English miles, where they make hay for the winter, which they bring home in a boat. They live here very cheap, getting money from the vessels which stress of weather, or other causes, bring into their harbour. I suspect, by their furniture, that they smuggle a little. I can now credit the account of the other houses, which I last night thought exaggerated.

I have been conversing with one of my companions respecting the

10 *Nootka Sound*: a channel between the west coast of Canada and Vancouver Island, the subject to rival claims by Britain and Spain. In February 1789, Spain's attempt to enforce its sovereignty over the area led to a confrontation between the governments of the two nations known as the Nootka Crisis. A major war over the issue was averted by the three Nootka Conventions (1790, 1793, and 1794).

11 *queen's ware*: glazed domestic pottery.

laws and regulations of Norway. He is a man with a great portion of common sense, and heart,—yes, a warm heart. This is not the first time I have remarked heart without sentiment: they are distinct. The former depends on the rectitude of the feelings, on truth of sympathy: these characters have more tenderness than passion; the latter has a higher source; call it imagination, genius, or what you will, it is something very different. I have been laughing with these simple, worthy *folk*, to give you one of my half score Danish words, and letting as much of my heart flow out in sympathy as they can take. Adieu! I must trip up the rocks. The rain is over. Let me catch pleasure on the wing—I may be melancholy to-morrow. Now all my nerves keep time with the melody of nature. Ah! let me be happy whilst I can. The tear starts as I think of it. I must fly from thought, and find refuge from sorrow in a strong imagination—the only solace for a feeling heart. Phantoms of bliss! ideal forms of excellence! again inclose me in your magic circle, and wipe clear from my remembrance the disappointments which render the sympathy painful, which experience rather increases than damps; by giving the indulgence of feeling the sanction of reason.

Once more farewell!

PART SIX

NORTH AMERICA

A LADY'S LIFE IN THE ROCKY MOUNTAINS

Isabella Bird

Isabella Bird (1831–1904) was an English explorer, writer, photographer, naturalist and the first female Fellow of the Royal Geographical Society. She suffered from poor health and eventually her doctors advised her to adopt nature as her cure. She took their wise counsel to heart, perhaps more literally than they intended – donning Hawaiian riding dress and trekking on horseback round the American Wild West, to encounter rattlesnakes, pumas and grizzly bears. Her collection of entertaining letters to her sister, keeping her abreast of all her adventures, was published as *A Lady's Life in the Rocky Mountains.*

Letter 1: Lake Tahoe, September 2

Lake Tahoe—Morning in San Francisco—Dust—A Pacific mail-train—Digger Indians—Cape Horn—A mountain hotel—A pioneer—A Truckee livery stable—A mountain stream—Finding a bear—Tahoe.

I have found a dream of beauty at which one might look all one's life and sigh. Not lovable, like the Sandwich Islands, but beautiful in its own way! A strictly North American beauty—snow-splotched mountains, huge pines, red-woods, sugar pines, silver spruce; a crystalline atmosphere, waves of the richest color; and a pine-hung lake which mirrors all beauty on its surface. Lake Tahoe is before me, a sheet of water twenty-two miles long by ten broad, and in some places

1,700 feet deep. It lies at a height of 6,000 feet, and the snow-crowned summits which wall it in are from 8,000 to 11,000 feet in altitude. The air is keen and elastic. There is no sound but the distant and slightly musical ring of the lumberer's axe.

It is a weariness to go back, even in thought, to the clang of San Francisco, which I left in its cold morning fog early yesterday, driving to the Oakland ferry through streets with side-walks heaped with thousands of cantaloupe and water-melons, tomatoes, cucumbers, squashes, pears, grapes, peaches, apricots—all of startling size as compared with any I ever saw before. Other streets were piled with sacks of flour, left out all night, owing to the security from rain at this season. I pass hastily over the early part of the journey, the crossing the bay in a fog as chill as November, the number of "lunch baskets," which gave the car the look of conveying a great picnic party, the last view of the Pacific, on which I had looked for nearly a year, the fierce sunshine and brilliant sky inland, the look of long RAINLESSNESS, which one may not call drought, the valleys with sides crimson with the poison oak, the dusty vineyards, with great purple clusters thick among the leaves, and between the vines great dusty melons lying on the dusty earth. From off the boundless harvest fields the grain was carried in June, and it is now stacked in sacks along the track, awaiting freightage. California is a "land flowing with milk and honey." The barns are bursting with fullness. In the dusty orchards the apple and pear branches are supported, that they may not break down under the weight of fruit; melons, tomatoes, and squashes of gigantic size lie almost unheeded on the ground; fat cattle, gorged almost to repletion, shade themselves under the oaks; superb "red" horses shine, not with grooming, but with condition; and thriving farms everywhere show on what a solid basis the prosperity of the "Golden State" is founded. Very uninviting, however rich, was the blazing Sacramento Valley, and very repulsive the city of Sacramento, which, at a distance of 125 miles from the Pacific, has an elevation of only thirty feet. The mercury stood at 103 degrees in the shade, and the fine white dust was stifling.

In the late afternoon we began the ascent of the Sierras, whose sawlike points had been in sight for many miles. The dusty fertility was all left behind, the country became rocky and gravelly, and deeply scored by streams bearing the muddy wash of the mountain gold mines down to the muddier Sacramento. There were long broken ridges and deep ravines, the ridges becoming longer, the ravines deeper, the pines thicker and larger, as we ascended into a cool atmosphere of exquisite purity, and before 6 P.M. the last traces of cultivation and the last hardwood trees were left behind.[1]

At Colfax, a station at a height of 2,400 feet, I got out and walked the length of the train. First came two great gaudy engines, the Grizzly Bear and the White Fox, with their respective tenders loaded with logs of wood, the engines with great, solitary, reflecting lamps in front above the cow guards, a quantity of polished brass-work, comfortable glass houses, and well-stuffed seats for the engine-drivers. The engines and tenders were succeeded by a baggage car, the latter loaded with bullion and valuable parcels, and in charge of two "express agents." Each of these cars is forty-five feet long. Then came two cars loaded with peaches and grapes; then two "silver palace" cars, each sixty feet long; then a smoking car, at that time occupied mainly by Chinamen; and then five ordinary passenger cars, with platforms like all the others, making altogether a train about 700 feet in length.

The platforms of the four front cars were clustered over with Digger Indians, with their squaws, children, and gear. They are perfect savages, without any aptitude for even aboriginal civilization, and are altogether the most degraded of the ill-fated tribes which are dying out before the white races. They were all very diminutive, five feet one inch being, I should think, about the average height, with flat noses, wide mouths, and black hair, cut straight above the eyes and hanging lank and long at the back and sides. The squaws wore their hair thickly plastered with pitch, and a broad band of the same across their noses and cheeks. They carried their infants on their backs, strapped to boards. The clothing of both sexes was a ragged,

1 In consequence of the unobserved omission of a date to my letters having been pointed out to me, I take this opportunity of stating that I traveled in Colorado in the autumn and early winter of 1873, on my way to England from the Sandwich Islands. The letters are a faithful picture of the country and state of society as it then was; but friends who have returned from the West within the last six months tell me that things are rapidly changing, that the frame house is replacing the log cabin, and that the footprints of elk and bighorn may be sought for in vain on the dewy slopes of Estes Park.—I.L.B. (Author's note to the third edition, January 16, 1880.)

dirty combination of coarse woolen cloth and hide, the moccasins being unornamented. They were all hideous and filthy, and swarming with vermin. The men carried short bows and arrows, one of them, who appeared to be the chief, having a lynx's skin for a quiver. A few had fishing tackle, but the bystanders said that they lived almost entirely upon grasshoppers. They were a most impressive incongruity in the midst of the tokens of an omnipotent civilization.

The light of the sinking sun from that time glorified the Sierras, and as the dew fell, aromatic odors made the still air sweet. On a single track, sometimes carried on a narrow ledge excavated from the mountain side by men lowered from the top in baskets, overhanging ravines from 2,000 to 3,000 feet deep, the monster train SNAKED its way upwards, stopping sometimes in front of a few frame houses, at others where nothing was to be seen but a log cabin with a few Chinamen hanging about it, but where trails on the sides of the ravines pointed to a gold country above and below. So sharp and frequent are the curves on some parts of the ascent, that on looking out of the window one could seldom see more than a part of the train at once. At Cape Horn, where the track curves round the ledge of a precipice 2,500 feet in depth, it is correct to be frightened, and a fashion of holding the breath and shutting the eyes prevails, but my fears were reserved for the crossing of a trestle bridge over a very deep chasm, which is itself approached by a sharp curve. This bridge appeared to be overlapped by the cars so as to produce the effect of looking down directly into a wild gulch, with a torrent raging along it at an immense depth below.

Shivering in the keen, frosty air near the summit pass of the Sierras, we entered the "snow-sheds," wooden galleries, which for about fifty miles shut out all the splendid views of the region, as given in dioramas, not even allowing a glimpse of "the Gem of the Sierras," the lovely Donner Lake. One of these sheds is twenty-seven miles long. In a few hours the mercury had fallen from 103 degrees to 29 degrees, and we had ascended 6,987 feet in 105 miles! After passing through the sheds, we had several grand views of a pine forest on fire before reaching Truckee at 11 P.M. having traveled 258 miles. Truckee, the center of the "lumbering region" of the Sierras, is usually spoken of as "a rough mountain town," and Mr. W. had told me that all the roughs of the district congregated there, that there were nightly pistol affrays in barrooms, etc., but as he admitted that a lady was sure of respect, and Mr. G. strongly advised me to stay and see the lakes, I got out, much dazed, and very stupid with sleep, envying the people in the sleeping car, who were already unconscious on their luxurious couches. The cars drew up in a street—if street that could be called which was only a wide, cleared space, intersected by rails, with here and there a stump, and great piles of sawn logs bulking big in the moonlight, and a number of irregular clap-board, steep-roofed houses, many of them with open fronts, glaring with light and crowded with men. We had pulled up at the door of a rough Western hotel, with a partially open front, being a bar-room crowded with men drinking and smoking, and the space between it and the cars was a moving mass of loafers and passengers. On the tracks, engines, tolling heavy bells, were mightily moving, the glare from their cyclopean eyes dulling the light of a forest which was burning fitfully on a mountain side; and on open spaces great fires of pine logs were burning cheerily, with groups of men round them. A band was playing noisily, and the unholy sound of tom-toms was not far off. Mountains—the Sierras of many a fireside dream—seemed to wall in the town, and great pines stood out, sharp and clear cut, against a sky in which a moon and stars were shining frostily. It was a sharp frost at that great height, and when an "irrepressible nigger," who seemed to represent the hotel establishment, deposited me and my carpetbag in a room which answered for "the parlor," I was glad to find some remains of pine knots still alight in the stove. A man came in and said that when the cars were gone he would try to get me a room, but they were so full that it would be a very poor one. The crowd was solely masculine. It was then 11:30 P.M., and I had not had a meal since 6 A.M.; but when I asked hopefully for a hot supper, with tea, I was told that no supper could be got at that hour; but in half an hour the same man returned with a small cup of cold, weak tea, and a small slice of bread, which looked as if it had been much handled.

I asked the Negro factotum about the hire of horses, and presently a man came in from the bar who, he said, could supply my needs. This man, the very type of a Western pioneer, bowed, threw himself into a rocking-chair, drew a spittoon beside him, cut a fresh quid of tobacco, began to chew energetically, and put his feet, cased in miry high boots, into which his trousers were tucked, on the top of the stove. He said he had horses which would both "lope" and trot, that some ladies preferred the Mexican saddle, that I could ride alone in perfect safety; and after a route had been devised, I hired a horse for two days. This man wore a pioneer's badge as one of the earliest settlers of California, but he had moved on as one place after another had become too civilized for him, "but nothing," he added, "was likely to change much in Truckee." I was afterwards told that the usual regular hours of sleep are not observed there. The accommodation is too limited for the population of 2,000,[2] which is masculine mainly, and is liable to frequent temporary additions, and beds are occupied continuously, though by different occupants, throughout the greater part of the twenty-four hours. Consequently I found the bed and room allotted to me quite tumbled looking. Men's coats and sticks were hanging up, miry boots were littered about, and a rifle was in one corner. There was no window to the outer air, but I slept soundly, being only once awoke by an increase of the same din in which I had fallen asleep, varied by three pistol shots fired in rapid succession.

This morning Truckee wore a totally different aspect. The crowds of the night before had disappeared. There were heaps of ashes where the fires had been. A sleepy German waiter seemed the only person about the premises, the open drinking saloons were nearly empty, and only a few sleepy-looking loafers hung about in what is called the street. It might have been Sunday; but they say that it brings a great accession of throng and jollity. Public worship has died out at present; work is discontinued on Sunday, but the day is given up to pleasure. Putting a minimum of indispensables into a bag, and slipping on my Hawaiian riding dress[3] over a silk skirt, and a dust

2 Nelson's Guide to the Central Pacific Railroad.

3 For the benefit of other lady travelers, I wish to explain that my "Hawaiian riding dress" is the "American Lady's Mountain Dress," a half-fitting jacket, a skirt reaching to the ankles, and full Turkish trousers gathered into frills falling over the boots,—a thoroughly serviceable and feminine costume for mountaineering and other rough traveling, as in the Alps or any other part of the world.—I.L.B. (Author's note to the second edition, November 27, 1879.)

cloak over all, I stealthily crossed the plaza to the livery stable, the largest building in Truckee, where twelve fine horses were stabled in stalls on each side of a broad drive. My friend of the evening before showed me his "rig," three velvet-covered side-saddles almost without horns. Some ladies, he said, used the horn of the Mexican saddle, but none "in the part" rode cavalier fashion. I felt abashed. I could not ride any distance in the conventional mode, and was just going to give up this splendid "ravage," when the man said, "Ride your own fashion; here, at Truckee, if anywhere in the world, people can do as they like." Blissful Truckee! In no time a large grey horse was "rigged out" in a handsome silver-bossed Mexican saddle, with ornamental leather tassels hanging from the stirrup guards, and a housing of black bear's-skin. I strapped my silk skirt on the saddle, deposited my cloak in the corn-bin, and was safely on the horse's back before his owner had time to devise any way of mounting me. Neither he nor any of the loafers who had assembled showed the slightest sign of astonishment, but all were as respectful as possible. Once on horseback my embarrassment disappeared, and I rode through Truckee, whose irregular, steep-roofed houses and shanties, set down in a clearing and surrounded closely by mountain and forest, looked like a temporary encampment; passed under the Pacific Railroad; and then for twelve miles followed the windings of the Truckee River, a clear, rushing, mountain stream, in which immense pine logs had gone aground not to be floated off till the next freshet, a loud-tongued, rollicking stream of ice-cold water, on whose banks no ferns or trailers hang, and which leaves no greenness along its turbulent progress.

All was bright with that brilliancy of sky and atmosphere, that blaze of sunshine and universal glitter, which I never saw till I came to California, combined with an elasticity in the air which removed all lassitude, and gives one spirit enough for anything. On either side of the Truckee great sierras rose like walls, castellated, embattled, rifted, skirted and crowned with pines of enormous size, the walls now and then breaking apart to show some snow-slashed peak rising into a heaven of intense, unclouded, sunny blue. At this altitude of 6,000 feet one must learn to be content with varieties of Coniferae, for, except for aspens, which spring up in some places where the pines have been cleared away, and for cotton-woods, which at a lower level fringe the streams, there is nothing but the bear cherry, the raspberry, the gooseberry, the wild grape, and the wild currant. None of these grew near the Truckee, but I feasted my eyes on pines[4] which, though not so large as the Wellingtonia of the Yosemite, are really gigantic, attaining a height of 250 feet, their huge stems, the warm red of cedar wood, rising straight and branchless for a third of their height, their diameter from seven to fifteen feet, their shape that of a larch, but with the needles long and dark, and cones a foot long. Pines cleft the sky; they were massed wherever level ground occurred; they stood over the Truckee at right angles, or lay across it in prostrate grandeur. Their stumps and carcasses were everywhere; and smooth "shoots" on the sierras marked where they were shot down as "felled timber," to be floated off by the river. To them this wild region owes its scattered population, and the sharp ring of the lumberer's axe mingles with the cries of wild beasts and the roar of mountain torrents.

The track is a soft, natural, wagon road, very pleasant to ride on. The horse was much too big for me, and had plans of his own; but now and then, where the ground admitted to it, I tried his heavy "lope" with much amusement. I met nobody, and passed nothing on the road but a freight wagon, drawn by twenty-two oxen, guided by three fine-looking men, who had some difficulty in making room for me to pass their awkward convoy. After I had ridden about ten miles the road went up a steep hill in the forest, turned abruptly, and through the blue gloom of the great pines which rose from the ravine in which the river was then hid, came glimpses of two mountains, about 11,000 feet in height, whose bald grey summits were crowned with pure snow. It was one of those glorious surprises in scenery which make one feel as if one must bow down and worship. The forest was thick, and had an undergrowth of dwarf spruce and brambles, but as the horse had become fidgety and "scary" on the track, I turned off in the idea of taking a short cut, and was sitting carelessly, shortening my stirrup, when a great, dark, hairy beast rose, crashing and snorting, out of the

4 Pinus Lambertina.

tangle just in front of me. I had only a glimpse of him, and thought that my imagination had magnified a wild boar, but it was a bear. The horse snorted and plunged violently, as if he would go down to the river, and then turned, still plunging, up a steep bank, when, finding that I must come off, I threw myself off on the right side, where the ground rose considerably, so that I had not far to fall. I got up covered with dust, but neither shaken nor bruised. It was truly grotesque and humiliating. The bear ran in one direction, and the horse in another. I hurried after the latter, and twice he stopped till I was close to him, then turned round and cantered away. After walking about a mile in deep dust, I picked up first the saddle-blanket and next my bag, and soon came upon the horse, standing facing me, and shaking all over. I thought I should catch him then, but when I went up to him he turned round, threw up his heels several times, rushed off the track, galloped in circles, bucking, kicking, and plunging for some time, and then throwing up his heels as an act of final defiance, went off at full speed in the direction of Truckee, with the saddle over his shoulders and the great wooden stirrups thumping his sides, while I trudged ignominiously along in the dust, laboriously carrying the bag and saddle-blanket.

I walked for nearly an hour, heated and hungry, when to my joy I saw the ox-team halted across the top of a gorge, and one of the teamsters leading the horse towards me. The young man said that, seeing the horse coming, they had drawn the team across the road to stop him, and remembering that he had passed them with a lady on him, they feared that there had been an accident, and had just saddled one of their own horses to go in search of me. He brought me some water to wash the dust from my face, and re-saddled the horse, but the animal snorted and plunged for some time before he would let me mount, and then sidled along in such a nervous and scared way, that the teamster walked for some distance by me to see that I was "all right." He said that the woods in the neighborhood of Tahoe had been full of brown and grizzly bears for some days, but that no one was in any danger from them. I took a long gallop beyond the scene of my tumble to quiet the horse, who was most restless and troublesome.

Then the scenery became truly magnificent and bright with life.

Crested blue-jays darted through the dark pines, squirrels in hundreds scampered through the forest, red dragon-flies flashed like "living light," exquisite chipmunks ran across the track, but only a dusty blue lupin here and there reminded me of earth's fairer children. Then the river became broad and still, and mirrored in its transparent depths regal pines, straight as an arrow, with rich yellow and green lichen clinging to their stems, and firs and balsam pines filling up the spaces between them, the gorge opened, and this mountain-girdled lake lay before me, with its margin broken up into bays and promontories, most picturesquely clothed by huge sugar pines. It lay dimpling and scintillating beneath the noonday sun, as entirely unspoilt as fifteen years ago, when its pure loveliness was known only to trappers and Indians. One man lives on it the whole year round; otherwise early October strips its shores of their few inhabitants, and thereafter, for seven months, it is rarely accessible except on snowshoes. It never freezes. In the dense forests which bound it, and drape two-thirds of its gaunt sierras, are hordes of grizzlies, brown bears, wolves, elk, deer, chipmunks, martens, minks, skunks, foxes, squirrels, and snakes. On its margin I found an irregular wooden inn, with a lumber-wagon at the door, on which was the carcass of a large grizzly bear, shot behind the house this morning. I had intended to ride ten miles farther, but, finding that the trail in some places was a "blind" one, and being bewitched by the beauty and serenity of Tahoe, I have remained here sketching, reveling in the view from the veranda, and strolling in the forest. At this height there is frost every night of the year, and my fingers are benumbed.

The beauty is entrancing. The sinking sun is out of sight behind the western Sierras, and all the pine-hung promontories on this side of the water are rich indigo, just reddened with lake, deepening here and there into Tyrian purple. The peaks above, which still catch the sun, are bright rose-red, and all the mountains on the other side are pink; and pink, too, are the far-off summits on which the snow-drifts rest. Indigo, red, and orange tints stain the still water, which lies solemn and dark against the shore, under the shadow of stately pines. An hour later, and a moon nearly full—not a pale, flat disc, but a radiant sphere—has wheeled up into the flushed sky. The sunset has passed through every stage of beauty, through every glory of color, through riot and triumph, through pathos and tenderness, into a long, dreamy, painless rest, succeeded by the profound solemnity of the moonlight, and a stillness broken only by the night cries of beasts in the aromatic forests.

I.L.B.

DIRT WORK

Christine Byl

Christine Byl (1973–present) is a writer and wilderness enthusiast who has spent most of her life in America's most remote regions. *Dirt Work* is Byl's account of 15 years spent trail crewing in Montana and Alaska – maintaining mountain trails, clearing trees, shifting boulders and blasting through snowdrifts. Even though Byl now runs a trail design business along with her husband, she still lives 'off the grid' – in a yurt in Alaska along with a couple of retired sled dogs.

North Fork: River

Dirt is an old word, an earthy word. It inhabits its meaning as it sits on your tongue when you speak it, onomatopoeia made flesh. "Dirt" never came out of Caesar's mouth; it can't be declined in a lyrical list. There is nothing fancy or trilling about the sound of dirt. It's not dressed up like "excrement" or "detritus," unlike "organic matter" or even "humus." From Old Norse, it made its way into Middle English as *drit*—the filth that collected on the soles of Chaucer's travelers' shoes. Dirt stands alone, underneath everything, hidden in the creases of our skin, blowing in the air. It's solid and unglamorous. *Old.*

Perhaps because of its permanence, dirt is a comfort. It comes from the purest elements: rain, rock, ice, wind. Glaciers form and move slowly, carving rock and mineral thrust up from Earth's core; ice melts into rivers, coursing through the path of least resistance, forcing incremental change. When rivers and air meet, condensation forms. Weather results, and weather makes dirt. Water from the sky—snow, sleet, downpours, sprinkles—impacts the surface of the Earth in small drops and wide puddles and rushing currents. Wind blows across it all, urging dirt and water onward, to drift and finally come to rest in a distant place. There are molecules of dirt on Boulder Pass that blew in from Egypt's pyramids; the mud caked in my boot treads may have once cradled the bones of some delicate, gossamer wing.

The North Fork is the only place in the Lower 48 I've seen a wolf. Driving south down the road, back to West Glacier, long past dark on an October night. We'd had a few beers, a big dinner at the saloon, and I leaned my head back against the seat in the drowse between wake and sleep, listening to soft pedal-steel on the radio, washboard ruts vibrating my thighs. The truck lurched as Gabe tapped his foot on the brake and stuck his arm out in front of me, an instinctive gesture. "Look," he whispered, "wolf." I opened my eyes. Gabe turned the wheel slightly, casting headlights toward the shoulder. Twenty feet ahead, it stood just off the road in profile, as still as if zapped in midstride.

If you've ever seen a coyote and wondered, *Could that be a wolf?* it wasn't. I've seen a coyote and wondered the same thing. Seeing a wolf I did not wonder. Even if I hadn't known anything about how large wolves are, how long their snouts, their legs, I think I would have known. The world seemed to close in around the edges of my perception until *it was only me and the wolf, our eyes locked, some ancient knowledge passing*—stop. Did I think this? Please. That wolf cared nothing for ancient knowledge, and in any case, I had little of it to give. To the wolf, I was neither augur nor soul mate, only an obstacle in the terrain, an odd creature that inched close. Its eyes were distinct, its gaze forward. We sat that way for a minute, probably less. The wolf walked slow, out of the beam of our lights and along the length of the passenger side of the truck, five, eight feet away. Gabe switched off the lights. My window was rolled down a third. It was too dark to see well but I could hear it outside the window. The night's noise went on around us, I'm sure, the squeak of a far-off rusted fence gate, a wind chime clattering in the eaves of an abandoned barn, but I remember those moments as if the world were muted, as if the wolf and I were the only things passing before a set stage. No Gabe. No truck. When it reached the tailgate, the wolf cut across the road and trotted down into the ditch line and up again, vanished into the woods between the river and us. Gabe and I sat in the truck in the dark. No talk. No touch. For a minute, just dark.

Of all the animals I've seen over the years, all the brief glimpses and long stares, I remember the wolf more clearly than many. Not so much the motions of it, not where the wolf walked and how long it took and what I thought when it disappeared. But I remember its eyes reflecting light, how the shoulder muscles undulated beneath the thick beginnings of its winter coat. I remember that it didn't run. It never seemed wary, or curious. Not canny, smart, devious, or fierce. We crossed its path and it regarded us briefly before making its way toward pups in a den, a deer kill buried in a hole, or miles more hungry walking under the slim moon. That night, whether because of culture or nature, my wishful tilt toward wildness or an evolutionary hunch, I felt the borders of physicality and transcendence shift until one allowed the other in, and when the wolf slipped into the woods, I wanted to follow it. I wanted to dip my face to the river to drink, tear flesh with my teeth, flatten myself a bed of needles with a circling pace before sleeping. Never mind the blood on my face. Never mind the cold.

When it's clear in the North Fork and you're having a beer at a picnic table outside the saloon, you can see east across the river valley to the mountains, twenty miles away. Long Knife, Kintla, Rainbow, Bowman, Vulture, Nashukin. Beyond those, more, and beyond those, still more, over the divide to the east side of the park, the rain shadow where red talus slopes run into prairie's edge. Gunsight, Bearhat, Two Medicine, Sentinel, Apikuni, Rain Shadow, Bad Marriage. Animal names, Native names, white men's names—mountain names. Rainbow Peak's name nods to three snowy couloirs on the south face that mimic, in monochrome, the spooned arcs of refracted sun. *Kintla* is the Kootenai word for sack: the drainage that leads up to that peak is like a loose bag, wide at the bottom, drawn tight at the top where the creek rockets down off the cliffs through a tapered gap. The summit ridge of Gunsight looks like the notch on the muzzle of a shotgun, from such height the world a target below.

Most peaks have other names, too, names that aren't on the map, the ones chosen by those who have slept and played and traveled and worked in them. *Cabin mountain; the peak where the snow stays year round. Thirsty Pass. The blond bear's mountain, the ridge I climbed in a hailstorm, the one where you left a shovel lying in the thimbleberries, the summit where two old friends died.* Names are our most condensed narrative, the one-, two-, three-word stories we tell ourselves about places we know, or wish to.

The mountains in the North Fork, as in all of the park, were formed by the creative force of tectonic upheaval and glacial revisions. Near a large body of water, an open meadow, or above tree line where the view is unobstructed, geology's alchemy is evident. Eras ago, through compression and uplift and carving, dirt and rock, water and ice turned into mountains. And since then, over centuries, the process reverses. A hard rain, hot summer sun, the freeze and thaw of the darkest days. A forest fire, the warming Arctic's winds. Mountains revert again to dirt and rock, water and ice.

From the high peaks, or the passes below them, you can see glaciers hanging shiny gray in the sun, scant remnants of the ones that shaped this land. Some of them are named, too: Agassiz, Weasel-Collar, Harris, Thunderbird, Two-Oceans. They look impressive, but not vast; small, really, in the context of the world's great ice fields. It's hard to believe these little patches of ice could have once dominated the faces that tower above them. Earth's constant scientific lesson: size is never the whole story. A new reality has emerged in the years since I first discovered Glacier. If I have children, and if they do, those kids won't see a glacier in the park. Like the grizzly bear on California's state flag, the story in Glacier's name will be a nod to something gone, the fact of language no longer matched to the truth of place. How startling, that a world I knew so well could vanish. And that despite my loving it, *in* my loving it, I helped it disappear.

What is *wild?* To Henry David Thoreau, it's "the thrill of savage delight" at a woodchuck in his path, and the urge to sink his teeth in; it's "the preservation of the world." Gary Snyder says the wild is the process and essence of nature, an ordering of impermanence. Annie Dillard gives a lyric: a cat's bloody paws on a pillowcase, things whole and things broken. To Edward Abbey, wild is the one true place, and there are many of them. Wallace Stegner says wilderness is "the geography of hope."

In margins, bedrooms, maps, and minds, wild hovers, lingers, skulks.

KLEE WYCK

Emily Carr

Emily Carr (1871–1945) was a Canadian artist and writer who made her name painting, in the Modernist style, the villages and totem poles of the indigenous people of the Pacific Northwest region of Canada. They called her Klee Wyck – Laughing One. Her book of the same name, *Klee Wyck,* is a series of literary sketches of her journeys among the First Nation peoples.

Sailing to Yan

At the appointed time I sat on the beach waiting for the Indian. He did not come and there was no sign of his boat.

An Indian woman came down the bank carrying a heavy not-walking-age child. A slim girl of twelve was with her. She carried a paddle and going to a light canoe that was high on the sand, she began to drag it towards the sea.

The woman put the baby into the canoe and she and the girl grunted and shunted the canoe into the water, then they beckoned to me.

"Go now," said the woman.

"Go where?"

"Yan.—My man tell me come take you go Yan."

"But—the baby—?"

Between Yan and Masset lay ugly waters—I could not—no, I really could not—a tippy little canoe—a woman with her arms full of baby—and a girl child——!

The girl was rigging a ragged flour sack in the canoe for a sail. The pole was already placed, the rag flapped limply round it. The wind and the waves were crisp and sparkling. They were ready, waiting to bulge the sack and toss the canoe.

"How can you manage the canoe and the baby?" I asked the woman and hung back.

Pointing to the bow seat, the woman commanded, "Sit down."

I got in and sat.

The woman waded out holding the canoe and easing it about in the sand until it was afloat. Then she got in and clamped the child between her knees. Her paddle worked without noise among the waves. The wind filled the flour sack as beautifully as if it had been a silk sail.

The canoe took the water as a beaver launches himself—with a silent scoot.

The straight young girl with black hair and eyes and the lank print dress that clung to her childish shape, held the sail rope and humoured the whimsical little canoe. The sack now bulged with wind as tight as once it had bulged with flour. The woman's paddle advised the canoe just how to cut each wave.

We streaked across the water and were at Yan before I remembered to be frightened. The canoe grumbled over the pebbly beach and we got out.

We lit a fire on the beach and ate.

The brave old totems stood solemnly round the bay. Behind them were the old houses of Yan, and behind that again was the forest. All around was a blaze of rosy pink fireweed, rioting from the rich black soil and bursting into loose delicate blossoms, each head pointing straight to the sky.

Nobody lived in Yan. Yan's people had moved to the newer village of Masset, where there was a store, an Indian agent and a church.

Sometimes Indians came over to Yan to cultivate a few patches of garden. When they went away again the stare in the empty hollows of the totem eyes followed them across the sea, as the mournful eyes of chained dogs follow their retreating masters.

Just one carved face smiled in the village of Yan. It was on a low mortuary pole and was that of a man wearing a very, very high hat of honour. The grin showed his every tooth. On the pole which stood next sat a great wooden eagle. He looked down his nose with a dour expression as a big sister looks when a little sister laughs in church.

The first point at the end of Yan beach was low and covered with coarse rushes. Over it you could see other headlands—point after point… jutting out, on and on… beyond the wide sweep of Yan beach to the edge of the world.

There was lots of work for me to do in Yan. I went down the beach far away from the Indians. At first it was hot, but by and by haze came creeping over the farther points, blotting them out one after the other as if it were suddenly aware that you had been allowed to see too much. The mist came nearer and nearer till it caught Yan too in its woolly whiteness. It stole my totem poles; only the closest ones were left and they were just grey streaks in the mist. I saw myself as a wet rag sticking up in a tub of suds. When the woolly mist began to thread and fall down in rain I went to find the woman.

She had opened one of the houses and was sitting on the floor close to a low fire. The baby was asleep in her lap. Under her shawl she and the child were one big heap in the half-dark of the house. The young girl hugged her knees and looked into the fire. I sat in to warm myself and my clothes steamed. The fire hissed and crackled at us.

I said to the woman, "How old is your baby?"

"Ten month. He not my baby. That," pointing to the girl, "not my chile too."

"Whom do they belong to?"

"Me. One woman give to me. All my chiles die—I got lots, lots dead baby. My fliend solly me 'cause I got no more chile so she give this an' this for mine."

"Gave her children away? Didn't she love them?"

"She love plenty lots. She cly, cly—no eat—no sleep—cly, cly—all time cly."

"Then why did she give her children away?"

"I big fliend for that woman—she solly me—she got lots more baby, so she give this and this for me."

She folded the sleeping child in her shawl and laid him down. Then she lifted up some loose boards lying on the earth floor and there was a pit. She knelt, dipped her hand in and pulled out an axe. Then she brought wood from the beach and chopped as many sticks as we had used for our fire. She laid them near the fire stones, and put the axe in the pit and covered it again. That done, she put the fire out carefully and padlocked the door.

The girl child guiding the little canoe with the flour-sack sail slipped us back through the quiet mist to Masset.

LAST FLIGHT

Amelia Earhart

Amelia Earhart (1897–unknown) transformed herself from tomboy to fashion icon, feminist, author and America's 'queen of the air'. A pioneering aviator whose iconic leather flying jacket is still coveted by women today, she racked up an awe-inspiring list of 'firsts', most notably making the first female solo nonstop transatlantic flight in a bright red plane and scaring cattle when she landed in Ireland. She vanished somewhere over the Pacific in 1937, seemingly without trace (although enthusiasts are still searching), while attempting to circumnavigate the globe. *Last Flight*, published posthumously, is an account of the trip.

A Pilot Grows Up

I worked in a hospital during the war. From that experience I decided that medicine interested me most. Whether or not medicine needed me I did not question. So I enrolled at Columbia University in New York and started in to do the peculiar things they do who would be physicians. I fed orange juice to mice and dissected cockroaches. I have never seen a cockroach since but I remember that the creature has an extraordinarily large brain.

However, I could not forget airplanes.

I went to California for a summer vacation and found air meets, as distinct from wartime exhibitions, just beginning. I went to every one and finally one day came a chance to ride. Frank Hawks took me on the first hop. He was then a barnstorming pilot on the west coast, unknown to the fame he later acquired. By the time I had got two or three hundred feet off the ground I knew I had to fly.

I think my mother realized before I did how much airplanes were beginning to mean to me, for she helped me buy the first one. It was second-hand, painted bright yellow, and one of the first light airplanes developed in this country. The motor was so rough that my feet went to sleep after more than a few minutes on the rudder bar. I had a system of lending the plane for demonstration so as not to be charged storage. Hangar rental would have annihilated my salary.

After a year my longest hop was from Long Beach to Pasadena, about 40 miles. Still I all but set off to cross the continent by air. The fact that I couldn't buy gasoline myself forced me to compromise and drive a car with Mother along. I am sure I wouldn't be here to tell the tale if I had carried out the original plan.

I did what flying I could afford in the next few years and then the "Friendship" came along. I was working in Denison House in Boston, one of America's oldest social settlements.

"Phone for you, Miss Earhart."

"Tell 'em I'm busy." At the moment I was the center of an eager swarm of Chinese and Syrian neighborhood children, piling in for games and classes.

"Says it's important."

So I excused myself and went to listen to a man's voice asking me whether I was interested in doing something dangerous in the air. At first I thought the conversation was a joke and said so. Several times before I had been approached by bootleggers who promised rich reward and no danger—"Absolutely no danger to you, Leddy."

The frank admission of risk stirred my curiosity. References were demanded and supplied. Good references. An appointment was arranged for that evening.

"Would you like to fly the Atlantic?"

My reply was a prompt "Yes"—provided the equipment was all right and the crew capable. Nine years ago flying oceans was less commonplace than today, and my own experience as a pilot was limited to a few hundred hours in small planes which work and finances permitted.

So I went to New York and met the man entrusted with the quaint commission of finding a woman willing to fly the Atlantic. The candidate, I gathered, should be a flyer herself, with social graces, education, charm and, perchance, pulchritude.

His appraisal left me discomforted. Somehow this seeker for

feminine perfection seemed unimpressed. Anyway, I showed my pilot's license (it happened to be the first granted an American woman by the F.A.I.) and inwardly prepared to start back for Boston.

But he felt that, having come so far, I might as well meet the representatives of Mrs. Frederick Guest, whose generosity was making the flight possible, and at whose insistence a woman was to be taken along. Those representatives were David T. Layman, Jr., and John S. Phipps, before which masculine jury I made my next appearance. It should have been slightly embarrassing, for if I were found wanting in too many ways I would be counted out. On the other hand, if I were just too fascinating, the gallant gentlemen might be loath to risk drowning me. Anyone could see the meeting was a crisis.

A few days later the verdict came. The flight actually would be made and I could go if I wished. Naturally I couldn't say "No." Who would refuse an invitation to such a shining adventure?

Followed, in due course, after weeks of mechanical preparation, efforts to get the monoplane "Friendship" off from the gray waters of Boston Harbor. There were chill before-dawn gettings-up, with breakfasts snatched and thermos bottles filled at an all-night lunch counter. Brief voyages on the tugboat *Sadie Ross* to the anchored plane, followed by the sputter of the motors awakening to Mechanic Lou Gordon's coaxing and their later full-throated roar when Pilot "Bill" Stultz gave them the gun—and I crouched on the fuselage floor hoping we were really off.

Thrice we failed, dragging back to Boston for more long days of waiting. Waiting is apt to be so much harder than *going*, with the excitement of movement, of getting off, of adventure-around-the-corner.

Finally one morning the "Friendship" took off successfully, and Stultz, Gordon, and I transferred ourselves to Newfoundland. After thirteen days of weary waiting at Trepassey (how well I remember the alternating diet of mutton and rabbits!) the Atlantic flight started. Twenty hours and forty minutes later we tied up to a buoy off Burryport, Wales. I recall desperately waving a towel; one friendly soul ashore pulled off his coat and waved back. But beyond that for an hour nothing happened. It took persistence to arouse interest in an itinerant trans-Atlantic plane.

I myself did no piloting on that trip. But I gained experience. In London I was introduced to Lady Mary Heath, the then very active Irish woman flyer. She had just made a record flight from London to Cape Town and I purchased the small plane she had used. It wore on its chest a number of medals given her at various stops she made on the long route.

After the pleasant accident of being the first woman to cross the Atlantic by air, I was launched into a life full of interest. Aviation offered such fun as crossing the continent in planes large and small, trying the whirling rotors of an autogiro, making record flights. With these activities came opportunity to know women everywhere who shared my conviction that there is so much women can do in the modern world and should be permitted to do irrespective of their sex. Probably my greatest satisfaction was to indicate by example now and then, that women can sometimes do things themselves if given the chance.

Here I should add that the "Friendship" flight brought me something even dearer than such opportunities. That Man-who-was-to-find-a-girl-to-fly-the-Atlantic, who found me and then managed the flight, was George Palmer Putnam. In 1931 we married. Mostly, my flying has been solo, but the preparation for it wasn't. Without my husband's help and encouragement I could not have attempted what I have. Ours has been a contented and reasonable partnership, he with his solo jobs and I with mine. But always with work and play together, conducted under a satisfactory system of dual control.

I was hardly home when I started off to fly the continent—my 1924 ambition four years late. Lady Heath's plane was very small. It had folding wings so that it actually could fit in a garage. I cranked the motor by standing behind the propeller and pulling it down with one hand. The plane was so light I could pick it up by the tail and drag it easily around the field.

At that time I was full of missionary zeal for the cause of aviation. I refused to wear the high-bred aviation togs of the moment. Instead I simply wore a dress or suit. I carried no chute and instead of a helmet used a close-fitting hat. I stepped into the airplane with as much nonchalance as I could muster, hoping that onlookers would be persuaded that flying was nothing more than an everyday occurrence. I refused even to wear goggles, obviously. However, I put them on as I taxied to the end of the field and wore them while flying, being sure to take them off shortly after I landed.

That was thoroughly informal flying. Pilots landed in pastures, race courses, even golf links where they were still enough of a novelty to be welcome.

In those days domestic animals scurried to the fancied protection of trees and barns when the flying monsters roared above them. Now along the airways there's not enough curiosity left for a self-respecting cow even to lift her head to see what goes on in the sky. She's just bored. Stories of that happy-go-lucky period should be put together in a saga to regale the scientific, precision flyers of tomorrow.

Nineteen-twenty-nine was the year of the women's derby from California to Cleveland, the first time a cross-country race had ever been sponsored for women alone. I felt I needed a new plane for this extraordinary sporting event. So I traded in the faithful little Avion for my first Lockheed Vega. It was a third-hand clunk but to me a heavenly chariot.

I crossed the continent again from New York to California to stop at the Lockheed factory. I thought possibly there might be a few adjustments necessary before I entered the race. There I met the great Wiley Post for the first time. Wiley Post had not then had his vision of stratosphere flying, and was simply a routine check pilot in the employ of the Lockheed company.

It fell to him to take my airplane up for test. Having circled the field once, he came down and proceeded to tell everyone within ear-shot that my lovely airplane was the foulest he had ever flown. Of course the worse he made the plane, the better pilot I became. The fact that I should have been able to herd such a hopeless piece of mechanism across the continent successfully was the one bright spot in the ensuing half hour.

Finally Lockheed officials were so impressed by my prowess (or so sorry for me) that they traded me a brand new plane. The clunk was never flown again.

The Derby produced one of the gems which belong in the folklore of aviation. Something went wrong with her motor and Ruth Elder made a forced landing in a field thickly inhabited by cattle. The bovine population crowded around her plane and proceeded to lick the paint off the wings—there seemed to be something in the "doped" finish that appealed to them. Meanwhile, Ruth snuggled down in the safety of the cockpit. "You see," she explained, "I didn't know much about such things and was uncertain as to the sex of the visitors. My plane was red—very red. And I'd always heard what bulls did to *that*."... Apparently the cows were cows.

After the "Friendship" flight I did not immediately plan to fly the Atlantic alone. But later as I gained in experience and looked back over the years I decided that I had had enough to try to make it solo. Lockheed #2 was then about three years old. It had been completely reconditioned and a new and larger engine put in. By the spring of 1932 plane and pilot were ready.

Oddly, one of my clearest memories of the Atlantic solo concerns not the flight itself but my departure from home. On May 19th the weather outlook was so unpromising we had abandoned hope of getting off that day. So I had driven in to New York from our home in Westchester. Just before noon an urgent message caught up with me immediately to get in touch with Mr. Putnam at the Weather Bureau.

Our phone conversation was brief.

"It looks like the break we've waited for," he said. "Doc Kimball says this afternoon is fine to get to Newfoundland—St. John's anyway. And by tomorrow the Atlantic looks as good as you're likely to get it for some time."

I asked a few questions. A threatening "low" on the first leg of the route had dissipated to the southeast; a "high" seemed to be moving in promisingly beyond Newfoundland.

"Okeh! We'll start," I said. Mr. Putnam agreed he would corral Bernt Balchen, my technical adviser who was to go with me to Newfoundland to be sure that everything was as right as could be before I hopped off. I explained I would have to rush back to Rye to get my flying clothes and maps. We arranged to meet at two o'clock at the city end of the George Washington Bridge, which leads across the Hudson toward Teterboro Airport in New Jersey, where my plane waited.

As fast as I dared—traffic cops being what they are—I drove the twenty-five miles to Rye. Five minutes was enough to pick up my things. Plus a lingering few more to drink in the beauty of a lovely treasured sight. Beside and below our bedroom windows were dogwood trees, their blossoms in luxuriant full flower, unbelievable bouquets of white and pink flecked with the sunshine of spring. Those sweet blooms smiled at me a radiant farewell.... That is a memory I have never forgotten.

Looking back, there are less cheering recollections of that night over the Atlantic. Of seeing, for instance, the flames lick through the exhaust collector ring and wondering, in a detached way, whether one would prefer drowning to incineration. Of the five hours of storm, during black midnight, when I kept right side up by instruments alone, buffeted about as I never was before. Of much beside, not the least the feeling of fine loneliness and of realization that the machine I rode was doing its best and required from me the best I had.

And one further fact of the flight, which I've not set down in words before. I carried a barograph, an instrument which records on a disc the course of the plane, its rate of ascent and descent, its levels of flight all co-ordinated with clocked time. My tell-tale disc could tell a tale. At one point it recorded an almost vertical drop of three thousand feet. It started at an altitude of something over 3000 feet, and ended—well, something above the water. That happened when the plane suddenly "iced up" and went into a spin. How long we spun I do not know. I do know that I tried my best to do exactly what one should do with a spinning plane, and regained flying control as the warmth of the lower altitude melted the ice. As we righted and held level again, through the blackness below I could see the white-caps too close for comfort.

All that was five full years ago, a long time to recall little things. So I wonder if Bernt Balchen remembers as I do the brief words he said to me as I left Harbor Grace. They were: "Okeh. So-long. Good luck."

THIS COLD HEAVEN

Gretel Ehrlich

Gretel Ehrlich (1946–present) is an American travel writer, poet and essayist. She's passionate about Greenland – the realm of the Great Dark, an unearthly landscape that she finds enthralling with its ice pavilions, polar bears and nomadic Inuit. *This Cold Heaven: Seven Seasons in Greenland* is her poetic account of her own travels in the company of indigenous Greenlanders, mingled with stories of others who've had similar experiences there.

Nanuq: The Polar Bear, 1999

An eyelid had been drawn down over Greenland since December and now it had lifted, revealing a puzzle of ice whose floating pieces—*kassut*—had been knocked apart by sun and sea currents and welded back together by wet snow. The ice had sheared off from a tangle of frozen rivers, fjords, and oceans, then thawed, the many becoming one until its threads were picked up again and turned back into separate waterways.

The ice had come in mid-October and now, in April, it covered the entire polar north. Like old skin, it was pinched and pocked, pressed up into hummocks and bejeweled by old and young calf ice rising here and there in beveled outcrops, hacked at by thirsty travelers such as ourselves in search of something to melt for drinking water.

Six hundred miles to the north, the rotating umbilicus of the North Pole was still sloshing around, held by its collar of continents, each body of land separated from others at its northern extremes by more frozen seas and straits pinched up into corridors of pressure ice. Now scientists were preparing to put a long line 2.6 miles down into that polar navel, not to catch halibut, but to read the currents, water temperature, salinity, and thickness of ice, to catch the rhythms of the ocean-atmosphere exchange.

Jens, Ilaitsuk, their five-year-old grandson Meqesuq, and I drove out onto that white puzzle of collisions and annealments and headed north in search of polar bears. Their friend and brother-in-law, Mikele Kristiansen, joined us. We were on two sleds, thin splinters moving across ice. The *iparautaq* (whip) snapped above each team of fifteen dogs and ice unscrolled beneath us as Greenland's mountains sailed by.

Since my last visit, Jens had begun getting gray at the temples and had gained weight. He now rued his "Eskimo bank account"—his potbelly—wishing he could find a good diet, and despaired over the struggle required to keep northern hunters from losing their traditions. He also worried about climate changes, how the spring months were colder, the summers rainier, the autumns stormier, and the thinning of the ice. Jens's friend Mikele, younger, thinner, and more agile, was at the height of his prowess—a keen intelligence that allowed him to get almost any animal he hunted. He joined us because he needed new polar bear pants for the coming winter. As we slalomed between jutting pieces of rough ice, his brown skin and high cheekbones shone in the pale transparency of spring light.

Meqesuq had crawled up to the front of Jens's sled and sat in his grandfather's lap. The frigid wind blew in his face but he didn't care. He wanted to know if I'd come all the way to Greenland from California by dogsled. He didn't know there was any other way to travel, had never seen a car, a train, a field, a tree, or a highway. Even at the close of the twentieth century, he still belonged to the Polar Eskimos, who shared an ice age culture that began thousands of years ago and had flourished in relative isolation.

We churned through fresh-fallen snow and skidded sideways on ice. I rested my hand on Jens's rifle laid on caribou skins and tucked under a blue nylon lash rope. "*Issiktuq* [it is getting cold]," Ilaitsuk said. Even though it was April, it felt more like February or March. Ilaitsuk and I had already changed into winter clothes: *annuraat ammit*, skins; *nannuk*, polar bear pants; *kapatak*, anoraks; polar bear *kamikpak*, boots made of polar bear skin lined with Arctic hare; and *aiqqat*, sealskin mittens with a dog-hair ruff at the wrists. We were headed north in search of animals whose skins we could make into more clothes.

By chance we were following the track of a sled that was carrying a coffin. Two days before, a young hunter had shot himself on the ice in front of twenty schoolchildren and his body was being taken home to Siorapaluk. Accident or suicide? Nobody knew for sure. "There are troubles everywhere. Even here," Ilaitsuk said, clasping the shoulder of her tiny grandson.

"*Harru, harru*" (go left), Jens yelled to the dogs. We swerved around a flat slab of ice that looked like a gravestone. "*Atsuk, atsuk*" (go right). We corrected our course. When his grandson mimicked his commands, Jens turned and smiled.

Wind belted out of the north, covering Jens's whiskered face as well as the muzzles of the dogs with rime ice. The dogs were still recovering from the outbreak of distemper that had killed half their numbers in the northern villages. Jens's and Mikele's teams had dwindled to three or four dogs. Friends from west Greenland sent replacements and those youngsters were still being trained.

One of Jens's dogs was sick and kept falling behind. Jens jumped off the moving sled and, at a run, picked the dog up, threw him into the midst of the pack, then hopped back on. The dog was gaunt and his gait was uneven; he quickly fell behind. Sometimes he was dragged alongside the sled by his trace line, other times he hobbled, never really pulling. Finally, Jens stopped and lifted the dog onto the front of the sled. We set out again, now five instead of four on the sled.

We stopped to make tea. The old kitchen box was set on end and the Primus stove was lit and placed inside the box to shelter the flame from wind. We hacked at a piece of young ice with an iron pole, stuffed the chips into the pot, and melted them for tea water. A whole frozen halibut was stuck head first into the snow and Mikele, Ilaitsuk, and Jens began cutting off chunks of "frozen sushi." The dogs rolled in the snow to cool themselves while we stood and shivered. When the water came to a boil, tea was made. "Is this the same box that went all the way to Alaska with you?" I asked Jens. He nodded.

The closer we got to Siorapaluk, the colder it got. The sled carrying the coffin made deep tracks, as if the finality of death was weighing the sled down. Jens untied the crippled dog from the front stanchion of the sled and threw him into the pack with the others. He hobbled along with less trouble. Appearances count: it wouldn't look good to arrive in a village with an injured dog. We slid around a bend: Robertson Fjord opened up. At the head of the fjord, three glaciers lapped at the sea ice with white tongues and the ice cap rose pale and still behind snowy mountains. Where one began and the other ended was hard to tell. Then, on the far, east-facing side of the fjord, the village of Siorapaluk came into view.

We made camp as usual on the ice in front of the village, pushing the two sleds together to serve as our *illeq*—our sleeping platform—and raising the canvas tent over the sleds. When I looked up, something caught my eye. The funeral procession had already started. Six men were carrying the coffin up the snowy path above the houses. The singing sounded faint. Wind took the strains of music and blew them out the end of the fjord away from us. Mourners gathered in a knot as the casket was set down on the snow, blessed, then pushed into a shed where it would stay until the ground thawed enough for burial. My eyes moved west: on the horizon a mirage shimmered, compressing the roots of the mountains and lifting them above ice and mirrored light, an errant stripe of geography, or a human life that no longer fit earth's puzzle.

As soon as the sun went behind the mountains the temperature plummeted. It was well below zero. All of us crowded into the tent. Shoulder to shoulder, leg to leg, we were bodies seeking other bodies for warmth.

Later. The sound of three hundred dogs crooning woke me. I looked across the row of bodies stuffed into sleeping bags, at Jens's barrel chest and face pressed wide by cold and wind. He was holding his grandson. They both opened their eyes: two moon faces smiled at the canine chorus. There were gunshots.

Mikele stuck his head out of the tent, then fell back on the *illeq*, grunting. "They shot at something but missed," he said.

"At what?" I asked.

"*Nanuq, imaqa*" (Maybe a polar bear), he said, smiling mischievously.

*

Bright sun, frigid breeze. It must have been midday. We sat in silence watching ice melt for tea water. "*Issi*," Ilaitsuk said again. We broke camp quietly. The crippled dog was tied away from the others, since he wouldn't be coming with us, and the tent was taken down. The pace was deceptive: it looked laid back because Inuit hunters don't waste energy and work quickly, with the utmost efficiency. Before I knew it, Jens was hooking the trace lines into the *urhiq*, to ivory hook that tied the dogs to the sled. I grabbed Meqesuq and made a flying leap as Ilaitsuk and Jens jumped aboard the already fast-moving sled. Jens laughed at his grandson for not being ready and the boy cried, which made Jens laugh harder. Mikele raced past us grinning. That was the Eskimo way of teaching children a sense of humor and the necessity of acting with precision—lessons that would later save their lives.

As we glided away from Siorapaluk on ocean ice another mirage appeared. This one lifted a band of cloud, and beneath it a light shone. We slid from a deception resembling a mirror. It seemed to be taunting us: could we see anything, could we even see ourselves? After eight years of traveling in the Arctic, I knew less and less. The complexities of ice would take a lifetime to learn. It was one thing for one moment, and quite another in the next. Now, as we moved, the mirage moved: the mirrored ice was not something in which you could gaze at yourself nor an instrument of self-knowledge. Instead, it only saw us—specks on ice, smaller than the *uttoq*—the seals that hauled out in the spring to bask in the sun when there was any.

Snow began pelting us in the face. "The weather and the hunter are not such good friends," Jens said. "If a hunter waits for good weather he may starve. But he may starve anyway. That's how it is here and always has been."

When we stopped to rest the dogs rolled in snow, then slept. We drank and peed. I laid out my topographical map. North of Siorapaluk the details stopped. There were no more human habitations but only seldom-visited places: Inglefield Land, Humboldt Glacier, Washington Land, Hall, Nyeboe, Warming, Wulff, Nares, Freuchen, and Peary Land, all the way over the top of Greenland at 83 degrees north latitude to the east side of the island, most of which was also uninhabited.

Snow deepened and the four-mile-per-hour dogtrot slowed to a walk. On our right brown cliffs rose in sheer folds striped with avalanche chutes, crisscrossed by the tracks of Arctic hares. "*Ukaleq, ukaleq*," Ilaitsuk cried out. Jens whistled the dogs to a stop. "There, there," she pointed excitedly. The rabbits meant food, and their hides provided liners for kamiks. We looked: they were white against a white slope and hopped behind boulders. No luck. On the ice, there were no seals. What would the five of us plus thirty dogs eat that evening?

Rounding a rocky knob, we saw a large bay open up; we crossed its wide mouth. Looking inward, I saw a field of talcum powder, then a cliff of ice—the snout of an enormous glacier made of turquoise and light, carrying streambed debris like rooftop ornaments. I glassed it with binoculars: my eyes darted into caves, bumped over pinnacles and fractures, traced the sensual, inward deformations of ice, the overturned folds and the weathered foliations that told the story of a glacier's life: its contortions, fractures, movements, birth, and rebirth; how it appeared to be static but wasn't; how its fins and flippers of ice were bent up by canyon walls; how, in summer, its snout, on touching sea water, lifted up, floated, and calved enormous icebergs—its life almost human.

Above the terminus, the glacier was curvaceous; its seeming motionlessness was in reality a slow coming apart. Its surface was fractured and crosscut—a grid for a city that had not yet been built. Bands of color revealed the rhythm of ablation and accumulation for what it was: the noise and silence of time. Above that was the ice cap. At its edge, rows of twenty-foot-long icicles hung like beaded curtains in front of caves, obstructing entry and exit as if to say: give up now, it is too big to know.

At the last minute we changed course. We were hungry and followed a lead in ice. We veered out into the frozen ocean looking for seals. Snow came on hard as the cowl of a storm approached, rising from behind the mountains of Ellesmere Island. There were breathing holes all along the crack, but no *uttoq*—no seals basking on the ice.

We went west toward the storm. Then it closed over us and all afternoon and evening we traveled without being able to see.

Once a hunter told me about getting vertigo: "Sometimes when we were on our dogsleds and there was bad fog or snow, we felt lost. We couldn't tell where the sky was, where the ice. It felt like we were moving upside down."

Two ravens appeared out of the white, jeering at us as we zigzagged from one frozen-over crack in the ice to another. We hadn't eaten meat for two days and our hunger was a kind of group ache. All was white. We stopped for tea, pulling the two sleds close together and lashing a tarp between them as a windbreak. We scrounged through our duffles for food. I found a jar of peanut butter but was dismayed to see the words "reduced fat" on the label. Never mind. I spread it on a cracker, then drank tea, and split a bittersweet chocolate bar with Ilaitsuk. Bittersweet was what I was feeling that day: happy to be in Greenland again among friends, but getting hungrier with each bite I took.

It was easy to see how episodes of famine could sweep through the Arctic; how quickly hunting could go bad, how hunger dominated. Before stores and helicopters, pan-Arctic cannibalism was commonplace. When the food ran out, they ate their dogs and boiled sealskins to make soup. When that was gone, eating human flesh—the remains of those who had already starved—was the key to survival, repellent as it was.

We headed north again, crossing back over a large piece of frozen ocean. The sound of the sled pushing through snow was oceanic. Rabbit tracks crisscrossed in front of us but we saw no animals. The edge of the storm frayed and light flooded through. Everything was made of chipped crystal: snow, ice, air. Meqesuq asked his grandmother for his sunglasses. It had become a ritual: on, off, on, off, and we adults were the caretakers of the precious things. He put them on and turned to us: he was pure Hollywood and he knew it.

How wonderfully relaxing it was to travel with another woman. Ilaitsuk and I tipped our faces up to the sun. Its warmth was a blessing, and for a few moments we closed our eyes and dozed. A yell shook us awake. Ilaitsuk scrambled to her knees. Far ahead, Mikele's sled was moving fast and he was half standing. "*Nanuq! Nanuq!*" he cried, pointing. A polar bear and her small cub were trotting across the head of a wide bay.

"*Puquoq, puquoq,*" Jens yelled, as his dogs took off in that direction. Mikele had already cut two of his dogs loose and they chased the bear. He released two more. The snow was deep and the little cub couldn't keep up. The mother stopped, wheeled around, and ran back for her baby, but Mikele's loose dogs caught up and held the bear at bay.

Now our sled was between the cub and the she-bear. Repeatedly, she whirled around to go back to her cub. The dogs closed in, not harming her, just threatening. She pawed, snarled, and ran again. Ilaitsuk told me that because the bear had a cub, she would not be shot, that Mikele would soon release her. Then something went terribly wrong: one of the dogs spied the cub. Before we could get there, the dog was on the cub and went for its jugular. We rushed to the cub's rescue, but the distances were so great and the going was so slow that by the time we got there, the dog was shaking the young bear by its neck and had been joined by others. Mikele and Jens leaped off their sleds and beat the dogs away with their whip handles, but it was too late. The cub was badly hurt.

When the dogs had been dispersed, we stayed with the cub while Mikele caught up with the mother. The cub was alive but weak. A large flap of skin and flesh hung down from the neck. If I'd had a tranquilizer dart, we could have sewn him up, but we had nothing. Dazed and weak, he was still feisty enough to snarl and scratch. Jens approached, throwing a soft loop around the cub's leg to hold him close to the sled and keep him away from the loose dogs.

We let the young cub rest. He was whiter than his mother and his button nose and eyes were black holes in a world of white. Maybe he would recover enough for us to send him back to his mother. Far ahead, the she-bear started to get away, but the loose dogs caught up with her again. Near the far side of the fjord, the bear darted west, taking refuge next to the wall of a half-crumbled iceberg. Mikele caught up as his dogs began to tire. The bear stood in her icy enclosure, coming out to charge the dogs as they approached—not so close that they would get hurt and not so far away that she could escape. She no longer looked for her cub; she was trying to survive.

The sun was out and the bear was hot. She scooped up a pawful of snow from the ground and ate it to ease her growing thirst. The slab of ice against which she rested was blue and shaped like a wide inverted V, its sides melting in the spring sun. The dogs surrounded her in a semicircle, jumping forward to snap at her, testing their own courage, but leaping back when she charged them.

Five hundred yards behind Mikele, we watched over the cub. If we got too close, he snarled. Sometimes he stood up, but he was weak and began panting. His eyes rolled back. He staggered and was dead.

Jens tied a loop around the cub's neck and dragged it like a toy behind the sled. Its skin would be used, and maybe the meat.

Mikele turned as we approached. "Is the cub dead?" he asked.

Jens said that it was. I knew what was going to happen next and begged Jens to spare the mother even if her cub was dead. She was young and beautiful and she would have more babies. "It's up to Mikele," he said. Mikele, whose polar bear pants were worn almost all the way through, considered, then quietly loaded his rifle.

Meqesuq and I sat on the side of the sled. Tears streamed from our eyes. Jens looked at us and chuckled—not at our softheartedness, but our naïveté. To think that they could pass up a bear for what he considered sentimental reasons was absurd.

The loose dogs continued to hold the bear at bay. I got off the sled and walked closer to her. She could have attacked me, but she had eyes only for the dogs who taunted her. After a long time she rested against the cool wall, licking its ice. Then she turned and looked toward Ellesmere Island. Standing on her toes, she laid her elbow on the top of the berg and scanned the frozen sea, searching for a way out. I rooted for her: "Go, go," I whispered loudly. These were the last moments of her life and I was watching them tick by. How was this possible? Did she know she was doomed? Of course not. But she knew enough to be making plans.

Once again I pleaded for her life, but only got questioning stares from the hunters. Again, she peeked over the top of the ice, but slumped back halfheartedly. She was tired and there was no escape.

The dogs began to lose interest. They turned away from the bear and licked their small wounds. She stood alone in her icy chamber, waiting. Ilaitsuk covered Meqesuq's ears as Mikele slowly raised his rifle. The boy was frightened. He had already seen the cub die and he didn't want to see any more. Standing in deep snow, I felt like a witness to an execution.

The bear was now close enough to jump forward and get me in one swipe. I don't know why she didn't. At the same time, I understood how important it was for a hunter to kill a polar bear. She would be a source of food and her skin would be used for much-needed winter clothing. I looked down at my own body: I too was wearing polar bear pants and boots and it was solely because of them that I was warm.

The bear bent forward, half standing, half sitting, exhausted and bewildered, then slouched down and sat. Did she wonder where her cub was? I wanted to carry her dead baby to her. But she couldn't know any of this and it would make no difference if she did. The world, for her, held no clues about human ambivalence, and she gave me the same hard stare she would give a seal. After all, I was just part of the food chain.

It was the same stare Mikele gave her now, not hard from lack of feeling, but from the necessity to survive. Predator and prey. In the Arctic, you never knew which side of that coin you'd find yourself on, and you lived by your wits, as did the bear and the seal, the dog and the fox, the raven, dovekie, and hare.

The bear's fur was pale yellow and the ice wall was blue. The sun was hot. Time melted. What I knew about life and death, cold and hunger, seemed irrelevant. There were three gunshots. A paw went up in agony, scratching the ice wall as she went down. Then she rolled on her back and was dead.

DESTINATIONS

Jan Morris

Jan Morris (1926–present) is a Welsh historian, writer and journalist. Jan, who until 1972 was James, rejects the description 'travel writer' – saying she writes about places, not journeys, as the essays in *Destinations* illustrate. Highlights of her long journalistic career include being the first to report on Sir Edmund Hillary's successful ascent of Everest in 1953 and 'the miserable Suez intervention' in 1956. She is also known for *Pax Britannica*, a history of the British Empire, and *Venice*. She declares herself in favour of life ending at the biblical three score years and ten. Note, she is now in her nineties!

Panama: An Imperial Specimen

They have a TV program in England in which a panel of eminent antiquarians inspects curios and objets d'art presented for its assessment by eager collectors. "*Nice enough little piece,*" they say. "*You inherited it from your grandmother did you Mrs. Thompson? Well, it's not quite a first-class example, I don't think—something a little greenish about the glaze, wouldn't you say, Francis?—but still a nice little thing, very pleasing, well worth hanging on to Mrs. Thompson.*"

In such a consultative capacity, as an aficionado of historical curiosities, did I fly into Central America one day to inspect that well-known collectors' item, that controversial but beguiling example of diplomatic craftsmanship, the Panama Situation. I will not pretend to you that it was always a specialty of mine. When I awoke in my hotel room in Panama City the morning after my arrival, I did not know whether it was the Atlantic or the Pacific Ocean I could see extending, bounded by hump-backed islands and speckled with shrimp boats, grayish and steamy outside my window. It was the Pacific actually, but as the waiter said when he brought my breakfast, I need not feel ashamed of myself—hardly anybody knows for sure.

Geographically Panama, which occupies the narrowest sliver of land in Central America, is a confusingly contorted country. Dividing as it does, almost symmetrically, North from South America, and calling itself, almost incessantly, the Bridge between the Oceans, it ought to run north and south, but instead goes perversely, and unreliably, east to west. The Pacific is south of Panama, the Atlantic north; the sun rises over the Caribbean; to go to the States from Panama City one sets off, ignorantly protesting, in a southwesterly direction. Moreover, the country is surrounded by states whose location most people are vague about, like Costa Rica and Colombia, besides having a history that few foreigners can grasp, a population rather less than Detroit's, and a name that nobody knows the meaning of, some translating Panama as "Lots of Fish," some as "Many Butterflies," and some rather feebly as "Big Trees."

Nevertheless, the moment I stepped out into the drizzle of Via España (for it was the rainy season and those shrimp boats lay there hangdog and apparently waterlogged in the bay), I recognized the genre. The Panama Situation is a late classic of the imperial form. It possesses all the true imperial elements; a distant and tremendous dominant power, an anxious settler community, a subject people united only in resentment, dubious historical origins, a sleazy tropical setting, above all a specific raison d'être.

In the annals of Empires there is no artifact more charged with passion and purpose than a canal, for great works of irrigation and navigation were always hallmarks of imperial grandeur, and sometimes its excuses too. Wherever Emperors ruled in foreign parts, they commemorated themselves with mighty waterworks, as though to demonstrate their mastery not merely over the lesser breeds, but over nature herself. In Mesopotamia the rulers of Babylon brought the desert to life; in Egypt the Pharoahs linked the Mediterranean with the Indian Ocean; grand aqueducts marked the progress of Rome across Europe; in India the Victorians summoned new provinces into existence by their monumental dams and conduits. The Suez Canal, though the British did not actually build it, became so inescapable an emblem of their imperialism that the phrase "East of Suez" was a synonym for Empire itself, and the Empire's desperate attempt to keep control of the waterway became in the end its bitter curtain call. Nearly always the constructions were destined to outlive their sponsoring sovereignties, and when all the substance of command had faded, the drums were silenced with the rhetoric, then the great work lingered on, crumbling more slowly down the centuries, like the last ironic smile of the Cheshire cat.

The greatest single work of the American Empire is the Panama Canal, the fifty-mile waterway which, bisecting the Republic of Panama, links the Pacific and the Atlantic oceans, and has for more than sixty years given the United States an overwhelming presence at the junction of the Americas. The Canal is the truest meaning of the Panamanian Republic, though Panamanians hate one to say so, but no less is it a terrific expression of American imperialism in its original and simplest sense, older by far than the complexities of Vietnam, the CIA or the conglomerates. It was bred by Big Stick out of Manifest Destiny, two thoroughbreds of American assertion with which, around the turn of the 20th century, the Americans hoped to keep up with the galloping European Empires. *"Take up the White Man's Burden,"* Rudyard Kipling had abjured the Americans, and nobody responded more boisterously to the call than Theodore Roosevelt, "Theodore Rex," who had already more or less arranged the acquisition of the Philippines, and was to see in the construction of the Panama Canal, with its emphasis on skill, strength and usefulness, a truly Kiplingesque consummation of American splendor.

Like most great imperialist enterprises, it had murky beginnings. It was an old dream, of course—for generations people had thought of piercing the isthmus, and Panama indeed had come into existence as a place of transit between the Atlantic and the Pacific. Here the conquistadors girded themselves for their assaults upon the Inca kingdoms, and here, by mule track from one coast to the other, the booty was assembled for shipment to Spain or plunder by English pirates. Here the gold-rush men staggered through swamp and jungle on their way to California, and here, as far back as the 1850s, the Panama Railroad Company of New York laid a line across the isthmus and. carried $750 million of gold bullion back to the East from California. The Panama Situation, by which this ancient function became subject to American expansionist instincts, was born in the early 1900s. Until then Panama had formed part of a province of the Colombian Republic, subject to the neglectful authority of Bogotá: it was the prospect of the Canal, giving the isthmus an incalculable international importance, which enabled the local nationalists to break away and establish their own hopeful if infinitesimal state.

Here was the American chance. Ferdinand de Lesseps, the French genius of the Suez Canal, had already begun work on a cutting through Panama, but had made a terrible mess of it all, sinking deeper every year in shame and corruption—the Panama Scandal, it is called in the French history books, and it is said that de Lesseps's bribery of the French press was so thorough that even *L'Écho des Sociétés Chorales* got its payoff. The Company went bankrupt, and so in 1903 Washington stepped in. By guaranteeing the independence of the new Panama Republic, by a frank flourish of the Big Stick in fact, President Roosevelt arranged that the Panama Canal would be a great work of American enterprise, a marvel to posterity and an earnest of American greatness forever. As Suez was to the British, Panama would be to the United States; not just a commercial enterprise, not only a strategic convenience, but a grand talismanic truth, the ships of all the nations passing symbolically beneath the Stars and Stripes from one half of the world to the other. "I took Panama!" Teddy Roosevelt cried, and he was echoing, consciously perhaps, Disraeli's celebrated report to his monarch, when with a loan from the Rothschilds he bought Britain's way into the Suez Canal: "Madam, the Canal is yours."

A proper degree of skulduggery was involved. The Panamanians, being inexperienced in power politics, had employed a French commission agent, the astute Philippe Bunau-Varilla, to present their case to Washington, offering in effect a canal concession in return for cash and protection. Bunau-Varilla had good personal reasons for wanting an agreement, since he stood to gain financially himself, and he had very soon drawn up the terms of a treaty. By the time the Panamanian leaders got to Washington themselves, he and John Hay, the U.S. secretary of state, had already signed it. The entire future of the Panamanian state had been decided by a Frenchman and an American; and Hay himself frankly told the Senate, when the treaty came up for ratification, that it was "very satisfactory, vastly advantageous to the United States, and we must confess, not so advantageous to Panama." The Senate, naturally, ratified it at once, for what it promised the Americans, give or take an interpretation or two, was not just the right to build and operate a canal across the isthmus of Panama, but the right to establish a colony of their own around it, with all the rights of sovereignty, inalienable, complete and in perpetuity.

The Panamanians were paid a modest fee—$10 million down, $250,000 yearly annuity—and could certainly be assured that no revengeful Colombian gunboat would be permitted to bombard Panama City. But the Americans were given sovereign powers over a swath of land ten miles wide running clean across the new Republic, dividing it absolutely in half. The Panamanians would have no share in the profits of the Canal: the Americans would have the right to do almost anything they pleased in the Canal Zone, to have a monopoly of all trans-isthmian communications forever, and even to keep order within the Panamanian cities of Colón and Panama City, which were not in the Zone at all.

Roosevelt was delighted. The uncompleted French works, with the railroad, were handed over to the United States government, represented by a Panama Canal Commission, and before long 45,000 men had poured into Panama, from the States, from the West Indies, from Spain, even from Greece and Italy, to build the all-American canal.

In 1906 Roosevelt went down in person to inspect progress. It was the first time an American President had ever left the country during his term of office, and it was like a Pageant of Destiny in some celebratory festival; all among the dredgers and the steam hammers, the toiling thousands of workers, the jungle clearings and the swamp causeways, the President strode bull-like and resolute, in knickerbockers and straw hat. Here was the American Empire, the White Man's Burden heroically shouldered! Sweeping irresistibly through marsh and shrub, defying disease, employing all the latest instruments of science and engineering, tremendously the Americans were cutting their ditch between the oceans. It was, said Roosevelt, one of the great works of the world. More than that, declared the editor of *Panama and the Canal in Picture and Prose*, it was "the most gigantic engineering undertaking since the dawn of time." The Canal was the equivalent of a ditch ten feet deep and fifty-five feet wide clean across the United States, Maine to Oregon, or a hole 16.2 feet square from the North to the South Pole. It was Colossal! It was Historical! It was AMERICAN!

Seventy years later it is still there, and in essence nothing much has changed in the relationship between Panama and the United States. But a situation that seemed the very latest thing in 1906, the most modern product of expansionist policy, is now a period piece. Though it can still give pleasure to enthusiasts like me, and still raise a frisson in true-blue all-American hearts, still good taste has outgrown it over the years—don't you agree, Francis? It has lost its atavistic punch, and is riddled anyway, I am sorry to have to say, with rot and woodworm.

The natives are restless, for the Republic of Panama has greatly changed its temper since those hapless delegates, morosely surveying the terms of their treaty, returned to their bewildered compatriots in 1903. They are frustrated, unfulfilled, and their national life has come to revolve around a grievance—as though in a subtle and insidious way they have been deprived of potency.

There is a shabby corner of Panama City which effectively conveys, I think, this flavor. It is down by the markets, in the old Spanish part of the city, and is pervaded by a powerful odor of dismembered bullock and gutted codfish, but it is not without beauty either, for here the wooden tenements open out to reveal a small shingly beach upon the bay, a fine sweep of sea, and the white high-rise buildings of the city's posher quarters to the east. This is a busy place, but not frenzied. There is something expectant to the scene, something calculated perhaps, as though everyone is waiting for an interesting event to occur—as though the whole city is waiting, indeed, for some grand and undefined denouement.

In the market entrance a leisurely row of men and women is selling lottery chances, sitting on the ground with legs stretched out, carpeted by green and yellow tickets. Facing the beach are a couple of open-fronted cafes, at whose counters one or two layabouts are meditatively or perhaps narcotically slumped. Whorelike ladies are here and there, giggling mildly with construction men or swapping symptoms with colleagues, and from the door of the marine police station a couple of lean gendarmes, heavily armed and darkly spectacled, look broodingly across the square, as though they are wondering whom to electrocute next. Above the beach there is a pile of rubbish; and there in ghoulish concentration half a dozen vultures pick away among the garbage, looking for bones and offal, or perhaps corpses, sometimes flapping their huge wings in appreciation, or taking off heavily among the rooftops, trailing strings of gristle.

Yet if it is a squalid scene, smelly too, it is very easily transformed. The Panamanians are people of great charm, and any one of those stagey characters, tart, cop, hardhat or beachcomber, will respond with grace to a greeting or an inquiry. Physically Panama may not be a very prepossessing Republic, but it has a quick and courteous style, even down there among the scavengers. Can it be you yourself, you momentarily wonder, that they have been expecting, like one of those theatrical tableaux that need only a director's click to bring them to life? But no, when they have given you your directions, and you look back upon the scene as you walk away toward the cathedral, that spell of anticipatory suspension has fallen upon it once more, and everyone is waiting for Godot again.

Panama lacks *settledness*. Perhaps it always has. Perhaps it is something to do with its functions of transit. It has always attracted the rootless, raffish kind, from the lusty Welsh pirate Henry Morgan, who with his compatriot John Morris sacked Old Panama in 1671, to the Spanish developers, American bankers, Russian cultural delegates and French arms salesmen who still fish hopefully in its somewhat polluted waters. Panama is a community of gamblers, jockeys, boxers and cockfighters, a place where characters habitually disappear to, or re-emerge from, in old-fashioned thrillers. Its greatest institution is the National Lottery, which holds the entire population in its grip, and it has traditionally been a great entrepôt of the drug trade, in whose profit, if we are to believe a line of gossip peddled almost everywhere in the modern world, many of its most prominent citizens have shared (you do know, don't you, about the Archbishop of Canterbury and the Corsican Connection?).

It lives for, by, around and because of the Canal, just as its churches, convents and caravanserai arose around the mule tracks of the Spaniards. Tourist guides speak glossily of mountain resorts, delectable island beaches, unspoilt Indian tribes and colorful country markets, but really Panama *is* the Canal. "If you're going to Gibraltar, dear," says one lady to another in a favorite Victorian cartoon, "you must on no account miss seeing the Rock"; and similarly one might say that if you are visiting Panama, you should keep your eyes open for the Canal. Probably a third of the population lives in one or other of the two Canalside cities, Colón at the Atlantic end, Panama City at the Pacific, and the whole texture of their lives, their manners and mores, their outlooks, their incomes, is influenced by the presence of the waterway.

This makes for an embattled feeling, too, as though they are struggling always to keep their dignity, or even their identity. The city of Colón is bisected by a rather grand boulevard, tree lined and ornamented with heroic statuary, Nationhood, Motherhood, Christopher Columbus, that kind of thing; but all around the Paseo del Centenario oozes the contagion of the Canal, in duty-free zones and sailors' bars, in yachts impounded for drug smuggling and seamen arrested for midnight brawls, in Hindu emporia and cut-price camera shops, in the shrill and gaudy bustle of Front Street, where generations of travelers have come ashore to be deftly clipped or comforted. Educated Panamanians try hard to maintain their Castilian poise, but it is hard to seem very composed on the edge of all this racket, and diligently though the National Cultural Institute presents its folk festivals and piano recitals, wittily and caustically though the Panama bourgeoisie observes the passing charade, still it must be said that the Republic of Panama, as Lord Rosebery once observed of the entire African continent, is not much of a place for a gentleman.

Wistfully they keep trying. I was taken to the theater one night to see the Cuban National Ballet, with its celebrated *première danseuse*, Alicia Alonso. It is a dear little theater, exuberantly embellished with gilt and flourishes, and the balletgoers were dressed in their slinky best and greeted each other with cousinly enthusiasm, since they all seemed to be related; but no less than that seamier ensemble beside the market, I thought, did the occasion seem to express some sense of yearning, some *jamais vu*. When the music struck up it was played only on a wavering record player, and the ballet itself turned out to be largely propaganda, emancipated peasants greeting a golden dawn, or marching shoulder to shoulder toward the revolution. The Panamanians greeted these exhortations halfheartedly, and there was some booing, not from the gallery but from the dress circle, where Aunt Elisa sat decorously with her nephew the professor.

Panama is a kind of police state, but not the most awful kind, for unlike some of its neighbors it has an easygoing tradition of politics. The family oligarchy which, until 1968, ran the place in quadrillelike succession was venal perhaps, but not often cruel: the revolutionary government which has succeeded it does not, I am assured, habitually murder its opponents, or incarcerate too many critics on its penal island. Exile rather than execution is the rule, and sometimes a dissident even returns from banishment and lives happily enough ever after.

Still, all the paraphernalia of despotism is there. The press is entirely controlled, all political parties are banned and the statutory portraits of the chief, General Omar Torrijos Herrera, gaze lugubriously from cobblers' shops and gas stations. There is a genial president of the Republic, who keeps live white herons in the hall of his presidency beside the sea, their cages lined daily with clean white copies of the morning newspapers. There is a ministry of civilians, mostly from the middle classes. There is even an impotent National Legislature, in a showy new Legislative Palace. The true core of the state, though, the state itself perhaps, is the National Guard, part army, part police, which brought General Torrijos into power seven years ago and keeps him there now.

This all-powerful gendarmerie is no joke. In other countries there is often something tragicomic about military despotisms, with their preposterously epauletted generalissimos and their strutting, puffed-up majors, but there is nothing laughable about the National Guard of Panama. Expensively equipped, well trained and disciplined, it is like a formidable praetorian guard implanted immovably in the heart of the Republic, with fingers in almost every Panamanian activity. Its elite battalions, the Tigers and the Pumas, are enough to scare any dissident into conformity, and its intelligence is said to be omniscient, so that people think twice before telling anecdotes about it.

The fortress headquarters of the force is in El Chorrillo, another of the less inviting quarters of Panama City, and a baleful place it is, being surrounded by slums, gas storage tanks and the city prison. As it happens I spent a couple of hours inside it, for I had arranged to meet the guard's chief of security, Colonel Manuel Noriega, and since he never in the event turned up, a common enough Panamanian practice, I was left to kick up my heels and pursue my fancies deep in his bunkerlike suite of rooms—now and then looked in upon by obliging orderlies, soothed by music from a local uplift program called the *Bright Sounds of Inspiration*, but otherwise all on my own.

How strange, to sit alone in the lair of an unknown security chief! I had heard conflicting reports of Colonel Noriega. He was sinister, he was not bad really, he had hypnotic eyes, watch out for his hands, he liked art, he knew all about interrogation. Certainly he looked after himself in his bunker. Steel doors enclosed it, with armed sentries and closed-circuit TV in his outer office, within the shuttered gates of the building itself, within the guarded wires of the headquarters compound. It was bugged, no doubt, and it had no windows, only skylights. The longer I sat there, and the more boldly I opened doors and peered around the place, the more vividly I seemed to see the absent colonel, and perhaps the autocracy he enforced. Here, through the left-hand door, was the sybaritic side of him, the sensual side, all done up in chrome and white leather, with thick sexy carpeting, and bright pictures of girls and landscapes, and a well-stocked cocktail cabinet, and a very strong suggestion of self-indulgence. Here, through the right-hand door, was his machismo: his big black TV console, with its six steady pictures of exits and entrances, his library of books on counterinsurgency and military intelligence, a huge photograph of himself parachuting out of an aircraft, and above the door an automatic rifle of the Egyptian Army, brought home from Sinai by the Panamanian contingent to the UN peace-keeping force.

Here and there I diffidently pottered, while the *Bright Sounds of Inspiration* wallowed on, and gradually there overcame me a feeling of despair, familiar to any student of the ends of Empires. Those adolescent symbols of manhood and virility! Those second-rate pictures! Those manuals of violence and repression! We are ruled by children, I thought, and all the agonies of state and ideology are only games for little soldiers.

At 3:30 next morning, before the dawn broke, there was a rap at my door, and looking out of my hotel window I saw two National Guardsmen pacing around the deserted patio far below. I feared the worst—perhaps they had put me on film down at the colonel's bunker?—and, jumping swiftly back into bed again, took my usual emergency action and pulled the sheets over my head.

Nothing more happened, but still for a moment I had experienced the chill uncertainty that is the worst part of autocracy. The Panama Situation, like many another experience of late imperialism, is especially disturbing because nobody knows what lies beyond it. What kind of a place will Panama be, if ever it is resolved? Will the traveling prove more gratifying than the arrival? The revolutionary government is a government of pragmatic response, rather than original initiative. Beyond a generally reformist or populist bias it has no true ideology of its own. If it has a communist emphasis, and certainly several of its civilian members have Marxist sympathies and backgrounds, that is partly because in imperialist situations communism habitually thrives. General Torrijos himself has invested in that least Marxian of properties, an estate in Spain (bought indeed, I am told, from the widow of Cuba's fascist reactionary colonialist puppet, Batista). Stylistically his models have varied from Moshe Dayan to Fidel Castro, and in recent pictures he looks for all the world like any other Pentagon general posing for a publicity handout. Ideologically he probably belongs, if he belongs to any company, only to the eclectic society of the dictators, living more by charisma than conviction. He does not often appear in Panama City these days, preferring his seaside estate some sixty miles out of town; but his bodyguard is always thick around his villa in the capital, and in his trellised garage there one may see his gleaming white Jaguar, ready perhaps for hasty getaways.

All these uncertainties, though, these unexpressed yearnings and expectancies, these unsatisfied aspirations, the very tone and temperament of modern Panama, find their focus in the presence of the Canal. It is the alien-controlled Canal which has, paradoxically, deprived the Panamanians of their vocation and their self-esteem; it is the Canal which binds them together; it is the Canal which enables the dictator to command their loyalty and pride.

Colonia Americana... No! runs the chorus of one of the regime's official Revolutionary Marches:

> Es nuestro el Canal
> No somos, ni seremos
> Di ninguna otra Nación.

—"We are not, nor shall we be, of any other nation." For in a world turned upside down since Teddy Roosevelt's day, the Panamanians look with an ever-growing resentment toward the imperial presence deposited, like some vast pyramid from earlier ages or a survivor from some vanished species, gigantically in the middle of their little state.

> *The Republic of Panama grants to the United States all the rights, powers and authority within the zone mentioned and described in Article II of this agreement... which the United States would possess and exercise if it were the sovereign of the territory within which said lands and waters are located to the entire exclusion of the exercise by the Republic of Panama of any such sovereign rights, power or authority.*

The American presence in Panama is based upon two abstractions:

power and pride. Both are inescapable. For most of its length the Canal Zone, 553 square miles of it, is remote from large Panamanian settlements, but at its two extremities its border forms the limit of a Panamanian city. Suddenly, across a city street, or at the end of an avenue, the Latin jumble of life evaporates, the rickety dark tenements disappear, the rubbish-strewn gutters give way to almost obsessively tended lawns and everything is plumper, richer, duller—*as if these streets,* the Panama poet Manuel Orestes Nieto has written, *and their stop lights / and highway signs / were controlled by computers / from Washington itself.* In the days of that other Empire, the British Raj in India, Englishmen of imagination often liked to escape from the ordered incorruptibility of their own territories into the jumbled domains of the independent and often atrocious maharajahs; and I must say that whenever I crossed the unmarked frontier out of the Republic of Panama into the Canal Zone, I felt I was taking a retrograde step, out of reality into pretense.

An impressive pretense, mind. The Panama Canal is exceedingly well run, to a textbook precision. The United States Defense Department not only operates the Canal itself, it also governs the Canal Zone. In its representatives are all virtue and authority delegated. The governor of the Zone, usually a lieutenant-general of engineers, is also president of the Panama Canal Company. The company may sound like a corporation, and indeed a representative of the *New York Times* was down there recently soliciting its advertising, but it is really wholly owned by the Defense Department: its toll rates are decreed by Washington and are supposed only to cover the cost of working the Canal. There is no private property in the Canal Zone and no private commerce. Even the supermarkets are government owned, and when you expect a Zone TV program to break for soap powder or shampoos, instead you get advice about calling the Fire Brigade, or elevating messages about the history of the 193rd Infantry.

It is a terribly institutional place, run so authoritarianly that there is not even a school board, let alone an elected legislature. Its judges, its radio announcers, its storekeepers, its railwaymen, its funeral parlor managers are one and all government servants. It is thick with notices, mostly prohibitive—CONSUMPTION OF ALCOHOLIC LIQUOR IN ANY

Vehicle Is Prohibited, Swimming Is Not Permitted between Dawn and Dusk—and even its friendly neighborhood signs are apt to have an organizational flavor, like Welcome to the Dredging Division. The Canal Zone is intensely *bland*. Panamanians often find it stifling in its pallor. Its architecture is mostly a kind of Hispanic Beaux Arts, and most of its buildings seem to look more or less the same, whether they are Lock Control Stations or Mrs. Dugdale's residence, but the governor's house is very desirable in white clapboard, with flower-painted fans and awned patios, while the headquarters of the company and government, standing magnificently on a crest above the company town of Balboa, looks half like the Forbidden City of Peking, and half like a post office (there is a large statue of Theodore Roosevelt in its central rotunda, and when I offered to wipe its nose, the cleaning lady being unable to reach that high, she said, "Yeah, he does get kinda snotty").

This is a truly imperial enclave, jammed with expertise and experience. It has been doing the same job for sixty years now and it all goes with a very professional glide. The great lock gates swing smoothly open. The sluices spill their overflow. The tugs adeptly maneuver. The pilots, leaning from their bridges as they pass through the locks, murmur a pleasantry over their walkie-talkies or wave a languid hand to Joe in the control tower. Down at marine headquarters the great register of vessels builds up year by year, so that the computer knows not simply the size, speed and shape of a ship, but the way she handles too, her mechanical idiosyncrasies, even the kind of meal the pilot is likely to get. Well oiled, well practiced, well documented—the Canal Zone Regulations fill 314 pages of the Federal Code—the mechanism has come to seem organic, as though the passing of the vessels is a natural phenomenon, and the locks are no more than steps in the landscape, or a convenient kind of cascade.

Teddy was right, though—it really was one of the world's great works when they built it long ago. It was cut through some of the nastiest country in the world, so unhealthy that 25,000 men are said to have died during the construction of the Panama Railroad, infested with noxious insects and jealous reptiles, lethal with malaria and yellow fever, tangled with jungle and soggy with swamp. It entailed building the biggest dam in the world to create the largest man-made lake, digging the largest excavation in history through the Continental Divide, and raising and lowering ships, by the largest locks ever conceived, 85 feet up at one end of the Canal, 85 feet down at the other. The very idea of the Canal was inspiring: Goethe himself had responded to the poetry of it, long before, and James Bryce the historian called it "the greatest liberty man has ever taken with nature."

Everything, Balboa on the Pacific to Cristobal on the Atlantic, was made to a pattern, giving the work an aesthetic unity too—Frederick Law Olmsted, the creator of New York's Central Park, approved the landscaping—and method, consistency, care, were embedded into the Canal's very structure, making it a kind of philosophical enclave, too, in that tropical environment. Everything was self-sufficient, self-reliant; only one percent of the labor force was Panamanian, and the Canal was built almost without reference to the Panamanian government. The Canal's own surgeons eradicated yellow fever from the Zone, having discovered that it was carried by mosquitoes. The Canal's own engineers invented the electric "mules" which, like land-borne tugs or the horses of earlier waterways, manipulated ships through the locks. And through all the great work, which took ten years to complete, there ran that conscious thread of American destiny, as the skills, guts and dollars of the United States drove the great ditch through the Divide to link sea with shining sea. It was a deliberately imperial enterprise. They called one of the construction towns Empire.

Almost from the start, too, the Americans saw it not just as a waterway, but as a power base. This was inevitable. Just as the possession of Suez enabled the British to keep a grip on the whole Middle East, so Panama was America's key to the command of the Americas. It obviated the need for a two-ocean Navy and it gave the Washington strategists an invaluable foothold in Latin America. They have never looked back. American forces have been based in the Canal Zone since 1911, and since 1963 Quarry Heights, just over the Zone border outside Panama City, has been the headquarters of United States

Southern Command, responsible for all American military activities in Central and South America.

There is no pretending that this base is there for the defense of the Canal itself, as the original treaty allowed. Its purpose is strategic, a command post for the whole of Latin America, a staging point, a training camp, a military laboratory. Every kind of military establishment has used the Canal Zone, from medical research teams to intelligence agencies, and today it teems with activities overt and concealed, and bristles with military acronyms—USARSA and IAAFA and COMUSNAVSO, MILGPs and MAAGs and MTTS and TATs. Here the Army has its Jungle Training School. From here the Green Berets dispatch their counterinsurgency training teams throughout Latin America—among their most successful pupils were the Bolivian rangers who hunted down Ché Guevara. Here, too, is the School of the Americas, specializing in counterrevolution (or as the military put it, "internal security and civic action requirements"); its alumni include many a Latin American security chief, war minister and intelligence director, and it is particularly busy at the moment training Chileans to keep their country in order. There are schools of Air Force technique too, and tropical laboratories of several kinds, and from the Canal Zone are coordinated all the contingency plans for American intervention in Latin American affairs, with or without the help of the CIA.

For within the Zone, in the very heart of Latin America, the American establishment may do what it pleases. It is like having a room of one's own, with one's very own lock and key, and a private telephone line, inside one's neighbor's house. The hills around Quarry Heights bristle with masts, aerials and suggestive bumps, and are tunneled through, like Gibraltar, with secret caverns; and whenever I looked up to those grassy knolls, beyond the parklike lawns of Balboa, the royal palms and the monument to Colonel George Washington Goethals Erected by His Fellow Americans—whenever I looked up there, I seemed to hear the hum of the ciphered messages, on their way to Washington, and see the wary flicker of their electronics.

*

These are reasons, right or wrong, for the American presence in the Canal Zone. Below them lie emotions. "It is not the critic that counts," Theodore Roosevelt cried when he visited the Canal in 1906. "The credit belongs to the man who is actually in the arena; whose face is scarred by dust and sweat and blood; who knows the great enthusiasms, the great devotions, so that his place shall never be with those cold and timid souls who know neither victory nor defeat...." This kind of rhetoric, imperfectly enunciated, still infuses the Americanism of the Canal Zone. Deeper by far than the goings-on of Green Berets or MILGPs lies an old American pride in achievement. This gives the Zone community a very old-fashioned, almost touching air, a nostalgic assertion of myth that is a kind of mirror image of Panamanian aspirations across the border—the one people hungering for a chimerical fulfillment, the other pining for a half-legendary past. The average age of American civilians in the Zone strikes me as fairly high and their affinities are often with the South, with New Orleans, which is almost the Canal's home port, so to speak, with Louisiana upon whose laws the Zone's legal system is patterned. They are likely to be patriots, Veterans of Foreign Wars, bicentennialists, people of the Flag and the Oath, family men, lodge members. They read the Panama edition of the *Miami Herald* over cheeseburgers in government canteens, and award second prizes to artifacts called Things and Strings in exhibitions of work by the National League of American Penwomen. Their husbands attend the Nathaniel J. Owen Branch of the American Legion. Their daughters go to proms. They are not Ugly Americans, not at all, but you might judge them, well, *plain*, perhaps.

I have much sympathy for them, for in all these attitudes they are only being true to themselves. They have been brought up to believe that they are serving a great American institution, the Panama Canal. It is as American in their eyes as Kleenex or George Wallace, and for them it reflects the American genius, the American dream, as truly today as it did when the first ship sailed through it. There is a plaque in the headquarters rotunda put up there in 1955 by the American Society of Engineers. "A Modern Civil Engineering Wonder of the U.S.," it says of the Panama Canal, and never for a moment does it suggest that the Canal is not in the U.S. at all. Americans built it,

Americans run it, Americans own it; many of its American employees seldom enter the Republic of Panama from one year to the next—there used to be a policeman who boasted he had never set foot in the place for thirty years. Of the 15,000 people who work the Canal today, 12,000 are Panamanians, but none of them are senior executives and only two of the two hundred Canal pilots are local men. The Panama Canal remains what it always was: a self-sufficient, self-reliant, self-perpetuating, American organism.

And this conviction is accentuated by the unchanging nature of the Canal itself. In fact it is fast getting out of date, being too small for many modern ships, so that the big container vessels have to squeeze their way through the locks like Victorian dames in bustles edging their way through drawing-room doors. There have long been plans to build a newer bigger one, probably without locks at all, but in the meantime the Canal still works exactly as it always did, often with its original equipment. The original dials and gauges, familiar to generations of American operators, still record the rise of the lock water in the high control towers. The electric mules still trundle archaically up and down, Japanese built in their latest models but still doing precisely the same job they always did. It is a very dated wonder and this adds a true pathos to the pride its servants have in it. They live in a world where Big is still Beautiful, where engineering marvels can still move the spirit, where a statistic is still believed, and you can still raise a gasp with the revelation that the stone handled in the construction of the Panama Canal would be enough for 28 Giza pyramids, or 190,438 average American homes. Manifest Destiny is alive, well and rather endearing in the duplexes of Balboa and Cristobal.

There they stand then, at the end of 1975, the classic opponents in an archetypal performance of Empire. They have been opponents from the start, ever since it dawned upon the Panamanians that the 1903 Treaty had robbed them of a birthright, but the animosity has built up steadily through the years, through the brave American heyday, through the chicaneries of banana republic and conglomerate, through the ignominies of Vietnam and Watergate—through a whole era of history in which imperialism as an idea has been discredited, and America as an imperial power has lost faith and persuasion.

The Panamanians now demand an altogether new relationship. They do not, at the moment anyway, demand the immediate withdrawal of American power from the Zone; but they want the arrangements to end altogether by the year 2000, and in the meantime they want to see the Canal gradually handed over to Panamanian control, they want substantial parts of the Zone given back to them and they want Panamanian sovereignty fully recognized. There is absolutely no way in which they can enforce these demands physically, the disparity between the two peoples being as great as ever—140 to 1. Today for the first time, though, they may well enforce them diplomatically, for Panama now has behind her the support of many countries and the threatened encouragement of many more.

When the British were fighting to keep control of Suez, the antagonism was complete, Britons and Egyptians having very little in common, seldom mixing, and pursuing diametrically opposite aims. In Panama it is different. For one thing, though the Canal Zone forms so distant an enclave within the Republic, still it is not physically insulated. Anyone can cross from one side to the other. There are no barriers, check points or wire fences, not even a *cordon sanitaire* (though in Panama City the wide highway called Avenida de los Mártires does form an unfortunate sort of No Man's Land, avidly photographed for TV documentaries, between the lawns of Quarry Heights and the fetid tenements of El Chorrillo). Many Panamanians commute from the Republic to the Zone—some Americans, too. There have been thousands of intermarriages over the years, so that for myself, as I wandered around the Zone, I often found it hard to know whether a cop, a functionary or even a soldier was American or Panamanian. The cultures overlap, as the British and the Egyptian never did: half America has grown up with the awareness of a Spanish past and all Panama has grown up with the consciousness of a gringo present. These antagonists are anything but strangers. They know each other very well indeed, and have more in common than they care to admit.

Then again, though Panamanians prefer not to recognize the fact publicly, they share many self-interests. General Torrijos would not be the chief he is without his American military training. Colonel Noriega perfected his machismo at the School of the Americas. The National Guard is armed with American weapons and advised by an American military mission (MAAG, I think, or it may be MILGP): when its battalion went to the Middle East, every item of its equipment was supplied by the United States, even down to the *socks*. The revolutionary government itself might well have been overthrown by now were it not for tacit American support (interspersed, they tell me, by CIA threats to have the chief of state contracted for, but then we all know how effective *they* are).

Economically, it pays Panama handsomely to be within the American orbit, and especially perhaps beneath the guns of the Canal Zone. The U.S. dollar is official currency, the Panamanians never having printed their own banknotes, and it is unlikely that USSOUTHCOM would ever let the Republic disintegrate into chaos; but the Panamanians impose few prissy restrictions on exchange, interest rates or accessibility, so that the canny investor in Panama City can enjoy the best of many worlds. Wherever you look in the capital there is a foreign bank or a company headquarters, and the Panamanian flag is so particularly convenient that more than 1000 merchant ships, nearly all American owned, gratefully fly it. Panama enjoys the highest living standards in Central America, and there is no denying that this is partly because the Americans are there.

So it is an amorphous emergency, blurred at the edges, slow in coming. There have been the customary riots now and then, the standard breaking of Embassy windows, the normal breaking of diplomatic relations, the usual student protests. The Avenida de los Mártires was renamed for Panamanian students killed in a 1964 affray—it used to be called Fourth of July Avenue. There have been several attempts to replace the Treaty, and it has been repeatedly modified, each time to give the Panamanians a little more self-respect or a little more cash; but only now is the confrontation really coming to a head, each side knowing that if a limit is not soon set upon the American presence in Panama, real trouble is on the way. On the American side intentions remain half-veiled. On the Panamanian side they are very clear: the Americans must be out of Panama altogether in twenty-five years, leaving the Republic of Panama in complete control, technically, economically and militarily, of the Most Gigantic Engineering Undertaking since the Dawn of Time.

If you drive from Panama City to Colón, along the highway magnificently called the Carretera Transistmica, you are traveling more or less parallel with the Canal, without entering the Canal Zone (for a Treaty modification of 1955 kindly allowed the Panamanians to have a road of their own across the isthmus). Everything is highly Panamanian. The villages you pass through are cheerfully wayward, littered with 7-Up signs, buses with pictures, banana-sellers' booths and ravaged, abandoned automobiles. The country is jungly, hummocky and unlovely. There is a kind of aimless shabbiness to it all, shambled, benevolent but not picturesque. At one or two places, though, a side road will take you to a vantage point above the Canal itself, and there, spread out before you between the hills, you may see an almost allegorical antithesis. There the tiled houses of the Americans nestle in their gardens. There the big ships sail across Gatun Lake, their high funnels and superstructures gliding grandly among the islands. There are the trim installations of USGOG or AMPLIG or COMSWAM. There everything seems cool, ordered, prosperous and private. It is like looking through the lodge gates at some unapproachable estate.

The Panama Situation, like so many of its kind, is embodied in *contrast.* Of course not all the Americans of the Canal Zone are stinking rich—none of them indeed are as rich as rich Panamanians. They are, however, undeniably exclusive and they have made the Zone a world of their own. Once you cross that Zone border, though you may be only a hundred yards from your own home, nothing is Panamanian. The signs, the systems, the language, the ambiance—all are American. If you are caught speeding, you will be taken before an American judge in an American court. If you need a cup of coffee, you will be unable to buy one without a Zone card. The Stars and Stripes fly everywhere—only since 1964 has the Panama flag flown within the Zone, and even now it does not often show.

It is the apparency of it all that is so provocative. It so happens that in Panama City a spit of the Zone protrudes directly in front of the Legislative Palace, so that while the Legislature is within the Republic, the lawns before it are in the Zone. On that very spot the Zone authorities, every morning of the year, hoist the American flag—in tandem, indeed, with the Panamanian, but giving the distinct impression, to foreigners as to touchier Panamanians, that they claim a tacit suzerainty not just over the Zone but over Panama itself.

In fact the Americans are not sovereign even within the Zone. Even M. Bunau-Varilla did not allow for that. They are the owners of the Canal Zone soil, just as a householder owns the title to his garden, and they possess all the rights of government, the Panamanians having specifically given up all claim to power or authority. But the United States was given those rights, even in 1963, only "*as if it were the sovereign of the territory.*" America did not acquire the Canal Zone in the sense that she acquired Alaska, say, or Hawaii. She enjoys no sovereign right of cession or conquest, which is why the Zone never became a territory of the United States. The American presence in Panama is analogous only to the Treaty Ports of pre-revolutionary China, where the several powers, while dimly recognizing the sovereignty of the Celestial Kingdom, ruled themselves and the local citizenry by their own laws and with their own authority. And just as the foreign garrisons, clubs, parks and department stores of Shanghai now seem like images of another age, so the American presence in the Canal Zone is already one of history's anachronisms.

Legally the Americans might maintain the status quo indefinitely. "We own this place," as one Canal Zone resident explained it to me, "it's as simple as that. It's ours for all time. It's a bit of America." Perhaps even a court of law, though, would not hold Panama to such an agreement, concluded in such doubtful circumstances, in such different times. The 1903 Treaty is a true text of the Imperial Age, presupposing that Western civilization would dominate mankind for centuries: but only a Frenchman and an American, perhaps, deciding between them the entire future of a third country, could make its provisions, like Rome herself, actually *eternal*! Even Hitler envisaged only a 1000-year Reich! Even Churchill, contemplating the British Empire's finest hour, gave it only a millennium!

> Take up the White Man's Burden,
> And reap his old reward
> The blame of those ye better
> The hate of those ye guard!

You must not suppose that I do not understand. I know the glory of the distant flag! I have heard the bugles call! From the island of Perico, at the Pacific end of the Canal, there is a magnificent view of Panama Bay and the Canal entrance. From there the scene looks immensely powerful. The city straggles eastward along the shore, ramparted and steepled at one end, skyscrapered at the other; the lawns and villas of the Canal Zone, topped with aerials and ringed around by harbor installations, run away to the west. The high steel arch of the Bridge of the Americas takes the Pan-American highway magnificently across the waterway, and through the humpbacked islands offshore, sometimes green and blue in the sunshine, sometimes black with sudden rainstorms, ships are always moving, steadily and silently out of the Pacific.

High on the flank of Perico, shut off by wire fences and severe injunctions (TRASH AND LITTER GENERATED IN THIS AREA WILL BE DEPOSITED IN YELLOW TRASH CANS) there stands an observation post, the first American station on the Pacific side; it has probably been there since the Canal was built. Its platforms are open-fronted and it perches on the hillside with a campaigning air, a hammocky, mosquito-net, semaphore and heliograph, sepia, Sam Browne air. I could not see if anyone was actually on watch beneath its eaves, when I went out there on my last afternoon in Panama, but I was powerfully moved anyway by the spectacle of that ever loyal lookout, ever watchful, ever faithful down the years. What generations of Americans looked proudly out from there, in the days when American power really was the hope and glory of the world! It seemed to me to stand in the truest line of the imperial monuments, the best of the genre, the line of the Khyber and Hadrian's Wall, the Saharan forts and the Venetian castles—the kind that make you wonder what kind of men once served their Empire there, how bravely they stood their ground, and how gracefully, when the time came, they pulled the flag down and departed. [1975]

NOTHING TO DECLARE

Mary Morris

Mary Morris (1947–present) is an American author and professor at New York's Sarah Lawrence College. Everything she writes marks a significant moment in her life, which is perhaps why *Nothing to Declare: Memoirs of a Woman Traveling Alone* was named one of the 20th century's top travel memoirs by Suite 101. She has, after all, infiltrated New Age groups in South America, crossed Siberia and sailed down the Mississippi in a houseboat, journeys with potential for many significant moments. But wherever she is, Mary feels the tug of the American Midwest – environmental magnetism is apparently very strong there.

The woman who ran the blue door bakery did have rooms to rent and at dusk the next day she took me to see them. We drove down the hill away from the center of town. We left the cobbled streets with bougainvillea vines and turned up a dirt road lined with mud huts, garbage, diseased animals, children in tattered rags. When I asked where we were going, she replied, "San Antonio." And that was all.

She was a cold, calculating person whom I would simply call "the Señora" and who'd take only cash for rent. In the middle of these slums in the neighborhood called San Antonio, the Señora had built some town houses. One of them had been vacated recently, and she showed it to me. It had a living room, kitchen, and small patio on the ground floor. Two bedrooms upstairs. Upstairs the front of the town house had French doors and a small balcony, but the back wall had no windows. I should have suspected that someone was building a house on the other side, but I did not. The sound of construction would punctuate my days. A small, winding staircase went to the roof, where I'd read and do the wash in the afternoons. From the roof

I could see the sierra—the pale lavender hills and the stretch of high desert, the cactus men and wildflowers.

It was the only place I considered. "I'll take it," I said.

I never would have moved to the neighborhood called San Antonio if I'd known better. For that part of town was different from the other parts. Very few Americans lived there. It was too far from the center of things. I would have to walk half an hour up a dusty hill to get to market. It was the poorest part; it was where the servants who served the wealthy lived and where others struggled just to get by. It was the dustiest, dirtiest place, where the Mexicans would call me "*gringita*" and my own mother, when she heard me describe it, would beg me to leave. I had no idea what I was doing when I moved into San Antonio. But I am grateful for the mistake I made.

I had come to Mexico with two suitcases and an electric typewriter, and the next day I brought them by taxi to my town house, whose name I noticed as I dragged my belongings from the cab: the *Departamentos Toros* (bull apartments). I am a Taurus and as I stood beneath the sign with the name of the apartment, I thought this must be a good omen, to move into a place named after my astrological sign. I spent the day settling in. But as dusk came, I realized I knew no one, was about a mile from town, and had no food in the house.

Climbing the winding stairs to the roof terrace, I saw the vast Mexican desert stretching before me, the sun setting in strips of brilliant scarlet across the horizon. The town with the pink steeple of the church seemed far away. I saw the birds—large, black, noisy birds—which every evening at dusk flew to the center of the town to stand guard over the promenade. And then, as I'd do many evenings after that, struck by the prospect of the evening alone, I followed them.

I changed my clothes, put on a pair of walking shoes, and headed up the hill—a climb I'd never get used to. But I went to the place where the birds were going. It seems I have always followed the birds, or have wanted to follow them. The loud chirps, thousands of them, grew piercing as I approached the jardín.

The birds were bedding down for the night and the promenade

was in process. I sat on a bench to watch. It is odd to sit in a place where you know absolutely no one. There was not a familiar face, not even the possibility of someone passing whom I might know. I was here a perfect stranger.

After a while I got up and headed down a road. I paused in front of a bar lit in amber. Inside Mexican men drank and laughed. There were no Mexican women, but there were a few Americans, so I thought it would be all right. I went in and ordered a beer. I sat for perhaps half an hour, until it grew dark. People were all around me and I thought to myself how I should try to make conversation, but I found I could think of nothing to say. I was sure that someone would come up to me and say something like, "Been in town long?" or "So where'd you come from?" But no one did. I ordered another beer and nursed it slowly, realizing I did not want to go home. I watched the people around me. Mexicans laughing and talking with blond American women. Other Americans huddled in corners. One man, whom I'd later know as Harold, sat in his pajamas, which he wore when he went on a binge.

I took it all in, and then, at about ten o'clock, I walked home. I descended the hill, toward the bus stop, until I reached the turnoff to San Antonio. At the turnoff is the dirt road, about a quarter mile long; it is walled on both sides. If you are attacked while walking down this road, you have no place to go.

For the first time, I walked that quarter mile at night alone. Every shadow, every sound, made me turn. I behaved like a hunted thing. It is not easy to move through the world alone, and it is never easy for a woman. You must keep your wits about you. You mustn't get yourself into dark places you can't get out of. Keep money you can get to, an exit behind you, and some language at your fingertips. You should know how to strike a proud pose, curse like a sailor, kick like a mule, and scream out your brother's name, though he may be three thousand miles away. And you mustn't be a fool.

Brace yourself for tremendous emptiness and great surprise. Anything can happen. The bad things that have occurred in my travels—and in my life in general—have happened because I wasn't prepared. At times I wonder that I am still alive.

WILD

Cheryl Strayed

Cheryl Strayed (1968–present) is an American memoirist, essayist, novelist and podcast host. Strayed has not sailed effortlessly through life – her mother's death affected her deeply, she was divorced and she struggled with eating disorders and heroin addiction. But she walked it all off, literally, trekking 1,100 miles along the Pacific Crest Trail, which follows the US West Coast, a 'wilderness path in our backyard'. *Wild*, her memoir of the experience, reached No.1 on the *New York Times* bestseller list and was adapted into a movie starring Reese Witherspoon.

Into a Primal Gear

Oregon was a hopscotch in my mind. I skipped it, spun it, leapt it in my imagination all the way from Crater Lake to the Bridge of the Gods. Eighty-five miles to my next box at a place called Shelter Cove Resort. One hundred and forty-three miles beyond that to my final box at Olallie Lake. Then I'd be on the home-stretch to the Columbia River: 106 miles to the town of Cascade Locks, with a stop for a holy-shit-I-can't-believe-I'm-almost-there drink at Timberline Lodge on Mount Hood at the midpoint of that final stretch.

But that still added up to 334 miles to hike.

The good thing, I quickly understood, was that no matter what happened in those 334 miles, there would be fresh berries along the way. Huckleberries and blueberries, salmonberries and blackberries, all of them plump for the picking for miles along the trail. I raked the bushes with my hands as I walked, sometimes stopping to fill my hat, as I made my way leisurely through the Mount Thielsen and Diamond Peak Wildernesses.

It was cold. It was hot. The tree-bark-plucked-dead-chicken flesh on my hips grew another layer. My feet stopped bleeding and blistering, but they still hurt like hell. I hiked a few half days, going only seven or eight miles in an effort to alleviate the pain, but it did little good. They hurt deep. Sometimes as I walked, it felt like they were actually broken, like they belonged in casts instead of boots. Like I'd done something profound and irreversible to them by carrying all this weight over so many miles of punishing terrain. This, and yet I was stronger than ever. Even with that tremendous pack of mine, I was capable of hammering out the big miles now, though at day's end I was still pretty much shattered.

The PCT had gotten easier for me, but that was different from it getting easy.

There were pleasant mornings and lovely swaths of afternoon, ten-mile stretches that I'd glide right over while barely feeling a thing. I loved getting lost in the rhythm of my steps and the click of my ski pole against the trail; the silence and the songs and sentences in my head. I loved the mountains and the rocks and the deer and rabbits that bolted off into the trees and the beetles and frogs that scrambled across the trail. But there would always come the point in each day when I didn't love it anymore, when it was monotonous and hard and my mind shifted into a primal gear that was void of anything but forward motion and I walked until walking became unbearable, until I believed I couldn't walk even one more step, and I stopped and made camp and efficiently did all the tasks that making camp required, all in an effort to get as quickly as possible to the blessed moment when I could collapse, utterly demolished, in my tent.

That's how I felt by the time I dragged into the Shelter Cove Resort: spent and bored with the trail, empty of every single thing except gratitude I was there. I'd hopped another of my squares in the Oregon hopscotch. Shelter Cove Resort was a store surrounded by a rustic set of cabins on a wide green lawn that sat on the shore of a big lake called Odell that was rimmed by green forests. I stepped onto the porch of the store and went inside. There were short rows of snacks and fishing lures and a cooler with drinks inside. I found a bottle of Snapple lemonade, got a bag of chips, and walked to the counter.

"You a PCT hiker?" the man who stood behind the cash register asked me. When I nodded, he gestured to a window at the back of the store. "The post office is closed until tomorrow morning, but you can camp for free at a spot we've got nearby. And there are showers that'll cost you a buck."

I had only ten dollars left—as I'd now come to expect, my stops in Ashland and Crater Lake National Park had been pricier than I'd imagined they'd be—but I knew I had twenty dollars in the box I'd get the next morning, so when I handed the man my money to pay for the drink and the chips, I asked him for some quarters for the shower.

Outside, I cracked open the lemonade and chips and ate them as I made my way toward the little wooden bathhouse the man had pointed out, my anticipation tremendous. When I stepped inside, I was pleased to see that it was a one-person affair. I locked the door behind me, and it was my own domain. I'd have slept inside it if they'd let me. I took off my clothes and looked at myself in the scratched-up mirror. It wasn't only my feet that had been destroyed by the trail, but it seemed my hair had been too—made coarser and strangely doubled in thickness, sprung alive by layers of dried sweat and trail dust, as if I were slowly but surely turning into a cross between Farrah Fawcett in her glory days and Gunga Din at his worst.

I put my coins in the little coin box, stepped into the shower, and luxuriated under the hot water, scrubbing myself with the sliver of soap someone had left there until it dissolved completely in my hands. Afterwards, I dried off with the same bandanna I used to wash my cooking pot and spoon with lake and creek water and dressed again in my dirty clothes. I hoisted Monster on and walked back to the store feeling a thousand times better. There was a wide porch in front with a long bench that ran along its sides. I sat down on it and looked out at Odell Lake while brushing my wet hair with my fingers. Olallie Lake and then Timberline Lodge and then Cascade Locks, I was thinking.

Skip, hop, spin, done.

"Are you Cheryl?" a man asked as he came out of the store. Within a moment, two other men had stepped out behind him. I knew immediately by their sweat-stained T-shirts they were PCT hikers, though they didn't have their packs. They were young and handsome, bearded and tan and dirty, equal parts incredibly muscular and incredibly thin. One was tall. One was blond. One had intense eyes.

I was so very glad I'd taken that shower.

"Yes," I said.

"We've been following you a long way," said the blond one, a smile blooming across his thin face.

"We knew we were going to catch you today," said the one with the intense eyes. "We saw your tracks on the trail."

"We've been reading your notes in the trail register," added the tall one.

"We were trying to figure out how old you'd be," said the blond one.

"How old did you think I'd be?" I asked, smiling like a maniac.

"We thought either about our age or fifty," said the one with the intense eyes.

"I hope you're not disappointed," I said, and we laughed and blushed.

They were Rick, Josh, and Richie, all of them three or four years younger than me. They were from Portland, Eugene, and New Orleans, respectively. They'd all gone to college together at an insular Minnesota liberal arts school an hour outside the Twin Cities.

"I'm from Minnesota!" I exclaimed when they told me, but they knew that already, from my notes in the trail register.

"You don't have a trail name yet?" one of them asked me.

"Not that I know of," I said.

They had a trail name: the Three Young Bucks, which they'd been given by other hikers in southern California, they told me. The name fit. They were three young and buckish men. They'd come all the way from the Mexican border. They hadn't skipped the snow like everyone else. They'd hiked over it, right through it—regardless of the fact that it was a record snow year—and because they'd done so, they were at the back of the Mexico-to-Canada thru-hiker pack, which is how, at this late date, they'd met me. They hadn't met Tom, Doug, Greg, Matt, Albert, Brent, Stacy, Trina, Rex, Sam, Helen, John, or Sarah. They hadn't even stopped in Ashland. They hadn't danced to the Dead or eaten chewable opium or had sex with anyone pressed up against a rock on a beach. They'd just plowed right on through, hiking twenty-some miles a day, gaining on me since the moment I'd leapfrogged north of them when I'd bypassed to Sierra City. They weren't just three young bucks. They were three young extraordinary hiking machines.

Being in their company felt like a holiday.

We walked to the campsite the store set aside for us, where the Three Young Bucks had already ditched their packs, and we cooked dinner and talked and told stories about things both on and off the trail. I liked them immensely. We clicked. They were sweet, cute, funny, kind guys and they made me forget how ruined I'd felt just an hour before. In their honor, I made the freeze-dried raspberry cobbler I'd been carrying for weeks, saving it for a special occasion. When it was done, we ate it with four spoons from my pot and then slept in a row under the stars.

In the morning, we collected our boxes and took them back to our camp to reorganize our packs before heading on. I opened my box and pushed my hands through the smooth ziplock bags of food, feeling for the envelope that would contain my twenty-dollar bill. It had become such a familiar thrill for me now, that envelope with the money inside, but this time I couldn't find it. I dumped everything out and ran my fingers along the folds inside the box, searching for it, but it wasn't there. I didn't know why. It just wasn't. I had six dollars and twelve cents.

"Shit," I said.

"What?" asked one of the Young Bucks.

"Nothing," I said. It was embarrassing to me that I was constantly broke, that no one was standing invisibly behind me with a credit card or a bank account.

I loaded my food into my old blue bag, sick with the knowledge that I'd have to hike 143 miles to my next box with only six dollars and twelve cents in my pocket. At least I didn't need money where I was going, I reasoned, in order to calm myself. I was heading through the heart of Oregon—over Willamette Pass and McKenzie Pass and Santiam Pass, through the Three Sisters and Mount Washington and Mount Jefferson Wildernesses—and there'd be no place to spend my six dollars and twelve cents anyway, right?

I hiked out an hour later with the Three Young Bucks, crisscrossing with them all day; occasionally we stopped together for breaks.

I was amazed by what they ate and how they ate it. They were like barbarians loose upon the land, shoving three Snickers bars apiece into their mouths on a single fifteen-minute break, though they were thin as sticks. When they took off their shirts, their ribs showed right through. I'd lost weight too, but not as much as the men—an unjust pattern I'd observed across the board in the other male and female hikers I'd met that summer as well—but I didn't much care anymore whether I was fat or thin. I cared only about getting more food. I was a barbarian too, my hunger voracious and monumental. I'd reached the point where if a character in one of the novels I was reading happened to be eating, I had to skip over the scene because it simply hurt too much to read about what I wanted and couldn't have.

I said goodbye to the Three Young Bucks that afternoon. They were going to push on a few miles past where I planned to camp because in addition to being three young incredible hiking machines, they were eager to reach Santiam Pass, where they'd be getting off the trail for a few days to visit friends and family. While they were living it up, showering and sleeping in actual beds and eating foods I didn't even want to imagine, I'd get ahead of them again and they'd once more be following my tracks.

"Catch me if you can," I said, hoping they would, sad to part ways with them so soon. I camped alone near a pond that evening still aglow from having met them, thinking about the stories they'd told me, as I massaged my feet after dinner. Another one of my blackened toenails was separating from my toe. I gave it a tug and it came all the way off. I tossed it into the grass.

Now the PCT and I were tied. The score was 5–5.

I sat in my tent with my feet propped up on my food bag, reading the book I'd gotten in my box—Maria Dermoût's *The Ten Thousand Things*—until I couldn't keep my eyes open anymore. I turned off my headlamp and lay in the dark. As I dozed off, I heard an owl in a tree directly overhead. *Who-whoo, who-whoo*, it hooted with a call that was at once so strong and so gentle that I woke up.

"Who-whoo," I called back to it, and the owl was silent.

"Who-whoo," I tried again.

"Who-whoo," it replied.

*

I hiked into the Three Sisters Wilderness, named for the South, North, and Middle Sister mountains in its boundaries. Each of the Sister peaks was more than 10,000 feet high, the third-, fourth-, and fifth-highest peaks in Oregon. They were the crown jewels among a relatively close gathering of volcanic peaks I'd be passing in the coming week, but I couldn't see them yet as I approached from the south on the PCT, singing songs and reciting scraps of poems in my head as I hiked through a tall forest of Douglas firs, white pines, and mountain hemlocks, past lakes and ponds.

A couple of days after I'd said goodbye to the Three Young Bucks, I took a detour a mile off the trail to the Elk Lake Resort, a place mentioned in my guidebook. It was a little lakeside store that catered to fishermen, much like the Shelter Cove Resort, only it had a café that served burgers. I hadn't planned to make the detour, but when I reached the trail junction on the PCT, my endless hunger won out. I arrived just before eleven in the morning. I was the only person in the place aside from the man who worked there. I scanned the menu, did the math, and ordered a cheeseburger and fries and a small Coke; then I sat eating them in a rapture, backed by walls lined with fishing lures. My bill was six dollars and ten cents. For the first time in my entire life, I couldn't leave a tip. To leave the two pennies I had left would've seemed an insult. I pulled out a little rectangle of stamps I had in the ziplock bag that held my driver's license and placed it near my plate.

"I'm sorry—I don't have anything extra, but I left you something else," I said, too embarrassed to say what it was.

The man only shook his head and murmured something I couldn't make out.

I walked down to the empty little beach along Elk Lake with the two pennies in my hand, wondering if I should toss them into the water and make a wish. I decided against it and put them in my shorts pocket, just in case I needed two cents between now and the Olallie Lake ranger station, which was still a sobering hundred miles away. Having nothing more than those two pennies was both horrible and just the slightest bit funny, the way being flat broke at times seemed to me. As I stood there gazing at Elk Lake, it occurred to me for the first time that growing up poor had come in handy. I probably wouldn't have been fearless enough to go on such a trip with so little money if I hadn't grown up without it. I'd always thought of my family's economic standing in terms of what I didn't get: camp and lessons and travel and college tuition and the inexplicable ease that comes when you've got access to a credit card that someone else is paying off. But now I could see the line between this and that—between a childhood in which I saw my mother and stepfather forging ahead over and over again with two pennies in their pocket and my own general sense that I could do it too. Before I left, I hadn't calculated how much my journey would reasonably be expected to cost and saved up that amount plus enough to be my cushion against unexpected expenses. If I'd done that, I wouldn't have been here, eighty-some days out on the PCT, broke, but okay—getting to do what I wanted to do even though a reasonable person would have said I couldn't afford to do it.

I hiked on, ascending to a 6,500-foot viewpoint from which I could see the peaks to the north and east: Bachelor Butte and glaciated Broken Top and—highest of them all—South Sister, which rose to 10,358 feet. My guidebook told me that it was the youngest, tallest, and most symmetrical of the Three Sisters. It was composed of over two dozen different kinds of volcanic rock, but it all looked like one reddish-brown mountain to me, its upper slopes laced with snow. As I hiked into the day, the air shifted and warmed again and I felt as if I were back in California, with the heat and the way the vistas opened up for miles across the rocky and green land.

Now that I was officially among the Three Sisters, I didn't have the trail to myself anymore. On the high rocky meadows I passed day hikers and short-term backpackers and a Boy Scout troop out for an overnight. I stopped to talk to some of them. *Do you have a gun? Are you afraid?* they asked in an echo of what I'd been hearing all summer. *No, no*, I said, laughing a little. I met a pair of men my age who'd served in Iraq during Desert Storm and were still in the army, both of them captains. They were clean-cut, strapping, and handsome, seemingly straight off a recruitment poster. We took a long afternoon break together near a creek, into which they'd placed two cans of beer to cool. It was their last night out on a five-day trip. They'd hauled those two cans the whole time so they could drink them on the final night to celebrate.

They wanted to know everything about my trip. How it felt to walk all those days; the things I'd seen and the people I'd met and what in the hell had happened to my feet. They insisted on lifting my pack and were stupefied to find that it was heavier than either of theirs. They got ready to hike away and I wished them well, still lounging in the sun on the creek's bank.

"Hey, Cheryl," one of them turned to holler once he was almost out of sight on the trail. "We left one of the beers for you in the creek. We did it this way so you can't say no. We *want* you to have it 'cause you're tougher than us."

I laughed and thanked them and went down to the creek to retrieve it, feeling flattered and lifted. I drank the beer that night near Obsidian Falls, which was named for the jet-black glass shards that wondrously cover the trail, making each step an ever-shifting clatter beneath me, as if I were walking across layers upon layers of broken china.

I was less wonder-struck the next day as I walked over McKenzie Pass into the Mount Washington Wilderness, and the trail became rockier still as I crossed the basalt flows of Belknap Crater and Little Belknap. These weren't pretty shiny shards of rock among spring green meadows. Now I was walking over a five-mile swath of black volcanic rocks that ranged in size from baseball to soccer ball, my ankles and knees constantly twisting. The landscape was exposed and desolate, the sun searing relentlessly down on me as I struggled along in the direction of Mount Washington. When I made it to the other side of the craters, I walked gratefully among the trees and realized the crowds had disappeared. I was alone again, just the trail and me.

The following day I hiked over Santiam Pass and crossed into the Mount Jefferson Wilderness, named for the dark and stately summit to my north. I hiked past the rocky multipeaked Three Fingered Jack, which rose like a fractured hand into the sky, and continued hiking into the evening as the sun disappeared behind a blanket of clouds and a thick mist slowly enveloped me. The day had been hot, but within thirty minutes the temperature dropped 20 degrees as the wind picked up and then suddenly stilled. I walked as quickly as I could up the trail, the sweat dripping from my body in spite of the chill, searching for a place to camp. It was precariously close to dark, but there was no place flat or clear enough to pitch my tent. By the time I found a spot near a small pond, it was as if I were inside a cloud, the air eerily still and silent. In the time it took me to pitch my tent and filter a bottle of water with my insufferably slow water purifier, the wind started up again in great violent gasps, whipping the branches of the trees overhead. I'd never been in a mountain storm. *I'm not afraid*, I reminded myself as I crawled into my tent without eating dinner, feeling too vulnerable outside, though I knew my tent offered little protection. I sat in expectant wonder and fear, bracing for a mighty storm that never came.

An hour after dark, the air went still again and I heard coyotes yipping in the distance, as if they were celebrating the fact that the coast was clear. August had turned to September; the temperatures at night were almost always bitingly cold. I got out of my tent to pee, wearing my hat and gloves. When I scanned the trees with my headlamp, they caught on something, and I froze as the reflection of two bright pairs of eyes gazed back at me.

I never found out whose they were. An instant later they were gone.

PART SEVEN

SOUTH AMERICA

ALONE IN THE SKY

Jean Batten

Jean Batten (1909–1982) was a New Zealand-born aviatrix. Inspired by the record-breaking flights being made in the 1920s, she travelled to England and learned to fly. She purloined money from a string of hopeful, but ultimately disappointed, young men to fund her expeditions, flying from England to Australia in 1934, across the South Atlantic in 1935, and making the first ever direct flight from England to New Zealand, solo, in 1936. She blazed a trail for modern airline routes, yet died in obscurity. But she'd had her moment in the sun, and *Alone in the Sky* is the story of those glory years.

Rio de Janeiro

On arrival at Natal I had considered the idea of flying on to New York and seeing the United States, but owing to the further expense involved decided instead to fly southward and see Rio de Janeiro, Montevideo, and Buenos Aires before shipping the Gull back to England.

The flight southward was an interesting one: storms had been forecast, but I was not expecting the series of fierce tropical rainstorms which I encountered. More than once I nearly turned back. The storms, although of almost monsoonal intensity, did not extend over a very great area, however, and it seldom took more than ten or fifteen minutes to fly through any of them. On one occasion, flying low over the tree-tops, I opened the windows, for the heat was intense and great columns of steam arose from the hot jungle. A strong exotic perfume was wafted into the cabin, and I realized that among the trees of the steaming jungle must be thousands of glorious orchids. Often I would look down and search the dark green, tropical vegetation for some glimpse of the lovely flowers. Although I knew that some of the rarest orchids were to be found growing on the tree-tops there was no sign of their exquisite colouring in the jungle beneath. Here and there I would see great purple patches of bourgainvillæa.

Gazing down on the tropical vegetation as mile after mile slipped by on the long flight southward, I began to realize the vastness of the great country to which I had flown. I tried to remember some of the overwhelming details I had come across while studying the flying conditions in Brazil before setting out from England. The fourth largest country in the world, with an area of 3,300,000 square miles, approximately four-fifths the size of Europe, with a seaboard of 4000 miles, there seemed very little that the great country was unable to produce. With the rarest of orchids and exquisite Morpho blue butterflies (whose wings are used for jewellery), the wonderful mineral riches and infinite variety of precious gems, the huge coffee and cotton plantations, great cattle stations, and the thousand million acres of timber-producing forest area which form only a percentage of its vast natural resources Brazil seems to the flyer a world in itself. I remembered how my host at Natal had smiled at my disappointment when it was found that there was no room for the huge pineapples which had been brought to the aerodrome for me. "Perhaps it will be alright there," I said, balancing one of the large fruits on top of the auxiliary oil-tank, where it had looked so comical. Realizing that it might fall forward and interfere with the controls I reluctantly removed it from the cockpit. There were plenty of pineapples to be had in Rio, my friend assured me. A ripple of amusement ran round the crowd at my astonishment on learning that nearly ninety million pineapples were exported each year from Brazil.

Innumerable little islands dotted some of the great rivers as they curved towards the Atlantic. Flying low over them, I searched vainly for a glimpse of any crocodiles such as I had seen on my flights over Sumatra, in the Dutch East Indies. There was no sign of life, however, but swimming in the deep waters were probably shoals of the deadly little Pirana fish which live in many of the Brazilian rivers. These fish, although so tiny, swim in vast shoals and are particularly vicious. They set upon any living thing entering the water, and within a few minutes will have nibbled every ounce of flesh off the bones. One story I heard was of a man who, when trying to cross a river, was attacked by a shoal of these fish and dragged under the water. Only a few hours later his skeleton was found without a single piece of flesh left on the bones.

One of the most interesting-looking cities over which I flew was San Salvador, or Bahia as it was marked on my map. There were innumerable churches to be seen, and it is said that at one time there was a church for every day of the year. I believe the full name of this city, the third largest in Brazil, is Bahia de São Salvador de todos os Santos, meaning "Bay of the Holy Saviour of all Saints." At one time Bahia was the capital of Brazil, long before Rio de Janeiro was discovered by the Portuguese sailors, who thought that the harbour was the mouth of a great river and named it Rio de Janeiro—"River of January."

Flying over Bahia I saw that it was built partly on the side of the bay and partly on a plateau about two hundred feet high. Connecting the lower part of the town to the upper I could see a high white lift. It appeared to be a very prosperous town, and I learned later that it is the centre of the cocoa and tobacco trades, also that it was from Bahia that the navel orange was transplanted to California.

Only fifty miles north of Rio a bad petrol leak exhausted my fuel supply; fortunately I was able to land safely on a beach. I telegraphed to Rio, and kind military pilots from the Campo dos Affonsos air base brought succour on this occasion. When the thirsty Gull was replenished I flew on to the Brazilian capital.

Never shall I forget the magnificent scene which met my eyes when I arrived over Rio de Janeiro. The sun was setting, and the last rays picked out the red wings of the escorting military Waco biplanes, which followed the Gull in perfect formation. As we crossed a promontory where the green-clad mountains rose sheer from the sea I suddenly beheld a sight which made me hold my breath. Rio de Janeiro… lovely, colourful, unbelievably beautiful Rio… well worth flying nearly seven thousand miles from London to see. The great blue harbour was shown on my map as being about fifteen miles long by seven wide. Rising sheer to a height of 1000 feet at the entrance of the harbour was a great granite rock, which I immediately recognized as the famous Sugar Loaf. Many green-clad islands dotted the harbour, looking almost like peaks of some subterranean mountain range. On a strip of land about six miles long between the great jungle-covered mountains and the sea lay the city of Rio de Janeiro. It looked almost as if the towering mountains had drawn back to allow the gem of a city to be displayed in this superb setting. Accentuated by the last rays of the sun, the Organ Mountains, thirty miles away, looked close enough for me to lean out of the cabin window and touch one of the fantastic peaks, soaring over 7000 feet into the sky, to earn the apt description of "the fingers of God." Towering above the palatial villas, gardens, and plazas in the centre of the city was a jagged rocky peak—the Corcovado (Hunchback) Mountain, well over 2000 feet in height. As I gazed in wonderment at the great mountain I was fascinated and could scarcely believe my eyes, for on the summit stood a gigantic white figure of Christ, completely dominating the city.

The city was suddenly transformed into a fairy city, for almost as if by magic myriads of tiny white lights flashed on. Rio… exquisitely beautiful by day, wondrously so by night. The thousands of lights outlined the city, and hung like festoons round all the silvery beaches and coves. In the fast-fading light I could just distinguish the long promenades, and the wide, straight line of the most beautiful of all avenues, the Avenida Rio Branco, over a mile in length, with its three rows of tall, stately palm-trees.

There was a large crowd at the military aerodrome of Campo dos Affonsos. As I landed and taxied up to the tarmac the aeroplane was quickly surrounded by enthusiastic people, while dozens of cameras clicked a welcome. From that moment until I left Rio and flew on to Buenos Aires some days later I received the most wonderful hospitality from the people in Rio, including a large number of British residents. A big reception was given at the British Embassy. The scene was one of great brilliance, for there were many lovely women present, and their beautiful gowns and jewellery were admirably set off by the smart uniforms of the men. I learned that the British Ambassador, Sir Hugh Gurney, was to present me to the President of the Republic of Brazil, Dr Vargas, who had taken a great interest in my flight from England to his country.

High up in the mountains, at a restaurant set amid the most glorious scenery, with a superb view of the vast Atlantic, a luncheon was given in my honour by Colonel Ivor Borges and the officers of the military air force and their wives. As I turned my gaze from the magnificent scenery and walked on to the wide, cool verandah I was deeply moved by the genuine enthusiasm and the smiling faces around me. The scene was again a brilliant one, the women in their bright colours looking like so many orchids amid the smart gold-trimmed white uniforms of the officers. It was announced that I was to be made an honorary officer of the military airforce, and I felt very proud of the lovely gold badge which was presented to me.

That night a dinner was given by the Royal Empire Society at which several hundred people were present, including the British Ambassador and Lady Gurney. Speeches were made by the President and the Ambassador, and I felt deeply moved by the poetic text of a speech delivered by the head of the Brazilian Press, who spoke in fluent English. During the evening I was presented with an exquisite Brazilian diamond set in a platinum brooch by the British community as a token of admiration for my flight, which, it was said, not only demonstrated the capability of the modern aeroplane and engine, but did a great deal for British prestige in South America.

The following day I visited the Director of Civil Aviation and heard all about the new aerodrome being made in Rio. The site for this aerodrome, which was already in course of construction, was on a promontory near the wide Avenida Rio Branco, and almost in the heart of the city. Part of the harbour was being reclaimed, and the aerodrome when finished promised to be one of the largest and most modern in the world. "You must fly back to Brazil when it is ready," the smiling Director of Aviation said, as he gave me a design of the projected airport.

Just before leaving I learned that the *fonctionnaires*—the girls working in the Department of Aviation—wished to meet me. I was delighted by the warmth of their welcome as they crowded round and congratulated me. Suddenly there was a hush, and the group of pretty Brazilian girls parted to allow their spokeswoman to come forward. Although she spoke in Portuguese it was not difficult for me to interpret the words, for her dark eyes alone were eloquent enough. She handed me a small case, and on opening it I saw a lovely aquamarine. The girls were pleased at my appreciation of their gift as I gazed entranced at the gem. Resting on the pale satin lining of the case it resembled the translucent blue of the water lapping up on to the creamy beaches of Rio, where its shallowness and transparency toned the sapphire shade of the deeper waters to pastel tints.

A visit to the headquarters of the naval air force followed, and to my joy I learned that it was the intention of the Aviação Naval to make me an honorary officer in the force. The naval air base was on the large island of Gobernador, and I found that British aeroplanes were used for training purposes.

The following morning a flight of aeroplanes from the naval base flew over to the military aerodrome of Campo dos Affonsos, and officially I was presented with the gold wings and diploma making me an honorary officer of the force. The Colonel and officers were very charming, and I accompanied them back to their base in my own aeroplane. It was a glorious afternoon, and the city was bathed in strong sunlight, so before returning to the military aerodrome I decided to fly once more over Rio and explore the numerous little beaches, coves, and islands with which the great harbour abounds. Leaving the island of Gobernador and the naval base I flew first round the Sugar Loaf rock, guarding the entrance to the harbour, then low along the silver strand of the Copacabana beach. Speeding back, I passed once again over Rio, along the palm-lined *avenidas*, and circled the site for the new airport. I put the machine into a climb and soon gained height, then at an altitude of well over two thousand feet flew round the shoulders of the giant statue of Christ on top of the Corcovado Mountain. At close quarters it appeared to dwarf everything in the city so far below. I felt almost awed by the immensity of the majestic figure, standing as it does two hundred feet high on the peak of the mighty Corcovado. Gliding down again, I flew for miles up the harbour, passing over unbelievably beautiful little palm-fringed islands encircled by silvery beaches. On some of the islands were coconut plantations, and I could see the tall graceful palms clustered closely together as if afraid of slipping into the limpid sapphire water surrounding them.

Turning back at length to the military aerodrome I landed, and then drove into Rio.

An English lady kindly offered to lend me several light frocks, for the costume I had brought with me was too warm for Rio. The heat seemed very sudden, for only a few days previously I had left the chilly autumn of the Northern Hemisphere. It was with a very critical eye that I surveyed the gowns, for that day was to be a momentous one in my life. I was to be presented to the President of Brazil that afternoon, so the selection of a suitable frock had assumed a position of great importance. I chose a pale pink linen frock with white organdie trimming.

With a spray or orchids adorning it I went to join the Ambassador at the appointed hour. We drove along the wide, palm-lined *avenidas* to the President's house. On entering we were shown into a large cool room with a highly polished parquet floor. The furniture was upholstered in brocade, and between the large gilt-framed mirrors on the walls were several portraits in oils. An attaché in a dazzling white uniform embroidered with gold cord escorted us into another room, where we awaited an audience with the President. It was only a matter of a few minutes before the door opened and a man wearing a tropical suit advanced and warmly greeted the Ambassador. It was President Vargas. On being presented I found him very friendly and unaffected as he spoke to me of my flight and congratulated me on the record I had established. He said that the Brazilian nation wished officially to show its appreciation of my achievement. It had been decided to confer on me the decoration of Officer of the Order of the Southern Cross in recognition of my flight, which had linked England with Brazil in the fastest time in history. Taking a green and gold leather case from the desk by his side the President opened the box and produced the insignia of the Order of the Cruzeiro do Sul. It was a gold cross with a centre medallion of blue enamel, on which were embossed in gold the stars of the Southern Cross constellation. The cross was joined to a pale blue ribbon by a green enamel link representing a laurel wreath. Pinning the decoration to the bodice of my dress the President shook my hand warmly. The first British woman other than Royalty to receive this decoration—no wonder I felt pleased. Although the

President was such a busy man he courteously agreed to pose for a photograph, which was taken on the terrace of his beautiful house.

The following day I drove to the aerodrome and made preparations for refuelling the aeroplane, as I had received cordial invitations to visit both Uruguay and Argentina before leaving South America.

I felt very reluctant to leave Rio de Janeiro, for apart from the fascination I felt for the beautiful city I had made many friends and enjoyed wonderful hospitality during my stay. Although it was very early when I arrived at the aerodrome a large crowd had assembled to see me take off on my flight to Buenos Aires, 1350 miles farther south. As strong head winds were predicted I wished to take off at dawn in order to arrive at Buenos Aires in daylight.

The aeroplane looked like burnished steel when it was wheeled out on to the tarmac, for it had been carefully washed and polished, and the windows and metal fittings were gleaming. The blue-and-green star symbol of the Brazilian Air Force had been painted on the rudder, and I had never seen the Gull look so smart. A squadron of aeroplanes was to escort me for a few miles, and the Colonel had detailed a fighter aircraft to accompany my aeroplane as far as Santos, 200 miles south-west of Rio. After shaking hands with friends and bidding them good-bye I was just about to step into my aeroplane when an officer hurried forward and asked me to wait for a few minutes, as the Colonel wished to make a presentation. Almost before the officer had finished speaking the Colonel appeared and walked across the tarmac towards us. He was carrying something in his arms, and as he drew near I saw that it was a bronze statue. "On behalf of the officers of the Aviação Militar I wish to present you with this trophy as a token of our great admiration of your magnificent flight from England," said the Colonel.

I looked at the statue which he presented to me. It was a beautifully wrought bronze female figure. She was poised on a globe representing the world on which were embossed the stars of the Southern Cross. In one hand was an olive branch of peace, and in the other a scroll on which the words "Conquête de l'Air" were written. The statue was mounted on Brazilian marble, and a gold plate bore a suitable inscription.

I was quite sure that all the British people present felt as proud as myself at this signal honour. "I wish it was possible to take the statue with me," I said.

"Yes, do," said some one in the crowd, who added, "then your aeroplane won't take off and you will have to stay in Rio."

"That's a very good idea," I replied laughingly, and handed back the lovely trophy, which was so heavy that I could scarcely lift it.

It was arranged that the statue would be safely packed and sent to England for me. Thanking the Colonel for the beautiful present, and once again for the kindness I had received from the Aviação Militar, I said good-bye and climbed into the cockpit. Waving a final farewell I taxied to the end of the aerodrome, and took off to join the squadron of military Waco aeroplanes circling overhead. Rounding the high mountain almost overhanging the aerodrome I drew level with the other machines and recognized the pilots, whom I now knew quite well. We flew in formation for some distance, then one by one the escorting machines drew close to my aeroplane, while the pilots waved a last good-bye and flashed back to the aerodrome.

UNPUBLISHED WRITINGS

Adela Breton

Adela Breton (1849–1923) was an English explorer and archaeological artist. She grew up in Bath, famed for its Roman remains, so an interest in archaeology was born early. She was also artistic, and had an 'inherent propensity to wander', so she headed for Mexico. She rode around, demurely side-saddle, with her trusty guide, Pablo, although an observer wrote: '... her appearance is utterly at variance with her real self. She seems to court discomfort at any cost.' She painted ruined temples and life-size replicas of the wall paintings of the Aztecs, and since many of these have since faded, historians remain grateful to her. She left no book, only a collection of unpublished writings.

A Letter from Adela Breton to Frederic Ward Putnam from Zinapecuaro, Michoacán, Mexico

Sept. 7th

Dear Professor Putnam,

I have to thank you very much for sending me a pamphlet on symbolism in American art. It is most interesting, the drawings so good, and I only wish it contained more of the original paper – have any of your workers made a collection of the portraits of Quetzalcoatl? I see one as the feathered snake among your illustrations – there are a good many scattered among the various codex, also a small gold one in the Museum of Mexico, a statue of him with blue eyes at the Castillo de Teano near Tihuatlan, State of Vera Cruz, and doubtless many others. I have one of the small terracotta figures from Sahuano, Lake Chapala, which is entirely intended for him—

I am very vexed to hear from your secretary that you wrote me a letter which has gone astray. Mexican post offices are not what they should be—

I have sent you some pieces of obsidian from the old workings here, on the chance that you may care for them. There are a quantity about the size to hold in the hand, rounded, and look as if they had been used as hammers.

I have sent two – the workings are on a hill close to this town, and consist of pits like wells, some of which communicate by horizontal galleries, and three small caves, now much filled up with earth washed in. Great mounds of obsidian debris over the surface, and complete absence of the so-called 'cores', just as I have noticed in all the workings I have examined, except the island in the lake of Magdalene, about which I wrote to you. I have sent you a box, with a few scraps from the ancient site, which is about 3 miles away or rather one of the sites, the chief. There are several hills which have been fortified, and have remains of buildings, and one has two large stone mounds on a levelled platform on top. One of them is said to have a chamber (or cave) under it, with steps down, and skulls have been found there, but as the entrance changes its position (!) it is not easy to find, and I have made 3 trials in vain. The grass and bushes are now thick, and fields covered with maize, so it is not a good time for hunting for small objects. I have sent some small chips of obsidian because though some are doubtless mere fragments, others look as if they had been painted purposely for use and they are curiously blunt, instead of having the usual sharp edges. Tzinapecuaro means 'place of obsidian' in Tarasco and was the chief place for obtaining it in Michoacán, but I have not found any really good worked pieces. I should imagine that it was inhabited very early, as though it is in 'tierra fuega' it is very sheltered, and there are a number of hot springs near and the sierra for hunting, and lake Cuitzeo for fishing, so an experienced person might find paleolithic implements. How do you distinguish them (except by position) from unfinished Neolithic implements? Some of those figured in one of the books you gave me look the same as those one finds scattered about Mexico. I sent you a broken stone implement – at least I suppose it broken, but all those I have found are the same size, and they could scarcely always break at the same place. It seems a pity to leave them lying about the fields—

Sept. 22 All this time I have not been able to send this as I have been suffering from fever and fatigue. It is very difficult to keep well in this country, except on the gulf side, where the Northerns keep the air fresh. In other parts, it seems permanently infected with fever and influenza—

I spent July at Patzcuaro, hoping to study the Tarasco people, but both my servant and I had more or less fever all the time. I went several times to the ancient capital Tzintzuntzan. It seems to have been a very large place, and part of it, the palaces and yácatas and fortress, are on the opposite side of a volcanic mountain round which the houses and gardens must have been—

Of course an Indian town does cover a great deal of ground when each house stands like a little farm in its fields and distance is nothing to these people – the postman at Zacapu walks 16 leagues a day, 6 days in the week over a rough hilly road with no shade – and they think nothing of 20 or 22 leagues. The soldiers are expected to march that.

It does seem a pity to call these varied nations 'Indians' – the Tarascos are a thoroughly Mongol type, and the Chichimeca, who are mixed up with them, are also not in the least one's idea of 'Indians'. However, I suppose the popular idea of an 'Indian' is a personage who wears feathers and smokes a calumet, and lives in a 'lodge' and talks about 'braves'. The Tarascos seem to have smoked much more than the Tlaxcala people, as the remains of pipes are much more common, and some are in the style of the mound pipes—

I have now come on to Valle de Santiago, in the state of Guanaxuato. The interest here is geological as there are several enormous craters containing lakes, close to the town. These Spanish-built towns are far less interesting than the real old ones as regards the people and I was suspicious to find here, one of the old Indian dances still surviving. It was performed on the National festival, the dancers wearing silvery crowns surmounted by feathers quite in the traditional style—

At Zapotlan, Jalisco, now called Ciudad Guzmán in Holy Week, the Indians make the most beautiful palm-like arrangements of flowers which look like feathers to carry in the processions. They gave quite an idea of how gorgeous the ancient decorations must have been—

In coming round Lake Cuitzeo on my way here, I stopped at a town called Sant' Ana Maya. The people looked Maya, and some one had a wonderful talent for Mosaic, which adorned the borders of the flowerbeds in the public garden.

I sent you rough copies of sketches of two of the figures from the mound of Guadalupe. You may have correspondents at Guadalajara who could get them for you, if you cared to have them for the museum. They are much broken as to arms and legs and I thought them dear at 5 dollars each, Mexican. But the tattooing seemed interesting and they are marvellous well finished as regards individual character. There was a very good one of a woman which I had not time to copy. The railway was to be finished part of the way by now, and there is also a stage which runs to Itzatlan, only a few miles from the Hacienda of Guadalupe, where the figures are kept. There are also quantities of shell ornaments from the Mound – A great many figures from it have already been dispersed which is the greatest pity. It is 2 days ride from Guadalajara to Itzatlan by Teuchitlán and Ahualulco. Please excuse this long letter. If you do not care to keep the sketches and plans, would you kindly send them to Major Breton R.E. Horseguards, Whitehall, London, England.

Believe me
Yours Faithfully,
Adela Breton

Extract from Adela Breton's diaries, as sent to Alfred Tozzer

Chichen days

1900. February 20 to April 1. Nearly died of fever, ticks and hunger. Took the Maudslay plates of sculptured Chamber E [the Lower Temple] and coloured them, the colour being often visible in the hollows of the reliefs, or sunk into the stone where the surface is weathered. It also varies according to the light.

In Temple A [the Upper Temple] traced and coloured the southern part of west wall frescoes and the piece over the door. Went over carefully the Maudslay plates, [for his great book on Mexican archaeology], for corrections and compared the inscription in Casa Colorada with the plate. Made a careful coloured drawing with full details, of the façade of the Monjas annexe. Stayed part of the time in the Akab Tzib. (Visited Uxmal)

1901. (To Izamal and Ake) At Chichen Jan 24 to March 8. Continued copying colours and correcting Maudslay plates. Stayed in Akab Tzib. Pitonillas [small snakes] awful. Traced and coloured garden scene, east wall of fresco. Worked at improving Maudslay's plates of the lintel and drew the underside. Many visitors and talking, and did little except a coloured drawing of the Door, looking outwards. (Stayed 10 days at Uxmal, and visited Labna and Loltun).

1902. At Chichen February 4 to May 2. Cleaned west wall of fresco, traced and coloured copy. Also part of east side. Lived in cottage from Feb 22. ... Traced and coloured fresco in vault of long upper chamber, Monjas, with scaffold. (Visited ruins at Oxkintoc near Maxcanu, and Chacmultun.)

1902–3. At Chichen December 23 to May 4, in same cottage. Used 36 yards of paper 27 ins wide, doing fresco. Photographed North Building of Ball Court and began copying reliefs. Did south wall of fresco, having cleaned out the bats. This wall required much time to clean and study, especially the Sacrifice stone in the vault. Drew and coloured, (two views each) the fifteen caryatid figures found by Bolio in the outer chamber, buried by Dr Le Plongeon who found them standing there, buried in rubbish from fallen roof. They were then taken to the National Museum in Mexico. Also I made out and drew the sculptured table (not all found) that rested on the figures. Photographed them in their right positions, they having had the numbers painted on them by Dr Le Plongeon who photographed them as found...

1904. At Chichen, in Temple A, April 9 to June 9. Traced and coloured north wall of fresco, very hard to make out, finished other bits. Worked at North Building reliefs, putting details on enlarged photos, and making drawings of them. Copied objects from cenote, [the sacred lake] brought by Mr Thompson. Suffered greatly from the huge flying chinches.

1907. Ten days at Chichen, correcting drawings. (Five weeks at Acanceh, tracing and colouring painted reliefs).

TEACHING A STONE TO TALK

Annie Dillard

Annie Dillard (1945–present) is a Pulitzer-prize-winning American author and poet. In her own words, 'the way to learn about a writer is to read the text.' And in *Teaching a Stone to Talk*, a series of 14 short narrative essays about her travels, she explores the world of natural facts and human meanings, sharing her powerful sense of wonder at the natural world with her readers. The essay 'Life on the Rocks: The Galápagos' won the New York Women's Press Club award.

Life on the Rocks: The Galápagos

I

First there was nothing, and although you know with your reason that nothing is nothing, it is easier to visualize it as a limitless slosh of sea – say, the Pacific. Then energy contracted into matter, and although you know that even an invisible gas is matter, it is easier to visualize it as a massive squeeze of volcanic lava spattered inchoate from the secret pit of the ocean and hardening mute and intractable on nothing's lapping shore – like a series of islands, an archipelago. Like: the Galápagos. Then a softer strain of matter began to twitch. It was a kind of shaped water; it flowed, hardening here and there at its tips. There were blue-green algae; there were tortoises.

The ice rolled up, the ice rolled back, and I knelt on a plain of lava boulders in the islands called Galápagos, stroking a giant tortoise's neck. The tortoise closed its eyes and stretched its neck to its greatest height and vulnerability. I rubbed that neck, and when I pulled away my hand, my palm was green with a slick of single-celled algae. I stared at the algae, and at the tortoise, the way you stare at any life on a lava flow, and thought: Well – here we all are.

Being here is being here on the rocks. These Galapagonian rocks, one of them seventy-five miles long, have dried under the equatorial sun between five and six hundred miles west of the South American continent; they lie at the latitude of the Republic of Ecuador, to which they belong.

There is a way a small island rises from the ocean affronting all reason. It is a chunk of chaos pounded into visibility *ex nihilo*: here rough, here smooth, shaped just so by a matrix of physical necessities too weird to contemplate, here instead of there, here instead of not at all. It is a fantastic utterance, as though I were to open my mouth and emit a French horn, or a vase, or a knob of tellurium. It smacks of folly, of first causes.

I think of the island called Daphnecita, little Daphne, on which I never set foot. It's in half of my few photographs, though, because it obsessed me: a dome of gray lava like a pitted loaf, the size of the Plaza Hotel, glazed with guano and crawling with red-orange crabs. Sometimes I attributed to this island's cliff face a surly, infantile consciousness, as though it were sulking in the silent moment after it had just shouted, to the sea and the sky, "I didn't ask to be born." Or sometimes it aged to a raging adolescent, a kid who's just learned that the game is fixed, demanding, "What did you have me for, if you're just going to push me around?" Daphnecita: again, a wise old island, mute, leading the life of pure creaturehood open to any antelope or saint. After you've blown the ocean sky-high, what's there to say? What if we the people had the sense or grace to live as cooled islands in an archipelago live, with dignity, passion, and no comment?

It is worth flying to Guayaquil, Ecuador, and then to Baltra in the Galápagos just to see the rocks. But these rocks are animal gardens. They are home to a Hieronymus Bosch assortment of windblown, stowaway, castaway, flotsam, and shipwrecked creatures. Most exist nowhere else on earth. These reptiles and insects, small mammals and birds, evolved unmolested on the various islands on which they were cast into unique species adapted to the boulder-wrecked shores, the cactus deserts of the lowlands, or the elevated jungles of the large islands' interiors. You come for the animals. You come to see the curious shapes soft proteins can take, to impress yourself with their reality, and to greet them.

You walk among clattering four-foot marine iguanas heaped on the shore lava, and on each other, like slag. You swim with penguins; you watch flightless cormorants dance beside you, ignoring you, waving the black nubs of their useless wings. Here are nesting blue-footed boobies, real birds with real feathers, whose legs and feet are nevertheless patently fake, manufactured by Mattel. The tortoises are big as stoves. The enormous land iguanas at your feet change color in the sunlight, from gold to blotchy red as you watch.

There is always some creature going about its beautiful business. I missed the boat back to my ship, and was left behind momentarily on uninhabited South Plaza island, because I was watching the Audubon's shearwaters. These dark pelagic birds flick along pleated seas in stitching flocks, flailing their wings rapidly – because if they don't, they'll stall. A shearwater must fly fast, or not at all. Consequently it has evolved two nice behaviors which serve to bring it into its nest alive. The nest is a shearwater-sized hole in the lava cliff. The shearwater circles over the water, ranging out from the nest a quarter of a mile, and veers gradually toward the cliff, making passes at its nest. If the flight angle is precisely right, the bird will fold its wings at the hole's entrance and stall directly onto its floor. The angle is perhaps seldom right, however; one shearwater I watched made a dozen suicidal-looking passes before it vanished into a chink. The other behavior is spectacular. It involves choosing the nest hole in a site below a prominent rock with a downward-angled face. The shearwater comes careering in at full tilt, claps its wings, stalls itself into the rock, and the rock, acting as a backboard, banks it home.

The animals are tame. They have not been persecuted, and show no fear of man. You pass among them as though you were wind, spindrift, sunlight, leaves. The songbirds are tame. On Hood Island I sat beside a nesting waved albatross while a mockingbird scratched in my hair, another mockingbird jabbed at my fingernail, and a third mockingbird made an exquisite progression of pokes at my bare feet up the long series of eyelets in my basketball shoes. The marine iguanas are tame. One settler, Carl Angermeyer, built his house on the site of a marine iguana colony. The gray iguanas, instead of moving out, moved up on the roof, which is corrugated steel. Twice daily on the patio, Angermeyer feeds them a mixture of boiled rice and tuna fish from a plastic basin. Their names are all, unaccountably, Annie. Angermeyer beats on the basin with a long-handled spoon, calling, "Here AnnieAnnie-AnnieAnnie" – and the spiny reptiles, fifty or sixty strong, click along the steel roof, finger their way down the lava boulder and mortar walls, and swarm round his bare legs to elbow into the basin and be elbowed out again smeared with a mash of boiled rice on their bellies and on their protuberant, black, plated lips.

The wild hawk is tame. The Galápagos hawk is related to North America's Swainson's hawk; I have read that if you take pains, you can walk up and pat it. I never tried. We people don't walk up and pat each other; enough is enough. The animals' critical distance and mine tended to coincide, so we could enjoy an easy sociability without threat of violence or unwonted intimacy. The hawk, which is not notably sociable, nevertheless endures even a blundering approach, and is apparently as content to perch on a scrub tree at your shoulder as anyplace else.

In the Galápagos, even the flies are tame. Although most of the land is Ecuadorian national park, and as such rigidly protected, I confess I gave the evolutionary ball an offsides shove by dispatching every fly that bit me, marveling the while at its pristine ignorance, its blithe failure to register a flight trigger at the sweep of my descending hand – an insouciance that was almost, but not quite, disarming. After you kill a fly, you pick it up and feed it to a lava lizard, a bright-throated four-inch lizard that scavenges everywhere in the arid lowlands. And you walk on, passing among the innocent mobs on every rock hillside; or you sit, and they come to you.

We are strangers and sojourners, soft dots on the rocks. You have walked along the strand and seen where birds have landed, walked, and flown; their tracks begin in sand, and go, and suddenly end. Our tracks do that: but we go down. And stay down. While we're here, during the seasons our tents are pitched in the light, we pass among each other crying "greetings" in a thousand tongues, and "welcome," and "good-bye." Inhabitants of uncrowded colonies tend to offer the stranger famously warm hospitality – and such are the Galápagos sea lions. Theirs is the greeting the first creatures must have given Adam – a hero's welcome, a universal and undeserved huzzah. Go, and be greeted by sea lions.

I was sitting with ship's naturalist Soames Summerhays on a sand beach under cliffs on uninhabited Hood Island. The white beach was a havoc of lava boulders black as clinkers, sleek with spray, and lambent as brass in the sinking sun. To our left a dozen sea lions were body-surfing in the long green combers that rose, translucent, half a mile offshore. When the combers broke, the shoreline boulders rolled. I could feel the roar in the rough rock on which I sat; I could hear the grate inside each long backsweeping sea, the rumble of a rolled million rocks muffled in splashes and the seethe before the next wave's heave.

To our right, a sea lion slipped from the ocean. It was a young bull; in another few years he would be dangerous, bellowing at intruders and biting off great dirty chunks of the ones he caught. Now this young bull, which weighed maybe 120 pounds, sprawled silhouetted in the late light, slick as a drop of quicksilver, his glistening whiskers radii of gold like any crown. He hauled his packed bulk toward us up the long beach; he flung himself with an enormous surge of fur-clad muscle onto the boulder where I sat. "Soames," I said – very quietly, "he's here because *we're* here, isn't he?" The naturalist nodded. I felt water drip on my elbow behind me, then the fragile scrape of whiskers, and finally the wet warmth and weight of a muzzle, as the creature settled to sleep on my arm. I was catching on to sea lions.

Walk into the water. Instantly sea lions surround you, even if none has been in sight. To say that they come to play with you is not especially anthropomorphic. Animals play. The bull sea lions are off patrolling their territorial shores; these are the cows and young, which range freely. A five-foot sea lion peers intently into your face, then urges her muzzle gently against your underwater mask and searches your eyes without blinking. Next she rolls upside down and slides along the length of your floating body, rolls again, and casts a long glance back at your eyes. You are, I believe, supposed to follow, and think up something clever in return. You can play games with sea lions in the water using shells or bits of leaf, if you are willing. You can spin on your vertical axis and a sea lion will swim circles around you, keeping her face always six inches from yours, as though she were tethered. You can make a game of touching their back flippers, say, and the sea lions will understand at once; somersaulting conveniently before your clumsy hands, they will give you an excellent field of back flippers.

And when you leave the water, they follow. They don't want you to go. They porpoise to the shore, popping their heads up when they lose you and casting about, then speeding to your side and emitting a choked series of vocal notes. If you won't relent, they disappear, barking; but if you sit on the beach with so much as a foot in the water, two or three will station with you, floating on their backs and saying, Urr.

Few people come to the Galápagos. Buccaneers used to anchor in the bays to avoid pursuit, to rest, and to lighter on fresh water. The world's whaling ships stopped here as well, to glut their holds with fresh meat in the form of giant tortoises. The whalers used to let the tortoises bang around on deck for a few days to empty their guts; then they stacked them below on their backs to live – if you call that living – without food or water for a year. When they wanted fresh meat, they killed one.

Early inhabitants of the islands were a desiccated assortment of grouches, cranks, and ships' deserters. These hardies shot, poisoned, and enslaved each other off, leaving behind a fecund gang of feral goats, cats, dogs, and pigs whose descendants skulk in the sloping jungles and take their tortoise hatchlings neat. Now scientists at the Charles Darwin Research Station, on the island of Santa Cruz, rear the tortoise hatchlings for several years until their shells are tough enough to resist the crunch; then they release them in the wilds of their respective islands. Today, some few thousand people live on three of the islands; settlers from Ecuador, Norway, Germany, and France make a livestock or pineapple living from the rich volcanic soils. The settlers themselves seem to embody a high degree of courteous and conscious humanity, perhaps because of their relative isolation.

On the island of Santa Cruz, eleven fellow passengers and I climb in an open truck up the Galápagos' longest road; we shift to horses, burros, and mules, and visit the lonely farm of Alf Kastdalen. He came to the islands as a child with his immigrant parents from Norway. Now a broad, blond man in his late forties with children of his own, he lives in an isolated house of finished timbers imported from the mainland, on four hundred acres he claimed from the jungle by hand. He raises cattle. He walks us round part of his farm, smiling expansively and meeting our chatter with a willing, open gaze and kind words. The pasture looks like any pasture – but the rocks under the grass are round lava ankle-breakers, the copses are a tangle of thorny bamboo and bromeliads, and the bordering trees dripping in epiphytes are breadfruit, papaya, avocado, and orange.

Kastdalen's isolated house is heaped with books in three languages. He knows animal husbandry; he also knows botany and zoology. He feeds us soup, chicken worth chewing for, green *naranjilla* juice, noodles, pork in big chunks, marinated mixed vegetables, rice, and bowl after bowl of bright mixed fruits.

And his isolated Norwegian mother sees us off; our beasts are ready. We will ride down the mud forest track to the truck at the Ecuadorian settlement, down the long road to the boat, and across the bay to the ship. I lean down to catch her words. She is gazing at me with enormous warmth. "Your hair," she says softly. I am blond. *Adiós*.

II

Charles Darwin came to the Galápagos in 1835, on the *Beagle*; he was twenty-six. He threw the marine iguanas as far as he could into the water; he rode the tortoises and sampled their meat. He noticed that the tortoises' carapaces varied wildly from island to island; so also did the forms of various mockingbirds. He made collections. Nine years later he wrote in a letter, "I am almost convinced (quite contrary to the opinion I started with) that species are not (it is like confessing a murder) immutable." In 1859 he published *On the Origin of Species*, and in 1871 *The Descent of Man.* It is fashionable now to disparage Darwin's originality; not even the surliest of his detractors, however, faults his painstaking methods or denies his impact.

Darwinism today is more properly called neo-Darwinism. It is organic evolutionary theory informed by the spate of new data from modern genetics, molecular biology, paleobiology – from the new wave of the biologic revolution which spread after Darwin's announcement like a tsunami. The data are not all in. Crucial first appearances of major invertebrate groups are missing from the fossil record – but these early forms, sometimes modified larvae, tended to be fragile either by virtue of their actual malleability or by virtue of their scarcity and rapid variation into "hardened," successful forms. Lack of proof in this direction doesn't worry scientists. What neo-Darwinism seriously lacks, however, is a description of the actual mechanism of mutation in the chromosomal nucleotides.

In the larger sense, neo-Darwinism also lacks, for many, sheer plausibility. The triplet splendors of random mutation, natural selection, and Mendelian inheritance are neither energies nor gods; the words merely describe a gibbering tumult of materials. Many things are unexplained, many discrepancies unaccounted for. Appending a very modified neo-Lamarckism to Darwinism would solve many problems – and create new ones. Neo-Lamarckism holds, without any proof, that certain useful acquired characteristics may be inherited. Read C. H. Waddington, *The Strategy of the Genes*, and Arthur Koestler, *The Ghost in the Machine.* The Lamarckism/Darwinism issue is not only complex, hinging perhaps on whether DNA can be copied from RNA, but also politically hot. The upshot of it all is that while a form of Lamarckism holds sway in Russia, neo-Darwinism is supreme in the West, and its basic assumptions, though variously modified, are not overthrown.

So much for scientists. The rest of us didn't hear Darwin as a signal to dive down into the wet nucleus of a cell and surface with handfuls of strange new objects. We were still worried about the book with the unfortunate word in the title: *The Descent of Man.* It was dismaying to imagine great-grandma and great-grandpa effecting a literal, nimble descent from some liana-covered tree to terra firma, scratching themselves, and demanding bananas.

Fundamentalist Christians, of course, still reject Darwinism because it conflicts with the creation account in Genesis. Fundamentalist Christians have a very bad press. Ill feeling surfaces when, from time to time in small towns, they object again to the public schools' teaching evolutionary theory. Tragically, these people feel they have to make a choice between the Bible and modern science. They live and work in the same world as we, and know the derision they face from people whose areas of ignorance are perhaps different, who dismantled their mangers when they moved to town and threw out the baby with the straw.

Even less appealing in their response to the new evolutionary picture were, and are, the social Darwinists. Social Darwinists seized Herbert Spencer's phrase, "the survival of the fittest," applied it to capitalism, and used it to sanction ruthless and corrupt business practices. A social Darwinist is unlikely to identify himself with the term; social Darwinism is, as the saying goes, not a religion but a way of life. A modern social Darwinist wrote the slogan "If you're so smart, why ain't you rich?" The notion still obtains, I believe, wherever people seek power: that the race is to the swift, that everybody is in the race, with varying and merited degrees of success or failure, and that reward is its own virtue.

Philosophy reacted to Darwin with unaccustomed good cheer.

William Paley's fixed and harmonious universe was gone, and with it its meticulous watchmaker god. Nobody mourned. Instead philosophy shrugged and turned its attention from first and final causes to analysis of certain values here in time. "Faith in progress," the man-in-the-street philosophy, collapsed in two world wars. Philosophers were more guarded; pragmatically, they held a very refined "faith in process" – which, it would seem, could hardly lose. Christian thinkers, too, outside of Fundamentalism, examined with fresh eyes the world's burgeoning change. Some Protestants, taking their cue from Whitehead, posited a dynamic god who lives alongside the universe, himself charged and changed by the process of becoming. Catholic Pierre Teilhard de Chardin, a paleontologist, examined the evolution of species itself, and discovered in that flow a surge toward complexity and consciousness, a free ascent capped with man and propelled from within and attracted from without by god, the holy freedom and awareness that is creation's beginning and end. And so forth. Like flatworms, like languages, ideas evolve. And they evolve, as Arthur Koestler suggests, not from hardened final forms, but from the softest plasmic germs in a cell's heart, in the nub of a word's root, in the supple flux of an open mind.

Darwin gave us time. Before Darwin (and Huxley, Wallace, et al) there was in the nineteenth century what must have been a fairly nauseating period: people knew about fossils of extinct species, but did not yet know about organic evolution. They thought the fossils were litter from a series of past creations. At any rate, for many, this creation, the world as we know it, had begun in 4004 B.C., a date set by Irish Archbishop James Ussher in the seventeenth century. We were all crouched in a small room against the comforting back wall, awaiting the millennium which had been gathering impetus since Adam and Eve. Up there was a universe, and down here would be a small strip of man come and gone, created, taught, redeemed, and gathered up in a bright twinkling, like a sprinkling of confetti torn from colored papers, tossed from windows, and swept from the streets by morning.

The Darwinian revolution knocked out the back wall, revealing eerie lighted landscapes as far back as we can see. Almost at once, Albert Einstein and astronomers with reflector telescopes and radio telescopes knocked out the other walls and the ceiling, leaving us sunlit, exposed, and drifting – leaving us puckers, albeit evolving puckers, on the inbound curve of space-time.

III

It all began in the Galápagos, with these finches. The finches in the Galápagos are called Darwin's finches; they are everywhere in the islands, sparrowlike, and almost identical but for their differing beaks. At first Darwin scarcely noticed their importance. But by 1839, when he revised his *Journal* of the *Beagle* voyage, he added a key sentence about the finches' beaks: "Seeing this gradation and diversity of structure in one small, intimately related group of birds, one might really fancy that from an original paucity of birds in this archipelago, one species had been taken and modified for different ends." And so it was.

The finches come when called. I don't know why it works, but it does. Scientists in the Galápagos have passed down the call: you say psssssh psssssh psssssh psssssh psssssh until you run out of breath; then you say it again until the island runs out of birds. You stand on a flat of sand by a shallow lagoon rimmed in mangrove thickets and call the birds right out of the sky. It works anywhere, from island to island.

Once, on the island of James, I was standing propped against a leafless *palo santo* tree on a semiarid inland slope, when the naturalist called the birds.

From other leafless *palo santo* trees flew the yellow warblers, speckling the air with bright bounced sun. Gray mockingbirds came running. And from the green prickly pear cactus, from the thorny acacias, sere grasses, bracken and manzanilla, from the loose black lava, the bare dust, the fern-hung mouths of caverns or the tops of sunlit logs – came the finches. They fell in from every direction like colored bits in a turning kaleidoscope. They circled and homed to a vortex, like a whirlwind of chips, like draining water. The tree on which I leaned was the vortex. A dry series of puffs hit my cheeks. Then a rough pulse from the tree's thin trunk met my palm and rang up my arm – and another, and another. The tree trunk agitated against my hand like a captured cricket: I looked up. The lighting birds were rocking the tree.

It was an appearing act: before there were barren branches; now there were birds like leaves.

Darwin's finches are not brightly colored; they are black, gray, brown, or faintly olive. Their names are even duller: the large ground finch, the medium ground finch, the small ground finch; the large insectivorous tree finch; the vegetarian tree finch; the cactus ground finch, and so forth. But the beaks are interesting, and the beaks' origins even more so.

Some finches wield chunky parrot beaks modified for cracking seeds. Some have slender warbler beaks, short for nabbing insects, long for probing plants. One sports the long chisel beak of a woodpecker; it bores wood for insect grubs and often uses a twig or cactus spine as a pickle fork when the grub won't dislodge. They have all evolved, fanwise, from one bird.

The finches evolved in isolation. So did everything else on earth. With the finches, you can see how it happened. The Galápagos islands are near enough to the mainland that some strays could hazard there; they are far enough away that those strays could evolve in isolation from parent species. And the separate islands are near enough to each other for further dispersal, further isolation, and the eventual reassembling of distinct species. (In other words, finches blew to the Galápagos, blew to various islands, evolved into differing species, and blew back together again.) The tree finches and the ground finches, the woodpecker finch and the warbler finch, veered into being on isolated rocks. The witless green sea shaped those beaks as surely as it shaped the beaches. Now on the finches in the *palo santo* tree you see adaptive radiation's results, a fluorescent splay of horn. It is as though an archipelago were an arpeggio, a rapid series of distinct but related notes. If the Galápagos had been one unified island, there would be one dull note, one super-dull finch.

IV

Now let me carry matters to an imaginary, and impossible, extreme. If the earth were one unified island, a smooth ball, we would all be one species, a tremulous muck. The fact is that when you get down to this business of species formation, you eventually hit some form of reproductive isolation. Cells tend to fuse. Cells tend to engulf each other; primitive creatures tend to move in on each other and on us, to colonize, aggregate, blur. (Within species, individuals have evolved immune reactions, which help preserve individual integrity; you might reject my liver – or someday my brain.) As much of the world's energy seems to be devoted to keeping us apart as was directed to bringing us here in the first place. All sorts of different creatures can mate and produce fertile offspring: two species of snapdragon, for instance, or mallard and pintail ducks. But they don't. They live apart, so they don't mate. When you scratch the varying behaviors and conditions behind reproductive isolation, you find, ultimately, geographical isolation. Once the isolation has occurred, of course, forms harden out, enforcing reproductive isolation, so that snapdragons will never mate with pintail ducks.

Geography is the key, the crucial accident of birth. A piece of protein could be a snail, a sea lion, or a systems analyst, but it had to start somewhere. This is not science; it is merely metaphor. And the landscape in which the protein "starts" shapes its end as surely as bowls shape water.

We have all, as it were, blown back together like the finches, and it's hard to imagine the isolation from parent species in which we evolved. The frail beginnings of great phyla are lost in the crushed histories of cells. Now we see the embellishments of random chromosomal mutations selected by natural selection and preserved in geographically isolate gene pools as *faits accomplis,* as the differentiated fringe of brittle knobs that is life as we know it. The process is still going on, but there is no turning back; it happened, in the cells. Geographical determination is not the cow-caught-in-a-crevice business I make it seem. I'm dealing in imagery, working toward a picture.

Geography is life's limiting factor. Speciation – life itself – is ultimately a matter of warm and cool currents, rich and bare soils, deserts and forests, fresh and salt waters, deltas and jungles and plains. Species arise in isolation. A plaster cast is as intricate as its mold; life is a gloss on geography. And if you dig your fists into the earth and crumble geography, you strike geology. Climate is the wind of the mineral earth's rondure, tilt, and orbit modified by local geological conditions. The Pacific Ocean, the Negev Desert, and the rain forest in Brazil are local geological conditions. So are the slow carp pools and splashing trout riffles of any backyard creek. It is all, God help us, a matter of rocks.

The rocks shape life like hands around swelling dough. In Virginia, the salamanders vary from mountain ridge to mountain ridge; so do the fiddle tunes the old men play. All this is because it is hard to move from mountain to mountain. These are not merely anomalous details. This is what life is all about: salamanders, fiddle tunes, you and me and things, the split and burr of it all, the fizz into particulars. No mountains and one salamander, one fiddle tune, would be a lesser world. No continents, no fiddlers. No possum, no sop, no taters. The earth, without form, is void.

The mountains are time's machines; in effect, they roll out protoplasm like printers' rollers pressing out news. But life is already part of the landscape, a limiting factor in space; life too shapes life. Geology's rocks and climate have already become Brazil's rain forest, yielding shocking bright birds. To say that all life is an interconnected membrane, a weft of linkages like chain mail, is truism. But in this case, too, the Galápagos islands afford a clear picture.

On Santa Cruz island, for instance, the saddleback carapaces of tortoises enable them to stretch high and reach the succulent pads of prickly pear cactus. But the prickly pear cactus on that island, and on other tortoise islands, has evolved a treelike habit; those lower pads get harder to come by. Without limiting factors, the two populations could stretch right into the stratosphere.

Ça va. It goes on everywhere, tit for tat, action and reaction, triggers and inhibitors ascending in a spiral like spatting butterflies. Within life, we are pushing each other around. How many animal forms have evolved just so because there are, for instance, trees? We pass the nitrogen around, and vital gases; we feed and nest, plucking this and that and planting seeds. The protoplasm responds, nudged and nudging, bearing the news.

*

And the rocks themselves shall be moved. The rocks themselves are not pure necessity, given, like vast, complex molds around which the rest of us swirl. They heave to their own necessities, to stirrings and prickings from within and without.

The mountains are no more fixed than the stars. Granite, for example, contains much oxygen and is relatively light. It "floats." When granite forms under the earth's crust, great chunks of it bob up, I read somewhere, like dumplings. The continents themselves are beautiful pea-green boats. The Galápagos archipelago as a whole is surfing toward Ecuador; South America is sliding toward the Galápagos; North America, too, is sailing westward. We're on floating islands, shaky ground.

So the rocks shape life, and then life shapes life, and the rocks are moving. The completed picture needs one more element: life shapes the rocks.

Life is more than a live green scum on a dead pool, a shimmering scurf like slime mold on rock. Look at the planet. Everywhere freedom twines its way around necessity, inventing new strings of occasions, lassoing time and putting it through its varied and spirited paces. Everywhere live things lash at the rocks. Softness is vulnerable, but it has a will; tube worms bore and coral atolls rise. Lichens in delicate lobes are chewing the granite mountains; forests in serried ranks trammel the hills. Man has more freedom than other live things; anti-entropically, he batters a bigger dent in the given, damming the rivers, planting the plains, drawing in his mind's eye dotted lines between the stars.

The old ark's a moverin'. Each live thing wags its home waters, rumples the turf, rearranges the air. The rocks press out protoplasm; the protoplasm pummels the rocks. It could be that this is the one world, and that world a bright snarl.

*

Like boys on dolphins, the continents ride their crustal plates. New lands shoulder up from the waves, and old lands buckle under. The very landscapes heave; change burgeons into change. Gray granite bobs up, red clay compresses; yellow sandstone tilts, surging in forests, incised by streams. The mountains tremble, the ice rasps back and forth, and the protoplasm furls in shock waves, up the rock valleys and down, ramifying possibilities, riddling the mountains. Life and the rocks, like spirit and matter, are a fringed matrix, lapped and lapping, clasping and held. It is like hand washing hand. It is like hand washing hand and the whole tumult hurled. The planet spins, rapt inside its intricate mists. The galaxy is a flung thing, loose in the night, and our solar system is one of many dotted campfires ringed with tossed rocks. What shall we sing?

What shall we sing, while the fire burns down? We can sing only specifics, time's rambling tune, the places we have seen, the faces we have known. I will sing you the Galápagos islands, the sea lions soft on the rocks. It's all still happening there, in real light, the cool currents upwelling, the finches falling on the wind, the shearwaters looping the waves. I could go back, or I could go on; or I could sit down, like Kubla Khan:

> Weave a circle round him thrice,
>   And close your eyes with holy dread,
> For he on honey-dew hath fed,
>   And drunk the milk of Paradise.

CRYING WITH COCKROACHES

Marianne du Toit

Marianne du Toit (1970–present) is a South African adventurer and photographer. In May 2002, du Toit set out to follow in the footsteps of the Swiss adventurer Aimé Félix Tschiffely who rode the 10,000 miles from Buenos Aires to New York in the 1920's on two Criollo horses – the breed which gauchos' favour for their qualities of endurance. *Crying with Cockroaches: Argentina to New York with Two Horses* is her account of the gruelling journey. But her trip wasn't one of self-indulgence – she was raising money to build an equestrian centre for disabled children in Ireland. A wild woman with wonderful ambition, and a worthy one with whom to complete this anthology.

Forty Days and Forty Nights

Second in length only to Africa's Nile, the Amazon River carries the greatest volume of water of any river in the world. It flows eastward about 6,275 kilometres through South America from its source in the Andes to its mouth at the Atlantic Ocean. Navigable for almost its entire length, it provides an important commercial route through the continent.

The Trans Amazon Highway is impassable for much of the year and the rivers are the only practical means of communication and transport. I found myself making arrangements to get myself and the horses on a five-day boat trip, exploring the waterways of the Rio Madeira, the Amazon's longest tributary, linking the city of Porto Velho with Manaus, 901 kilometres on.

While in Porto Velho, I was fortunate to meet Frank, a Dutchman, and his North American colleague, Brian, both of whom worked on contract for a US telecommunications company. Frank and I got on very well and it helped that they both spoke Portuguese and so could assist with some of my preparations.

It was also Frank who told me it would be impossible to go on horseback from Manaus to Venezuela as one had to pass through a private Indian Reserve.

"Although you're allowed to enter the Reserve, it's prohibited to stop in that area and with you travelling on a horse, it'll take more than three days to cross," he informed me.

He also told me how the Indians living there are still used to their old ways and I shivered when he mentioned cannibalism.

From what I gathered, the Manaus Boa Vista Highway, called the BR-174, has a violent history. Its 125 kilometre stretch of road cuts across the 25,000 square kilometres Reserve called the Terra Indigena Waimiri Atroaris.

The Waimiri-Atroari Indians live deep in the Amazon Rainforest in this part of Northern Brazil. Their territory is one of the most feared and impenetrable in the Amazon. Having been in constant open warfare for over 300 years, the Waimiri fiercely defended their land against the construction of the road, combating the forces of the Brazilian army. The retaliations against the Indians were always disproportionate. They were unequal battles, first in terms of weapons – one side using firearms, the other, bows and arrows. Furthermore, 300 Brazilians were arrayed against a much smaller number of Indians according to the reports of casualties on both sides. These were unjust wars in which one side attacked while the other defended their territory, their honour and their communities.

With right on their side they fought to reoccupy their traditional territories, part of which was occupied by a large mining company. In 1968 a Catholic priest and seven nuns were found dead in Waimiri territory and more than 200 soldiers were killed by poison arrows during the confrontation. The number of Waimiri killed in retaliation was never released. The Waimiri-Atroari were simply reacting against repeated acts of plundering and violence against them. Since the sixties and seventies, when the BR-174 highway was built, they have been dominated and subjugated by the Army. In this process, 2000 Indians disappeared and their lands were reduced by four-fifths. A hydroelectric power plant, which led to severe flooding within the Waimiri territory, also caused irreversible damage to the Indians' habitat.

But the Waimiri-Atroari faced up to these challenges and negotiated with Brazilian officialdom so that today they enjoy secure reservation boundaries, cultural vigour and population growth.

A local man called Geraldo worked as an agent for the ferries in Porto Velho. For two days we rushed through the city on his powerful bike, visiting different boat companies. Despite the fact that I love motorbikes, I was in a state every time I sat behind him, clinging to his midriff with all my might as he sped through the busy streets, far too fast. More frightening was the fact that I was never given a crash helmet to wear.

"You're doing a hundred, Geraldo!" I shouted one morning as we zigzagged around. "This is madness, we're going to crash."

He turned his head side-ways and grinned. "Relax. I know what I'm doing."

It turned out he did not.

Two days before my departure, I could not get hold of him on his phone. I knew he had had a late night (I was invited to the party but declined) and left a message for him to ring me on Frank's phone. When he finally returned my call I did not recognise his voice.

"I cannot speak," he mumbled in a croaky murmur.

I had to pass the phone to Frank who shook his head for the duration of the conversation, making a lot of sympathetic noises.

It turned out that Geraldo had been involved in a very serious accident on his motorbike when on the way back from the party. He had fractured his skull and broken numerous bones including ribs.

Before the accident Geraldo had made arrangements with a cargo boat to transport me and the horses up the Amazon after it became clear that the passenger ferries would not accommodate us. They were not keen on having animals on board and mentioned potential difficulties with health and safety. I cannot say I was overly disappointed, especially after I had been on one of those ferries. Hammocks were lined up like sardines in a tin and I was told theft could be a problem.

A day before our departure, Frank and Brian helped me to cart bags of sawdust to the port. These would go on the surface of the barge area where a section was cordoned off for the horses.

The barge was about 20x6 metres and also carried four cars and hordes of bags of spaghetti and beans. I pitched my tent between the bags of food and the cars. The small boat pushing the barge was managed by a laid-back and very friendly crew, the captain, his assistant, a mechanic and his wife who did the cooking. Accompanying us would be a missionary and his son, from Brazil, and later, a duck.

On the day I was told we would be leaving I rode the horses to the harbour wearing only knee-length shorts, a sleeveless top and trainers. The neighbourhoods we passed through had a distinct market atmosphere about them, with music stores blaring out their sounds, traders shouting out their wares and stallholders chattering on about their predominantly cheap plastic goods. Every other lamppost seemed to have had a loudspeaker attached to it. We received a lot of friendly stares, thumbs up and waves as we headed down towards the port. My spirits were high and I did not even get annoyed at some men making flirtatious gestures. I even gave a group of jubilant kids a spin on Tusa.

Not too far from the port a car stopped. I barely recognised Geraldo in the passenger seat. He looked terrible. His eyes were bloodshot and swollen and the area around them was badly bruised. He still had dried blood on his face, ears and neck.

"You should have stayed in hospital," I scolded him.

He shook his head, "No, now I work for you."

The port area was bustling when we arrived around 6 p.m. A man suggested the horses jump from one barge to the other but I insisted on finding two wooden planks so they could cross safely. Mise strolled on as if she did that kind of thing just about every day and true to his nature, Tusa boarded more warily, his legs trembling slightly.

I loved the atmosphere on the boat and had a real feeling of excitement, knowing that the journey up the river was going to be a memorable and unusual one.

Before the sun went down, I fed the horses a cocktail of wheat and proteins in their brand new powder-blue buckets. While the crew was still getting everything loaded, I crawled into my tent, fatigued yet pleased and gratified. I was asleep when we eventually got moving.

*

I awoke the following morning to a beautiful sunrise and the sound of water splashing against the barge. I peeked through my tent and felt on top of the world when I realised that we were actually cruising up the Amazon. Completely relaxed and in great form I made my way over to the little kitchen, checking on the horses first. They were standing around calmly waiting for their buckets to be filled with more food. I attached a rope to a bucket and scooped water from the river.

Sipping coffee and tucking into crackers, I sat in my chair (purchased especially for the boat trip) on the tiny deck, watching the world go by, contemplating life. I had absolutely nothing to do and nowhere to go. Dense, lush vegetation and towering trees lined the river and the odd, small settlement nestled in the forest or on the shores. For the sake of the horses I was happy it was an overcast day.

That evening I sat in the opening of the kitchen, my feet dangling over the side of the boat, eating spaghetti. Life was good. I had a beer and asked Valcilene the cook if she would like one too. She declined politely.

"I suffer from depression and shouldn't drink or smoke."

I found her openness very interesting although it was not the first time in Brazil that somebody, without shame or embarrassment, had admitted to being depressed. They stated their condition simply as a fact of life.

These were tranquil, easygoing days. Occasionally pink-grey river dolphins surfaced, a sight which never ceased to amaze and excite me. I wished that the days would pass by even more slowly. One day though was particularly hot. I asked the men what we could do for protection for the horses. They brought out large plastic sheets to tie over the area where the horses were standing. However, the horses were disturbed by the noisy, flapping sounds of the sheets in the wind and I feared they might jump overboard. Noticing that Tusa was sweating profusely they cut open the sides to allow for more air to blow through.

Mise was in heat again and bullied Tusa, giving him playful bites which hurt I was sure. She also intimidated him when they were eating, moving over to his bowl, pushing his head away. They had a container each but somehow Mise must have thought that Tusa's food was better.

A number of people living on the edges of the river made their living from providing food and provisions to the passing boats. They arrived in a type of motorised canoe and attached this to the moving boat, using a rope. The inside of their canoes were filled not only with a number of family members but also with everything ranging from fruits to fish or a slaughtered animal. This is how we acquired the duck but in this case he was still alive. He was tied up in different places on the boat and I made sure he had food and water. On one occasion the crew even chucked him into the river for a brief spell to cool down. I dreaded the moment of his slaughter and had an urge to throw him overboard, pretending he had escaped.

For lunch one day Valcilene prepared fish we got the day before. I took pictures from the top deck as she cut them open expertly, tossing their bloody insides into the river. Later, I noticed the heads and dismembered parts floating in a pot. I could not stomach the white, uninviting pieces of fish, their eyes still intact, and made my excuses not to join in the meal.

The horses' diet worried me. So when one day we passed close to the banks of the river, I ran to the side of the barge, went down on my knees and started to pull reeds sticking out of the water. Soon, I was joined by some of the crew who helped to gather a good quota for the horses. They loved the bit of greenery and afterwards their systems appeared much more regular.

A full bladder at night turned out to be the biggest hassle on board. First of all I had to get out of my tent in the dark and make my way over to the toilet, stepping carefully on the narrow side of the barge past metal obstacles and bags of dried food. A wrong step to the left would have seen me plunging into the perilous waters of the great river.

The toilet, next to the noisy engine, was the smallest I had ever encountered, much smaller than those on planes. Not only was it a struggle to get my pants up and down, but to actually sit on the toilet was an achievement in itself with my knees almost pressed to my ears. When I stood up, my head knocked against the ceiling. A kind of squatting position was mercifully possible due to a strip of wood attached to the wall on the front left on which I could distribute my weight. The tiny room was newly renovated and the combined smells of fresh paint, lavatory and engine, made for a nauseating experience.

I woke up one morning around 3 a.m. bursting to go. Once I had reached the toilet I discovered the door was locked. I had to make a decision fast and walked to the back of the boat and dropped my pants. I grabbed on to a metal hook that was fixed to the deck and literally hanging over the edge of the boat with my bottom hovering over the mighty Amazon, I managed to find relief. The flow seemed to last forever and I could feel my arms and legs tiring from the strain of holding my own weight.

Later, back in the tent I could not help smiling to myself at the thought of what a sight that must have been.

EXTENDED COPYRIGHT

Delia Akeley: *Jungle Portraits*

Felicity Aston: *Alone in Antarctica*

Mary Barker: *Station Life in New Zealand*

Jean Batten: *Alone in the Sky*

Gertrude Bell: *Syria*

Isabella Bird: *A Lady's Life in the Rocky Mountains*

Nellie Bly: *Around the World in Seventy-Two Days*

Adela Breton: *Unpublished Writings*

of Archaeology & Ethnology, Harvard University. This letter reprinted by permission of Peabody Museum of Archaeology & Ethnology, Harvard University.

Madeleine Bunting: *Love of Country*
© Madeleine Bunting, 2016. Published by Granta Books in 2016. This excerpt reprinted by permission of Granta Books.

Christine Byl: *Dirt Work*
© Christine Byl, 2013. Published by Beacon Press books. This excerpt reprinted by permission of Beacon Press.

Mildred Cable and Francesca French: *The Gobi Desert*
© Mildred Cable and Francesca French, 1942. First published by Hodder and Stoughton Ltd. Published by Trotamundas Press Ltd. in 2008. This excerpt reprinted by permission of Trotamundas Press Ltd.

Emily Carr: *Klee Wyck*
© Emily Carr, 1941. Published by Douglas & McIntyre in 2003.

Penelope Chetwode: *Two Middle-Aged Ladies in Andalusia*
© Paul Betjeman, 1963. First published by John Murray in 1963. Published by Eland Publishing Limited in 2012. This excerpt reprinted by permission of Eland Publishing Limited.

Robyn Davidson: *Tracks*
© Robyn Davidson, 1980, 2012. First published by Jonathan Cape Ltd in 1980. Published by Bloomsbury Publishing Plc in 2012. This excerpt reprinted by permission of Bloomsbury Publishing Plc.

Josie Dew: *Long Cloud Ride*
© Josie Dew 2007. Published by Sphere, an imprint of Little, Brown Book Group Limited. This excerpt reprinted by permission of Little, Brown Book Group.

Annie Dillard: *Teaching a Stone to Talk*
© Annie Dillard, 1982. First published by Harper & Row, a division of HarperCollins Publishers in 1982. Reprinted by the permission of Russell & Volkening as agents for the author.

Christina Dodwell: *A Traveller on Horseback*
© Christina Dodwell, 1989. Published by Long Riders' Guild Press in 2004. This excerpt reprinted courtesy of Christina Dodwell and The Long Riders' Guild Press in 1987.

Amelia Earhart: *Last Flight*
© Amelia Earhart, 1937. First published by Harcourt, Brace and Company, Inc. Published by Trotamundas Press Ltd. in 2008. This excerpt reprinted by permission of Trotamundas Press Ltd.

Isabelle Eberhardt: *The Passionate Nomad*
© Isabelle Eberhardt, 1900–1903. Published by Virago Press Limited in 1987.

Amelia Edwards: *A Thousand Miles Up the Nile*
© Amelia Edwards, 1877. Published by Parkway Publishing in 1993.

Gretel Ehrlich: *This Cold Heaven*
© Gretel Ehrlich, 2001. Published by Fourth Estate, a division of HarperCollins Publishers Ltd. in 2002. Reprinted by permission of HarperCollins Publishers Ltd.

Catherine Fairweather: *Oman's Empty Quarter*
© Catherine Fairweather, 2018. Reprinted by permission of the author.

Rosita Forbes: *Forbidden Road*
© Rosita Forbes, 1937. Published by Long Riders' Guild Press.

Imogen Lycett Green: *Grandmother's Footsteps*
© Imogen Lycett Green, 1994. Published by Macmillan, London in 1994. Reproduced with permission of the Licensor through PLSclear.

Juanita Harrison: *My Great, Wide, Beautiful World*
© Juanita Harrison, 1936. First published by The Macmillan Company in 1936. Published by Forgotten Books in 2015.

Sarah Hobson: *Through Persia in Disguise*
© Sarah Hobson, 1973. First Published by The Travel Book Club in 1974. Published by John Murray Press, an imprint of Hodder & Stoughton.

Ernestine Hill: *The Great Australian Loneliness*
© Ernestine Hill, 1940. Published by Robertson and Mullens Limited in 1940.

Gretchen Legler: *On The Ice:*
© Gretchen Legler, 2005. Published by Minneapolis: Milkweed Editions in 2005. This excerpt reprinted with permission from Milkweed Editions. milkweed.org

Anna Leonowens: *The English Governess at the Siamese Court*
© Anna Harriette Leonowens, 1869. Published by University of Chicago Press.

Ella Maillart: *The Cruel Way*
© Ella K. Maillart, 1947. First published by William Heineman in 1947. This excerpt reprinted by permission of David Higham.

Beryl Markham: *West with the Night*
© Beryl Markham, 1942, 1983. First published by Houghton Mifflin Company in 1942. This excerpt reprinted by permission of Pollinger Limited (www.pollingerltd.com) on behalf of the Estate of Beryl Markham.

Kate Marsden: *On Sledge and Horseback to Outcast Siberian Lepers*
© Kate Marsden, 1892. Published by Century Hutchinson Group.

Jan Morris: *Destinations*
© Rolling Stone Press and Jan Morris, 1980. Published by Oxford University Press in 1982. This excerpt reprinted by permission of Oxford University Press.

Mary Morris: *Nothing to Declare*
© Mary Morris, 1988. First published by Houghton Mifflin Company in 1988. This excerpt reprinted by permission of Mary Morris.

Dervla Murphy: *South from the Limpopo*
© Dervla Murphy, 1997. First published by John Murray in 1997. Published by Eland Publishing Limited in 2016. This excerpt reprinted by permission of Eland Publishing Limited and the author.

Bella Pollen: *A Snapshot of Afghanistan*
© Bella Pollen, 2018. Reprinted by permission of the author.

Lois Pryce: *Red Tape and White Knuckles*
© Lois Pryce, 2008. Published by Century in 2008. Reprinted by permission of The Random House Group Limited.

Vita Sackville-West: *Passenger to Teheran*
© the Estate of Vita Sackville-West, 1926. First published by Hogarth Press in 1926. Published by Cockbird Press in 1990. This excerpt reprinted by permission of Curtis Brown Group Ltd, London on behalf of The Beneficiaries of the Estate of Vita Sackville-West.

Mary Lee Settle: *Turkish Reflections*
© Mary Lee Settle, 1991. Published by Touchstone in 1991. This excerpt reprinted bypermission of Simon & Schuster, Inc. All rights reserved.

Nan Shepherd: *The Living Mountain*
© Nan Shepherd, 2008. First published by Aberdeen University Press in 1977. Published by Cannongate Books in 2011. This excerpt reprinted by permission of Cannongate Books.

Lady Hester Stanhope: *The Life and Letters of Lady Hester Stanthorpe*
© Catherine Cleveland, 1914. First published by John Murray in 1914. Published by Forgotten Books in 2017.

Cheryl Strayed: *Wild*
© Cheryl Strayed, 2012. Published by Alfred A. Knopf, an imprint of the Knopf Doubleday Publishing Group, a division of Penguin Random House in 2012. This excerpt reprinted by permission of Alfred A. Knopf, an imprint of the Knopf Doubleday Publishing Group, a division of Penguin Random House LLC. All rights reserved.

Junko Tabei: *Honouring High Places*
© Junko Tabei and Helen Y. Rolfe, 2017. Published by Rocky Mountain Books in 2017. This excerpt reprinted courtesy of Rocky Mountain Books.

Marianne du Toit: *Crying with Cockroaches*
© Marianne du Toit, 2007. First published by Liendl Publishing in 2006. This excerpt reprinted by permission of the author.

Flora Tristan: *London Journal 1840*
© Flora Tristan, 1840. English translation © Dennis Palmer and Giselle Pincetl, 1980. English edition first published by George Prior Publishers in 1980.

Ethel Tweedie: *A Girl's Ride in Iceland*
© Ethel Brilliana Tweedie, 1894. Published by Dodo Press in 2008.

Aloha Wanderwell: *Call to Adventure!*
© The Nile Baker Estate, 2013. Originally published by Raddon Craftmen, Inc. 1939.

Edith Wharton: *In Morocco*
© Edith Wharton, 1919. First published by Charles Scribner's Sons. Published by Tauris Parke Paperbacks in 2004.

Sara Wheeler: *Access All Areas*

Mary Wollstonecraft: *Letters Written During a Short Residence in Sweden Norway and Denmark*